Artificial Intelligence and Digitisation in Education

Artificial Intelligence and Digitisation in Education

Editors
Aerum Khan
Jasim Ahmad

SHIPRA

And the project is funded by ICSSR, New delhi

₹895; US$ 30
ISBN: 978-93-91978-48-8

2025
First Published in India

Artificial Intelligence and Digitisation in Education

Published by:
SHIPRA PUBLICATIONS
LG 18-19, Pankaj Central Market
I.P. Ext., Patparganj, Delhi 110092, India
91 11 2223 5152; 96500 28065, 98105 22367
info@shiprapublication.com
www.shiprapublication.com

Foreword

I would like to congratulate the entire team of JICE-2024 for organizing such a great conference, on a very relevant and pertinent topic, which provided platform for learning about the artificial intelligence and digitization in a collaborative manner. Rapid technological advancements have a huge impact on the educational environment, resulting in rapid incorporation into educational practices. With the advancement of technology, it has become imperative in the arena of progressive education, providing a multitude of advantages for both students and teachers. Technology allows for individualized learning paths adapted to specific student requirements, encourages cooperation and communication between students and instructors, and gives access to a plethora of educational materials regardless of location. The instant accessibility of extensive e-resources empowers learners to understand the subject matters beyond the textbooks, fostering self-directed learning. With innovations such as artificial intelligence, virtual reality, and online learning platforms, educators are adopting new tools and approaches to improve teaching and learning experiences.

The COVID-19 epidemic has hastened the global adoption of digital education, with numerous educational organizations shifting to online and distance learning to maintain the continuity of education. This transition has underlined the need for digital literacy for students and educators, as well as the necessity for fair access to technology as well as internet connectivity.

The book in hand '*Artificial Intelligence and Digitization in Education*'has an array of chapters that examine essential topics of contemporary education, such as digitalisation, artificial intelligence (AI), and technology addiction. It discusses the integration of digital tools and platforms in educational settings in depth, emphasizing their role in increasing accessibility and flexibility. Furthermore, it investigates the implications of artificial intelligence in education, offering light on its potential to transform teaching and learning methods. Furthermore, the book investigates the topic of technology addiction, providing insights into its effects on students' well-being and academic achievement. Together, these chapters provide a comprehensive grasp of the changing face of education in the digital era.

In light of changing technology environments digitizing education has become an essential necessity. This paradigm shift aims to improve accessibility, adaptability, and instructional efficacy by seamlessly integrating digital tools, platforms, and resources into educational frameworks. Leveraging a multitude of digital resources, such as interactive simulations, virtual classrooms, educational software, online learning platforms, and multimedia materials etc have become a necessity to adapt to the changing needs of educators and students.

Artificial intelligence (AI) is playing an increasingly important role in altering many sectors of education. AI technologies are being used to improve teaching and learning processes, personalize learning experiences, increase educational outcomes, and automate administrative activities. AI has enormous potential to transform education by personalizing learning experiences, boosting educational outcomes, and optimizing administrative operations. Challenges in integrating AI in education include protecting data privacy, addressing equitable difficulties, and promoting ethical use. As artificial intelligence evolves, its impact on education is projected to expand, profoundly affecting the future of teaching and learning.

The proverb "excess of everything is bad" is especially relevant to the topic of technology addiction and its effects on mental health. While technology has provided unparalleled ease and connectivity, overuse of digital gadgets and online activities can lead to addiction and negative psychological repercussions. Excessive use of social media, online gaming, and other digital platforms can lead to addictive behaviors, which are defined by a compulsive drive to engage despite negative consequences. This addiction can exacerbate mental health conditions such as anxiety, despair, and loneliness by interrupting sleep habits and interfering with real-world social connections. To maintain mental well-being and overall health, it is critical to strike a balance and utilize technology with moderation.

This book provides insights into the multidimensional nature of digital education by covering a wide range of topics in-depth. It explores subjects including how to use technology to educate and learn, how to leverage digital tools and platforms for teaching, and how digitalisation has affected teaching methods. The book also examines the advantages and difficulties of digital education, covering topics like equity, quality, and accessibility. It offers real-world examples, case studies, and best practices to highlight efficient methods for utilizing digital technology in the classroom. The book also explores new developments and trends in digital education, illuminating creative thinking and technological breakthroughs that are reshaping the industry.

It will continue to be an indispensable resource for scholars, educators, and policymakers as they work through the rapidly changing field of digital education. It will keep giving guidance on best practices and new trends as well as thoughts and viewpoints on how to incorporate technology into teaching and learning. This book will operate as a guide for being informed and adjusting to new developments as technology advances and shapes educational methods.

Its extensive encompassing of digital education in a range of settings will guarantee its continued applicability for many years to come.

I congratulate the conference convener Prof. Jasim Ahmad for organizing the international conference on such a big scale and producing this edited volume as a by-product of the conference. The efforts of the editors and contributors is highly appreciated for doing high level academic work in a timely manner and in a key area of today's significance. It is hoped that the book will prove significant contributions towards academics and will be highly useful for students and teachers.

Prof. Jessy Abraham
Head, IASE
Jamia Millia Islamia
New Delhi

Acknowledgements

It gives us immense pleasure to recall all the university officers, faculty members, and the funding agency who helped at all stages of Jamia International Conference on Education (JICE-2024), whose final product is in your hand in the form of a book.

We first and foremost thank Hon'ble Vice Chancellor, and Registrar, Jamia Millia Islamia for guiding us at all stages of the conference.

We are indebted to Prof. H.C.S. Rathore, Chairperson, NRC, NCTE and former Vice Chancellor, Central University of South Bihar, and Prof. Dhananjay Joshi, Vice Chancellor, Delhi Teachers University for gracing the occasions of Inaugural and Valedictory sessions respectively as chief guest. We thank Prof. Jyotsna Pattnaik, California State University, Long Beach, USA, Prof. Theodoros Karakasidis, University of Thessaly, Greece, for delivering the keynote address during inaugural and valedictory functions and Prof. Joey Martinez Dela Cruz, University of Abra, Philippines, for his plenary talk in the valedictory session of the conference.

The Dean, Façulty of Education, Prof. Sara Begum; and Head, Department of Teacher Training and Non-formal Education, Prof. Jessy Abraham for extending all kinds of support throughout the conference planning and execution. Without their support, it could not have materialized in such a grand way.

We acknowledge and thank our superannuated faculty members Prof. Mohammad Akhtar Siddiqui, former Chairman, NCTE, for delivering the keynote address, Prof. Najma Amin, Prof. Shoeb Abdullah, Prof. Ahrar Hussain and Prof. Ilyas Husain for chairing the technical sessions and guiding us whenever we approached them for their support and guidance. We also thank Prof. Mohd. Miyan, former Vice Chancellor, MANUU, and Prof. Talat Aziz, former Dean, Faculty of Education, JMI for their benign presence in the inaugural session and the moral support they provided throughout the preparation of the conference.

We acknowledge and thank the key members of the conference organizing team — Prof. Naheed Zahoor, Prof. Kartar Singh, Prof. Kaushal Kishore, Prof. Savita Kaushal, Prof. Roohi Fatima, Dr. Dori Lal, Dr. Ajit Kumar Bohet, Dr. Sameer Babu M, Dr. Ansar Ahmad, Dr. Raisa Khan, Dr. Sajjad Ahmad, Dr. Andleeb, Dr. Sarita Kumari, Dr. Shadma Yasmeen, Dr. Aysha, Dr. Saman Zaki and Ms. Nazneen for their constant support and contributions towards the organization of JICE-2024.x

Thanks are due to all faculty members from both departments, Department of Teacher Training and Non-formal Education (IASE) and Department of

Educational Studies for their cooperation in reviewing papers, convening/ chairing/ co-chairing technical sessions and doing all the associated work during the entire process of JICE-2024.

We must thank the Indian Council of Social Science Research (ICSSR), the agency which funded the organization of the international conference JICE-2024. Without the financial support of ICSSR, it would not be possible to organize the conference on such a big scale.

It is important to mention that we decided to publish ISBN books instead of publishing papers in the form of proceedings with a vision to make the researchers' work wider dissemination. It is generally observed that proceedings are read by a fewer number of people, but books are more read as it reaches in the form of course material for certain programmes and are useful for teachers as well as students. This book will be very useful for teachers and students of Education in the specified area of study. We thank and acknowledge the worthwhile and important piece of work contributed by researchers and faculty members for their presentation in the conference and allowing us to publish it in the form of a chapter in an edited book with ISBN Number. We thank them all and wish to have the same support, motivation and encouragement in our future conferences.

We acknowledge the utmost efforts and untiring day and night work of our scholars —Mr. Md. Ashique Husain, Ms. Zahra Kazmi, Ms. Soumya Panigrahi, Ms. Ambrin Khanam, Ms. Aditi Tiwari, Ms. Sehar Nigar, Ms. Shahla Naz, Mr. Sajuddin Saifi, Mr. Haroon Salmani, Mr. Mohd. Noor Alam, Ms Sania Noor, Mr. Dhananjay Kumar, Ms. Humaira Khatoon, Mr. Dheeraj Kumar, Ms. Maria Waseem, Ms. Samra Jamal, Ms. Shaista Tanweer, Mr. Mohammad Haider Raza, Mr. Nisar Ahmad, Ms. Khushnuda Bano, Dr. Noor Alam, and Mr. Taj Mohammad in timely completion of all necessary preparations of the conference and its publication work including this book. We wish them all great success in their future endeavours.

Special appreciation is due to Ms. Soumya Priyadarsani Panigrahi, research scholar, IASE for her sincere, dedicated and rigorous efforts towards the content management and proofing of the manuscript.

We would like to extend our sincere thanks to all the contributors for their insightful work in the area. We would also like to convey our gratitude to those who have put great efforts and supported us during the publication of this book.

Editors

Contents

1

Introduction

The intersection of artificial intelligence (AI) and digitalisation with education represents a transformative force that is reshaping learning environments, pedagogical approaches, and educational outcomes. As technology continues to evolve and permeate every aspect of society, it becomes increasingly imperative to explore the implications, challenges, and opportunities of AI and digitalisation in education.

In this edited volume, titled Artificial Intelligence and Digitisation in Education we bring together a diverse group of scholars, researchers, educators, and practitioners who have contributed their expertise and insights to elucidate the multifaceted dynamics of this rapidly evolving landscape.

Ms. Soumya Priyadarsani Panigrahi and Jasim Ahmad together authored the chapter on Journey of ICT in Indian Education. This chapter examines the transformative path of ICT. It investigates the underlying policies and frameworks that laid the groundwork for ICT in education, followed by an examination of important government actions and stakeholder participation. The chapter concludes with a consideration of the dramatic acceleration in digital education caused by the COVID-19 epidemic, focusing on the shift to online learning, the persistent digital gap, and the innovative answers that arose. This chapter gives a comprehensive overview of the dynamic environment of ICT in Indian education through reflection on success stories, best practices, and lessons learned, as well as ideas for future improvements to provide equitable and excellent education for everyone.

Md. Ashique Husain and Jasim Ahmad together authored a chapter on digital learning platforms and MOOCs as new initiatives. This paper explores the opportunities and challenges presented by this innovative approach to higher education. This paper delves into these opportunities and challenges in detail, highlighting the need for careful planning, technological infrastructure, pedagogical innovation, and policy support to harness the full potential of e-Learning Platforms and MOOCs in higher education. By navigating these opportunities and challenges effectively, institutions can create a dynamic and inclusive educational ecosystem that meets the Needs of the 21st century and beyond.

Ms. Pallavi Jain, Dr. Harish Kumar and Dr. Anup Kumar Rajput together wrote the chapter 'Examining the Role of Digital Storytelling in

Enhancing Writing Skills'. This chapter presents a segment of examination into the pedagogical integration of digital storytelling within the domain of writing skills instruction. The strategic amalgamation of technology into the educational landscape affords students a potent means to enhance their writing skills. Within this context, our research seeks to illuminate the impact of digital storytelling on students' writing skill proficiencies, with a specific focus on the organization of ideas, word choice, sentence fluency, and overall performance. In tandem, it endeavours to delve into the nuanced perspectives of students regarding the incorporation of digital storytelling into their writing practices.

Dr. M. Ponnambaleswari and Aswathy, C.K. explored the adoption of Learning Management Systems (LMS) by B.Ed. students. This paper delves into the acceptance of Learning Management Systems (LMS) by Bachelor of Education (B.Ed.) students. In the dynamic realm of educational technology, LMS platforms have emerged as indispensable tools for facilitating online teaching and learning. Acting as digital aids, these systems play a pivotal role in the educational journey of students and teachers alike. B.Ed. students stand out as trailblazers in embracing the potential of LMS in their academic pursuits. This study aims to elucidate the driving factors behind the widespread acceptance of LMS among B.Ed. students.

Mohd Noor Alam and Dr. Aerum Khan wrote a chapter on utilisation of cloud-based learning platforms. The chapter studies the perception of secondary school students of using cloud-based learning platforms in teaching-learning. The findings of the study highlights lack of awareness among students regarding cloud-based learning platforms and low registration and utilization indicate the need for widespread awareness campaigns to enhance their adoption in both teaching and learning.

Diksha Dhanda wrote about the importance of developing an e-learning style model. This chapter delves into an analysis of existing models for e-learning styles, identifying their limitations and shortcomings. It argues that the evolving digital landscape necessitates the development of a specific model tailored to e-learning styles. With the increasing importance of Information and Communication Technology (ICT) skills in today's digital world, integrating ICT into education is crucial for preparing learners for technological demands. However, despite the widespread adoption of ICT, there exists a disconnect between learners' individual needs and the available technology. While frameworks like TPACK and COI offer guidance on ICT integration, they lack specificity regarding what precisely should be integrated. To address this gap and optimize educational experiences, the paper advocates for the creation of an e-learning style model that aligns ICT tools with learner preferences, ultimately aiming to enhance learning outcomes in the digital era.

Samra Jamal and Aerum Khan together wrote a chapter on the perception of education through digital learning. The chapter aims to explore the landscape of education through digital learning methods, focusing on the availability and accessibility of the Internet, gadgets, and devices. Additionally, it seeks to understand the motivational aspirations of learners in utilizing digital learning platforms. Conducted as a qualitative research study, the paper utilized open-ended questionnaires to gather insights from undergraduate-level participants in teacher training programs.

Mohammad Amir Khan's chapter on the role of digitalisation and ICT-based learning in higher education showcases the efforts made by digitalisation in bringing changes to the education sector, including the provision of creative solutions that improve teaching, learning, and administrative procedures. The chapter discusses a wide range of associated services and programs, such as video conferencing and remote learning. These technologies are employed in education, specifically to create learning environments to assist and enhance student learning. Further the function and impact of ICTs are discussed, as well as it talks about how they may support growth and development in the future.

Madhurima Pal and Prof. Fauzia Khan wrote a chapter on the parent's views on the use of educational films as a teaching tool. This chapter aims to investigate the perspectives of parents regarding educational films and their efficacy as teaching-learning materials. With the continuous rise in the production of educational films, children are increasingly exposed to this medium both within and outside classroom settings, often through technological platforms. Given the crucial role parents play in a child's development, understanding their views on various aspects related to their child's education, including the use of educational films, is essential. Through this exploration, the chapter seeks to provide insights into parental perceptions, attitudes, and preferences regarding the utilization of educational films as a tool for enhancing learning experiences.

Dr. Vinod Kumar Kanvaria and Shruti Tomar together wrote a chapter on the novel applications and integration of machine learning in education. This research study examines the evolving intersection of Machine Learning (ML) and education, analyzing recent trends and applications observed over the past six years. It highlights three prominent trends: Predicting Learning Paths, Personalized Learning Paths, and advancements in Assessment, Grading, and Feedback systems, showcasing ML's transformative potential in educational methodologies. Through an analysis of 30 primary literature articles, the study aims to identify novel ML applications in education and explore methods for integrating ML into educational settings. By providing nuanced insights into ML's impact on teaching practices and learner-centered approaches, the study contributes to understanding ML's role in shaping the future of education.

Sadia Khalid and Dr. Aerum Khan together did a content review of the *Mann ki Baat* radio series. This chapter is a comprehensive content analysis of *Mann Ki Baat* episodes, focusing on topics related to education and associated issues such as Vedic Maths, promoting book gifting over bouquets, establishing Akshara Libraries, teaching sign language, converting waste to wealth, and advocating for local businesses. Through this analysis, researchers aim to pave the path for further investigation into the effectiveness of this flagship program in addressing educational concerns and promoting initiatives for societal development. By examining the content of *Mann Ki Baat* episodes, the study seeks to shed light on the program's impact and potential contributions to educational reform and social change.

Gulafshan Salam Khan did a review on podcasts as a tool to enhance language learning. This paper examines the role of podcasts in language learning, specifically targeting listening and speaking skills enhancement. Podcasts serve as innovative and effective computer-based learning tools that aid in improving language learners' listening and pronunciation abilities. They offer independent learning materials, lectures by educators, and expert presentations accessible within learning management systems. The chapter explores how the integration of podcasts into traditional teaching methods can influence educational outcomes, emphasizing the importance of both students' and teachers' active engagement in podcast utilization. Ultimately, the study aims to evaluate the impact of podcasting on language education and its potential to revolutionize conventional teaching approaches.

Abdul Badi in his paper delved into the investigation of teachers' perspectives on online learning and the challenges they encounter. The study focuses on educators from Government and Government Aided Urdu Medium Schools in Delhi, India, employing a descriptive survey methodology. The author utilizes a self-structured closed-ended questionnaire as the primary data collection tool to gain insights into teachers' perceptions of online education. Through this exploration, the paper aims to provide valuable insights into prospects towards online learning and the obstacles the teachers face, contributing to the enhancement of online education effectiveness in Urdu medium schools.

Pavitra Rana and Sarita Kumari wrote a chapter on disruptive technologies, digital India, and the digital divide. This chapter evaluates the readiness of technological infrastructure to accommodate disruptive technologies and their potential implications for education. Through an analysis of advantages and challenges, it examines the transformative impact disruptive technologies may have on the educational landscape. By assessing the readiness of existing infrastructure, the study aims to anticipate and address potential barriers to the effective integration of disruptive technologies in education. Ultimately, the chapter seeks to provide insights into the opportunities and challenges posed by disruptive technologies, offering recommendations for optimizing their utilization in educational settings to enhance teaching and learning outcomes.

Stuti Shandilya explored augmented reality through a technological intervention that transforms the idea of new age learning. This chapter examines the efficacy of Augmented Reality (AR) in transforming learning into an engaging and enjoyable experience, thereby fostering a renewed emphasis on the intrinsic joy of learning. By reviewing the impact of AR technology on educational outcomes, it explores how AR can reinvigorate learning environments and motivate learners to pursue excellence. In contrast to the current competitive learning landscape, AR offers the potential to reignite students' enthusiasm for learning by providing immersive and interactive experiences. The paper aims to highlight the transformative potential of AR in promoting a holistic approach to education that prioritizes enjoyment and intrinsic motivation.

Naresh Kumar wrote a chapter on the volunteers' experience with implementing Vidyanjali 2.0 portals in schools. This paper discusses the challenges encountered by volunteers during their involvement in the implementation of Vidyanjali 2.0 portals in schools, drawing from the author's firsthand experience as a volunteer. Vidyanjali 2.0 aims to facilitate volunteer engagement in educational activities within schools. Through personal experiences and observations, the author highlights the obstacles faced by volunteers in effectively contributing to educational initiatives. By sharing insights gained from direct involvement, the paper provides a valuable perspective on the challenges inherent in implementing Vidyanjali 2.0 and offers recommendations for addressing these issues to enhance volunteer participation and impact in school settings.

Sadiya Saheen and Dr. Aerum Khan explored the awareness, perception, preparedness and challenges of school students regarding the use of AI applications in their paper. The sample of the study consisted of 55 school students of Delhi schools. A purposive sampling technique was used. A questionnaire, consisting of both open and closed-ended questions was constructed to collect data from students. The findings suggest that there is optimism for using AI applications, but more education may be needed to ensure that school students have a deeper understanding of AI and its potential benefits and drawbacks. The results also suggest that while there is a general positive view of AI, there is a need to ensure that AI-enabled tools are reliable, accurate, and effective in meeting the needs of diverse types of learners.

Dr. Zainab Musheer wrote the chapter 'Impact of AI-Driven Classroom Assistants on Teacher Workload'. Utilizing a survey-based approach, this study delves into the experiences of educators, seeking to uncover the intricacies of AI integration in their daily instructional routines. The survey instrument is carefully crafted to assess key variables such as time allocation, task distribution, and the perceived effectiveness of AI in supporting teaching responsibilities. By employing a survey-centric approach, the study seeks to provide a nuanced understanding of teachers' experiences and perspectives regarding the integration of AI tools in their classrooms. The findings of this research contribute valuable insights into the multifaceted relationship between AI and teacher workload, shedding light on the potential benefits and challenges associated with the incorporation of AI-driven classroom assistants. The outcomes of this study aim to inform educational stakeholders, policymakers, and technology developers about the implications of AI implementation for teachers, with the ultimate goal of fostering informed decision-making and promoting the effective integration of AI technologies in educational settings.

Mufti Shahla and Mahmood Ahmad Khan authored the chapter 'Artificial Intelligence in Education: Impact on Learning and Creativity'. This study was conducted to understand the impact of AI on learning and creative thinking. A qualitative research approach, leveraging the use of literature review as a research design was used and effectively facilitated the realisation of the study purpose. A systematic search of numerous online databases published between 2019 to 2023 which covered the connection between AI and learning, AI and creativity resulted in the investigation of21 studies. This study was conducted on PRISMA guidelines. This study investigates the intricate relationship between AI and learning, AI and students' creative thinking ability acknowledging the potential paradox wherein AI may serve as both a facilitator and a constraint. In the end, it also suggests adopting a balanced approach towards AI.

Dr. Uzma Siddiqui wrote the chapter 'Artificial Intelligence Usage in Academic Writing among Research Scholars'. This descriptive study aims to evaluate awareness, perceptions, and opinions towards the uses of AI in academic writing among research scholars at Aligarh Muslim University, Aligarh, Uttar Pradesh. The data collection was carried out using online questionnaires on a convenience sample of 213 research scholars enrolled in the faculties of Arts and Social Sciences respectively. The results of the statistical analysis of data revealed that overall, scholars had good awareness of AI. Moreover, the majority of the students had positive perceptions about the concept and uses of AI. The findings of this study imply that incorporating AI into curricula at an early stage is a great way to prepare students and researchers for the widespread usage of AI in their future careers.

Babita authored the chapter 'Navigating Intellectual Property Rights in the Era of AI'. This chapter explores how the use of AI and machine learning can affect the protection of intellectual property in the education sector, how educational institutions can understand the importance of safeguarding intellectual rights and oversight, and how critical issues of intellectual rights in the context of AI utilization for the education sector have been deliberated upon. It ensures that technological advancements not only bring benefits to education but also assist in safeguarding intellectual property from negative impacts. Moreover, it indicates the need for stronger policies and procedures in educational institutions to safeguard the intellectual rights and privacy of children.

Irum Alvi wrote the chapter 'Impact of AI for Advancing Technical and Soft Skills in Engineering Education'. The study scrutinizes the NEP 2020 document to identify and analyze themes, sub-themes, and themes, to comprehensively understand the document's approach towards the use of AI for fostering excellence in technical and soft skills. The next part presents an empirical and quantitative analysis based on raw data collected from 540 Technical Students from Kota, Rajasthan using an online structured questionnaire to delve into these themes and offer insights into the students' perceptions and experiences. The data was analyzed using SPSS v 26 for patterns and trends that assess students' perceptions on themes identified using qualitative methods, namely Curricular Adaptation, Skill Emphasis, Pedagogical Strategies, Ethical and Responsible AI Use, Teacher Training and Capacity Building, Assessment and Evaluation, Equity and Access, Research and Innovation, Industry Collaboration and Future Readiness. The findings have immense practical and managerial implications for AI integrations in education and contribute to informed decision-making, implementation of innovative teaching and training in Technical institutes, and preparation of an efficient workforce for the contemporary globalized market.

Dr. Dhriti Tiwari and Dr. Sangeeta Suman wrote the chapter 'Machine Learning: Navigating Promises and Pitfalls of AI'. This study is focused on the complex interplay between the possible benefits and innate difficulties posed by artificial intelligence (AI) in education. It sheds light on the potential of artificial intelligence (AI) in education, highlighting its ability to improve educational accessibility, customize learning experiences, and transform pedagogical approaches. Concurrently, through a thorough analysis of recent research, it examines the drawbacks of implementing AI, delving into worries about over-reliance and dependency, cognitive decline, reduced creativity, issues of attention and distraction, the possible loss of human touch in the learning process, and social isolation. This research contributes to the existing discourse by suggesting responsible AI integration strategies for promoting the harmonious coexistence of technology and pedagogy in educational settings.

Mohammad Haseen Ahmed authored the chapter 'Creating a Positive and Supportive Culture around AI in Education'. In this chapter, the author emphasizes the importance of raising awareness and understanding among educators and policymakers about the potential and challenges of AI, advocating for comprehensive training and professional development programs. Through practical strategies, case studies, and recommendations, the chapter aims to foster a culture of openness, collaboration, and innovation that supports the ethical and equitable use of AI in education, ultimately advancing the objectives and principles outlined in the Indian NEP-2020.

Babita Yadav and Manvi Yadav wrote the chapter 'Integration of AI in the Personalised Learning of Dyscalculia'. This chapter explores the applications of artificial intelligence in enhancing the learning outcome of dyscalculic students and its effectiveness in personalized learning. This innovative approach supports and aids the design of effective intervention plans tailored to the specific needs of students with dyscalculia. It facilitates the creation of learning content, tools and assessment processes that enhance their learning experiences. The data are sourced from various reputable studies and meticulously narrowed down to focus on personalized learning for students with dyscalculia.

Rajnee Gaur and Harmeet Kaur authored the chapter 'Artificial Intelligence in Education: Opportunities and Threats'. This study examines the complex environment of artificial intelligence (AI) in education intending to identify the possible risks as well as the exciting opportunities that come with its use. The authors explore the many uses of AI in educational contexts, such as automated assessment tools, intelligent tutoring systems, and personalised learning, through an extensive study of the literature.

Prachi Khanna and Dori Lal wrote a chapter on the effect of Artificial Intelligence on the learning and academic achievement of students. The primary emphasis of this research will be on understanding how university students interact with chat-bot learning platforms. The goal is to investigate how the use of these platforms influences students' performance and learning within the classroom setting. It also aims to determine whether it has a positive impact, such as improving learning outcomes, or it has any negative consequences, such as a potential decrease in academic performance or engagement.

Dr. Rohit authored the chapter on Digi-AI in performing arts education and explores the potential of Digi-AI, the merging of digital technologies and artificial intelligence, to revolutionize performing arts education across music, dance, and drama in India. Through mixed methods, we analyze the current landscape, identify challenges, and assess Digi-AI's impact on artistic learning. Emphasizing culturally sensitive integration, digital divide bridging, and ethical implementation, our findings offer concrete recommendations and guide future research. This study charts a course for leveraging Digi-AI to nurture artistic expression, democratize access, and shape the future of performing arts education in India and beyond.

Tahira Akhtar, Shabnama Nadir and Prof. Mohammad Yusoof together wrote the chapter 'Digital Gaming Addiction, Academic Self-handicapping and Educational Aspiration'. This study investigates the interplay between digital gaming addiction, academic self-handicapping, and educational aspirations among secondary school students in the district of Baramulla, Kashmir. Using a sample of 100 students (50 male and 50 female) selected through random sampling, the study employs self-report measures to assess digital gaming addiction, academic self-handicapping, and educational aspirations.

By examining these variables, the paper aims to provide insights into the relationship between excessive gaming habits, academic behaviours, and students' aspirations for their educational future. Ultimately, the study seeks to shed light on the potential impacts of digital gaming addiction on academic performance and educational goals among secondary school students.

Merajul Hasan and Prof. Ujjwal Kumar Halder authored the chapter 'Internet Addiction among Undergraduate Students'. This chapter is an attempt to study Internet addiction among undergraduate students in the Uttar Dinajpur district of West Bengal. This chapter also aimed to explore the differences among college-level students in their Internet addiction in terms of different sub-samples of the population, followed by the survey method of descriptive research.

Sapna Raj authored the chapter 'Self Esteem and Body Image of Students Addicted to Social Media'. This research paper delves into the intricate dynamics of social media usage among college students pursuing Bachelor of Arts programs at Hindu College and Ramjas College, aiming to comprehend its impact on body image perceptions and self-esteem. The study also highlights significant gender-specific differences in the influence of social media on body image and self-esteem. Furthermore, the study offers valuable insights for educators, policymakers, and mental health professionals, emphasizing the importance of addressing gender-specific influences of social media on psychological well-being among the youth in higher education.

Altaf Ahmad Sheikh, Dr. Manzoor Ahmad Rather and Owaise Jan Kirmani have authored the chapter 'Digital Technologies and Online Learning Addiction: Impact on Mental Health'. This review chapter aims to explore the relationship between excessive usage of social networking sites/technologies and the development of online addiction among learners, along with its impact on mental health in the digital era. Conducted through a systematic search of online databases from 2011 to 2023, the study examines 15 relevant research studies. Findings suggest that prolonged technology use contributes to online addiction, leading to various mental health issues. Adhering to PRISMA guidelines, the study synthesizes secondary data from sources including the draft NEP 2020, publications, research papers, journals, and websites, providing valuable insights into the implications of digital technology on mental well-being.

2

Digital Transformation

Journey of ICT in Indian Education

Soumya Priyadarsani Panigrahi and Jasim Ahmad

Introduction

In recent years the education system in India has gone through a paradigm shift. One of the most powerful instruments that help in the transformation is ICT (Information and Communication Technology). In an age where technology is changing rapidly, the integration of ICT in education has been very crucial in order to prepare the next generation for the 21st century. Being a country with the largest population in the world, trying to achieve hundred per cent access to education for all while chasing the dream of quality education, integration of ICT in education was not easy. Keeping in mind India's digital divide, the major goal was to ensure that ICT integration leads to inclusion rather than further exclusion. The journey of ICT in education in India has gone through a dynamic interplay of technological advancements, policies to incorporate those advancements and initiatives to implement those policies.

Educational Landscape of India

Over time, the Indian education system revealed a rich tapestry woven with layers of adaptation and innovation. However, like India, the Indian educational landscape is diverse and complicated. With a population of 1.44 billion (as of January 2024) and a broad network of schools and colleges, India offers a high potential for ICT integration and at the same time makes this one of the most challenging tasks. Considering fast socio-economic changes and technological improvements, the Indian educational system faces an array of challenges, ranging from access inequities to quality problems. Despite a rich history of the education system, India is still struggling with issues of universal access, quality and equity in education delivery (MUNDHE, 2024).

ICT in Education

In India, where traditional educational paradigms frequently fail to fulfil the needs of a rapidly changing society, ICT emerges as a catalyst for transformation. ICT has the capacity to overcome geographical obstacles, bridge socio-economic differences, and provide learners with the knowledge and skills they need to succeed in the digital age by harnessing digital technology, interactive learning platforms, and online resources.

This chapter reflects on the growth of ICT in education in India, from its early stages to its current position as a crucial component of the country's education agenda. By exploring significant legislative initiatives, government programs, technology developments, and grassroots efforts, we hope to present a thorough picture of ICT in Indian education. We expect that our investigation will uncover new trends, best practices, and areas for future growth and innovation in the use of ICT for educational reform.

Radio – Means of Education in Indian Context

In June 1923, the first ever radio program was broadcast by the Radio Club of Bombay. In India, All India Radio (AIR) was established in 1936 and then renamed Akashvani in 1957. It is currently administered by Prasar Bharati, an autonomous public service broadcaster that has existed since 1997.

However, radio as a means of education was started in the British period in India. Several significant milestones highlighted the emergence of radio as an educational instrument in India:

- ***School Broadcast Project:*** The very first education project in radio was the School Broadcast Project, launched in 1937. It was targeted at elementary and secondary school students. This program was aired in Kolkata (Calcutta), Chennai (Madras), Mumbai (Bombay) and Delhi. In 1940 this program was also broadcast from Tiruchirapalli. The programs were in the Indian language and there was no specific curriculum. Though the programs were educational, the main focus was on entertainment. Madras commenced broadcasting for college students in 1939. The programs were in English. With no specific curriculum for a specific age group, this program was not very successful (UNESCO, 1949).
- ***Adult Education, Farm and Community:*** As a radio discussion program, Farm Radio Forum was started in Canada in 1941. It was then introduced in India in 1956. The program was initiated and sponsored by UNESCO. This program covered the issues in agriculture, rural education, development and literacy. The main objective was to use this program as an instrument for adult education. This program was a huge success in India (Samag, 2018). In 1965, it was determined to create Farm and Home Units in 10 AIR Stations to bring extensive Agricultural District and Comprehensive Agricultural Area Programs to the farming community. Farm School on Air, another accomplishment in rural radio, debuted in 1973. As a result, farmers' interest in and readiness to learn contemporary farming methods increased. Non-formal education is demonstrated by AIR's large farm

broadcasting production, as well as another 1970s invention aimed at rural audiences. Non-formal education broadcasts for rural youth aged 15 to 25 have commenced at AIR's five stations in Srinagar, Nagpur, Tiruchi, Shimla, and Jaipur. On February 15, 2004, launched a new project called narrowcasting to transform its hard-core agriculture program into 'The Voice of Farmers', or 'Kisanvani' (Source: https://www.aesanetwork.org/blog-191-the-continuing-relevance-of-all-india-radio-for-agricultural-development-in-the-digital-era/).

- ***Radio Pilot Project:*** In 1979-1980, the AIR along with the Department of Education, Government of Rajasthan launched this Language Learning Program. The objective was to facilitate Hindi learning as their first language for school-going students in 500 elementary schools in Jaipur and Ajmer districts through an experimental approach. The broadcasts were found to help children improve their vocabulary, so a similar effort was launched in Madhya Pradesh's Hoshangabad area.
- ***IGNOU-AIR:*** With the collaboration of IGNOU and AIR Shillong, Mumbai and Hyderabad, IGNOU-AIR was introduced in 1992. IGNOU-AIR Interactive Radio Counseling (IRC) was introduced in May 1998 for students at Open and Conventional Universities. AIR Bhopal and IGNOU piloted a year-long initiative to offer academic counselling and reply to student inquiries. The program proved successful and was expanded to additional AIR stations. Currently, All India Radio's 186 radio stations deliver one hour of Interactive Radio Counseling every Sunday. Gyan-vani was launched in 2001. It is the first exclusive radio program in India. It targets university students enrolled in various universities both traditional and open learning (Chandar & Sharma, 2003).

Impact and Challenges

In India, radio was introduced at a time when a large number of Indian citizens were still illiterate. Unlike print media which required reading to get the written information, radio was an easier option, especially among people in rural India. Also, the ability to penetrate in the remote and under-developed areas of India makes the impact of radio on people high. Unlike television where electricity and TV sets are essential requirements, radio was easily accessible at a much lower cost to the economically disadvantaged people of India. The programs on the radio are broadcast in various languages to ensure the inclusivity of languages in a multilingual country like India and catering to more and more people. According to its website, All India Radio (AIR) is one of the country's largest public service broadcasters, with 287 stations addressing 99 per cent of the population in 23 languages and 146 dialects (Gupta, 2022). Radio caters to a wide range of subjects in various fields. Radio played a critical role in increasing the rate of literacy, fostering vocational skills, and spreading essential knowledge, all of which contributed to the nation's overall socio-educational development.

Although it has numerous advantages, the usage of radio for teaching purposes in India has various problems and restrictions. The medium's intrinsic lack of interactivity reduced instructor-student engagement and feedback, which is an essential component of effective education. Another key problem was ensuring the quality and relevancy of educational content, which necessitated careful planning and competence to suit the population's different requirements. Technological concerns, including inadequate reception in certain rural places, hampered the clarity and reliability of broadcasts, lowering their effectiveness. Furthermore, as new media technologies such as television and later digital platforms arose, radio had to compete for attention and resources, frequently fighting to remain relevant. These issues combined to limit radio's effectiveness as a transformational teaching tool (Mann, 2023).

Innovation and Expansion through TVs and PCs

During the 1960s India started experimenting with educational broadcasting on television.

- ***Secondary School television project:*** With the Ford Foundation's assistance, the Directorate of Schools in Delhi developed educational programs in Physics, Chemistry, English, Hindi, Social Studies, and Geography in 1961. Two hundred fifty TV sets were installed in various schools in Delhi to watch these educational programs (Shaw, 2008).
- ***Krishi Darshan:*** Krishi Darshan as the name suggests was a project launched in 1966 with the aim to provide information related to agriculture. This program was only for 80 villages of Delhi's union territory.
- ***SITE:*** The SITE (Satellite Instructional Television Experiment) implemented in 1975 was a pioneering project that established TV as a means of education. The Government of India launched SITE through collaboration with the National Aeronautics and Space Administration (NASA) to air educational content in rural India. The project, encompassing over 2,400 communities across six states, aimed to deliver information on education, health, farming and family planning (Shaw, 2008).
- ***INSAT:*** In 1982, India launched its own satellite, after the success of SITE. In the same year, UGC introduced a program called INSAT for Education. The program was aimed at producing quality educational content for the students enrolled in under-graduate in various rural and suburban colleges. In 1984, UGC initiated the Countrywide Classroom initiative. It used INSAT satellites to telecast educational content for both schools and colleges. The programs were created to complement the teaching in the classroom, encompassing an array of subject areas such as

maths, social studies, and science. It also included content on vocational training (Shaw, 2008).

- ***Gyan Darshan:*** Gyan Darshan, an educational television station founded in 2000, was intended to offer high-quality educational content to students throughout India. It was a collaboration between the Ministry of Human Resource Development, Prasar Bharati, and IGNOU. Gyan Darshan aired a variety of instructional programs for school children, university students, and lifelong learners. The channel had an important role in increasing access to educational resources, particularly in remote and marginalized communities.
- ***EDUSAT:*** EDUSAT was launched in 2004, it is the first satellite of India that was exclusively for education. It was founded to deliver satellite-based open education to schools and colleges around the country. EDUSAT encouraged interactive classroom sessions, which allowed for two-way conversations between learners and their educators. This effort greatly expanded the quality and scope of education, especially in remote regions of India.
- ***SWAYAM Prabha:*** SWAYAM Prabha, a set of 40 DTH (Direct to Home) television channels, launched in 2017 to offer high-quality content for education around the clock. The channels provide an array of topics, appealing to learners from school to university. SWAYAM Prabha was created to narrow the digital gap by giving educational resources to learners who do not have an Internet connection. The channels are run by India's finest educational institutions, which ensures the content's quality and relevancy.

Impact and Challenges

The accessibility of fascinating and multi-sensory learning opportunities via television has considerably improved educational experiences in India, particularly in remote and impoverished communities with limited access to excellent education. Gyan Darshan, and later SWAYAM Prabha, broadened the breadth of educational programming by providing diverse content in multiple regional languages, encouraging inclusivity and supporting lifelong learning. Television's vast geographical coverage, combined with government efforts and the introduction of Direct-to-Home (DTH) services, ensured that educational programs reached even the most neglected regions.

The medium had various disadvantages, including a lack of interactivity, which hampered personalized participation and feedback. Technical and infrastructure issues, such as insufficient electricity and inadequate reception of signals in remote areas, hampered its efficacy. Despite becoming more inexpensive, TVs and subscriptions remained prohibitively expensive for some low-income homes. Maintaining the quality and relevance of educational content necessitated ongoing work and resources while promoting awareness of and encouraging TV as a regular source of education faced additional obstacles. Despite these challenges, television has had a significant impact on Indian education by improving learning experiences and supporting social growth.

Computers in Education

The 1980s saw the first wave of computer use in India's educational landscape, mainly in urban regions and higher education institutions. During this time, some educational institutions began to use mainframe computers and early personal computers (PCs). However, due to high costs and limited availability, computer penetration remained low, with usage restricted to a small sector of the population.

IIT Kanpur was a pioneer in computer-related education in India. The first computer-related classes began in August 1963 at IIT Kanpur, with a system deployed in the nation's first computer classroom (source: https://cse.iitk.ac.in/pages/AboutTheDepartment.html). However, CLASS was the first project that brought the computer to school. In 1984, the Government of India recognized the importance of ICT in education and A pilot project *Computer Literacy and Studies in Schools* (CLASS) was introduced (UNESCO, 1987). The National Policy on Education (NPE) was developed in 1986, emphasizing the importance of incorporating technology into education. The NPE's following revision in 1992 emphasized the need to use ICT to improve the quality of teaching and learning. Despite these legislative instructions, the implementation of ICT projects in education has remained limited due to infrastructure and resource restrictions. In July 1998, the then prime minister constituted a *National Task Force on Information Technology and Software Development*, which laid down specific recommendations on the introduction of IT in the education sector. During this time, instructional software began to gain popularity, although in limited numbers. Educational institutions and software companies began developing basic educational programs and apps for PCs, with a concentration on disciplines such as mathematics, science, and language acquisition. The availability of such software aided early attempts to use technology to enhance traditional classroom learning.

Impact and Challenges

The learning environment was transformed by the introduction of computers in education. Access to a vast array of information and educational resources was made possible by computers. The learning experience was enhanced by the development of computer-aided learning tools and instructional software. Higher education saw a surge in the popularity of computer science, contributing to the growth of India's IT industry.

The use of computers for education faced numerous challenges. Due to the high expense of computers, many schools, particularly in rural regions, did not have access to them. A lack of infrastructure, such as electricity and Internet access, was a considerable challenge. Furthermore, a dearth of computer-trained teachers hampered the successful implementation of computer literacy initiatives. The digital divide between cities and rural areas, as well as between socio-economic categories, remained a significant barrier.

Through Policies and Initiatives

In 2002, SSA (Sarva Shiksha Abhiyan) was launched with the aim of providing universal access to elementary education. It also tries to bridge the digital gap through computer education. In 2003, The National Programme on Technology Enhanced Learning (NPTEL) offered high-quality educational content online, with an initial focus on engineering and science fields. Since 2004, the Government of India has attempted a number of measures to incorporate ICT into education to ensure that future generations have the necessary digital competencies. The ICT in Schools initiative was aimed to give chances for secondary school pupils to develop their ICT skills and facilitate learning using cutting-edge technology (Asrani, 2020). The 2005 National Policy on Education (NPE) Amendment acknowledged the necessity for technology-enhanced learning and stressed the integration of ICT in education. The National Mission on Education through ICT (NMEICT) was launched in 2009 to use ICT to improve the quality of teaching and learning in higher education institutions.

NROER (National Repository of Open Educational Resources) was established by the National Council of Educational Research and Training (NCERT) in 2013. NROER is an online platform that provides open and free educational content. The repository contains digital textbooks, interactive information, films, and other educational tools that assist teachers and students in improving their learning experiences. In the year 2014, the *Digital India* Initiative was launched to transform India into a digitally enabled society and knowledge economy, with efforts promoting digital literacy and connectivity in education.

SWAYAM (Study Webs of Active-Learning for Young Aspiring Minds) was founded in 2017 to offer free online courses ranging from high school to university level on a variety of topics. In the same year, *SWAYAM Prabha* was launched. It was a group of 32 DTH channels that provided educational content for schools and higher education.

DIKSHA (Digital Infrastructure for School Education) was launched by NCERT in 2017 under the Ministry of Education, Government of India. This is an online platform that facilitates various digital resources such as e-books, videos and much more interactive content for school education according to the prescribed curriculum by the NCERT.

Pradhan Mantri e-Vidya Program was announced in 2019 as part of the New Education Policy (NEP) to encourage online education, which includes the creation of digital infrastructure and content. NEP 2020 emphasizes the revolutionary potential of computer integration in education and provides plans for using technology to improve educational access, equity, and quality at all levels of India's education system.

Thrived through Innovation in the Pandemic (COVID-19 Era)

Overview of the period after the COVID-19 pandemic, marked by a rapid shift to online learning and the acceleration of digital transformation in education. The shutdown of schools and universities during lockdowns resulted in a rapid transition to online learning. Virtual classrooms, video conferencing tools, and learning management systems (LMS) have become necessary for providing educational content remotely. Platforms such as Zoom, Google Classroom, and Microsoft Teams witnessed increased usage as educators and students transitioned to online teaching and learning (Panigrahi & Dwivedi, 2021).

Government Initiatives: The various existing resources such as SWAYAM, SWAYAM Prabha, NROER, e-pathshala and DIKSHA have played a crucial role in facing the pandemic and overcoming the shortness of the no physical school era. In April 2020, during the pandemic, the Government launched the program *VidyaDaan*. It is a national educational resource contribution programme. This effort sought to leverage the DIKSHA platform to improve the accessibility and quality of digital educational resources throughout the country. VidyaDaan played a crucial role in guaranteeing education continuity throughout COVID-19 restrictions and afterward, responding to the critical requirement for diversified and good-quality online educational resources. *PM e-vidya* was another initiative of GoI, launched in May 2020 for school education. The objective of this initiative was to unite all initiatives connected to digital, online, and on-air education. It intended to provide fair multi-mode access to education at the school level (Singh et al., 2021). In July 2020, *Manodarpan* was launched to provide psychological support to students and instructors at all levels during the pandemic situation. It aims to bridge the gap between home and school by fostering an understanding of the new "normal" and facilitating peer support, and positivity, promoting e-learning, and developing life skills to become resilient, caring, responsible independent learners, during the pandemic and afterwards (Panigrahi & Dwivedi, 2021).

Way Forward with Artificial Intelligence

AI is revolutionizing the education system by enabling personalized learning, adaptive assessments, high-quality material creation, and teacher support. Personalized learning adapts curriculum to each learner's specific needs, assuring interest and efficacy. Adaptive assessments modify in real-time to provide accurate measures of student achievement and identify areas for improvement. AI creates and curates appropriate instructional information, ensuring that it is current and consistent with curricular standards. Additionally, AI helps teachers by streamlining repetitive chores and providing data-driven analytics into student performance, allowing for more focused and effective education. AI is the need of the hour for the Indian education system (Saxena, 2022) (Dubey et al., 2022). This holistic approach highlights the vital role of AI in improving the quality and accessibility of education and is a requirement to integrate into the Indian education system. Keeping the importance of AI-integration in mind for the first time in India. In 2018, NITI Aayog, published a discussion paper named *NSAI* (National Strategy for Artificial Intelligence). The focus was on its implementation in key sectors and it considered education one of them. The paper emphasizes the role of AI in developing adaptive teaching-learning systems, smart tutoring, and individualized educational plans (NITI, 2022). Then it was also emphasized by NEP 202**0**. It is a groundbreaking strategy that stresses the incorporation of technology, especially artificial intelligence, into the Indian educational system. It promotes the use of AI to tailor learning experiences, improve educational quality, and assure equal access to education. The policy calls for the development of a National Educational Technology Forum (NETF) to enable the exchange of ideas and best practices around the use of technology in education (NEP, 2020). In 2022, UNESCO released the *State of the Education Report for India: Artificial Intelligence in Education*. This detailed paper illustrates AI's disruptive impact on the Indian educational system. It digs into how artificial intelligence technologies are being used to improve learning experiences, personalized education, and close access and quality gaps. The paper also addresses the obstacles and opportunities posed by AI integration in education, offering policymakers, educators, and stakeholders useful insights and ideas for properly using AI's promise. This initiative demonstrates UNESCO's commitment to promoting educational innovation and inclusion in India (UNESCO, 2022).

Planetcode, the Atal Innovation Mission's ATL AI-Base Module, the launch of INDIAai as the "central hub for everything AI in India and beyond," and the Central Board of Secondary Education's effort to integrate AI into the school curriculum are a few of the many commendable and much-needed steps taken toward AI education in India (Source: https://radhika-k-madhavan.medium.com/ai-in-india-history-and-evolution-28aba000504b).

The Ministry of Electronics and Information Technology (MeitY) introduced the "*Responsible AI for Youth*" program in 2020, and over 11,000 government school students finished the introductory AI course.

To get the country ready for an AI future, MeitY, NeGD, and NASSCOM collaborated to create the National AI Portal of India (*INDIAai*) in 2020. The portal offers a treasure trove of information on the rapidly expanding field of artificial intelligence, including research reports, datasets, case studies, educational institutions, courses, and articles.

AIRAWAT (AI Research, Analytics and Knowledge Dissemination Platform) is a platform initiated by the GoI, in order to provide a common computing platform for AI research and knowledge assimilation (source: https://www.meity.gov.in/emerging-technologies-division).

Santhigiri Vidyabhavan is the first-ever AI school that was launched in Kerala in 2023 (Source: https://indiaai.gov.in/news/india-s-first-ai-school-launched-in-kerala).

Anuvadini is a voice and document AI translation tool, it was launched in 2024 by the Ministry of Education and AICTE. This app was built to support twenty-two Indian regional as well as foreign languages.

An AI teacher named ***Iris*** was introduced to a Thiruvananthapuram school in Kerala, marking a first for the country (Source: https://www.hindustantimes.com/trending/indias-first-ai-teacher-iris-launched-in-a-kerala-school-here-s-what-you-need-to-know-101709732297049.html).

Challenges of AI Integration in Indian Education

Being the country with the largest population, where 64.13% (according to the World Bank report of 2022) of the population resides in rural areas, where villages are still struggling to connect with the world of the Internet, AI integration into education is difficult. Digital divides, disparity of resources and infrastructure are the most significant barriers to AI integration. For teachers to be prepared to use AI tools efficiently, there is also a great need for teacher training. Risks also arise from worries about data privacy and security since it is important to keep private student information safe from exploitation and breaches. Furthermore, a lot of money is needed for the development and application of AI technologies, which can be prohibitive for many educational institutions (UNESCO, 2022).

What does India need to focus on?

- An inclusive AI policy in order to cater the diverse needs of the students. This will make AI accessible and beneficial for every student.
- Investment in better digital infrastructures (computers, Internet, digital platforms etc.) to make AI integration easy and smooth. This will help in AI integration in rural and remote areas of India.
- Including AI literacy in teacher education. The teacher must be trained to teach. The only way AI integration in Indian education is feasible is only if the teachers are trained enough to educate the new generation.

- India must focus on collaboration. Collaboration of Government, NGOs, IT companies and educational institutions. Overcoming the various barriers to AI integration can be possible through this partnership.
- R&D (Research and Development) are another important aspect to be focused on. Any significant change in education is possible through quality research.
- Developing guidelines and setting standards for the ethical use of AI. One of the biggest fears of AI integration is data privacy and safety hence India needs strong guidelines that will lead to ethical use and eradicating the fear of data privacy.

Conclusion

From the initial days of radio broadcasting to the new age of Artificial Intelligence integration in the education system, the history of ICT evolution has made a dramatic transformation in India. This journey was not a smooth or easy one. It takes various policies, initiatives and research to make this possible. From the early days of radio broadcasts to the modern era of AI integration, the history of ICT in Indian education reveals a dramatic evolution characterized by advances in technology and changes in policy. In the beginning, radio was a crucial instrument for closing educational gaps, especially in underprivileged and rural areas. More interactive and captivating learning opportunities were made possible by the gradual expansion of educational resources through the introduction of computers and televisions. Programs such as SWAYAM Prabha and SITE demonstrate the government's determination to use technology to improve education. The most recent and potentially revolutionary stage of this journey is the integration of AI. AI has the potential to completely transform the way that education is provided and experienced by providing individualized learning, adaptive assessments, and data-driven insights. But there are a number of obstacles to this change, such as digital gaps, privacy issues with data, and the requirement for large investments in infrastructure and teacher preparation. In the future, AI has enormous potential to offer personalized learning experiences and democratize education, especially in rural areas. India can fully utilize AI by tackling the related issues with thoughtful investments, moral considerations, and inclusive legislation. By guaranteeing that every student, irrespective of their background, has access to a top-notch education, this will help to create a more inventive and equitable educational environment.

References

Chandar, U., & Sharma, R. (2003). Bridges to Effective Learning Through Radio. *International Review of Research in Open and Distance Learning*, *4*(1). https://doi.org/10.19173/irrodl.v4i1.118

Dubey, G., Hasan, M., & Alam, A. (2022). Artificial Intelligence (AI) and Indian Education System: Promising Applications, Potential Effectiveness and Challenges. https://www.researchgate.net/publication/362412596

Gupta, I.B. (2022). One Voice Many Languages, Colonial Radio in India. *Journal of Contemporary History*, *58*(1), 3–25. https://doi.org/10.1177/00220094221121869

Mann, R. (2023, October 1). *Challenges of radio as a mass medium in Indian society*. https://ignited.in/jasrae/article/download/14558/28920/72263?inline=1

Nag, B. (1989). Informatics Education in India: The CLASS Project For Secondary Students. Higher Education Policy, 2(4), 71–72. doi:10.1057/hep.1989.76

NEP (2020) (1): Policy document released by Government of India Retrieved on Retrieved June 8, 2024, from https://www.education.gov.in/sites/upload_files/mhrd/files/NEP_Final_English.pdf

NITI Aayog. (2022). Responsible-AI-AIForAll. In *https://www.niti.gov.in*. Retrieved June 8, 2024, from https://www.niti.gov.in/sites/default/files/2023-03/Responsible-AI-AIForAll-Approach-Document-for-India-Part-Principles-for-Responsible-AI.pdf

Panigrahi, S. P., & Dwivedi, S. K. (2021). A Study on Online Teaching Learning in School during Pandemic: Opportunities and Challenges. *Praxis International Journal of Social Science and Literature*, *4*(4), 48–54.

Samag, S.V. (2018). Rural Broadcasting by all India Radio is a Social Change Agent. *Journal of Emerging Technologies and Innovative Research (JETIR)*, *5*(3), 674–678. https://www.jetir.org

Saxena, R. (2022). Role of Artificial Intelligence in Indian Education System. *Integrated Journal for Research in Arts and Humanities*, *2*(5), 104–107. https://doi.org/10.55544/ijrah.2.5.16

Shaw, P. (2008). Television in Education. *Media Asia*, *35*(3), 198–204. https://doi.org/10.1080/01296612.2008.11726884

Singh, M., Adebayo, S.O., Saini, M., & Singh, J. (2021). Indian government E-learning initiatives in response to COVID-19 crisis: A case study on online learning in Indian higher education system. *Education and Information Technologies*, *26*(6), PMID: 34177350. https://doi.org/10.1007/s10639-021-10585-1

UNESCO. (1987). Prospects: quarterly review of education. In *UNESCO*. Retrieved June 8, 2024, from https://unesdoc.unesco.org/ark:/48223/pf0000078295

Web References

https://www.aesanetwork.org/blog-191-the-continuing-relevance-of-all-india-radio-for-agricultural-development-in-the-digital-era/

https://radhika-k-madhavan.medium.com/ai-in-india-history-and-evolution-28aba000504b

https://www.meity.gov.in/emerging-technologies-division

https://indiaai.gov.in/news/india-s-first-ai-school-launched-in-kerala

https://www.hindustantimes.com/trending/indias-first-ai-teacher-iris-launched-in-a-kerala-school-here-s-what-you-need-to-know-101709732297049.html).

3

Digital Learning Platforms and MOOCs as New Initiatives

Md. Ashique Husain and Jasim Ahmad

Introduction

The present situation has changed the norms of life be it social norms, educational norms. The increasing use of online teaching-learning tools is witnessing a tremendous change in education. This new way of learning has started especially with the corona pandemic. Online learning is also having an impact on students' academic achievement.

Now we are living in a global civilization and the whole world has become one vast village. Advancements in technology have affected the previous design, way of working and way of living our lives. Online teaching and learning as an environment are becoming beneficial for both students and teachers, which plays a very important role in achieving the goals of education in terms of curriculum. It is becoming more popular these days, and many institutions are working on creating better tools for e-learning. Higher education is being reformed with respect to traditional and online education.

Teaching and learning through online platforms have become very popular among teachers nowadays. This is not only due to the convenience and easy communication with the learners, but also since the platform enables learners to prepare for lessons in advance and motivates them to revise the material learned, as well as take any feedback from the instructors, provide advantage in exchanging ideas about the problem. Among the existing platforms, MOOCs is one of the most popular open sources globally.

Today, due to educational technology, the education system has progressed so much that under any circumstances, students can continue their education through Digital Learning Platform and teachers can also teach easily through Digital Platform. Online education is currently the best option as keeping schools, colleges and universities open sometimes creates problems for students. Schools have also adopted virtual platforms to conduct online classes. As a result, online education has evolved as an alternative to face-to-face classes to meet the needs of all levels of education, from pre-primary to university level. Accordingly, various stakeholders like government and private organizations and various voluntary organizations are trying their best to help each other through improving their Digital Learning platforms, apps and providing training to teachers to use these apps and platforms at an optimum level and more, efforts are being made by government and non-government organizations and individual organizations to support Higher Education to bring about a smooth transition to the virtual world. Skilling and motivating teachers, organizing counseling sessions for stakeholders like teachers, parents, and students. Making continuous efforts to provide suitable customized content for online classes is another way to facilitate Students Achievement. The Central Government has launched Swayam Prabha 34 DTH channels, Swayam, and PM e-Vidya platform with 12 new DTH channels, an initiative for every section to reach out to all sections of the society. These efforts have been designed keeping in mind the interests and needs of students from school education to university education and are proving beneficial for a large section of the population.

Information and Communication Technologies (ICT)

Information and Communication Technologies is the means of distribution of information and exchanging the idea, creation, collaboration, cooperation, storage, management, and dissemination of information via electronic means. In general, information and communication technology can be defined as a means by which remote areas or parts of the world are connected to an offline medium and convey the information there, like through Radio, Telephone, Computer, Internet, Smartphone, etc.

Technologies with different characteristics are emerging in the field of education and communication technology. In these specialized technologies, knowledge can be secured and protected through hardware and software and distributed over an extended period.

According to C-DEC, Department of IT, GoI: "The term Information and Communication Technology (ICT) refers to forms of Technology that are used to transmit, store, create, display, share or exchange information by electronic means. This broad definition of ICT includes such technologies as Radio, Television, Video, DVD, Satellite System, Computer and Network Hardware and software as well as the equipment and services associated with these technologies such as video conferencing, e-mails, and blogs."

Digital Learning Platform

Online learning methods provide exciting opportunities to broaden and holistically enhance the learning environment for diverse students. Gradually the demand for online teaching and learning is increasing, most of the professors have now started bringing their classes in an online medium environment. Now they are not only considering studying online but are also preparing and teaching online courses. Online teaching learning is very similar to face-to-face teaching learning, but it also has a unique set of skills, interests, attitudes, and requirements. Online teaching is very similar to face-to-face teaching except for the pace and delivery of content, both approaches are like each other. Instead of developing courses. Online learning is an emerging concept for better transaction of curriculum. Professors can use digital learning platform to prepare and deliver their courses and many other means of teaching. Using software allows instructors to get it right from the beginning. In digital learning platform it is recommended that the instructor should follow the following principles: (1) motivate student to participate, (2) enhance student participation, (3) encourage student collaboration, (4) encourage active and live learning, (5) give continuous feedback, (6) respect diversities of learner and their learning style. (7) address individual differences, (8) provide self-paced to the student, (9) give real life experience (10) encourage student understanding and reflection.

Some of the Digital Learning Platforms

I. *SWAYAM* — It is an acronym for the Study Webs of Active Learning for Young Aspiring Minds. Initiative taken by the Government of India, which encourages lifelong learning. It is a MOOCs platform for distance education that is aimed at offering varied forms of courses from School Education (Class IX) to University Education. SWAYAM was developed jointly by MHRD (now the Ministry of Education) and All India Council for Technical Education in 2014 with the help of Microsoft and is capable of hosting 2,000 courses.

II. *NPTEL* — NPTEL stands for the National Programme on Technology Enhanced Learning. It is an initiative by the Ministry of Education (formerly Ministry of Human Resource Development) in India to enhance the quality of engineering and science education in the country. NPTEL provides free online courses and study materials in various disciplines, including engineering, sciences, humanities, and management. The courses offered through NPTEL are developed by professors and experts from top Indian institutes, such as the Indian Institutes of Technology (IITs) and the Indian Institute of Science (IISc).

III. *mooKIT* — It is a light-weight MOOCs platform like EdX which is conceived, designed and developed by IIT Kanpur to deliver and manage courses online. mooKIT has been developed at the Computer Science department at IIT Kanpur with best breed features and state-of-art technology.

IV. *ITBX* — It is a MOOCs platform developed by IIT Bombay. This platform has been created for learners including academicians, students, researchers, professionals, administrative staff, and novice users, including educationally, socially, economically, physically disadvantaged groups or others that seek to transform themselves through cutting-edge technologies, innovative pedagogy, and rigorous courses.

V. *Coursera* — Offers a wide range of courses from universities and colleges around the world, covering diverse subjects.
VI. *edX*— Similar to Coursera, edX provides online courses from universities and institutions globally. It also offers MicroMasters and Professional Certificate programs.
VII. *Udacity* — Focuses on tech-related courses and nanodegree programs, providing hands-on projects and mentorship.
VIII. *Skillshare* — An online learning community that offers classes on a variety of creative skills, such as design, photography, and writing.
IX. *Udemy* — A platform where individuals can create and sell their courses on a wide range of topics, from business to personal development.
X. *Canvas* — A learning management system (LMS) used by educational institutions to manage and deliver online courses.
XI. *Blackboard* — Another popular LMS used by schools and universities for online learning and course management.
XII. *Duolingo* — A language-learning platform that offers a gamified approach to learning new languages.
XIII. *FutureLearn* — Offers a diverse range of courses from universities and cultural institutions, often with a global focus.
XIV. *Pluralsight* — Primarily focused on technology and software development courses, including IT certifications.

Massive Open Online Courses (MOOCs)

The term MOOCs was coined by Dave Cormier in 2008 in the University of Prince Edward Island for a course offered by University of Manitoba, i.e. "Connectivism and Connect Knowledge". MOOCs has thousands of registered users worldwide offering hundreds of courses. In the year 2011, some educational videos were developed by Stanford University professors and released through open online platforms supported with free web resources. This was the time when the use of MOOCs grew tremendously around the world, with their numbers ever increasing. All learners who use Internet resources can participate in MOOCs for free. Here the learner can participate in more than one course and can get all types of learning materials. Ultimately, it can be said that there is openness in MOOCs in terms of the role of the learner. Cormier and Siemens (2010) explain openness in their article by saying, "When learners step through our open doors, they can enter our workplace, engage in research, engage in discussion, and develop knowledge, are invited to contribute." MOOCs is an acronym for Massive Open Online Courses, in other words, we can say that there are four elements of MOOCs i.e., Massive, Open, Online, Courses.

i. *Massive*: There are huge logically unlimited participants.
ii. *Open*: It is open to all means anyone can access the course free of cost without entry qualification.
iii. *Online*: Means the full course is available on the Internet.
iv. *Course*: It offers a wide variety of complete courses and provide complete learning experiences.

MOOCs have Four Quadrants

I. *E-Content*: MOOCs provide E-content i.e. PPT, PDF, Text, Document that can be downloaded and printed.
II. *Video Lecture*: MOOCs provide explanatory videos, they can be 7-8 mins long, even can be of half an hour that can be viewed anytime, anywhere according to the need and convenience.
III. *Assessment Questions*: MOOCs provide close-ended assessment based on particular topic that can be attempted anytime and anywhere by the participants according to their pace and convenience.
IV. *Discussion forum*: In MOOCs platform, discussion forums are provided to engage the learner by the instructor in which participants are required to actively participate and clear their doubt.

Related Literature

Li Y (2019), worked on the title as "MOOCs in Higher Education: Opportunities and Challenges" discussed as learners can register on the MOOC platform for free, characterized by an open curriculum and excellent open-ended outcomes, making it widely popular around the world. MOOCs have brought great opportunities for learners to access high-quality courses more easily and for instructors to present their teaching capabilities on a larger platform. Also, MOOCs face challenges such as high dropout rates compared to high enrollment rates and lack of effective evaluation systems. The further development of MOOCs lies in blended learning by combining traditional classroom teaching and online teaching, the relationship between which is complementary.

Mallikarjuna (2018, August), worked on the title as "Digital Initiatives Online Learning Community Towards MOOCs and OER on Engineering Education". MOOCs have made education easy and accessible to anyone, anytime, anywhere across the world through the Internet and have made people's lives better by providing pace and quality education. The education system managed through advanced technologies and online teaching-learning will help India boost its growth, MOOCs are rapidly gaining popularity in the eyes of learners. MOOCs are proving to be exemplary in this direction for Indians who want quality based Global Education. Teachers work collaboratively within a framework to support each other through shared planning and curriculum development, access resources, and provide feedback to teachers in the professional learning community. Digital content will also help online learners find an appropriate pedagogy that will be reflective of and accountable to the content.

Pouezevara & Horn (2016, March), worked on the title as "Digital Initiatives Online Learning Community Towards MOOCs and OER on Engineering Education". discussed as large-scale MOOCs have attracted attention in recent years as both an opportunity and a threat in higher education around the world. "MOOCs for Development '' is increasingly becoming the focus of international conferences, journals, books and donor-funded projects. MOOCs and other forms of online learning to provide access to sources of expertise that may not be locally available or up-to-date in changing circumstances (job market learning-training or health crisis management) and to connect with a diverse set and development centers. The importance of education platforms has emerged as a new business model for sharing and developing new content to engage learners around the world, making it possible to offer courses at scale. The emerging different types of online education are now considered under the umbrella of "MOOCs", resulting in ambiguity in efforts to take stock of MOOCs for development; moreover, any type of MOOCs may not be designed for those populations. Making them accessible and relevant to those who need them most remains challenging due to indirect costs and technical, cultural and language barriers.

Biswas & Sarkar (2020), worked on the title as "MOOC: Challenges & Prospects in Indian Higher Education" discussed as MOOC is a web-based platform that provides a virtually unlimited number of students across the globe the opportunity for life-long learning through distance learning with the world's best institutions. One of the distinguishing features of MOOCs is the interactive sessions conducted between students, professors, and teaching assistants (TAs) along with the study/course. MOOCs are playing an important role in changing the nature of higher education. Courses designed for many participants, which can be accessed by anyone, anywhere, anytime, if they have an Internet connection, entry is open to all without any special qualifications, and are complete and free of charge. Delivering the entire course experience online (OpenUpEd, 2015). As more initiatives are launched, millions of people around the world continue to participate in MOOCs through a small but growing variety of courses and platforms; And they are attracting high levels of interest from reputed academic institutions, senior politicians, policymakers and popular media houses. On the other hand, they show that

MOOCs have the potential to challenge the closed and privileged nature of academic knowledge in traditional universities. Massive Open Online Courses (MOOCs) are a relatively recent entrant in the field of online learning but are still attracting a lot of attention from interested learners due to their "vastness" and "openness".

Sadiku et al., 2018, MOOCs are the latest initiative in the field of higher education and are becoming an integral part of the modern education system. Free participation, free access for everyone, are some of the features that are much needed in this era. Moreover, MOOCs help in getting education from the best faculty of any universities. It is also helpful for those who want to excel by gaining expertise in their area of interest and needs while in jobs (Chakraborty, 2016). MOOCs are known to build knowledge, abilities, skills, innovation and learning capabilities in their learners. In a great country like India, where most of the learners living in remote areas do not have adequate access to skill enhancement and quality education, MOOCs are playing an important role in bringing a quality education to those learners.

The Study

Objectives

1. To identify the various dimensions related to digital learning platforms.
2. To study the opportunities perceived by teachers and research scholars with respect to digital learning platforms and MOOCs.
3. To study the challenges faced by teachers and research scholars with regard to digital learning platforms and MOOCs.

Methodology

The present Study was a Descriptive Survey in nature. The population of the study constitute the teachers and research scholars of three central universities, namely Jamia Millia Islamia, Maulana Azad National Urdu University, and Aligarh Muslim University. The sample of the study constituted 100 teachers and research scholars of the above three central universities. But the response was received from 56 teachers and scholars only (20 teachers and 36 Research scholars). Hence the sample size remained 56 teachers and research scholars. Random sampling technique was used in this study. A self-prepared mixed questionnaire (Open & Close ended) was used for the Data Collection. The tool consisted of 36 items, 18 to study opportunities and another 18 to study challenges of the digital learning platforms and MOOCs. There were six dimensions each for Opportunities as well as challenges, dimensions under opportunities include: 1. Access and Inclusivity, 2. Cost-Efficiency and Affordability, 3. Flexibility and Convenience, 4. Globalization and Collaboration, 5. Personalization and Adaptive Learning, 6. Assessment and

Credentialing and Same way to identify the challenges dimension include: 1. Technological, 2. Pedagogical, 3. Access and Equity, 4. Quality Assurance, 5. Student Engagement and Support, 6. Assessment and Evaluation. Questionnaire contains 36 items in which 20 items are open ended and 16 items are close ended. The data was collected through Google form from the above specified University, the link is shared through Email and WhatsApp.

Result and Discussion

Objective 1

Discussion: To identify the various dimensions related to digital learning platforms and MOOCs the researcher has reviewed the study related to the same and identified six dimensions on each under opportunities dimension, include: 1. Access and Inclusivity, 2. Cost-Efficiency and Affordability, 3. Flexibility and Convenience, 4. Globalization and Collaboration, 5. Personalization and Adaptive Learning, 6. Assessment and Credentialing, and in the same way to identify the challenges dimension, include: 1. Technological, 2. Pedagogical, 3. Access and Equity, 4. Quality Assurance, 5. Student Engagement and Support, 6. Assessment and Evaluation

Objective 2

Findings related to Dimension I: Access and Inclusivity

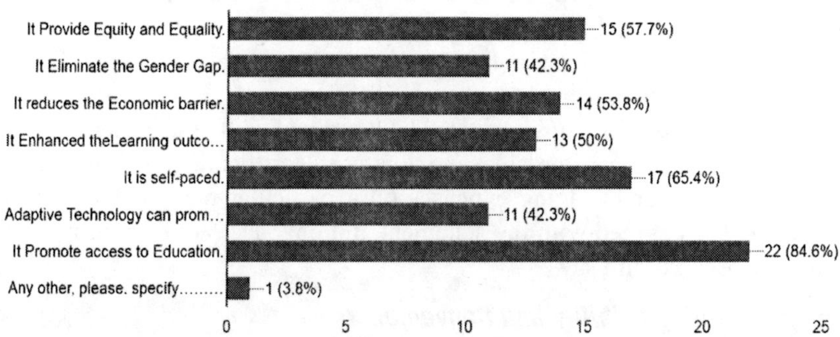

Figure 1.1: Respondents reply to the question, "How online Learning Platform and MOOCs help bridge the educational access gap for individuals in remote underserved areas?"

Discussion: As depicted in Figure 1.1, 57.7% said that online learning platform and MOOCs provide Equity and Equality, 42.3% said it eliminates the gender gap and 53.8% said it reduces the economic barrier, 50% of the respondents said it enhances the learning outcome, 65.4% said online learning platform and MOOCs is self-pace, 42.3% said that online learning platform and MOOCs adapt such technology that engages more and more participants, 84.6% said that it promotes access to education.

Findings related to Dimension I: Access and Inclusivity

Respondents reply on a five-point scale statement "online education is inclusive and accessible to people with disabilities".

Interpretation and discussion: 57.7% agree that online education is inclusive and accessible to people with disability, 23% of the respondents strongly agree with that thus we can adopt various assistive and adaptive technology easily, only 7.7% disagree with the statement.

Respondents reply on a three-point scale on a statement "Digital Learning Platforms accommodate learners from diverse cultural backgrounds and language."

Interpretation and discussion: 69.2% agree with the statement. as online education is held on a web and it is available for all at anytime, anywhere with the Internet, so online learning platform accumulates good number of participations from all areas of the country. 15.4% did not agree with the statement and 15.4% responded as "can't say".

Dimension II: Cost-Efficiency and Affordability Dimension

Respondents reply on the close ended statement "Which mode of education is cost effective or economical in terms of total expenditure on education by students/parents? 1. Online 2. Offline. 3. Can't say.

Interpretation and discussion: 68.26% responded as online mode of education is cost effective or economical whereas 22% said Offline and only 9.74% have responsed as can't say.

Respondents reply on a three-point scale with a statement "Digital Education is affordable and low-cost certification".

Interpretation and discussion: 73.1% agreed with the statement that Digital Education is affordable and low-cost certification, it reduces the accommodation and lodging expenses on a particular place, 15.4% of the respondent not agreed with the statement and only 11.5% of the respondent has responses as can't say.

Dimension III: Flexibility and Convenience

Respondents reply with an open-ended statement. "How does the flexibility of online learning platforms cater to individuals with busy schedules or other commitments, such as work or family responsibilities"?

Interpretation and discussion: On the basis of responses, a conclusion can be made that students can access course materials and lectures at their own pace and according to their own schedule, this flexibility allows individuals to balance their education with work, family responsibilities, or other commitments, making it an ideal option for busy students, the flexibility of time, where a person can avail a particular lecture or may give an exam whenever it is possible for them, makes online learning a convenient option for people with busy schedules, opportunity to learn easily and more flexible, we can revise our learning by watching videos again and again. One can learn as recorded lectures help the individuals to login anywhere, anytime. It provides additional support and motivation that in the worst scenario one can do preparation the way one wants. It will be managed with self-control and follow proper time management and protect us from any distraction.

Respondents reply on an open-ended statement "What technologies and tools are used to create interactive and engaging learning experiences in online courses.?"

Interpretation and discussion: On the basis of responses conclusion can be made that content being provided in small chunks and pieces fun-based assessment on small intervals providing chat options raising hands during discussions, showing response through various symbols. Besides that provisions of sharing windows slides and many more like: multimedia content and interactive task or assessments, multimedia content, gamification elements, real-time collaboration, and interactive assessments help captivate students' interest and motivate them to actively participate in their learning. There are several technologies for developing scalable and effective e-learning solutions, including Learning Management Systems (LMS), learning analytics, and mobile learning. Discussion forums and assessment questions are useful tools for engaging.

Dimension IV: Globalization and Collaboration

Respondent reply on an open-ended statement "What strategies and tools are used to create interactive and engaging learning experiences in online courses?".

Interpretation and discussion: An educator may use his creativity to make online interactive and engaging they can adopt collaborative approach, think pair and share, jigsaw, brainstorming, debates, discussions, short creative assignments online technique etc., two-way communication, adopt a flexible approach to student participation in the classroom, engaging students with gamification. Choose appropriate digital technologies. Offer regular feedback and use asynchronous tools wherever possible.

Respondents reply on a five-point scale on the statement "Digital learning platforms facilitate international collaboration and knowledge sharing among students and instructors from diverse geographic locations?

Interpretation and discussion: 34.6% strongly agreed with the statement and 34.6% agreed with the statement this is why because in Digital Learning platforms anyone from anywhere can register with a network and collaborate effectively there is no limitation of boundary and geographic circumstances. Only 11.5% of respondents did not agree with the statement.

Dimension V: Personalization and Adaptive Learning

Respondent reply on an open-ended statement "Can you discuss instances where MOOCs have been used to foster global communities of learners or to address global challenges?"

Interpretation and discussion: During COVID Digital Learning platform and MOOCs played very crucial role and almost all learning platforms saw record enrolments globally. Many are doing short term courses from Oxford Cambridge University in India, MOOCs offer an affordable, flexible way to learn new skills, advance a career, and deliver quality educational experiences. Challenges are many but still would like to point out a few that are having major challenges — Without intrinsic motivation you cannot learn effectively. If a learner is not having self-discipline sometimes they do not complete their course. It is asynchronous, so interaction in real-time is not possible, Due to poor Internet connectivity one faces hurdles. MOOCs have the potential to help individuals enjoy learning and acquire knowledge in a variety of ways. MOOCs are to learn for a variety of reasons, such as professional development, career transition, college preparation, supplemental learning, lifelong learning, and corporate e-learning and training. MOOCs enable access to quality education to as many people as possible and contribute to continuous education of various social groups. MOOCs can be addressed to unemployed people, helping them to develop certain skills needed for employability.

Respondents reply with an open-ended statement "How can educators strike a balance between automation and human interaction in online education to provide a personalized touch?"

Interpretation and discussion: Based on response, a conclusion can be made that two-way communication and participation made balance between automation and Human Interaction, many features in Google Meet, Zoom and other online platforms provide ample features to interact one to one interaction, they can guide and support learners. Enhance the social-emotional relationship with learners to help you achieve this balance, consider using technology to enhance, rather than replace, human interaction. Professors, mentors, and counsellors provide students with crucial support, guidance, and encouragement, nourishing their individual growth and potential, using multimedia tools including storytelling, real-life examples, to build connection while teaching. They must use different gestures, voice variation, expression, discussion among peers. These are some which will remove the gaps of social distance.

Dimension VI: Assessment and Credentialing

Respondents reply on an open-ended statement "What assessment methods are commonly used in online courses to measure student understanding and progress?"

Interpretation and discussion: On the basis of responses, we can use variety of assessment technique like: Online quizzes, Essay questions, Drag-and-drop activities, Online interviews, Dialogue, simulations, Online polls, Game-type activities, self and peer evaluation, brainstorming technique and review Forum posts.

Respondents reply on an open-ended statement "How can the credibility of online course certifications and badges be ensured, and how do they compare to traditional degrees in the job market?"

Interpretation and discussion: Many of the respondents said that if the course is being advised by faculty members of any prestigious university and by any senior who has already done the course and gone through recruitment process and has seen the relevance of the course then the time can be devoted to the course, credibility is increasing day by day. We should not forget that Microsoft certified courses were in market online since decades with very high credibility, Legitimate online degree programs are accredited by agencies recognized by either the Department of Education or the non-profit Council for Higher Education Accreditation, known as CHEA, Online courses with certificate are value addition they might not be eligibility certificates but definitely they are helpful for knowledge and skill upgradation.

Respondents reply on a five-point statement "Digital Portfolio in showcasing online learning achievement is valid source of Information."

Interpretation and discussion: 19.2% strongly agree and 38.5% respondent agree that Digital Portfolio in showcasing online learning achievement is valid source of Information, whereas 34.6% are neutral and only 7.7% of the respondent strongly disagree with the statement.

Objectives 3

Dimension I: Technological Dimension

Respondent response on an open-ended statement "What technological infrastructure challenges do institutions face when implementing online learning platforms?"

Interpretation and discussion: As depicted in Fig:1.2, from the responses we can conclude that there are many technological barriers or shortcomings of digital learning platforms and MOOCs to implement like lack of electricity, smart board, ICT lab, Internet connectivity, lack of familiarity with appliances, lack of infrastructure support etc.

Respondents reply on an open-ended statement "How do institutions ensure that students and faculty have access to necessary hardware and reliable Internet connections?" and "What cybersecurity concerns arise with the use of online learning platforms, and how can they be addressed?".

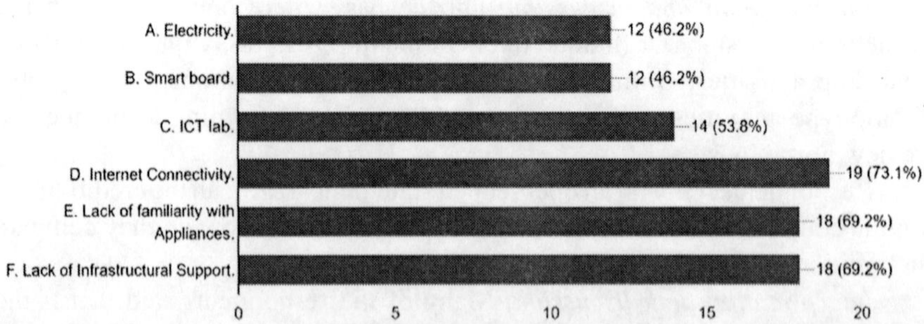

Figure 1.2: Respondents reply on the five-point scale statement Respondents reply on a five-point scale on the statement "What technological infrastructure challenges do institutions face when implementing online learning platforms?"

Interpretation and discussion: From the respondents we receive the responses, we can conclude that by providing them with a stable and secure digital infrastructure and digital device, identifying the hardware and software needs of the institution and availing the required amount of infrastructural support and removing logistic issues. Institutions must also ensure students are aware of the available support by promoting services across campus email, social media, advisers, faculty, IT websites, the learning management system and more. By establishing better Internet Service Technology and making students and Teachers more involved bit by bit to take it as a familiar method of education to gain more trust and reliability. Educational institutions allocate funds to invest and upgrade digital education and avail high Internet speed connections. Institute can provide discounted rates of laptop, tab, Internet access to students so that it will be affordable for all. Literacy of digital should be given to students. To take feedback Providing free Wi-Fi, encourage faculty to presume students are under-connected by constant testing, Sometimes Internet connection is not working properly so it is a big challenge for online platform, certificate fee payment related cyber threat. Cater by the partnership with the related cyber agency, identity theft, online bullying, malware attacks, password hacking etc, privacy breaches/ go through terms and conditions, leak of personal information, online stalking are some concerns. Having small groups that allow only registered members/ students from known background or at least from familiar or authentic background. One of the most well-known online cybersecurity learning and training platforms, Cybrary offers a massive catalogue of free, quality training for those interested in developing their IT skills. Educators have been refining their online learning system. Use end to end encryption, empower your students, regularly update content filters etc. Data gets hacked by using trusted software, leakage of sensitive data, confidentiality issues, hacking, malicious software are some of the cybersecurity concerns which require stringent cybersecurity systems. Data must then be protected to maintain confidentiality, integrity, and availability. Protecting against data manipulation, fraudulent user authentication and compromises in confidentiality are important security issues in e-Learning.

Dimension II: Pedagogical

Respondents reply on an Open-ended statement "What challenges do educators encounter when adapting their teaching methods to an online environment?".

Interpretation and discussion: From the responses received, we can conclude that many challenges educators encounter when adapting their teaching methods to an online environment like: Lack of practical knowledge, Improper planning, they do not have sufficient time, Learners were not fully digitalized, Lack of administrative support, Students misusing technology, Cost of new technology, Lack of motivation in students, Infrastructural problems, Digital literacy and Technical issues, Lack of in-person interaction, Lack of EdTech and online learning options for special needs of students, Course structure and quality, Time management issues, Lack of interaction with peers and instructors.

Dimension III and IV: Access and Equity and Quality Assurance

Respondents reply on a three-point scale statement "Digital Learning Platforms and MOOCs cater to the Individual Needs of Students?"

Interpretation and discussion: 69.2% of the individual responses as Yes and 11.5% of the individuals are responses as can't say, only 11.5% of the respondent responses as No, it means we can conclude that Digital Learning Platforms and MOOCs cater to the Individual Needs of Students.

Dimension V and VI: Student Engagement and Support Dimension and Assessment and Evaluation Dimension

Respondents reply on a five-point scale statement "Institutions are addressing concerns related to academic integrity and cheating in online assessments?"

Interpretation and discussion: 30.8% of the individual agree with the statement, 11.5% strongly agree with the responses, mainly considerable thing in this item is that 34.6% of the individual neutral with the statement means a mix response has arrived and yes we can conclude that institutions are not fully addressing concerns related to academic integrity and cheating in online assessments.

Conclusion

The increasing use of online teaching-learning tools is witnessing a tremendous change in education especially after the corona pandemic. Online learning is also having an impact on students' academic achievement. Online teaching and learning as an environment are becoming beneficial for both students and teachers, which plays a very important role in achieving the goals of education in terms of curriculum. It is becoming more popular these days, and many institutions are working on creating better tools for e-learning. Teaching and learning through online platforms have become very popular among teachers nowadays. This is not only due to the convenience and easy communication with the learners, but also since the platform enables learners to prepare for lessons in advance and motivates them to revise the material learned, as well as take any feedback from the instructors, provide advantage in exchanging ideas about the problem. Among the existing platforms, MOOCs is one of the most popular open sources globally. Digital learning platforms and Massive Open Online Courses (MOOCs) have ushered in a new era in higher education, presenting both unprecedented opportunities and unique challenges. On the positive side, these initiatives have democratized access to education, breaking down geographical barriers and providing flexible learning options for diverse learners. The vast array of courses and resources available online has empowered individuals to tailor their educational journeys to their specific needs and interests. However, with these opportunities come challenges that cannot be ignored. Issues such as the digital divide, ensuring the quality of online education, and the need for effective assessment and accreditation mechanisms pose significant hurdles. Moreover, the shift to digital learning demands a revaluation of traditional teaching methodologies and the development of new pedagogical strategies to engage and motivate learners in a virtual environment.

References

Suleiman, & Danmuchikwali. (n.d.). Digital education: opportunities, threats, and challenges. E-Presented at Its National E-Conference on Education and Development: Post Covid-19 Organized by School of Education, Lovely Professional University, Phagwara-India on 26th September, 2020. https://www.researchgate.net/publication/345378791_Digital_Education_Opportunities_Threats_and_Challenges/link/5fb9272ca6fdcc6cc6565463/download

Sadiku, Adebo, & Musa (2018, February). Online Teaching & Learning. *International Journals of Advanced Research in Computer Science and Software Engineering*, 8(2), 73–75. https://www.researchgate.net/publication/324821090_Online_Teaching_and_Learning/link/5c50b79fa6fdccd6b5d1e6d6/download

Seifert (2021, July 5). Students' Perceptions of Online Teaching and Learning. *Malaysian Online Journal of Educational Technology*, 9(3), 1–12. https://files.eric.ed.gov/fulltext/EJ1315213.pdf

University Grant Commission (n.d.). Blended Mode of Teaching and Learning: Concept Note. In ugc.ac.in. UGC. Retrieved September 14, 2023, from https://www.ugc.gov.in/pdfnews/6100340_Concept-Note-Blended-Mode-of-Teaching-and-Learning.pdf

Ghoshal (2020, August). Advantages and Disadvantages of Online Teaching Learning During Pandemic. *International Journal of Creative Research Thought*, 8(8), 982–985. https://ijcrt.org/papers/IJCRT2008120.pdf

Dung (2020, June 17). The Advantages and Disadvantages of Virtual Learning. *IOSR Journal of Research & Method in Education* (IOSR-JRME), 10(3), 45–48. https://iosrjournals.org/iosr-jrme/papers/Vol-10%20Issue-3/Series-5/H1003054548.pdf

Raad, & Odhabi (2021, May 17). Hybrid Learning Here to Stay! Frontiers in Education Technology, 4(2), 121–131. https://doi.org/10.22158/fet.v4n2p121

Kazui & Yalçın (2022, November 1). Investigation of the Effectiveness of Hybrid Learning on Academic Achievement: A Meta-Analysis Study. *International Journal of Progressive Education*, 18(1), 249–265. https://doi.org/10.29329/ijpe.2022.426.14

O'Byrne, W.I., & Pytash, K.E. (2015, August 28). Hybrid and Blended Learning. Journal of Adolescent & Adult Literacy, 59(2), 137–140. https://doi.org/10.1002/jaal.463

UNICEF, U., & EdTech Hub, E.H. (2022, March 4). Monitoring Hybrid Learning: A Short Guide. https://doi.org/10.53832/edtechhub.0072

Nwosisi, C., Ferreira, A., Rosenberg, W., & Walsh, K. (2016). A Study of the Flipped Classroom and Its Effectiveness in Flipping Thirty Percent of the Course Content, *International Journal of Information and Education Technology*, 6(5), 348–351. https://doi.org/10.7763/ijiet.2016.v6.712

Ozdamli & Asiksoy (2016, July 20). Flipped classroom approach. *World Journal on Educational Technology*: Current Issues, 8(2), 98–105. https://www.researchgate.net/publication/309890120_Flipped_Classroom_Approach/link/58a4a791a6fdcc0e075d01dd/download

Mushtaha, E., Abu Dabous, S., Alsyouf, I., Ahmed, A., & Raafat Abdraboh, N. (2022, November). The challenges and opportunities of online learning and teaching at engineering and theoretical colleges during the pandemic, *Ain Shams Engineering Journal*, 13(6), 101770. https://doi.org/10.1016/j.asej.2022.101770

Jindal & Chahal. (2018). Challenges and Opportunities for Online Education in India, *Pramana Research Journal*, 8(4). https://www.pramanaresearch.org/gallery/prj_c_ap_12.pdf

IGNOU (2018, March). BESE-135 Information and Communication Technology. Retrieved December 12, 2023, from https://egyankosh.ac.in/bitstream/123456789/46303/1/BESE-135B1E.pdf.

Sharma (Ed.). (n.d.). Information and Communication Technology Applications (DLIS108). Lovely Professional University. Retrieved December 12, 2023, from https://ebooks.lpude.in/library_and_info_sciences/BLIS/year_1/dlis108_information_and_communication_technology_applications.pdf

Rani (n.d.). Massive Open Online Courses (MOOCs). Mahatma Gandhi Central University, Motihari, Bihar. Retrieved December 12, 2023, from https://mgcub.ac.in/pdf/material/202004060200186 5899ae96e.pdf

Government of India Ministry of Human Resource Development Department of Higher Education. (2015). Guidelines for Development and Implementation of MOOCs. aicte-india.org. Retrieved December 12, 2023, from https://www.aicte-india.org/downloads/MHRD%20moocs%20guidelines%20updated.pdf

Baturay, M.H. (2015, February 1). An Overview of the World of MOOCs. Procedia - Social and Behavioral Sciences. https://doi.org/10.1016/j.sbspro.2015.01.685 (2021,

October). MOOCs in India: An Overview. *International Journal of Science and Research* (IJSR), 10(10), 461–463. https://doi.org/10.21275/SR211008112027

Pérez Zapata, B. (2020, December 23). https://www.atlantisjournal.org/index.php/atlantis/article/view/679. Atlantis. *Journal of the Spanish Association for Anglo-American Studies*, 42(2), 180–196. https://doi.org/10.28914/atlantis-2020-42.2.09

Mallikarjuna (2018, August). Digital Initiatives Online Learning Community Towards MOOCs and OER on Engineering Education. *Journal of Emerging Technologies and Innovative Research* (JETIR), 5(8), 673–677. https://www.jetir.org/papers/JETIRA006121.pdf

Pouezevara & Horn (2016, March). MOOCs and Online Education: Exploring the Potential for International Educational Development. RTI Press Publication. https://files.eric.ed.gov/fulltext/ED570099.pdf

Biswas & Sarkar (2020). MOOC: Challenges & Prospects in Indian Higher Education. *Journal of Information and Computational Science*, 10(2), 1015–1024. https://www.researchgate.net/publication/364329757_MOOC_Challenges_Prospects_in_Indian_Higher_Education

Pant, H.V., Lohani, M.C. & Pande, J. (2021). MOOCs in Higher Education. Advances in Human and Social Aspects of Technology, 58–77. https://doi.org/10.4018/978-1-7998-7844-5.ch004

4

Examining the Role of Digital Storytelling in Enhancing Writing Skills

Pallavi Jain, Harish Kumar and Anup Kumar Rajput

Introduction

Digital Storytelling

Digital storytelling, recognized as a multimedia educational tool, represents a contemporary iteration of the age-old tradition of storytelling (Dogan & Robin, 2009). While traditional methods involved communication through written narratives, books, and notebooks, the evolution of technology has given rise to a new era marked by digital storytelling, where pictures, music, and audio are seamlessly integrated through computers (Hett, 2012). The essence of digital storytelling lies in its ability to combine various media elements to enhance and refine spoken language, marking a modern interpretation of a longstanding artistic practice (Frazel, 2010).

In the words of Ohler (2008), digital storytelling harnesses personal digital technology to amalgamate diverse media components into a cohesive narrative (p.15). Robin (2006) emphasizes the integration of multimedia elements such as pictures, audios, and videos as a defining characteristic of digital storytelling, echoing the traditional storytelling structure. Consequently, all digital stories share a common foundation, combining digital graphics, audios, videos, and music to convey information while adhering to a specific theme and viewpoint. Typically, spanning a few minutes, digital stories serve multiple purposes, ranging from personal narrative sharing to the recounting of historical events and can be employed for informative or instructional objectives.

Numerous studies underscore the positive impact of digital storytelling on the learning environment, curriculum, and overall learning experiences (Sadik, 2008). According to Dogan and Robin (2009), engagement in digital storytelling cultivates technical, presentation, research, organizational, and writing skills. Moreover, it has been shown to augment learning motivation and problem-solving capabilities (Bumgarner, 2012; Hung, Hwang, & Huang, 2012). Academic achievements, attitudes, motivation, and learning strategies have also been found to develop through the incorporation of digital storytelling in educational settings (Kahraman, 2013; Demirer, 2013).

Furthermore, digital storytelling plays a crucial role in fostering self-confidence among students (Yüksel, 2011) and contributes to the enhancement of skills such as story organization, multimedia literacy, and writing skills (Bumgarner, 2012; Kulla-Abbot, 2006; Sylvester & Greenidge, 2009). In essence, the utilization of digital storytelling proves to be a multifaceted approach with far-reaching benefits in educational contexts.

Digital Storytelling and New Literacy

Reading or writing a text does not guarantee literacy among students in today's educational landscape. Students are now expected to not only comprehend and practice information but also to analyze, synthesize, evaluate, and compose it. In light of the escalating complexity and growth of information, students must possess multimedia literacy skills to navigate a diverse array of texts, encompassing traditional texts, visuals, and hypertexts (Thesen & Kara-Soteriou, 2011).

Traditional storytelling has historically been employed to enhance students' literacy skills by activating language skills such as reading, writing, listening, and speaking. Digital storytelling extends literacy into the digital realm by seamlessly integrating traditional and new literacy skills. Leveraging various digital tools, such as iMovie, Photostory, microphones, digital cameras, and scanners, students effectively engage in digital storytelling, integrating their understanding, problem-solving skills, and critical thinking abilities while creatively utilizing technology (Ohler, 2013).

Digital storytelling not only fosters traditional literacy skills like reading, writing, speaking, and communication but also cultivates new literacy skills crucial in multimedia environments. Several studies have highlighted the potential of digital storytelling in developing 21st-century skills, including technical, presentation, research, editing, and writing skills (Dogan & Robin, 2009; Dogan, 2012; Dogan, 2007). Additional research indicates that digital storytelling enhances multimedia literacy, the sense of voice, and story organization (Kulla-Abbot, 2006), as well as students' cultural identities, basic literacy, and new literacy by bridging extramural and intramural contexts (Skinner & Hagood, 2008).

Digital Storytelling and Writing Instruction

Within the realm of 21st century learning, the English language occupies a pivotal position, demanding students to master essential language skills, including listening, speaking, reading, and, notably, writing. Writing, deemed the most crucial skill, is intricately connected to the enhancement of the other language proficiencies, fostering improvements in listening, speaking, and reading skills indirectly (Saed & Al-Omari, 2014). Maghsoudi and Haririan (2013) underscore the role of writing in stimulating thinking, enhancing concentration, managing ideas, and nurturing summarization, analysis, and criticism abilities. The multifaceted function of writing encompasses informative reporting of events and storytelling (Abdel-Hack & Ahmed Helwa, 2014). However, students encounter challenges, including grammatical errors and content production (Teo, 2006), prompting the exploration of effective strategies to enhance their writing skills.

Abdel-Hack and Ahmed Helwa (2014) advocate for the incorporation of digital storytelling in the learning and teaching process as a solution to enhance writing skills. In the era of Web 2.0, various online tools offer opportunities to bolster students' writing abilities. Reinders (2011) defines digital storytelling as the integration of text, audio, music, videos, and photos to craft a digital story. Despite the prevalence of these tools, academic research supporting the notion that digital storytelling can elevate literacy standards in writing remains scarce (Garrard, 2011, as cited by Siti Mariam et al., 2016).

Numerous studies on the integration of digital storytelling in writing instruction have demonstrated its positive impact on student outcomes. Digital storytelling motivates students to craft more explicit and detailed narratives, expanding their audience (Foley, 2013; Sylvester & Greenidge, 2009; Vasudevan et al., 2010). It also heightens participation levels and boosts writing self-efficacy among students (Banaszewski, 2002; Bumgarner, 2012; Campbell, 2012; Hathorn, 2005). Additionally, digital storytelling encourages students to employ their unique styles (Lee, 2014), stimulates life experiences, fortifies the writing process (Bumgarner, 2012; Saunders, 2014), and increases the quantity of words, precision in sentences, and correctness of language use (Xin, 2013). Digital storytelling emerges as a tool for self-authoring processes (Davis, 2004) and facilitates the development of a shared language concerning writing identities and processes, particularly in primary schools using digital media (Foley, 2013). Through digital stories, students comprehend the organization of narratives and gain insights into reflection, editing, feedback processes (Kulla-Abott, 2006), and develop a deeper understanding of the revision process (Stojke, 2009).

Addressing the weaknesses in writing skills among ESL (English as a Second Language) students, researchers propose solutions such as leveraging online educational tools, notably digital storytelling, which has been found to enhance writing skills in various aspects (Abdel-Hack & Ahmed Helwa, 2014; Duman & Göcen, 2015; Leong & Jafre, 2018; Pardo, 2014; Rahimi & Yadollahi, 2017; Sepp & Bandi-Rao, 2015; Siti Mariam et al., 2016; Thonghattha et al., 2016; Tsigani & Nikolakopoulou, 2018; Yee & Kee, 2017). Despite numerous studies on writing skills, research specific to ESL middle school students' writing in India is limited. Consequently, there is a pressing need to investigate the impact of digital storytelling on the writing skills of Indian students belonging to middle school.

The Study

Inquiries

This research endeavours to address the following inquiries:

1. What is the effect of digital storytelling in improving ESL middle school students' writing essays in terms of organization of ideas, word choice, sentence fluency, and overall performance?
2. How do ESL students belonging to middle school perceive the utilization of digital storytelling in improving their essay writing proficiency?

Objectives

The objectives derived from the research questions are outlined as follows:

1. To assess the influence of digital storytelling on the enhancement of essay writing skills among ESL middle school students, focusing on the organization of ideas, word choice, sentence fluency, and overall performance.
2. To explore and comprehend the perspectives of middle school ESL students concerning the effectiveness of digital storytelling in enhancing their proficiency of essay writing.

Related Literature

This research is anchored in the constructivism theory, pioneered by Jean Piaget and Lev Vygotsky. Piaget's constructivism centres on cognitive development, while Vygotsky's work focuses on social constructivism (Sanders, 2016). These two psychologists are seminal figures in the constructivist paradigm. The theory posits that knowledge is constructed as students engage with the material, with two vital branches: cognitive constructivism, as advanced by Jean Piaget, and social constructivism, championed by Lev Vygotsky.

According to Piaget, students construct knowledge through their experiences, continually forming new schemata based on prior encounters. As affirmed by Sanders (2016), citing Piaget (1964), students are individual architects of knowledge, actively interpreting new information based on their existing cognitive frameworks (Elliot et al., 2000). This individualized knowledge construction process is termed individual or psychological constructivism. In contrast, Lev Vygotsky's social constructivism emphasizes collaborative knowledge construction during tasks requiring group problem-solving. This form of knowledge construction occurs through interactions with teachers, peers, and even family members at home, contributing to the construction of individual meaning (Elliot et al., 2000). The constructivist theory finds practical application in the context of writing tasks, where students apply their knowledge of construction processes.

Writing, as a form of human communication, represents the visual manifestation of language (Rahmawati, 2017). Byrne (1988) posits that writing involves encoding symbols to represent the sounds of language, arranged in a specific order to form words, and further organized to construct coherent sentences. The composition of multiple sentences, interconnected in a deliberate manner, gives rise to cohesive texts. Proficiency in writing demands mastery of skills such as vocabulary, grammar, content, mechanics, organization, and style (Anita, 2016; Hapsari & Sukavatee, 2018). Yee and Kee (2017) assert that effective writing requires the development and management of ideas, meticulous attention to spelling, punctuation, grammar, and other elements.

To imbue writing with meaning, writers follow distinct processes to complete writing tasks. These processes are typically categorized into two approaches: the product-based approach and the process-based approach. The product-based approach, rooted in traditional teaching methods, prioritizes the final product, often replicating a model text (Yee & Kee, 2017). Conversely, the process-based approach centers on the dynamic stages of writing, emphasizing the various activities and phases that contribute to language development (Yee & Kee, 2017). This approach involves planning, production, editing, revision, and the integration of content, collectively constituting the comprehensive writing process (Kelly & Melor, 2016). Tompkins (2008) delineates this process into five stages: prewriting, drafting, revising, editing, and publishing. The writing process aligns seamlessly with the principles of constructivism, particularly when conducted collaboratively, allowing writers to construct new knowledge through interaction.

In an American context, Sepp and Bandi-Rao (2015) examined the utilization of digital storytelling at a community college in New York City, observing significant improvements in the writing skills of 19 ESL students. Similarly, a study in Malaysia by Siti Mariam et al. (2016) focused on students' collaborative work with digital storytelling, revealing enhancements in writing skills. Rahimi and Yadollahi (2017) emphasized the positive impact of digital storytelling on literacy skills, including reading and writing. Leong and Jafre (2018) conducted a case study in Malaysia, reporting improvements in language skills, including writing, among primary five pupils.

Notably, digital storytelling has been associated with improvements in specific writing dimensions. Duman and Göcen (2015) found that digital storytelling enhanced students' word choice, leading to increased richness in vocabulary. Leong and Jafre (2018) reported participants' perceived improvement in vocabulary following digital storytelling implementation. Additionally, Pardo (2014) and Duman and Göcen (2015) observed enhanced sentence fluency, with fewer grammatical errors and improved grammar accuracy attributed to digital storytelling usage. Dollar and Tolu (2015) conducted a study in Turkey, confirming a good command of grammar rules and mechanics among participants following digital storytelling exposure.

Beyond linguistic aspects, digital storytelling has demonstrated efficacy in fostering creativity and enhancing writing content. Pardo (2014) and Duman and Göcen (2015) concurred that digital storytelling facilitated the development of original ideas. Yee and Kee (2017) conducted qualitative research in Malaysia, highlighting improvements in participants' writing quality, specifically in organization and content. The motivational aspect of digital storytelling in writing was evident in studies by Thonghattha et al. (2016) and Yee and Kee (2017), where increased motivation and a more enjoyable writing process were reported.

Given the array of studies showcasing the positive impact of digital storytelling on writing skills, this research aims to investigate the specific impact of digital storytelling on Indian ESL middle school students' writing skills. Despite the abundance of literature on ESL writing skills, the focus on Indian middle school students remains limited, reiterating the significance of this study in addressing this gap.

Methodology

This research aims to investigate the impact of digital storytelling on ESL middle school students' writing skills through a quasi-experimental study. To achieve this goal, a pre- and post-test design was implemented to assess the students' performance before and after the digital storytelling intervention, which spanned 16 hours of lesson time. The study focused on standard sixth-grade students in a middle school, comprising a controlled group and an experimental group. Importantly, both groups, as per information from their English teachers, had not been exposed to essay writing before the pre-test.

The experimental group underwent a 16-hour intervention where digital storytelling, incorporating multimedia elements and technology, was utilized to enhance writing skills. In contrast, the controlled group followed a traditional teaching approach, emphasizing foundational writing skills without the integration of technology-driven methods. This dichotomy allowed for a comparative analysis of the impact of digital storytelling on ESL middle school students' writing proficiency.

Following the intervention, both groups underwent a post-test to gauge their writing proficiency. In addition to quantitative data, qualitative insights were collected through semi-structured interviews with participants, adapted from Zainudin's (2016) research interview questions. The interview session took place after the post-test.

Data analysis included an examination of the pre- and post-test scores, assessing data normality, and calculating mean scores for both tests. The comparison of mean scores aimed to identify improvements after the intervention. Additionally, a comparison between the two groups was conducted to determine group performance. Further analysis involved assessing significant differences post-intervention and conducting tests to identify variations between the two groups. The interview data underwent thematic analysis to glean participants' perceptions of digital storytelling. This multifaceted approach, encompassing both quantitative and qualitative analyses, provides a comprehensive understanding of the impact of digital storytelling on ESL middle school students' writing skills.

To evaluate students' writing skills, considerations were given to writing quality, story components, and writing lengths. An essay writing question was administered, and the assessment of compositions was conducted using a rubric developed by the researcher. The rubric's validity was established through consultation with five experts. During the rubric development process, relevant features of digital storytelling from the literature Barrett, 2006; Demirer, 2013; Dogan, 2012; Frazel, 2010; Ohler, 2008; Robin, 2006; Sadik, 2008 were reviewed. The rubric comprised four key elements: organization of ideas, word choice, sentence fluency, and overall performance. These criteria were designed to systematically assess the quality of students' writing skills. The students' achievement levels were determined based on their scores within each specified criterion.

In addition to the quantitative assessment, a semi-structured interview protocol was developed adapted from Zainudin's (2016) research interview questions to gather qualitative insights from participants. Similar to the rubric development process, the interview protocol underwent validation by consulting experts in the field. The questions were refined to ensure clarity, depth, and alignment with the research objectives.

Findings

This study aimed to assess the impact of digital storytelling on the writing proficiency of ESL middle school students. All data were subjected to analysis using Statistical Package for the Social Sciences (SPSS) version 24.

Before delving into further analysis, it is imperative to ascertain the nature of data distribution within the sample, specifically whether it adheres to a normal distribution. Given that the number of samples selected is less than 50, the Shapiro-Wilk test proves to be a suitable method for this determination (Razali & Yap, 2011). Table 1 presents the results obtained from the Shapiro-Wilk test.

All collected data indicate a departure from normal distribution ($p < 0.05$), except for the overall post-test score for the experimental group, as well as the overall scores for both the pre-test and post-test for the controlled group ($p > 0.05$).

Table 1: Shapiro-Wilk Normality Test Result

Groups	*Tests*	*Organisation of Ideas*	*Sentence Fluency*	*Word Choice*	*Overall*
Experimental Group (n = 27)	Pre-test	0.000	0.000	0.000	0.013
	Post-test	0.02	0.001	0.004	0.118
Controlled Group (n = 25)	Pre-test	0.001	0.007	0.000	0.163
	Post-test	0.004	0.002	0.002	0.21

$p > 0.05$

Objective 1

To address this objective, data were gathered from the pre-test and post-test, subsequently analyzed to derive mean scores for both tests across both groups. Table 2 presents the outcomes of this analysis:

Table 2: Mean Scores Analysis

Groups	*Tests*	*Organisation of Ideas*	*Sentence Fluency*	*Word Choice*	*Overall*
Experimental Group (n = 27)	Pre-test	2.6	5.2	2.4	13.3
	Post-test	3.3	6.5	3.3	16.6
Controlled Group (n = 25)	Pre-test	3.0	5.5	2.8	14.5
	Post-test	3.2	6.2	3.2	15.9

The analysis reveals that all post-test scores surpass the corresponding pre-test scores across all categories. The data suggest that, in general, both groups exhibited enhancements in their writing skills from the pre-test to the post-test. The experimental group showed a more substantial improvement in all categories, indicating a positive impact of digital storytelling on essay writing skills. However, further statistical analysis is needed to validate the significance of these observed changes.

To delve deeper into the data, an inferential analysis was conducted to ascertain the significance of the observed improvements. The Wilcoxon Signed Rank test was deemed the most appropriate method for this analysis, given the non-normal distribution of the data, as indicated in Table 3.

Table 3 displays the Wilcoxon Signed Rank test results for the experimental group, revealing statistically significant improvements after the intervention in all categories. The sum of ranks and p-values for are consistently below the 0.05 threshold, indicating a significant positive impact of digital storytelling on the students' writing skills. These findings affirm that digital storytelling

Table 3: Wilcoxon Signed Rank test result for the experimental group.

	Sum of Ranks	*Asymp. Sig. (2-tailed)*	*Probability*
Organisation of Ideas	18.00	0.002	
Sentence Fluency	13.00	0.003	Significant difference
Word Choice	0.00	0.000	
Overall	12.00	0.000	

$p < 0.05$

Table 4: Wilcoxon Signed Rank test result for the controlled group

	Sum of Ranks	*Asymp. Sig. (2-tailed)*	*Probability*
Organisation of Ideas	32.50	0.317	No Significant difference
Sentence Fluency	12.00	0.020	
Word Choice	13.00	0.012	Significant difference
Overall	25.00	0.003	

$p < 0.05$

intervention led to notable enhancements in the organization of ideas, sentence fluency, word choice, and overall writing performance in a statistically significant manner for the experimental group. This proves that digital storytelling can improve students' writing skills.

Table 4 presents the Wilcoxon Signed Rank test results for the controlled group, revealing significant improvements in sentence fluency, word choice, and overall writing performance ($p < 0.05$). However, there is no significant difference in the organization of ideas ($p = 0.317$). The sum of ranks and p-values for sentence fluency, word choice, and overall performance consistently fall below the 0.05 threshold, signifying a noteworthy positive impact of the intervention on specific aspects of writing skills for the controlled group. This finding shows that the controlled group's improvement after they had learnt how to write an essay is significant but not significant for organization of ideas.

Objective 2

Following the collection of quantitative data, a semi-structured interview was conducted to address the research question. Fourteen participants took part in individual interviews, with data saturation achieved during interviews with participants thirteen and fourteen. Transcriptions of each interview were analyzed thematically, resulting in the identification of two distinct categories.

1. Digital Storytelling motivates students to write

The investigation delved into the influence of digital storytelling on students' motivation to write, as reflected in the interview responses. All participants were interviewed about their perceptions of digital storytelling, and a unanimous positive sentiment was expressed. Specifically, nine participants highlighted their interest in digital storytelling, citing factors such as the integration of pictures and the use of digital aids in the writing process as contributors to the appeal of digital storytelling for essay writing. One participant conveyed excitement about creating digital storytelling, while another found it "a bit easier" to write due to the inclusion of visual elements. An enthusiastic response was captured from a participant who cheerfully exclaimed, "Happy, happy!" as digital storytelling represented a novel and enjoyable experience. Furthermore, when asked about their willingness to engage in digital storytelling again, all participants responded affirmatively, indicating a collective eagerness to participate in future digital storytelling activities.

2. Digital Storytelling helps them to write better

The impact of digital storytelling on enhancing writing skills emerged as a notable theme in the participants' responses. Several participants acknowledged that digital storytelling played a crucial role in inspiring and generating ideas for essay writing, attributing this to the inclusion of pictures in digital storytelling.

"It gives me an idea to write the story."

"Because we can imagine the story and the characters."

"Yes, I can imagine more."

"I can generate more ideas and create an interesting story."

Interestingly, one participant expressed the challenge of incorporating pictures into her storytelling process, stating, "I need to think about what I can do with this picture." She clarified that adjusting her story to align with the pictures required careful consideration, adding, "After this, I need to write a story where I need to see the picture first."

Furthermore, participants emphasized that the digital storytelling process facilitated vocabulary improvement, as they actively searched for new words on various websites.

"My sentences in essay writing become longer."

"Because I can use new words."

"From the Internet dictionary, I find new words."

These findings collectively reiterate participants' positive perceptions of digital storytelling, recognizing its role in enhancing their writing skills.

Discussion

This study investigated the impact of digital storytelling on the writing skills of ESL students, utilizing an experimental group engaged in learning writing skills using digital storytelling and a controlled group using traditional methods. Data collection involved pre- and post-tests, supplemented by a semi-structured interview. Mean analyses demonstrated higher post-test scores, affirming digital storytelling's positive influence on writing skills, consistent with previous research outcomes (Abdel-Hack & Ahmed Helwa, 2014; Leong & Jafre, 2018; Saputro, 2013; Sepp & Bandi-Rao, 2015). Notably, improvements were observed in the organization of ideas, word choice, and sentence fluency post-digital storytelling treatment, validated by significant differences in the Wilcoxon Signed Rank test. These findings align with similar enhancements reported in prior studies (Duman & Göcen, 2015; Pardo, 2014; Yee & Kee, 2017). The integration of digital storytelling creation into the five stages of the writing process contributed to the experimental group's development of writing skills, emphasizing the constructive impact of this approach. Digital storytelling's features, such as the use of pictures, facilitated idea generation by providing clear visual contexts, supporting the participants' understanding of events or scenarios in the story (Robin, 2008). Additionally, the collaborative process of creating digital storytelling, guided by the Theory of Constructivism, facilitated knowledge construction through interactions with teachers and peers (Masek & Yamin, 2010). The interview findings concluded that digital storytelling motivates students to write, as participants found it interesting and exciting due to the engaging use of pictures. The incorporation of technology, particularly digital storytelling, attracted students to the writing process, aiding in forming a vivid image of their writing topics. Group work further enhanced motivation, allowing participants to generate ideas and improve sentence fluency and word choice through collaborative discussions, affirming the motivational impact of digital storytelling on writing skills (Thonghattha et al., 2016; Tsigani & Nikolakopoulou, 2018; Yee & Kee, 2017).

Conclusion

This study aims to assess the impact of digital storytelling on ESL students' writing skills, recognizing the significant role technology plays in modern life and its potential to engage students in writing. The findings highlight the positive influence of digital storytelling on enhancing students' writing abilities. However, it is crucial to clarify that this study does not assert digital storytelling as the definitive method ensuring improvement in writing; rather, it proposes digital storytelling as a tool for essay writing. The intention is to raise awareness among teachers about an alternative approach to teaching essay writing by incorporating digital storytelling into lessons. Additionally, this study contributes to existing literature on digital storytelling, offering unique findings that emphasize the variability of results based on different contexts. It also provides an intriguing option for future researchers to explore diverse outcomes. Time constraints were a significant factor in this experimental study, limited by a one-month period mandated by the school administration. The impending mid-year exams and the need to cover the syllabus added further constraints. For future research, it is recommended to allocate a longer intervention period to assess potential improvements more comprehensively. Alternative sampling methods, such as purposive sampling, could be explored. Furthermore, researchers may consider investigating the impact of digital storytelling on other language skills like listening, speaking, and reading. In the rich tapestry of language education, this study illuminates the transformative potential of digital storytelling, highlighting its capacity to not only enhance ESL students' writing skills but also to weave a narrative of innovative possibilities for future pedagogical explorations.

References

Abdel-Hack, E.M. & Ahmed Helwa, H.S.A. (2014). Using Digital Storytelling and Weblogs Instruction to Enhance EFL Narrative Writing and Critical Thinking Skills Among EFL Majors at Faculty of Education. *International Research Journals, 5*(1).

Adam, A.A.S. (2015). Developing EFL Learners' Narrative Writing Through Using Short Stories — The Case of Al-Baha University Students. *European Journal of English Language and Literature Studies, 3*(4): 1–8.

Alismail, H.A. (2015). Integrate Digital Storytelling in Education. *Journal of Education and Practice, 6*(9): 126–130.

Anita, R. (2016). Using "Storybird" for Teaching Narrative Writing. *Proceeding of the Fourth International Seminar on English Language and Teaching (ISELT-4)*, 230–239.

Banaszewski, T. (2002). Digital storytelling finds its place in the classroom. *Information Today.*

Barrett, H. (2006). Researching and evaluating digital storytelling as a deep learning tool. In C. Crawford, et al. (Eds.), *Proceedings of Society for Information Technology and Teacher Education International Conference 2006* (pp. 647–654). Chesapeake, VA: AACE.

Bumgarner, B.L. (2012). *Digital storytelling in writing: A case study of student teacher attitudes toward teaching with technology* (Doctoral Dissertation). Retrieved from ProQuest LLC (3533990).

Byrne, D. (1988). *Teaching Writing Skills*. London:Longman.

Campbell, T., (2012). Digital storytelling in an elementary classroom: Going beyond entertainment. *Procedia — Social and Behavioral Sciences, 69*, 385-393.

Chung, J. &Melor, M.Y. (2016). Digital Storytelling Production as a Learning Tool in Improving ESL Learners' Verbal. *Asian EFL Journal Professional Teaching Articles, 3*(90): 1–106.

Davis, A. (2004). Co-authoring identity: Digital storytelling in an urban middle school. *THEN: Technology, Humanities, Education, & Narrative.*

Demirer, V. (2013). *Use of e-storytelling in primary education and its effects*. (Doctoral Thesis, Necmettin Erbakan University Institute of Educational Sciences, Konya, Turkey).

Dogan, B. (2007). *Implementation of digital storytelling in the classroom by teachers trained in a digital storytelling workshop*. (Doctoral Dissertation). Retrieved from ProQuest LLC (3272583)

Dogan, B., & Robin, B. (2009). Educational uses of digital storytelling: Creating digital storytelling contests for K-12 students and teachers. In Gıbson et al. (Eds.). *Proceedings of society for information technology and Teacher Education International Conference 2009* (pp.633-638). Chesapeake, VA: AACE.

Dogan, B. (2012, March). Educational Uses of Digital Storytelling in K-12: Research Results of Digital Storytelling Contest (DISTCO) 2012. *In Society for Information Technology and Teacher Education International Conference* (Vol. 2012, No. 1, pp. 1353-1362).

Dollar, Y.K. & Tolu, A.T. (2015). My First Digital Story: A Case Study With 5th Grade Turkish English Language Learners. *ELT Research Journal, 4*(3): 172–185.

Demirer, V. (2013). *Use of e-storytelling in primary education and its effects*. (Doctoral Thesis, Necmettin Erbakan University Institute of Educational Sciences, Konya, Turkey).

Duman, B. & Göcen, G. (2015). The Effect of the Digital Storytelling Method on Pre-Service Teachers' Creative Writing Skills. *Anthropologist, 20*(1–2): 215–222.

Elliot, S.N., Kratochwill, T.R., Cook Littlefield, J. & Travers, J.F. (2000). *Educational Psychology: Effective Teaching, Effective Learning*. Third Edit. Boston: McGraw-Hill.

Foley, M.L. (2013). *Digital storytelling in primary-grade classrooms* (Doctoral Dissertation). Retrieved from ProQuest LLC (3560250).

Frazel, M. (2010). *Digital storytelling: Guide for educators*. Eugene, OR: International Society for Technology in Education (ISTE).

Garrard, D. (2011). A Case Study to Evaluate the Effectiveness of Digital Storytelling as a Narrative Writing. *Integration The Vlsi Journal*.

Hapsari, E.W. & Sukavatee, P. (2018). Second Language Writing Instruction: A Recent Practice in Indonesia. *Journal of Linguistic and English Teaching, 3*(1).

Hathorn, P.P. (2005). Using digital storytelling as a literacy tool for the inner-city middle school youth. *The Charter Schools Resource Journal*, 1(1), 32-38.

Hett, K. (2012). Technology-supported literacy in the classroom: Using audiobooks and digital storytelling to enhance literacy instruction. *Illinois Reading Council Journal, 40*(3), 3-13.

Hung, C.M., Hwang, G.J., & Huang, I. (2012). A project-based digital storytelling approach for improving students' learning motivation, problem-solving competence and learning achievement. *Educational Technology and Society, 15(4)*, 368-379.

Kahraman, Ö. (2013). *The effect of using teaching materials prepared by digital storytelling method at the engagement phase of the learning cycle on physics course achievement and motivation level.* (Doctoral Thesis, Balikesir University Institute of Science, Balıkesir, Turkey).

Kelly, J.D. & Melor, M.Y. (2016). The Effectiveness of Using Sentence Makers in Improving Writing Performance among Pupils in Lubok Antu Rural Schools *Proceeding of the International Conference on Education in the 21st Century*, 469–475.

Kulla-Abbott, M.T. (2006). *Developing literacy practices through digital storytelling.* (Doctoral Dissertation). Retrieved from ProQuest LLC (3285640).

Lee, L. (2014). Digital news stories: Building language learners' content knowledge and speaking skills. *Foreign Language Annals*, 47(2), 338-356.

Lembaga Peperiksaan Malaysia. (2018). Pengumuman Analisis Keputusan Sijil Pelajaran Malaysia.

Leong, C.H.A. & Jafre, M.Z.A. (2018). Young ESL Learners' Perception on the Effects of Using Digital Storytelling Application in English Language Learning. *Pertanika Journal of Social Science & Humanities, 26* (December): 179–198.

Maghsoudi, M. & Haririan, J. (2013). The Impact of Brainstorming Strategies Iranian EFL Learners' Writing Skill Regarding their Social Class Status. *International Journal of Language and Linguistics, 1*(1): 60.

Masek, A. & Yamin, S. (2010). Fostering Creativity from Constructivist Perspectives: A Literature Review. *RCEE & RHEd* (June): 1–10.

Ohler, J. (2008). *Digital storytelling in the classroom: New media pathways to literacy, learning, and creativity*. Thousand Oaks, CA: Corwin.

Ohler, J. (2013). *Digital storytelling in the classroom: New media pathways to literacy, learning, and creativity* (2nd Ed.). Thousand Oaks, CA: Corwin

Pardo, B.S. (2014). Digital Storytelling: A Case Study of the Creation, and Narration of a Story by EFL Learners El. *Digital Education Review,* (26): 74–84.

Piaget, J. (1964). Part I: Cognitive Development in Children: Piaget Development and Learning. *Journal of Research in Science Teaching, 2*(3): 176–186.

Rahimi, M. & Yadollahi, S. (2017). Effects of offline vs. online digital storytelling on the development of EFL learners' literacy skills. *Cogent Education, 4*(1): 1–13.

Rahmawati, O.I. (2017). Think-Pair-Share: A Technique to Enhance Students' Writing Skill. *Jurnal Pendidikan Edutama, 4*(1): 49–58.

Ramirez, Y.E.H. (2013). Writing Skill Enhancement When Creating Narrative Texts Through the Use of Collaborative Writing and the Storybird Web 2.0 Tool. *Colombian Applied Linguistics Journal, 15*(2): 166.

Razali, N.M. & Yap, B.W. (2011). Power Comparisons of Shapiro-Wilk, Kolmogorov-Smirnov, Lilliefors and Power comparisons of Shapiro-Wilk, Kolmogorov-Smirnov, Lilliefors and Anderson-Darling tests. *Journal of Statistical Modelling and Analytics, 2*(1): 21–33.

Reinders, H. (2011). Digital Storytelling in the Foreign Language Classroom. *Innovationinteaching.org 3* (April): 1–9.

Robin, B. (2006). The educational uses of digital storytelling. *In Society for Information Technology & Teacher Education International Conference* (Vol. 2006, No. 1, pp. 709-716).

Robin, B.R. (2008). Digital storytelling: A powerful technology tool for the 21st century classroom. *Theory into Practice, 47*(3): 220–228.

Sadik, A. (2008). Digital storytelling: a meaningful technology-integrated approach for engaged student learning. *Educational technology research and development*, 56(4), 487-506.

Saed, H.A. & Al-Omari, H.A. (2014). The Effectiveness of a Proposed Program Based on a Mind Mapping Strategy in Developing the Writing Achievement of Eleventh Grade EFLStudents in Jordan and Their Attitudes Towards Writing *Journal of Education and Practice, 5*(18): 88–110.

Sanders, S. (2016). Critical and Creative Thinkers in Mathematics Classrooms. *Journal of Student Engagement: Education Matters, 6*(1): 19–27.

Saputro, D.A.J. (2013). Digital Storytelling to Improve Students' Mastery in Writing Narrative. *Journal of English Language Teaching, 2*(1).

Saunders, J.M. (2014). Where writing happens: Elevating student writing and developing voice through digital storytelling. *Teaching/Writing: The Journal of Writing Teacher Education*, 3(1), 61-70.

Sepp, M. & Bandi-Rao, S. (2015). Creating an Effective Model for Digital Storytelling in the ESL Writing Class. *CUNY Academic Works, 2*(1): 76–88.

Siti Mariam, Z., Melor, M.Y., Nurhuda, M.N. & Parilah, M.S. (2016). Students' Experience of Using Storybird in Writing ESL Narrative Text. *Creative Education, 07*(15): 2107–2120.

Skinner, E., & Hagood, M.C. (2008). Developing literate identities with English language learners through digital storytelling. *The Reading Matrix: An International Online Journal, 8*(2), 12-38.

Stojke, A.E. (2009). *Digital storytelling as a tool for revision* (Doctoral Dissertation).

Sulaiman. (2017). Improving Students' Achievement in Writing Narrative Text Through Modelling Technique in the Second Semester of the Eight-Year Students of Public Junior High School 2 Blitar. *International Research-Based Education Journal, 1*(1).

Sylvester, R., & Greenidge, W.L. (2009). Digital storytelling: Extending the potential for struggling writers. *The Reading Teacher*, 63(4), 284-295.

Teo, A.K. (2006). Using a peer assisted writing activity to promote ESL/EFL students' narrative writing skills. *TESL Journal, 7*(8): 12–25.

Thonghattha, M., Kittichartchaowalit, K. & Kittisunthonphisarn, N. (2016). Effects of Using Storybird to Enhance Creative English Writing Ability of Mathayomsuksa III Students. *Proceeding of ISER 42nd International Conference,* 41–44.

Tompkins, G.E. (2008). *Teaching Writing: Balancing Process and Product.* 5th Ed. New Jersey: Pearson/Merrill Prentice Hall.

Trapsilo, P. (2016). A Think-Aloud Protocols as a Cognitive Strategy to Increase Students' Writing Narrative Skill, *Premise Journal*, *5*(1): 81–90.

Tsigani, C. & Nikolakopoulou, A. (2018). Digital Storytelling: A Creative Writing Study in the Foreign Language Classroom. *Educational Journal of the University of Patras UNESCO Chair, 5*(2): 68–80.

Vasudevan, L., Schultz, K., & Bateman, J. (2010). Rethinking composing in a digital age: Authoring literate identities through multimodal storytelling. *Written Communication, 27*(4), 442-468.

Wong, H. (1989). *The Development of a Qualitative Writing Scale*. Monograph. Pusat Bahasa.

Xin, J. (2013, August). Using digital stories in writing instruction for secondary students with disabilities. In 2013 *International Conference on Educational Research and Sports Education* (ERSE 2013). Atlantis.

Yee, B.C. & Kee, L.L. (2017). Digital Writing in English Language Writing Instruction. *International Research Journal of Language and Literature, 28*: 1–16.

Yüksel, P. (2011). *Using digital storytelling in early childhood education: A phenomenological study of teachers' experiences* (Doctoral Thesis, METU the Graduate School of Natural and Applied Sciences)

Zainudin, Z. (2016). Effect of Using Facebook in Collaborative Writing on ESL Students' Writing Apprehension. National University of Malaysia.

5

Learning Management Systems

Exploring Adoption by B.Ed. Students

M. Ponnambaleswari and Aswathy, C K

Introduction

The advent of Learning Management Systems (LMS) has transformed the educational landscape, offering a digital platform that empowers both educators and learners to manage, deliver, and enhance educational content and experiences. The integration of LMS into teacher education programs holds tremendous potential, providing a versatile platform for content management, fostering interaction, and granting access to a plethora of educational resources. B.Ed. students, as future educators, serve as not only learners but also as potential catalysts for change in the classrooms of the future. Their acceptance and adeptness in utilizing LMS can make a significant impact on the trajectory of education. This paper delves into the exploration of LMS acceptance among B.Ed. trainees, emphasizing the factors that influence acceptance and delving into the experiences of students with LMS. Through a focused examination of LMS acceptance in this specific context, the study contributes to the expanding body of knowledge concerning the seamless integration of technology in teacher education.

Learning Management System (LMS)

The Learning Management System (LMS) is an extensive set of tools and resources utilized by educators and institutions to oversee, deliver, and monitor educational content. It facilitates communication and interaction between learners and instructors, encompassing course administration, content creation, dissemination, assessment management, and collaborative spaces for discussion. LMS platforms serve as the foundation for online and blended learning, enabling learners to access resources, submit assignments, and engage in discussions from virtually any location with an Internet connection.

Adoption of LMS

Adoption of LMS among B.Ed. students signifies the degree of inclination and preparedness of individuals enrolled in the Bachelor of Education (B.Ed.)

program to embrace and utilize Learning Management Systems (LMS) as a fundamental platform for their educational endeavours. This readiness encompasses their willingness, openness, and eagerness to effectively engage with LMS technology and the diverse learning resources it offers.

B.Ed. Students

B.Ed. students refer to individuals who are currently enrolled in the Bachelor of Education program, actively participating in the prescribed coursework, practical teaching experiences, and other essential training activities integral to their teacher education journey. These students are committed to fulfilling the requirements of their B.Ed. degree and are immersed in a comprehensive educational experience that prepares them for their future roles as educators.

The Study

Objectives

1. To assess the overall acceptance of Learning Management Systems (LMS) among Bachelor of Education (B.Ed.) students by determining the percentage of those who consider LMS a valuable tool for their academic journey.
2. To evaluate the consensus among B.Ed. students regarding the ease of use and the perceived usefulness of LMS by calculating the percentage agreement on these aspects.
3. To analyse the percentage of B.Ed. students who endorse the idea that LMS facilitates collaboration and communication in the educational context.
4. To determine the percentage of B.Ed. trainees who express a sense of technological readiness and willingness to actively engage with LMS.
5. To calculate the percentage of B.Ed. trainees who believe that their experience with LMS sufficiently prepares them for their future career as teachers.

Related Literature

Factors Influencing Technology Adoption

The Technology Acceptance Model (TAM) developed by Davis (1989) is widely recognized as a theoretical framework for understanding the adoption and acceptance of technology. TAM posits that two primary factors influence technology acceptance: perceived ease of use (PEOU) and perceived usefulness (PU). According to the author, users are more likely to accept technology if they believe it will enhance their productivity and efficiency.

According to Roca et al., (2006), instructors play a crucial role in shaping technology acceptance. When instructors endorse and actively use LMS in their teaching, it sends a positive signal to trainees and encourages their adoption.

Research has shown that the usability and user-friendliness of technology significantly affect acceptance. When users perceive a system as easy to navigate and understand, they are more likely to embrace it (Al-Gahtani, 2016).

As per Gupta et al., (2019), effective technical support, including timely assistance and problem resolution, can enhance user confidence in using LMS. Users are more likely to accept technology when they feel supported.

Learning Management System in Teacher Education

In teacher education, the integration of LMS has several advantages, including the ability to facilitate communication between instructors and trainees, provide access to resources and materials, and support collaborative learning. Studies have shown that LMS can enhance engagement, collaboration, and the overall learning experience in teacher preparation programs (Ally & Samaka, 2013; Lim & Kim, 2019).

Ally and Samaka (2013) emphasize the role of Open Educational Resources (OER) in conjunction with LMS, highlighting their potential to bridge educational gaps and promote collaborative learning experiences. Lim and Kim (2019) provide empirical evidence of the positive impact of LMS on teacher education.

Marin et al. (2013) reported that LMS platforms facilitate increased interaction between students and instructors in teacher education programs.

The adoption of LMS empowers teacher trainees to take ownership of their learning journeys. Through LMS, trainees can navigate course content at their own pace, revisit materials, and pursue additional resources as needed. This self-directed approach fosters autonomy and critical thinking skills, attributes essential for educators (Alqurashi, 2019).

Methodology

To explore the acceptance of Learning Management Systems (LMS) among Bachelor of Education (B.Ed.) trainees, data was gathered using a survey methodology. The study employed a purposive sampling technique, selecting a sample of 180 B.Ed. students from Bangalore University. To collect data on the adoption of Learning Management Systems (LMS) among B.Ed. students, a questionnaire was utilized. The questionnaire was designed to assess participants' perspectives across four dimensions:

1. Ease of use and usefulness
2. Collaboration and communication
3. Technological readiness and willingness
4. Preparation for future career as a teacher

The questionnaire comprised a total of 20 items, with five items allocated to each dimension. These items encompassed both positive and negative statements, totalling 12 positive and 8 negative statements. Respondents were provided with binary options, choosing between "Yes" or "No" for each item.

Results

Data was gathered from a sample of 180 students enrolled in different B.Ed. Colleges under Bangalore University, utilizing the researcher-prepared questionnaire. The questionnaire focused on four dimensions, and the ensuing results are outlined below.

a) Ease of Use and Usefulness

- Universally, all students express a belief in the advantageous impact of integrating Learning Management Systems (LMS) into their B.Ed. program.
- 69.8% agree that the layout and design of the LMS platform are user-friendly, indicating a positive perception of its accessibility.
- A substantial 96.2% believe that LMS facilitates the organization and accessibility of theoretical learning materials, highlighting its effectiveness in managing educational resources.
- 79.2% express the belief that LMS has the potential to enhance their academic performance, reflecting a positive correlation between LMS adoption and academic outcomes.
- Among the surveyed students, 92.5% anticipate that LMS usage will contribute to more effective time management, indicating a perceived benefit in terms of organizational efficiency.

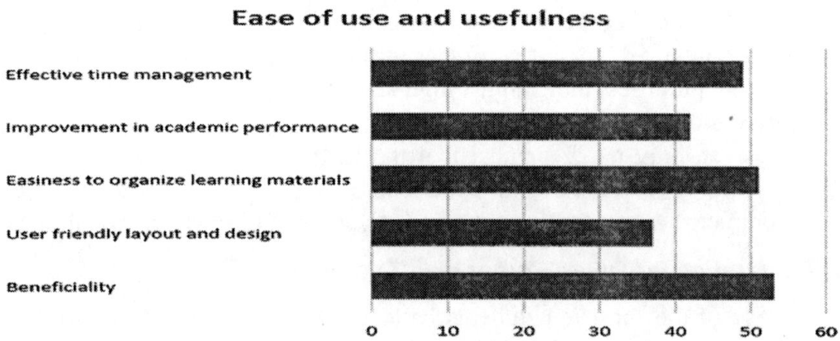

b) Collaboration and Communication

- An overwhelming 94.3% of the surveyed students believe that the adoption of LMS will enhance their collaborative abilities when working on group projects or assignments, indicating a positive perception of its potential for group work.

- 73.6% anticipate that LMS utilization will improve communication and information sharing among students enrolled in the B.Ed. program, underscoring its role in facilitating effective communication channels.
- 67.9% express the belief that LMS's collaborative tools are not particularly beneficial for group discussions and virtual meetings, indicating a nuanced perspective on the platform's collaborative features.
- A significant 98.1% believe that LMS will actively encourage participation in online discussions and forums, emphasizing its potential for fostering engagement and interaction.
- Furthermore, 94.3% anticipate that using the LMS will contribute to building a sense of community among students in the B.Ed. program, highlighting its potential to create a collaborative and supportive learning environment.

c) Technological Readiness and Willingness

- A significant 98.1% of the surveyed students' express comfort in using digital devices (such as computers, smartphones, and tablets) for academic activities, indicating a high level of technological familiarity among the respondents.
- In alignment with their preferred learning style, 92.5% agree that learning through an online platform like LMS is conducive to their educational preferences, showcasing a positive attitude toward digital learning methods.
- 71.7% convey a willingness to invest time and effort to become proficient in using the LMS, demonstrating a moderate yet positive inclination towards acquiring the necessary skills for effective utilization.
- A substantial 94.3% felt confident in their ability to use technology for learning purposes, indicating a high level of self-assurance in leveraging digital tools for educational pursuits.
- However, only 64.2% expect that the LMS will provide a wide range of learning materials and experiences, suggesting a more reserved anticipation regarding the comprehensiveness of the platform's offerings.

d) Preparation for Future Career as a Teacher

- 58.5% of the surveyed students believe that integrating LMS into their education will enhance their digital teaching skills, recognizing the significance of such skills in modern classrooms.
- A substantial 90.6% express the belief that LMS can provide valuable insights into best practices for student engagement and motivation, emphasizing the platform's potential role in enhancing teaching methodologies.

- 92.5% agree that using LMS will help them understand the importance of different learning styles and personalized instruction, showcasing an awareness of the platform's capacity to promote a student-centric approach.
- 71.7% are of the opinion that learning to use LMS will align with the evolving demands of 21st-century teaching, indicating a recognition of the platform's relevance in preparing educators for contemporary educational landscapes.
- An overwhelming 94.3% agree that the skills acquired through LMS usage will enhance their competitiveness in the job market as future educators, underlining the perceived professional advantages associated with incorporating LMS into their teacher training.

Therefore, it can be concluded that,

- A significant majority of B.Ed. trainees, accounting for 84.72%, acknowledge Learning Management Systems (LMS) as a valuable and beneficial tool for their academic journey.
- An overwhelming 87.54% express agreement regarding the ease of use and the overall usefulness of LMS in facilitating their educational endeavours.
- The majority, comprising 85.64%, believe that LMS plays a pivotal role in promoting collaboration and communication among peers.
- A substantial 84.16% exhibit a sense of technological readiness and willingness to engage with LMS, showcasing a positive attitude towards incorporating technology into their learning experience.
- The majority, constituting 81.52% affirm that LMS adequately prepares them for their future careers as teachers, highlighting the platform's perceived value in teacher training.

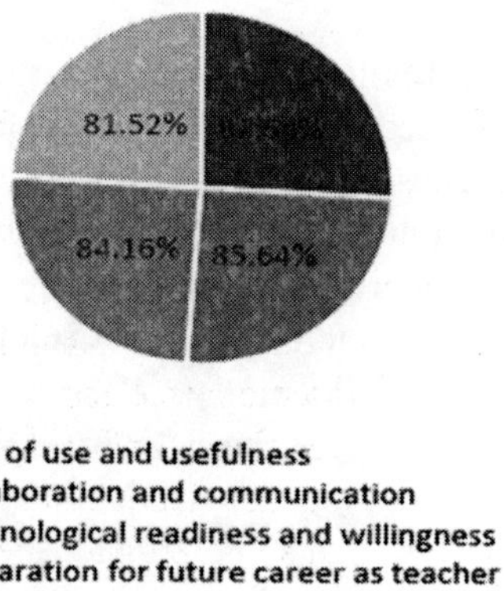

Conclusion

Drawing conclusions from the data collected, several key observations emerge:

- *Acceptance of Learning Management Systems (LMS)*: A significant majority of B.Ed. trainees, specifically 84.72%, acknowledge the value and benefit of Learning Management Systems (LMS) in their academic journey. This positive reception reflects a favourable attitude toward the incorporation of technology into their educational experience.
- *Ease of Use and Usefulness*: An overwhelming 87.54% find LMS to be user-friendly and valuable for their educational needs. This high level of agreement suggests that the LMS platform's layout, design, and functionality are generally well-received, contributing to a positive user experience.
- *Collaboration and Communication*: A substantial 85.64% believe that LMS plays a pivotal role in promoting collaboration and communication among peers. This finding underscores the platform's significance in fostering a sense of community and facilitating effective group projects and information sharing.
- *Technological Readiness and Willingness*: The data reveals that a majority of students, comprising 84.16%, express feeling technologically ready and willing to engage with the LMS. This positive disposition indicates a readiness to embrace digital tools for various academic activities.
- *Preparation for Future Teaching Careers*: The LMS is recognized as a valuable asset in preparing future educators. A noteworthy 81.52% of B.Ed. trainees believe that the LMS adequately equips them with essential skills and knowledge for their future teaching careers. This encompasses the enhancement of digital teaching skills, understanding diverse learning styles, and staying aligned with the evolving demands of 21st-century teaching.

In conclusion, the findings from this survey underscore the overall positive perception and acceptance of Learning Management Systems (LMS) among B.Ed. trainees. These systems are viewed as user-friendly, valuable for collaboration and communication, and effective in preparing future teachers for the demands of modern education. These insights provide valuable guidance for the integration and continued development of LMS platforms in the academic curriculum of B.Ed.

Bibliography

Abdelrahman, Beverly (2016), "Hybrid learning: perspectives of higher education faculty", *International Journal of Information Communication Technologies and Human Development* 8(1)

Al-Gahtani, S.S. (2016). Empirical investigation of e-learning acceptance and assimilation: A structural equation model. Applied Computing and Informatics, 14(1), 27-50.

Allen, I.E., & Seaman, J. (2016). Online report card—Tracking online education in the United States. Retrieved from http://online learningsurvey.com/reports/onlinereportcard.pdf

Ally, M., & Samaka, M. (2013). Open educational resources and mobile technology to narrow the learning divide. *The International Review of Research in Open and Distributed Learning*, 14(2), 14-27.

Alqurashi, E. (2016). Predicting student satisfaction and perceived learning within online learning environments. *Distance Education*, 37(2), 179-192.

Alqurashi, E. (2019). Self-directed learning in teacher education: The use of learning management systems. *Teaching in Higher Education*, 24(1), 30-47.

Behzad, M.; Adnan, N.; Naeem Malik, A.; Merchant, S.A. Technology-Embedded Hybrid Learning. Preprints 2018, 2018030229 (doi: 10.20944/preprints 201803.0229.v2).

Bolliger, D.U., & Inan, F.A. (2012). Development and validation of the Online Instructor Satisfaction Measure (OISM). *Educational Technology Research and Development*, 60(4), 703-719.

Bonk, C., Graham, C.: *The Handbook of Hybrid Learning*. John Wiley & Sons, New York (2006)

Davis, F.D. (1989). Perceived usefulness, perceived ease of use, and user acceptance of information technology. *MIS Quarterly*, 13(3), 319-340.

Garnham, C. & Kaleta, R. (2002). Introduction to hybrid courses. *Teaching with Technology Today*, 8(6). Retrieved September 21, 2005 from http://www.uwsa.edu/ttt/articles/garnham.htm

Gleason, B. & Greenhow, C. (2017). Hybrid Education: The Potential of Teaching and Learning with Robot-Mediated Communication. *Online Learning Journal, 21*(4),

Gupta, A., & Mohan, D. (2019). Factors influencing the acceptance of learning management systems in Indian universities: A structural equation modeling approach. Education and Information Technologies, 24(6), 3927-3947.

Johnson, M.L., & Brown, S.E. (2019). Exploring the Effectiveness of LMS in Blended Learning Environments. In Proceedings of the International Conference on e-Learning, (pp. 78-92). Academic Press.

Kajder, S. (2007). Unleashing potential with emerging technologies. In Beers, K. Probst, R. & Rief, L. (Eds.) Adolescent literacy: Promise into practice. Portsmouth, NH: Heineman.

Kanishka Bedi, 2011. A Methodology for Integrating Traditional Classroom Learning with Contemporary Online Learning, International Conference on Hybrid Learning

Khoo, H.E. (2003). Implementation of problem-based learning in Asian medical schools and students' perception of their experience. *Medical Education*, 37(5), 401-409

Koohang, A. & Durante, A. (2003). Learners' perceptions toward the web-based distance learning activities/assignments portion of an undergraduate hybrid instructional model. *Journal Information Technology Education*, 2, 105-113. Retrieved September 21, 2005 from http://www.jite.org/documents/Vol2/v2p105-113-78.pdf

Olapiriyakul, K., Scher, J.M.: A Guide to Establishing Hybrid Learning Courses: Employing Information Technology to Create a New Learning Experience and a Case Study. *Internet and Higher Education* 9, 287–301 (2006)

Owen P. Hall Jr. and John G. Mooney (2010). Hybrid Learning Systems: Meeting the Challenges of Graduate Management Education, International Conference on Hybrid Learning ICHL 2010: Hybrid Learning pp 35–48

Roca, J.C., Chiu, C. M., & Martínez, F.J. (2006). Understanding e-learning continuance intention: An extension of the Technology Acceptance Model. *International Journal of Human-Computer Studies*, 64(8), 683-696.

Smith, J.A. (2020). The Impact of Learning Management Systems on Student Engagement. Educational Technology Research and Development, 68(3), 145-162.

6

Utilisation of Cloud-based Learning Platform

Mohd Noor Alam and Aerum Khan

Introduction

Technological advancement has revolutionized the way of life in the last few decades. We are using technology in every walk of our life and cannot even imagine a day without the use of technology. Technology has also brought revolution in the field of education too. It provides a variety of solutions to improve the teaching-learning process and makes the teaching-learning process more accessible and flexible. Cloud-based technology is one of the innovative technologies that provides learning resources to the learners as per their needs and interest over the Internet. In this digital era, cloud-based learning platforms have revolutionized the way of acquiring knowledge and skills. These cloud-based learning platforms provide flexible, accessible and interactive educational experiences to the learners anywhere and anytime using the Internet connected device. Learners are no longer bound by the constraints of physical classrooms or rigid schedules.

The Indian government launched various cloud-based learning platforms such as SWAYAM, Swayam Prabha, e-pathshala, DIKHSA, PM-eVidya etc. SWAYAM and SWAYAM Prabha initiatives are proposed to go hand in hand supplementing and complementing each other (Kanjilal and Kaul, 2016). In 2009, the Ministry of Human Resource Development launched a centrally sponsored scheme, National Mission on Education through Information and Communication Technology (NMEICT) to leverage the potential of ICT in the teaching-learning process. The major ongoing initiatives are SWAYAM, SWAYAM Prabha, National Digital Library (NDL), e-Yantra, FOSSEE, Virtual Labs etc. (Draft of Digital Initiative in Higher Education, NMEICT). Evaluation Committee on NMEICT proposed the cloud-based learning architecture (Fig. 1) to implement a cloud computing platform for providing all the services required under NMEICT projects.

The proposed architecture connects all the broad themes of NMEICT together. The generated content in active form (virtual labs) and passive form (videos) reside on a distributed data server spread across the cloud. Connectivity ensures that end-users are always connected to the cloud services through various end-devices. The proposed architecture ensures that learning

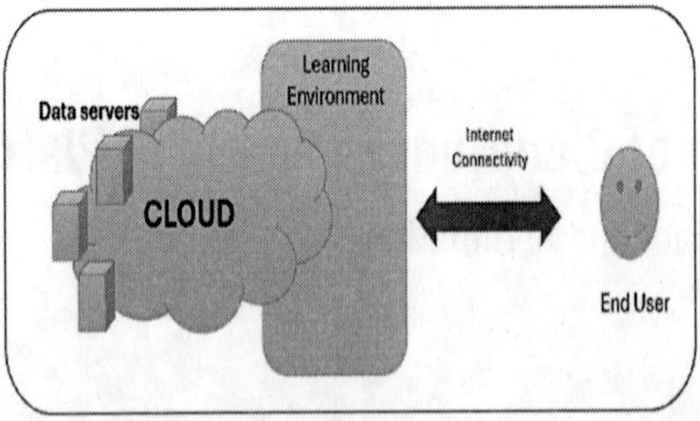

Figure 1: Cloud-Based Learning Architecture (Source — Report of the Evaluation Committee on NMEICT)

can happen anytime-anywhere paradigm. It would also minimize the need for technical expertise at the end-user premise since all the infrastructure resides in the cloud. (Report of Evaluation Committee on NMEICT).

Related Literature

Kanjilal and Kaul (2016), while examining the Digital India initiative of the Indian Government gives more insight on Study Webs of Active Learning for Young Aspiring Minds (SWAYAM) and other initiatives like National Mission on Education Through ICT (NMEICT), National Programme on Technology Enhanced Learning (NPTEL), a joint program of IITs (Indian Institutes of Technology) and IISc (Indian Institute of Science). SWAYAM is being seen as an instrument for self-actualization providing opportunities for life-long learning. Lateef, A.N. (2021), stated that Swayam Prabha is a good initiative by the MHRD, GoI. It provides higher education like all under one roof method. It is mentioned that the Swayam Prabha channels provide curriculum-based contents at undergraduate, post-graduate and school levels and cover different subject disciplines. Through SWAYAM (platform for offering Massive Open Online Courses MOOCs), all the courses would be certificate-ready after successful completion of the course. Brahma K. and Verma M.K. (2018), investigated the awareness and use of e-PG Pathshala Open Courseware by PG students of Mizoram University. It is found that only 54% of respondents are aware of e-PG Pathshala and nearly half of the respondents (46%) are not aware of e-PG Pathshala. It is recommended that the university should conduct awareness programmes for students to create more awareness about e-PG Pathshala with the involvement of teachers in this awareness programme. Vidyasagar D. (2022) mentioned that the e-Pathshala is a good solution on online teaching and learning in this COVID-19 pandemic and it is emerging as the best online teaching-learning methodology. Panda S. (2020) conducted a case study on e-PG Pathshala and found that the majority of the e-PG visitors is held by the continent Asa of e-PG Pathshala visitors among the world. It is also found that Uttar Pradesh has the highest number of e-PG visitors (514288) which was 17% of the total visitors. Rani, U.M. (2020), conducted a study on the effectiveness of e-Pathshala impact and found that there is no significant difference between the control group and experimental group while teaching subjects like English, Maths, and Science. The significant difference has been seen in the IV Science where the scores of the experimental group were much lower than the control group scores. It is suggested that e-Pathshala should be used more effectively, and teachers should be trained more to use it.

The aim of this research paper is to know the awareness level of secondary schools' students about the use of cloud-based learning platforms in the teaching learning process. This paper also investigates the applications of cloud-based learning platforms in secondary school education and the major challenges faced by the students in using these cloud-based learning platforms.

The Study

Objectives

1. To study the perception of secondary school students about the use of cloud-based learning platforms.
2. To find out the awareness level of students about the use of cloud-based learning platforms.
3. To study the application of cloud-based learning platforms in secondary school education.
4. To investigate the major challenges faced by students in using cloud-based learning platforms.

Methodology

In the present study, a quantitative research design was used to know the perception, usage and the challenges faced by the secondary school's students in using cloud-based learning platforms. The population for the present study consisted of secondary level students of Jamia Millia Islamia schools. A sample of 25 students was selected randomly for the present research. The researcher personally visited the two different schools and distributed 50 questionnaires among the students. Out of which 25 questionnaires were duly filled in by the students. The data was collected in the month of March 2023. In order to collect data, the researcher developed a self-constructed mixed questionnaire after reviewing related literature. The questionnaire contains 21 items (20 close ended and 1 Open ended). The data has been analyzed as per the objectives of research. MS-Excel has been used to analyze the collected data and the descriptive statistics including graphical representation and percentages are used to provide a general view.

Results

Demographic Information of the Students

Among 25 students, 60% are male and 40% are female. The sample has taken from Class IX and XI only in which 68% students are of Class XI and 32% students are of Class IX. 72% students are from senior secondary school while only 28% are from secondary school. 36% students are from science background, 20% from commerce background and 16% from arts background. The sample has been taken from two schools of Jamia Millia Islamia, 25 students were among the sample, in which 64% students are from Jamia Senior Sec. School while 36% are from Syed Abid Hussain Senior Sec. School.

Theme 1: Perception of using Cloud-based Learning Platforms

- *When asked "Have you ever used cloud-based learning platforms for self-learning?"*

Sixty-four percent students responded yes while 36% responded no.

- *Cloud-based Learning Platforms Known by Students?*

The majority of students, i.e. 80% know about e-pathshala and 24% students know about DIKSHA. PM e-Vidya and e-PG Pathshala is known by only 4% respectively while very few number of students know about other cloud-based learning platforms like SWAYAM, SWAYAM Prabha, PM e-Vidya, DIKSHA etc. Fig. 2.

- *Student's awareness about SWAYAM?*

The majority of students i.e. 80% have not heard about SWAYAM platform while only 20% are aware about it..

- *Student's awareness about SWAYAM Prabha?*

96% students are not aware about SWAYAM Prabha, they have not even heard about it. Only 4% have heard about SWAYAM Prabha.

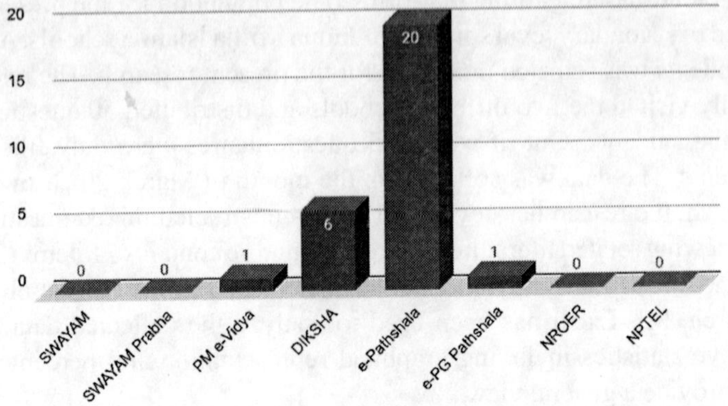

Figure 2: Cloud-based Learning Platforms Known by Students

< *Student's Awareness about PM E-Vidya?*

The Government of India launched the PM eVidya scheme in 2020 with the aim to protect the education of children during Covid-19 pandemic. The majority of students i.e. 84% have not heard about it while only 16% are aware about it..

< *Registration of students at SWAYAM?*

When asked about the registration at SWAYAM portal 96% students responded that they have never registered for any course. Only 4% have registered at SWAYAM portal for any course.

Theme 2: Application of cloud-based learning platforms

< *Students perception about cloud-based learning platforms?*

The result indicates that a majority of respondents i.e. 68% reported that cloud-based learning platforms help them to understand the concept easily while only 32% disagree .

< *Use of Cloud-based Learning Platforms to Download Books*

60% students have used cloud-based learning platforms for downloading books' pdf while 40% have not downloaded books from cloud-based learning platforms ever.

< *Students' Registration under DIKSHA App?*

Majority of respondents i.e. 92% have not registered for any course under DIKSHA app while only 8% have registered for the course.

< *Students' Response to Watch Videos Lectures on Cloud-based Learning Platforms?*

The results show that 76% of students like to watch video lectures on cloud-based learning platforms while 24% do not like to watch it

< *Students' Response to Download Books from DIKSHA App?*

The majority of respondents i.e. 48% do not download books from DIKSHA app/web while 12% strongly agreed and 28% agreed that they usually download books from DIKSHA app/web. 12% are neutral with the statement

< *Students' Response to Download Books from E-Pathshala?*

12% respondents strongly agreed and 32% agreed that they usually download books from e-Pathshala while 32% disagree and 32% are neutral with the statement.

< *Students' Response to Download Books from NCERT Websites?*

The majority of respondents i.e. 44% agreed and 40% strongly agreed that they usually download books from NCERT websites while only 16% are neutral with the statement

Theme 3: Comfort Level of using Cloud-Based Learning Platforms

< *Students' Comfortability in Using Technology?*

40% of respondents strongly agreed and 32% agreed that they are comfortable in using technology for self-learning while 24% respondents are neutral to the statement.

< *Students' response to watch video lectures on SWAYAM?*

Only 24% of respondents like and 24% of respondents do not like to watch video lectures on SWAYAM while the majority of respondents i.e. 52% are neutral to the statement.

< *Students' Response to Watch Video Lectures on SWAYAM Prabha?*

20% of respondents agreed while only 4% strongly agreed that they like to watch educational content broadcasted on SWAYAM Prabha channel. The majority of respondents i.e. 48% are neutral and 28% disagree with the statement.

Theme 4: Motivation Level of Using Cloud-based Learning Platforms

< *Students' Perception about Lectures on SWAYAM?*

Majority of respondents i.e. 40% disagree that lectures on SWAYAM help them to understand the topic better while 24% agreed and 4% strongly agreed with the statement.

< *Students' Perception About Lectures on SWAYAM Prabha?*

24% respondents agreed and 8% strongly agreed that the lectures on SWAYAM Prabha help them to understand the topic better while majority of respondents i.e. 36% disagree with the statement.

< *Students' Motivation about the use of Cloud-Based Learning Platforms?*

Majority of respondents i.e. 40% agreed and 16% strongly agreed that they are always motivated when they use cloud-based learning platforms while 20% disagree and 20% are neutral with the statement.

< *Course Done by Students on Cloud-based Learning Platforms?*

The majority of respondents i.e. 92% have not done any course from any cloud-based learning platforms.

Theme 5: Challenges in using Cloud-based Learning Platforms

The majority of respondents have not responded to this item. Some of the respondents raised the issue of the unavailability of Internet and instant doubt solutions regarding any topic. Two respondents reported that there is a lot of distraction while using cloud-based learning platforms.

Major Findings

1. The findings reveal that a significant portion of the surveyed students have not extensively utilized these platforms for self-learning. Specifically, only 36% of respondents have used cloud-based learning platforms for self-learning, indicating a notable gap in adoption.
2. Regarding awareness, a substantial percentage of students demonstrated limited knowledge about key platforms. For instance, only 20% had heard about SWAYAM (Study Webs of Active Learning for Young Aspiring Minds), and an even smaller percentage, merely 4%, were familiar with SWAYAM Prabha. The Government of India launched the PM eVidya scheme in 2020 with the aim to protect the education of children during Covid-19 pandemic. But the majority of students, i.e. 84% have not heard about it.
3. A mere 4% of students had registered for any courses on SWAYAM, suggesting a relatively low level of engagement with this particular platform. Interestingly, despite limited registration, a significant majority of students, 68%, believed that cloud-based learning platforms help them understand concepts more easily.
4. The findings provide a detailed insight into students' attitudes and preferences concerning technology-enabled learning, particularly on various platforms. A significant portion of teachers, comprising 36%, expressed comfort in using technology for self-learning, with 32% agreeing and 24% remaining neutral. This indicates a positive inclination toward incorporating technology into their learning practices.
5. When assessing motivation levels, 56% of students expressed being motivated when using cloud-based learning platforms, with 40% agreeing and 16% strongly agreeing. This suggests a positive correlation between the use of technology in learning and students' motivation.
6. The majority of students, i.e. 92% have not done any course from any cloud-based learning platforms even though they have not registered on these platforms.

Discussion

The findings highlight several important issues regarding the lack of awareness and utilization of cloud-based learning platforms among students. The study reveals that there is a significant gap in knowledge and awareness among students about prominent cloud-based learning platforms such as SWAYAM, SWAYAM Prabha, PM e-Vidya, and DIKSHA. Despite being flagship schemes of the Government of India, these platforms are not well-known or utilized by the majority of students.

One of the key implications of these findings is the need for an effective awareness campaign to familiarize students with these cloud-based learning platforms. Increasing awareness among students is crucial as they play a pivotal role in incorporating technology and online resources into their classroom learning. The government and educational institutions should take proactive measures to promote these platforms, provide training and support for teachers to enhance their digital skills, and emphasize the benefits of integrating cloud-based learning platforms into their teaching practices.

Despite the launch of initiatives like the PM eVidya scheme, which aimed to ensure uninterrupted education during the COVID-19 pandemic, the majority of students are unaware of these cloud-based learning platforms. This finding emphasizes the importance of not only targeting teachers but also students in awareness campaigns and providing them with the necessary information and resources to access and utilize these platforms effectively.

Furthermore, the study reveals that even among the students who are aware of these platforms, there is a significant lack of engagement. Most students have not registered or taken any courses on these cloud-based learning platforms. This finding points to the need for further investigation into the reasons behind the low participation rate. Factors such as accessibility, usability, relevance of available courses, and perceived value of online learning may influence students' decisions to enrol in courses through these platforms. Identifying and addressing these factors will be crucial to encourage greater student engagement and utilization of cloud-based learning platforms.

Overall, this study underscores the importance of raising awareness and promoting the adoption of cloud-based learning platforms among students. It highlights the need for effective awareness campaigns, targeted training programs, and support systems to overcome the barriers and challenges associated with the adoption and utilization of these platforms. By addressing these issues, policymakers, educators, and stakeholders can harness the potential of cloud-based learning platforms to enhance educational opportunities and improve learning outcomes for students.

Conclusion

In this digital era, Cloud-based technology is one of the innovative technologies that provide learning resources to the learners as per their needs and interest over the Internet. Cloud-based services refer to the wide range of services provided to the masses over the Internet without the need of internal infrastructure or hardware. These services are designed to provide easy, affordable access to resources. The Indian government has launched various cloud-based learning platforms in the last few decades to make education accessible and affordable for all. The need for an effective awareness campaign to familiarize students with these cloud-based learning platforms. Increasing awareness among students is crucial as they play a pivotal role in incorporating technology and online resources into their classroom learning. The government and educational institutions should take proactive measures to promote these platforms, provide training and support for teachers to enhance their digital skills, and emphasize the benefits of integrating cloud-based learning platforms into their teaching practices. There is a clear disconnect between the availability of cloud-based learning platforms and their utilization by teachers and students. Addressing this gap requires targeted efforts to increase awareness among both educators and learners, enabling them to leverage the benefits of these initiatives. By bridging the awareness gap, the Government of India can better support the education system and enhance access to quality learning opportunities for all.

References

Best J.W. & Kahn J.V. (1995), *Research in Education.* 7th Edition.

Brahma K. & Verma M.K. (2018), Awareness and Use of E-PG Pathshala Open Courseware by PG Students of Mizoram University: A Survey, *DELNET-Developing Library Network*, 211-224 Retrieved from https://www.researchgate.net/publication/324889005

DIKSHA https://diksha.gov.in/

E-Pathshalahttps://epathshala.nic.in/

Griethttp://www.nmeict.griet.ac.in/index.html

Hajam M.A. (2016), SWOT Analysis of e-PG Pathshala, *Professional Journal of Library and Information Technology,* Volume 6, Issue 2, 2016, ISSN 0976-7274 Retrieved from https://www.researchgate.net/publication/351356600

Khosla R. et al. (2020), The PM e-Vidya Scheme as an e-Learning Scheme for Disadvantaged Students in India During the COVID-19 Pandemic, *International Journal of Advanced Research* 8(07), 1018-10288, Retrieved from http://dx.doi.org/10.21474/IJAR01/11364

Latheef N.A. (2018), Gateway of Teaching and Learning: Role of Swayam Prabha, University News, *A Weekly Journal of Higher Education*, 11-15, Retrieved from https://www.researchgate.net/publication/355668425

Panda S. (2020), An Analysis of E-Content Modules of Indian OERs: A Case Study of E-Pg Pathshala Retrieved from https://www.researchgate.net/publication/348660914

Rani, U.M. (2020), Study on Effectiveness of E-Pathshala Impact, Retrieved from https://www.researchgate.net/publication/342600037

Report of the Evaluation Committee on NMEICT, Retrieved from http://13.235.123.225/wp-content/uploads/2020/04/documents/Evaluation%20Committee%20Report/NMEICT_Evaluation_Report.pdf

SWAYAM Government Portal; https://swayam.gov.in/

Swayam Prabha; https://www.swayamprabha.gov.in/index.php/home

Vidyasagar D. (2022), Accepting the Challenges of COVID-19: The E-Pathshala Project for Effective Online Teaching & Learning, Retrieved from https://www.researchgate.net/publication/358279857

7

Importance of Developing an E-Learning Style Model

Diksha Dhanda

Introduction

In the early stages of the use of ICT in education, computers were used as accompanying teaching tools. With the advancement in technology, the influence of the technological revolution in education was observed which showed a transformative shift in how education is received and delivered. In the modern educational landscape, ICT integration in teaching as well as learning has become a crucial component in forming educational practices. The change is not only about the inclusion of digital tools in the class but a fundamental shift in the pedagogical approach towards more flexible, and learner-centred learning. Education experimenters have been studying the learning styles ideas for long and proposed different models to classify and know the differences in how learners process and retain information. Still, these models substantially concentrate on the conventional classroom setting and may not completely address the requirements of a digital learning environment. The significance of developing an e-learning style model lies in its implicit ability to feed to the colourful learning preferences of learners by perfecting the learning issues.

Research has shown that by understanding learning styles, the quality of teaching and learning in education can be better which would lead to better achievement levels (Escuadro, 2023). It has been recommended by numerous educational technologists that relating and integrating different learning styles into e-learning design helps to design the course content which helps to feed to the individual preferences of learners (Periasamy, 2023). However, there are frameworks like TPACK, COI, and SMAR which help educators integrate technology in their teaching practices. But they are unable to specify what should be integrated, for example, the CoI (Community of Inquiry) framework identifies three types of presence i.e., cognitive, social, and teaching presence. It provides a theoretical foundation for designing and implementing online learning activities. But it too has some drawbacks as it does not consider individual learning preferences. Based on the learning preferences of online learners, the demand to go beyond conventional pedagogical bounds and fulfill the diversity of learner needs in digital surroundings requires establishing an e-learning style model. A model like this would account for variables like online involvement, digital knowledge, flexibility and colourful multimedia formats. Educators can thus produce a more productive and inclusive learning environment by matching educational strategies with the help of preferred digital learning styles of learners. Thus, re-evaluating ICT integration in teaching and learning is necessary.

Families of existing learning style models

The idea of learning styles has been integral to educational theory and practice which helps to understand how the learners absorb and process the information. Over the past, some learning models have been proposed to classify and explain these variations in a method that can improve teaching methodologies. Based on the existing review of literature, many models of learning styles have been put forth by educational technologists at different points in time which are regularly used in classroom teaching learning by educators. A summary of some of the most well-known and significant models in the subject of education is provided like the VARK Model, Kolb's Model, Felder-Silverman learning style model, etc. Moreover, the learning models are categorized into families like Constitutionally based models, Cognitive structure-based models, Flexibly stable learning preference-based models, and Personality type-based models (Liyanage et al., 2014). These models are based on the focus and learners' approaches to learning.

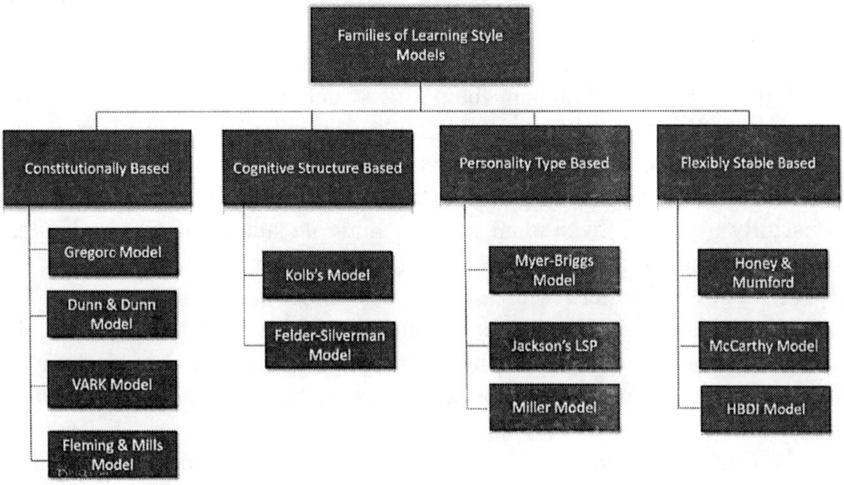

Figure 1: Families of Learning Style Model

1) ***Constitutionally-based learning style models*** are determined mainly by inherited traits or characteristics. This family includes models like the Gregorc model, Dunn and Dunn model, VARK model, etc.

Anthony Gregorc in the 1970s developed a model called the Gregorc Mind Styles Model that distributed learning styles grounded on how learners perceive and order information. These are concrete successional, abstract successional, abstract arbitrary, and concrete arbitrary which help educators to understand learner preferences in learning. This model emphasizes more on cognitive processing preferences while learning. Still, there's limited exploration on the effectiveness of this model and whether it is effective or not in an online environment as it has not been used in the digital environment. In short, to determine whether or not the concept works well in an online setting, further exploration is needed as there is limited exploration till now (Miller, 2004). For example, Min et al., 2018 in their study found that the model did not show significant teaching effectiveness for learners enrolled in online courses.

VARK Model was developed by Neil Fleming in 1987 and is a structure for comprehending various learning preferences. As the name suggests, it categorizes learners into four types like Visual learners, Audible learners, Reading-Writing learners, and Kinesthetic learners. This educational frame has been applied in several educational settings including online education but the exploration regarding its effectiveness in an online setting is limited. The available research emphasizes the application of the VARK model in online learning (Idrizi et al., 2018) and the impact of mobile VR on learner motivation and engagement for VARK learning styles (Manzoor, Mohd-Isa & Dollmat, 2022). Still, the advantages of applying this approach in an online setting are not supported by any dependable study. Thus, further exploration is demanded to know about its connection to online context.

Next, *the Dunn and Dunn model of Learning Style* was developed by Rita and Kenneth Dunn in the 1970s which helped to understand how learners prefer to learn. This model emphasizes substantially on factors like emotional, physiological, sociological, and emotional that help educators produce a conducive learning environment. Although this approach has been constantly used in conventional settings, multiple studies have revealed that in online literacy its effectiveness is limited. For example, (Oweini & Daouk, 2016) suggested further research to use this model in an online context. The model emphasizes the demand to match an individual learning style with the educational environment, but to the online environment, its connection may be limited because of its complexion which may not allow the customization of instruction to fit unique approaches to learning.

2) *Cognitive-structure based learning style model* reflects cognitive structure features of the learners like their ability to process and organize information.

It includes *Kolb's Model* proposed by David Kolb in 1984, which understands learning as a process. It suggests that education becomes successful when a learner progresses through a cycle of four stages: Concrete experience, Reflective observation, Abstract conceptualization, and Active experimentation. Based on these stages, Kolb distinguished between four types of learning for example: Diverging (focus on imagination), Assimilating (prefer logical approach), Converging (focus on problem-solving), and Accommodating (prefer intuitions). The model has been used in different educational settings including online education (Richmond, Cohen & Cummings). The existing research focuses on application of Kolb's theory in online distance education (Richmond, 2005), the measurement of learning styles of learners in online context (Pinchot, 2014), and the use of Kolb's model in online settings (Cohen, 2022). Nonetheless, every one of these studies were not sufficient to know the effectiveness of the model in an online environment.

Richard Felder and Linda Silverman proposed the *Felder-Silverman Model* in the 1980s. It categorizes learners into four dimensions according to how they choose to learn. Four categories of learners were Sensory-intuitive (sensory prefers concrete information and intuitive prefers abstract information), Visual-Verbal (visually learned by pictures and verbally learned by words), Active-Reflective (active learning by doing and reflective by thinking), and Sequential-Global (sequential follow logical paths and global learners make large jumps in understanding). In short, although the model has been used widely in different educational contexts including online learning environments, still, there has not been much study done on how successful the model is in these situations. The existing studies focus on the FSLM use for the design of online courses and learning analytics intervention approaches, rather than on its limitations in a virtual classroom (Joseph et al., 2022). So based on existing literature, its effectiveness remains inconclusive within the framework of online education. Thus, additional research studies must be conducted by the researchers.

3) *Personality-type based learning style model* views learning style as an element of a personality type that can affect how a learner approaches learning tasks.

It includes models like Briggs *Study Process Questionnaire (SPQ)* that was developed by John Briggs in the 1980s. This was used to know how learners approach their learning. This model states that a learner's approach to studying and learning can be divided into three types: Deep approach, Surface approach, and Achieving approach. The BSPQ is an extensively used instrument to access learning styles in online classes. Still, the available exploration is limited in addressing the effectiveness of BSPQ in online learning. Therefore, further research is needed to determine if the model is appropriate for learning online or not (Min et al., 2018).

Jackson's Learning Style Profiler (LSP) was created by Chris J. Jackson in the early 2000s. It is a psychometric tool used to assess individual learning preferences determined by their personality traits. It proposed that learning style is influenced by two key dimensions. Further, these dimensions are divided into four categories: Explorer, Planner, Expert, and Visionary.

4) *Flexibly stable* learning preferences-based models consider learning style as a stable and flexible long preference that can change over time.

This family includes models like the *4MAT Learning Style Model* which was created by Bernice McCarthy in 1972. This is an instructional design model featuring four distinct learning styles, each of which has unique learning strengths. It rests on the idea that the learner's cycle goes through four different literary styles. It provides a frame that helps to address various learning styles in educational settings. This model categorizes learners as Innovative Learners, Common Sense Learners, Dynamic Learners, and Analytic Learners. Studies have validated the model in primary, secondary, and advanced education (AlSaleem, 2019). But when we talk about online learning, the body of literature is lacking practical methods to address learning styles (Pinchot and Paullet, 2014). Thus, the effectiveness of the model remains inconclusive when considering online education. So further study is needed to know its suitability regarding the online environment.

Hermann Brain Dominance Instrument (HBDI) was developed by Ned Hermann in the 1970s. This tool was designed to assess the thinking preferences of learners. The idea behind this model was the conception of four different thinking styles of the brain, with each learner having a unique mode of thinking. This model's four brain quadrants are A Quadrant (Left Cerebral), B Quadrant (Left Limbic), C Quadrant (Right Limbic), and D Quadrant (Right Cerebral). But in the context of online learning this model needs to be investigated further.

Honey and Mumford in the 1980s developed a model called *Honey and Mumford learning styles* which was an extension of Kolb's learning theory. They divided learners into four categories – Activist, Theorist, Pragmatist, and Reflector. This model helped educators to develop a method of teaching that caters to unique learning styles of learners. But in case of self-instructional learning, education technologists warrant further research to explore the additional factors which influence achievement of learners (Oliveira et al., 2023).

The Study

Related Literature

Several case-studies were conducted by the educational technologists which incorporated the e-learning styles into consideration. The case-studies suggested that incorporating learning style models in education can lead to higher engagement, better performance, and improved outcomes in education.

Manochehr, (2007) conducted a case-study to compare the effects of e-learning with traditional learning, based on the learning styles of learners using Kolb's learning style Inventory. The study concluded that the learning style was irrelevant for traditional learning, but for e-learning, the learning style was important. Results revealed that learners with converger and assimilator style achieved a better result with e-learning.

Aldajah, Haik, and Moustafa, (2014) in a case-study of mechanical engineering students, found that the learning styles of students were balanced: intuitive-sensor, visual-verbal, active-reflective, and global-sequential. The global over the sequential style was preferred by the students. It was concluded by the researchers that by understanding and addressing these styles by the instructors could help to improve performance of students.

Idrizi, Filipposka, and Trajkovik, (2018) conducted a case-study on VARK learning styles and online education. They analyzed by their study how the results got affected by the learning styles during the course between two groups of two papers. They suggested the teachers be more aware and adjust to the needs and preferences of learners in online classes to attain the best results.

Clark, E., and Nguyen, F., (2021) in a case-study on multiple intelligences in schools where lessons were designed by the teachers which catered to the multiple intelligences. The results showed increased motivation level and deeper understanding of concepts by the learners.

Need and Significance

There are numerous further models proposed by the researchers to know about the learning preferences of learners in traditional classroom settings. Despite the widespread use of these learning style models in teaching and learning by educators, some shortcomings have been noted in educational research. So, the effectiveness and applicability of these models were challenged due to these shortcomings. Therefore, the existing learning style models cannot be used in online learning as these models were proposed keeping in mind the classroom environment. The requirements of both traditional classroom and online learning environments are different. The traditional models of learning do not account for the unique features of online learning like self-paced study and digital interaction. The existing models inculcate e-learning but they are based on the old pedagogical approaches of traditional style learning (Bruff, 2011). These models do not address the requirements of learners in a digital context very effectively.

After the pandemic, a sudden shift in education took place from traditional learning to e-learning which led to the widespread adoption of e-learning (Singh, 2022). The classroom content was designed according to the requirements of the learners based on e-learning. But they present the content in the same old traditional kind so they replicate the same activities that were performed earlier in classrooms. Educators generally use frameworks like TPACK (Technological Pedagogical Content Knowledge) and CoI (Community of Inquiry) in education. It generally helps the instructors to integrate technology into online courses. TPACK is based on integration of three types of knowledge i.e., content, pedagogical, and technological knowledge to provide a comprehensive approach to understand and implement technology in education. However, it describes how to integrate ICT in education but it does not specify what should be integrated specifically that would help achieving better results. Therefore, to address this gap, it becomes essential to consider the learning preferences of online learners as instructors would be able to create more effective and engaging learning experiences. Therefore, this approach could also help to address the lack of guidance provided by TPACK on how to integrate technology in learning based on the preferences of learners, thus, making it a valuable addition to the TPACK framework in the context of e-learning.

SAMR, for example, is another framework like TPACK, developed by Dr. Ruben Puentedura. It helps educators to design, create, and integrate technology-infused lessons into classrooms and categorize learners into four tiers as Substitution, Augmentation, Modification, and Redefinition. However, SAMR also does not specify what should be integrated in education based on learning preferences of online learners to achieve better outcomes. The pandemic led to increased reliance on technology and raised concerns about digital poverty and its impact on learners' well-being (Bashir et al., 2021).

Online learning includes various interactive elements and multimedia but the multimodal factors that are essential for gaining the attention of online learners may not be fully embraced by traditional models. There is no doubt that traditional learning style models help to provide valuable insights but their application in an online environment needs careful adaptation to address the unique demands of digital learning. Consequently, e-learning has the potential to be a useful educational instrument (Long, 2023). Therefore, it can be concluded that learning styles and preferences play a significant role in determining how the learners engage with e-learning content. So, by incorporating learning styles into the design and implementation of e-learning, educators can create very effective and engaging learning experiences for learners.

Conclusion

The significance of developing an e-learning style model is discussed here to make the teaching learning effective in an online environment. Due to the digital revolution in education and transformative shift in pedagogical approach towards e-learning, the need to develop a more inclusive, learner-centred, and flexible environment of learning is highlighted. An overview of existing traditional learning style models has been discussed along with the drawbacks of these models in online learning context by various educators in their studies, thus emphasizing the need for further research in this area. Additionally, the importance of the study is highlighted in light of the transformative shift from conventional learning to e-learning, especially after the pandemic. It emphasizes the significance of adapting instructional design to fully utilize the potential of technology in e-learning. Therefore, the researcher addresses the need to develop a new e-learning style model that would take into account the variables like digital literacy, online environment and multimodal preferences of the learners. ICT integration in teaching and learning is an irreversible trend, and the development of a model of e-learning style can be considered as a critical step towards maximizing its potential. The e-learning style model will not only enhance the learning experience and outcomes in an effective manner but also prepare both educators as well as learners for a more digitized future in education.

References

Dunn, R., Griggs, S.A., Olson, J., Beasley, M., and Gorman, B.S.(1995). *A meta-analytic validation of the Dunn and Dunn model of learning-style preferences*, 88(6), https://www.jstor.org/stable/27541998

Ginsburg, J.,(2001). *The Gregorc model of learning styles. Voices from the Classroom.* University of Toronto Press. https://doi.org/10.3138/9781442603059-022

Miller, L. (2005). *Using learning styles to evaluate computer-based instruction.* Computers in Human Behavior, 21(2), pages 287-306, https://doi.org/10.1016/j.chb.2004.02.011

Richmond, A.S., and Cummings, R. (2005). Implementing kolb's learning styles into online distance education. *International Journal of Technology in Teaching and Learning*, 1(1), 45-54

Zapalska, A., and Brozik, D. (2006). *Learning styles and online education.* Campus-wide Information Systems, 23(5), pages 325-335. doi: 10.1108/10650740610714080

Graf, S., Viola, S.R., and Leo, T. (2007). In-depth analysis of the Felder-Silverman learning style dimensions. *Journal of Research on Technology in Education*, 40(1), 79-83

Dag, F., and Gecer, A. (2009). *Relations between online learning and learning styles. Procedia-social and Behavioral Sciences*, 1(1), pages 862-871. doi: https://doi.org/10.1016/j.sbspro.2009.01.155

Sangvigit, P., and Mungsing, S.(2012). *Correlation of Honey & Mumford learning styles and online learning media preference.* International Journal of Computer Technology & Applications, 3(3), pages 1312-1317. ISSN: 2229-6093

Bruff, D.O., et.al., (2013). Wrapping a MOOC: Student perceptions of an experiment in blended learning. *Journal of Online Learning and Teaching*, 9(2), http://creativecommons.org/licenses/by-nc-sa/3.0/us/

Pinchot, J., and Paullet, K.(2014). Different keystrokes for different folks: Addressing learning styles in online education. *Information Systems Education Journal* (ISEDJ), 12(2), ISSN: 1545-679X, www.aitp-edsig.org/www.isedj.org

Prithishkumar, J., and Michael, S.A. (2014). *Understanding your student: using the VARK model.* National Library of Medicine, 60(2), doi: 10.4103/0022-3859.132337

Liyanage, P., Gunawardena, L., and Hirakawa, M. (2014). Using learning styles to enhance learning management systems. *International Journal of Advances in ICT for Emerging Regions*, 7(2), doi: 10.4038/icter.v7i2.7153

Hughes, M., Hughes, P., and Hodgkinson, I.R. (2017). *In pursuit of a 'whole- brain' approach to undergraduate teaching: implications of the Hermann brain dominance model. Studies in Higher Education*, 42(12), pages 2389-2405. doi: https://doi.org/10.1080/03075079.2016.1152463

El-Bishouty, M., Aldraiweesh, A., Alturki, U., and Tortorella, R. (2018). *Use of Felder and Silverman learning style model for online course design.* Educational Technology Research and Development, 67(3), doi: 10.1007/s11423-018-9634-6

Min, S., Chen, Y., Li, H., and Zuo, M. (2018*)*. A learning style model designed for online learning environments. *International Journal of Information and Education Technology*, 8(9):623-627, doi: 10.18178/ijiet.2018.8.9.1111

Idrizi, E., Filiposka, S., and Trajkovik, V. (2018). *VARK learning styles and online education: Case study*, Conference: ETAI 2018

Min.Q., Chen, Y., Liu, N., and Zuo, M. (2018). A Learning style model designed for online learning environments. *International Journal of Information and Education Technology*, 8(9), doi: 10.18178/ijiet.2018.8.9.1111

Periasamy, R. (2021). Learning styles on academic achievement of high school students in Salem district. *International Research Journal of Modernization in Engineering Technology and Science*, 3(2), e-ISSN: 2582-5208

El-Sabagh, H.A. (2021). Adaptive e-learning environment based on learning styles and its impact on development students' engagement. *International Journal of Educational Technology in Higher Education*, 18, Article no. 53, https://doi.org/10.1186/s41239-021-00289-4

Manzoor, S.R., Mohd-Isa, W., and Dollmat, K.S. (2021). *Post-pandemic e-learning: a pre-protocol to assess the impact of mobile VR on learner motivation and engagement for VARK learning styles*. National Library of Medicine, doi: 10.12688/f1000research.73311.2

Kaya, V.D., and Akpinar, B. (2021). Effects of the online learning environment designed with instruction activities model on academic achievements, attitudes, and retention of learning. *International Journal of Education*, 9(4), pages 59-77. doi: https://doi.org/10.34293/education.v9i4.4062

Joseph, I., Abraham, S., and Rajesh, N. (2022). *Exploring the effectiveness of learning path recommendation based on Felder-Silverman learning style model: a learning analytics intervention approach*, 60(6), doi: https://doi.org/10.1177/07356331211057816

Escuadro, S. (2023). *Learning styles: Why they are important in learning and development.* Retrieved from: https://www.edapp.com/blog/why-learning-styles-are-important/

Oliveira, A., et al., (2023). *Influence of learning styles on student performance in self-instructional courses*. PLoS One, 18(7), doi: 10.1371/journal.pone.0289036

8

Perception of Education through Digital Learning

Samra Jamal and Aerum Khan

Introduction

Technological developments have a broad impact in various aspects of the life sector, especially in the teaching and learning process (Vai & Sai & Sosulski, 2015). This is considered as one of the fundamental components of the United Nations Sustainable Development 2030 agenda is quality education. It aims to ensure inclusive and equitable quality education for all. In order to achieve this goal, digital technologies have essential tools and emerged as the best alternative mode of pedagogy. Digital technologies also fulfil the desired sustainable environment-friendly practices. This leads to decreased environmental pollution. Digital technologies have potential to bring efficiency vis- a- vis improved learning experiences and increase production.

These technologies have shown a positive impact on the entire education system. The recent pandemic of COVID-19 has led to more use of technological applications and strengthened it. Which brought a paradigm shift in the entire education system. Expansion of education through e-learning and digital learning is taking place all around the world. The availability of electronic and web-enabling technologies has a tremendous influence on the success of e-learning (Kramer, 2000). The role of advanced digital technologies such as the Internet, web-based tools, online applications to education has increased significantly during the last few years.

In order to make it more successful and align it with traditional methods of teaching to make it more effective, these systems must be designed and planned in a way that they serve the purpose of learning objectives for teachers as well as learners therefore scientific approach is required which is systematic in itself. As we know e-Learning does not have a universally accepted definition. The term has different interpretations by different people. E-learning is an umbrella term that is used to define a wide variety of electronic ways. That makes education accessible and process within reach of the learners. We can say e-learning is suited to flexible learning methods and distance learning.

Features of E-Learning

Distance learning has combined features of online-learning and e-Learning which overtook earlier technologies such as correspondence courses, educational TV, video conferencing.

- *Combination of Diverse Learning Tools:* Mixed learning tools give ample opportunity to students to widen their horizons, e-learning platforms use all the available online resources to best of their potential which consists of a number of devices that are accessible to the students and teachers.
- *Learning Management System:* A learning management system consists of proper schedules and a list of courses that are offered by it. The users can get easy access to the course by just scrolling through the list or catalogues.
- *User-friendly:* To diminish the monotony of traditional classroom, e-learning apps and websites can make learning more inclusive, individualized and more interactive through appealing design and aesthetics.

The epidemic of Covid-19 has left the education system to bring certain transformation towards an enhanced system of education. Even though the traditional method of teaching is very much there but system has to adapt itself according to the ever-increasing number of technical applications that are used to communicate and transaction of knowledge. Once we connect students outside the world it enhances their ability to construct new knowledge. Which is not possible in a traditional classroom because acquisition of knowledge is limited to the instructor.

The Study

Need and Rationale

The rate at which information technology (IT) is growing today is evident from the fact that it has invaded almost every part of our life. The Government of India has launched its National Mission on Education through Information and Communication Technology (NMEICT) in 2009 to provide the opportunity for all the teachers and experts in the country to pool their collective wisdom for the benefit of every Indian learner and to reduce the digital divide. E-Learning consists of computers and the Internet in or out of the classrooms. Web-based learning is meant by e-learning which is commonly referred to as electronic learning. After expansion of Internet services to all over the world. If today any person has any query, he/she first searches it on the Internet rather than looking into books or asking anyone. Therefore, education is not untouched with its implications. Hence this has led to the significance of E-learning in education.

There are many platforms that offer various e-content on different courses and subjects and topics completely on the Internet. Video conferencing, online classes, live lectures, emails provide opportunities to the participants to share their views and ideas on a particular subject. In this way it is a great platform to exchange views and provide quality content to the learners irrespective of their geographical location. Online learning is helpful to accommodate everyone's specific needs. It helps learners to be updated with latest practices and upgrade themselves accordingly. Taking into consideration all these aspects of digital technologies, this study was designed to understand the perception of digital learning /E-learning among students of teacher training programs.

Objectives

1. To study the level of awareness among students about digital technologies in education.
2. To study the perception if e-learning systems are well structured for the students.
3. To identify the significant challenges of digital technologies in education, which are encountered by the students.

Methodology

The present study was a pilot study which is done to probe into the awareness of digital learning and its various aspects pertaining to ease, challenges and structure of the content among students of the teacher training program of a central university in Delhi. The present study is a descriptive survey kind of research. The population for the present study was all the undergraduate students of the teacher training program of a central university. Sample was chosen by using purposive sampling technique which consists of all the students of D.El. Ed. The first-year student's sample size was 30. students were chosen through randomization. The tool was adapted by the researcher questionnaire which consists of mainly open-ended items to get in-depth information pertaining to the items. The first question was related to demographics. The tool was distributed in the presence of researchers. Once all the participants completed their responses they were collected by the researcher. Prior permission was taken by the concerned teachers and administration. Data was analyzed by qualitative as well as quantitative methods. Data was carefully analyzed by evaluation of responses and transcripts. Statements were realigned into coherent manner in an orderly way. Based on the theoretical framework of tools and related literature in the field, list of codes was developed during the initial analysis. Data was selected and coded and then analyzed; this way it has created various categories of codes identified. Many transcripts from the data were examined that had similar meanings before labelling a theme. Themes such as digital tools, inclusion of technology, CT, Online applications were some of the themes.

Delimitations

- The research was delimited to D.El.Ed. students of first year only.
- The research was delimited to central university of Delhi only.

Results and Discussion

The data obtained from the study was carefully evaluated. Participants' responses, transcripts and statements were realigned in a coherent and orderly category (Corbin & Strauss 2007). In-depth study was carried out to get better results, therefore serving the purpose of the research. List of codes were developed initially. Data was selected and codes were given accordingly. This way it has created various categories of codes identified. Many transcripts that have similar meaning were considered under a common theme. This way two main themes were identified which are accompanied by many subthemes. Two major themes were:

1. The E-Learning system provides better opportunities to learn.
2. The E-Learning system makes students independent learners.

Sub-themes that were identified are as follows:

1. ICT Skills
2. Applications
3. Digital tools
4. Use of videos in online learning
5. Online environment/offline environment
6. Network

The data obtained from the study revealed some remarkable responses. The tool consisted of eight items which were divided into two major themes, each theme consists of four items and each item was analyzed by going through all the responses pertaining to that item.

1. Almost 95% of the participants said yes participating in e-learning programs improves ICT skills. Almost 60% said yes that the e-learning system is easy to handle. 30% said it is difficult in the beginning but once we start using it then we find it easy. Almost 80% believed that it requires a good Internet connection with proper speed. Some of the students suggested that lessons can be revisited any time. Lectures are accessible as per need of individual students. This way it is also suitable for individualized learning. Any information is just a click away, 60% of the students have learnt to create links and how to invite and join the meeting. Some of the suggestions were that during an emergency such as Covid, this mode of teaching method has been very useful for the students and teachers, so that students could continue their education.
2. 60% of the responses suggested that students can learn anything anytime anywhere. They also suggested that students' attendance can be uploaded on google sheets and results can be uploaded on it very easily. It also saves our time and helps us to clear our doubts; while sitting at our home we get more sources to read from to broaden our knowledge base.

3. 50% of the participants said it provides ease to communicate with the instructor. Whereas 40% of the participants denied it. The data also revealed that e-learning systems provide opportunities to the learners to communicate with their teachers as well as to discuss with their groups to understand the concepts and theories in real time sessions. Whereas 30% of the participants said they are not comfortable to clear their doubts online as compared to offline. They find the physical classroom environment more suitable for this. Almost 30% of the students said that e-learning provides ease to communicate through various devices such as laptops, mobiles, computers, tablets etc. Some students said they had been distracted during online classes.
4. Whether digital-learning system has high availability – 50% said yes, 30% said no and 20% said can't say. Some said it is easily available in almost every state. On the other side, some said it is not easily available in rural areas. Because it lacks infrastructure in countries like India. Almost 30% of the participants said it will depend on the availability of Internet data. One student suggested this is not right to say because in urban cities we have more access to the Internet as compared to rural areas where access to the Internet is less.
5. Item number 5 revealed that almost 60% of the respondents said e-learning courses are well structured and clear. 20% said no it is not well structured and clear. 20% of participants said they do not have an idea about it.
   Some of the remarkable responses suggested connectivity and technical issues. Some of the students suggested that if e-learning courses are designed in stepwise manner then they are feasible otherwise students get better understanding of subject matter if it is taught in face-to-face manner. E-learning courses can inspire, excite actively engaged learners. Some students suggested e-learning is very structured because there is application for every task whether it is for PDF or any drawing.
6. Almost 60% of the participants said yes e-learning lessons help the students understand the subject better. 20% of the participants could not decide. And 20% said no, it is not better than offline mode.
7. 57% of the participants said e-learning programs motivate students to develop independent learning skills, 20% said no it does not develop independent learning skills. 20% of the participants did not have any idea about it.
   Some of the other responses were that it develops the habit of self-study because students only rely on material provided to them, students can plan their way of learning and they can analyze it. Evaluate and own learning skills.
8. 30% of the participants said no e-learning programs do not provide effective and frequent feedback. 20% of the participants said yes e-learning systems provide effective feedback. Almost 20% of the participants said they do not have any idea about it. Some of the suggestions where

feedback should be given in a timely manner ask your students what they want feedback on so they feel their specific needs are being met. Some of the responses suggested e-learning programs provide effective and frequent feedback but it is not better than offline mode because we could not interact among our peers like we did during offline classes.

Conclusion

These studies gave some very remarkable suggestions like more use of digital learning platforms for education has some negative effects on eyesight. This also makes learners addicted to their phones. Education through online mode lacks a social environment and no social interaction among peers is there. It also requires teachers to be fully trained in using ICT in their teaching practices. It also suggested in country like India large number of population is under poverty so, it is not possible for each student to have their own digital equipment. It is not possible for parents of disadvantaged group to provide them personal smartphones or other devices for better communication and clarity they require Internet without any hindrance and fast speed. If we make it available to rural areas of the country, it can reduce many geographic constraints which is beneficial for those who do not have access to it.

References

Brika, Mokhtar, Khalfa, Said & Chergui, Khalil (2022). E-Learning Research Trends in Higher Education in Light of Covid 19: A Bibliometric Analysis.

Gunasekaran, Angappa (2002). E-Learning: Research and Applications. Emerald Publishing. Industrial and Commercial Training Pennsylvania State University Harrisburg. 34(2):44-53.

Haleem, Abid, Javaia, Mohd. Qadri, Asim, Mohd. Suman, Rajiv (2022). Sustainable Operations and Computers. Understanding the Role of Digital Technologies in Education: A review. Volume 3, pages 275-285.

Nicols, M (2008). E-Learning in Context. E-Primer Series 1,1-28.

Vai, Marjorie & Sosulski, kristen (2015). Essentials of Online Course Design A Standard — Based Guide. 2nd Edition.

Wiguna, Wira, Ngurah, Gusti, I. (2022) Ganesha University of Education, Indonesia. *Journal of Educational Study*. Volume 2. Issue 1

Yeboah-Kumi Alex & Kim Yanghyun (2020). Exploring the Use of Digital Technologies from the Perspective of Diverse Learners In Online Learning Environments. University of Albany, NewYork, USA.

Zhou, L, & Zhang, D. (2008). Web 2.0 Impact on Student Learning Process. In KMC Ferrin et al. (eds). Proceedings of Society for Information Technology and Teacher Education International Conference (P.P. 2880-2882). AACE.

https://www.digitalclassworld.com.

9

Role of Digitalisation and ICT-Based Learning in Higher Education

Mohammad Amir Khan

Introduction

Digitalisation has brought about many changes to the education sector, including the provision of creative solutions that improve teaching, learning, and administrative procedures. Society is undergoing dramatic transformation thanks to ICT (Moldagali et al., 2022; Al-Ansi et al., 2021). They affect all facets of existence. In the same spirit, it is indisputable that ICT has a big influence on education. It adds effectiveness and excitement to the teaching-learning process (Coskun, 2015; Telukdarie & Munsamy, 2019). Any type of communication equipment or application, such as satellite systems, PCs, mobile phones, radios, TVs, and network hardware and software, is included in the wide category of information and communication technology, or ICT (Viberg & Mavroudi, 2019; Coskun, 2015). A wide range of associated services and programs, such as video conferencing and remote learning, are also included. These technologies are employed in education, specifically to create learning environments to assist and enhance student learning (Tømte, et al., 2019). One may classify ICT as a branch of educational technology. The function and impact of ICTs are discussed, as well as how they may support growth and development in the future. The educational system's inputs include teachers, students, classroom supplies, teaching equipment, and teaching strategies; its outputs are the amount and calibre of knowledge that students have acquired (Telukdarie & Munsamy, 2019; Al-Ansi et al., 2021). When ICT is properly integrated into the teaching and learning environment, there is a greater probability of education and higher production.

The quick adoption of ICT applications, which have drastically changed society, technology, and the economy (Toader et al., 2021; Karagiannidis et al., 2014). Teachers, administrators, and educational institutions all had to reconsider their responsibilities in the classroom and their future goals as a result of these developments. In the information era, a nation's capacity to support its economy depends on having an effective educational system. It is thought of as an input-output comparison study. According to Watson (2001), ICTs have completely changed how people operate today and are currently changing educational institutions (Ayu, 2020; Telukdarie & Munsamy, 2019). The educational system's inputs are its teachers, students, classroom materials, instructional aids, and methods; its outputs are the amount and calibre of knowledge that students have acquired. The likelihood of obtaining education and productivity is both boosted when ICT is properly integrated into the teaching and learning environment (Coskun, 2015; Toader et al., 2021). ICT gives students a variety of chances and helps instructors understand their new duties and responsibilities in the classroom. Many of the learning tactics used by instructors and students will alter as a result of the increasing usage of ICT. Technology will always play a part in school administration.

Emerging Trends in Education Sector

Digitalisation has had a huge and diverse influence on the education industry, changing the way that teaching and learning are carried out in important ways. Geographical boundaries have been broken down by the worldwide accessibility of educational materials and information brought about by digitalisation (Al-Ansi et al., 2021; Gamar & Tati, 2021). Because digital tools may be customized to meet varied learning demands, education can become more inclusive of students with a range of abilities. The advent of digitalisation has made remote and online learning possible, giving students the freedom to access instructional materials from any location with an Internet connection (Tømte, et al., 2019; Ayu, 2020). A blended learning strategy that combines in-person and online training is made possible by the integration of digital resources with conventional teaching methods (Watson, 2001). Multimedia components including movies, animations, and interactive simulations are included into digital platforms to improve student learning and engagement. In addition to making studying more fun, educational games and gamified learning environments may inspire students to take an active role in their education (Seethal & Menaka, 2019; Al-Ansi et al., 2021). Digital tools are able to adjust to the unique learning methods and speed of each student, offering customized learning experiences that meet their particular needs. By using data to inform decisions, learning analytics assists teachers in customizing education to students' needs and interests (Viberg & Mavroudi, 2019).

For learning to go successfully, all online-learning activities need to be supported by technology or software that acts as a bridge. As a more flexible form of instruction, online learning combines a range of learning strategies and technologies, such as computer-based learning, learning through video conferencing, and CD-ROMs, to deliver or activate instructional content or experiences (Muktiarni et al., 2019; Oliver, 2002). Applications such as Zoom, Google Classroom, Google Forms, and Google Meet are utilized in India to facilitate distant learning (Tømte, et al., 2019; Al-Ansi et al., 2021). The above stated technologies facilitate teacher-student interaction via video conferencing, resulting in a learning environment that is more like a classroom. Furthermore, it is imperative to tackle the obstacles caused by remote learning, particularly for educators. Teachers' psychological shifts and reluctance to change need to be acknowledged in addition to elements like the digital revolution in education. A significant change in one's job and environment necessitates the practice of effective coping and stress management strategies (Laurillard, 2005; Altmann et al., 2019). Thus, the present study tries to examine the role of digitalisation in the higher education system.

Increases Involvement and Promotes Cooperation

According to Muktiarni et al. (2019), it is anticipated that when technology is incorporated into the classroom, students would take a greater interest in the subjects they are learning. Technology provides educators with a multitude of methods to present the same material in novel ways, enhancing student engagement and making learning more pleasant (Coskun, 2015; Basri & Paramma, 2019. Using gamification in education, virtual field excursions, and other online learning resources are a few examples. Additionally, technology can promote more active learning, which is something that might be challenging to do in a typical lecture setting (Watson, 2001; Mondal & Mete, 2012). Participating in various online activities is one way for students to develop their teamwork abilities. For instance, trading papers or conversing with others on forums while working on different projects in virtual learning settings (Altmann et al., 2019; Toro & Joshi 2012). Technology may let students collaborate with each other in the same classroom, at the same school, or even at schools all across the world.

Increases Retention of Knowledge and Promotes Independent Learning

It is anticipated that students who are actively involved in and passionate about the material they are studying would retain more of it. As previously said, technology has the potential to facilitate active learning in the classroom, which is essential for increasing student recall of the subject matter (Abou El-Seoud, 2014; Basri & Paramma, 2019). It is possible to experiment with various sorts of technology and determine which ones help pupils remember their information the best (Tømte, et al., 2019). Because everyone has distinct learning methods and talents, no two people learn in the same manner. With the use of technology, learning may be more effectively tailored to each individual's needs. For example, students can study at their own speed, review difficult material, or go on to the next section if needed (Zhang et al., 2016). Furthermore, technology can provide kids who struggle or have disabilities greater chances.

Benefits for Teachers and Students

Using technology in the classroom may help teachers and students develop 21st century skills. Pupils can develop the skills necessary for success in the future. The development of communication, leadership, problem-solving, teamwork, and critical thinking abilities is emphasized in today's curriculum, along with raising productivity and motivation (Basri & Paramma, 2019; Toro & Joshi 2012). Technology may also help with the development of many other practical skills, such as drafting emails, adhering to proper online conduct, creating presentations, and identifying reliable from unreliable online sources. These are extremely useful skills that may be developed in the classroom. With so many materials available online, technology may enhance instruction (Oliver, 2002; Gamar & Tati, 2021). Teachers can utilize a variety of programs or trustworthy websites to enhance traditional teaching strategies and sustain student engagement.

Anyplace and Anytime Learning

The idea of offering educational sessions at several locations is not a novel one. For many years, educational institutions have provided remote learning opportunities, and a great deal of research and development has gone into creating efficient protocols and practices for this type of off-campus instruction (Al-Ansi et al., 2021; Toader et al., 2021). However, the use of technology has expanded the reach of this activity. While off-campus delivery was formerly an option for students who could not attend campuses, many more students may now choose to do so thanks to technology-enabled learning environments. Traditional classroom instruction has frequently been replaced with work-based learning environments where students may access courses and programs from their place of employment (Sarkar, 2012; Basri & Paramma, 2019). The benefits of providing education and training at the site of need extend beyond convenience and encompass financial savings from reduced travel and work-related time lost, as well as the placement and implementation of learning activities in pertinent and significant settings (Toro & Joshi 2012; Abou El-Seoud, 2014). Technology-enabled educational programs eliminate many of the temporal limitations that affect students with special needs in addition to providing geographic flexibility. Students are beginning to recognize that they may pursue their education at any time, place, or anywhere. Due to this flexibility, many more learners who were previously limited by other obligations have been able to take advantage of just-in-time learning possibilities.

The Study

Objectives

- To analyse the influence of digitalisation on the higher education sector.
- To examine the role of ICT-based learning in the education system.
- To investigate the pros and cons of digitalisation and ICT-based learning in the higher education sector.

Research Methodology

The current study is a conceptual-based study in which authors explore the existing literature to find out the prospects and challenges faced by the higher education sector. Qualitative Conceptual research is a process that involves examining and interpreting literature that has already been published on a particular subject (Altmann et al., 2019). Practical experimentation is not a component of conceptual research. It has to do with thoughts or notions that are abstract. It has to do with thoughts or notions that are conceptual. For a very long time, philosophers have employed conceptual inquiry to create new ideas or to reinterpret old ones.

Conclusion

All levels of higher education systems (HES) have seen changes in teaching and learning due to the growing use of information and communication technologies (ICTs), which has improved quality. Online and virtual settings are replacing traditional teaching and learning methods more frequently. When ICT is integrated into the educational system, the possibilities are virtually limitless. In addition to enhancing the in-class teaching and learning process, ICT use in education offers the advantage of e-learning. Technology has improved remote learning. Remote locations may be reached by the teaching community, and students can access a qualitative learning environment at any time and from any location. It is thought that integrating ICT into the classroom can make learning possibilities more accessible. With the use of cutting-edge teaching techniques, it can serve to raise educational standards, promote student learning, and facilitate systemic change or improved administration. Extrapolating from present practices and activities, the development and use of ICTs in education will continue to have a significant influence on who is teaching and learning as well as what is being taught, when and when learning occurs, and how and what is learnt. The temporal and geographical options that are now available will grow as long as ICTs are used in education more and more in the years to come. It is inevitable that ICTs will be included into higher education. The extremely high demand for post-secondary education has led to notable expansion in both public and private offerings.

References

Abou El-Seoud, M.S., Taj-Eddin, I.A., Seddiek, N., El-Khouly, M.M., & Nosseir, A. (2014). E-learning and students' motivation: A research study on the effect of e-learning on higher education. *International Journal of Emerging Technologies in Learning (Online)*, *9*(4), 20.

Al-Ansi, A.M., Garad, A., & Al-Ansi, A. (2021). ICT-based learning during Covid-19 outbreak: Advantages, opportunities and challenges. *Gagasan Pendidikan Indonesia*, *2*(1), 10-26.

Altmann, M., Clauss, A., Jantos, A., Lenk, F., Reeb, S., Safavi, A.A., & Schoop, E. (2019). Digitalisation in Higher Education.

Ayu, M. (2020). Online learning: Leading e-learning at higher education. *The Journal of English Literacy Education: The Teaching and Learning of English as a Foreign Language*, *7*(1), 47-54.

Basri, M., & Paramma, M.A. (2019). EFL students' perspective on the usefulness of ICT based learning in Indonesian higher education. *ELT Worldwide*, *6*(2), 105-120.

Coskun, Y.D. (2015). Promoting digital change in higher education: Evaluating the curriculum digitalisation. *Journal of International Education Research (JIER)*, *11*(3), 197-204.

Gamar, M.M., & Tati, A.D.R. (2021, February). Utilization of ICT-based learning media in local history learning. In *Journal of Physics: Conference Series* (Vol. 1764, No. 1, p. 012079). IOP Publishing.

Karagiannidis, C., Politis, P., & Karasavvidis, I. (2014). Research on e-Learning and ICT in Education. *Research on e-Learning and ICT in Education: Technological, Pedagogical and Instructional perspectives*.

Laurillard, D. (2005). E-learning in higher education. In *Changing higher education* (pp. 87-100). Routledge.

Moldagali, B., Sultanova, B., Akhtayeva, N., Suleimenova, A., & Akimbekova, S. (2022). Innovative Technologies: Digitalisation of Education. *Journal of Social Studies Education Research*, *13*(4), 209-224.

Mondal, A., & Mete, J. (2012). ICT in higher education: opportunities and challenges. *Institutions*, *21*(60), 4.

Muktiarni, M., Widiaty, I., Abdullah, A.G., Ana, A., & Yulia, C. (2019, December). Digitalisation trend in education during industry 4.0. In *Journal of Physics: Conference Series* (Vol. 1402, No. 7, p. 077070). IOP Publishing.

Oliver, R. (2002). The role of ICT in higher education for the 21st century: ICT as a change agent for education. *Retrieved April*, *14*, 2007.

Sarkar, S. (2012). The role of information and communication technology (ICT) in higher education for the 21st century. *Science*, *1*(1), 30-41.

Seethal, K., & Menaka, B. (2019). Digitalisation of education in 21st century: A Boon or bane. *Higher Education*, *43*, 196.

Telukdarie, A., & Munsamy, M. (2019, December). Digitisation of higher education institutions. In *2019 IEEE International Conference on Industrial Engineering and Engineering Management (IEEM)* (pp. 716-721). IEEE.

Toader, T., Safta, M., Titirişcă, C., & Firtescu, B. (2021). Effects of digitalisation on higher education in a sustainable development framework—Online learning challenges during the COVID-19 pandemic. *Sustainability*, *13*(11), 6444.

Tømte, C.E., Fossland, T., Aamodt, P.O., & Degn, L. (2019). Digitalisation in higher education: mapping institutional approaches for teaching and learning. *Quality in Higher Education*.

Toro, U., & Joshi, M. (2012). ICT in higher education: Review of literature from the period 2004-2011. *International Journal of Innovation, Management and Technology*, *3*(1), 20-23.

Toro, U., & Joshi, M.J. (2013). A review of literature on knowledge management using ICT in higher education. *International Journal of Computer Technology and Applications*, *4*(1), 62.

Viberg, O., & Mavroudi, A. (2019). Digitalisation of education: application and best practices.

Watson, D.M. (2001). Pedagogy before Technology: Re-thinking the Relationship between ICT and Teaching. Education and Information Technologies, 6, 4, 251-266

Zhang, J., Yang, J., Chang, M., & Chang, T. (2016). ICT in education in global context. *The Best Practices in K-12 Schools*.

10

Use of Educational Films as a Teaching Tool

The Parent's Views

Madhurima Pal and Fauzia Khan

Introduction

Technology is the need of the hour. Without technology, one cannot think of living. Especially in the 21st century where technology is dominant over others, how children relate to technological devices around them plays an important role in their concept learning process. Technological devices such as smartphones, computers, tablets or televisions have some wonderful features that create environments which appeal to more than one sensory organ (Başar & Elyildirim, 2021). Due to this, the use of technological devices among young children have increased rapidly.

Many studies have been carried out worldwide on the effect of information communication technologies on school education and their integration into school education. Technology as result of these studies, has been increasingly included in school education as of 2000s, and thus various practices have been carried out (Ekici, 2016). It was in fact with the advent of Covid-19 pandemic, the use of technology in the teaching-learning process grew rapidly. This contributed to the rapid use of films and documentaries into the classrooms.

Students are now exposed to many audio-visual resources in and outside the classrooms and home. Readily available educational films are most used in the classrooms such as documentaries, You-Tube videos, animated films, etc. Since parents are the ultimate stakeholders in education, their views on various aspects should also be considered for the growth of the education sector. Parents' views also depend on how and what education their children will receive. Hence, this study will try to study the views of parents on the use of educational films in the classroom as a teaching-learning material.

Related Literature

Ekici (2016), examined the views of parents regarding the use of technology in the early childhood period using a survey method. From this study, the views of parents on the use of technology in early childhood significantly differ by various factors like gender of the parents, gender of the children, level of parents' income and the type of school attended by the children. Further it was found that the views of parents on the use of technology in early childhood do not significantly differ by the factors like age of the children, working status of the mothers and number of children the parents have.

Sopekan (2020), studied the influence of cartoons on children's social behaviour from the perspective of parents using a survey research design where 100 parents participated in the study. Data was analysed using frequency counts and percentages. It was found that most of the children watched cartoons on a weekly and daily basis, most children watched cartoons which were violent where there were lots of fights, violent heroes and characters shouted and abused one another. Parents were neutral about the influence of violent cartoons on behaviour of children. It was concluded by the recommendation that training programmes should be organised for guardians and parents by the organisation or government on influence of media on social behaviour and development of the children. Parents were also recommended to examine the content of cartoons which they provide for their own children to ensure they do not have violent elements and also, they should educate their children on acceptable societal and family values.

Media use and attitudes report 2022, showed most parents were concerned about content which their children saw online such as whether it is age-appropriate or not, language used in the content. Parents had few concerns about the content shown. Parents concerned whether children gave out personal details of people or whether they are seeing any content age-inappropriate online or TV. Most parents were less confident in keeping their child safe online.

Downes et al. (2020), conducted a survey to study about the beliefs of parents about associations to their elementary children usage of Technology at home. Thus, findings showed significant associations for the demographic characteristics such as age, gender education, ethnicity of parents and first language of parents as determinants of their beliefs about use of Technology by their children. It was further found that the immigrant parents might consider misconceptions on 21st century literacies and hence there should be an attempt to assist them to provide technology support and 21st century literacy for their own children.

Al-Ali et al. (2018), conducted a study to assess parents' beliefs and knowledge about effects of violent media on children's aggressive behaviour. According to the results, children spent on average 4.83h watching TV, 3.20h playing video games, 1.07h listening to music and 0.52h of reading as pleasure. Study found parents have moderate level of knowledge on effect of media. The children of parents who have adequate knowledge about media effect spent less time watching TV playing video games and listening to music. Most of the parents concerned about amount of violent-content and sexual-content children see on TV or in movies.

Okoro & Chima (2017), tried to explore the perception of parents' influence of cartoon films on children's data was collected by 393 respondents using a survey method. Findings revealed that parents have a negative perception of the influence of cartoons on children which ranges from desensitisation violence and sexual immorality. Study found children had negative impact by the harmful contents of cartoons as it promotes negative behaviours among the children which leads to a general distortion from reality due to desensitisation from pain or pain of others. The study was concluded by the recommendation that parents should be selective of the kind of cartoon which their children watch so that desired influence is generated.

Basar & Elyildirim (2021), tried to determine the role of multimedia in concept learning of preschool children. Case study was used as a tool for analysing the data qualitatively from 21 parents. The results from this study indicated that children spent most of their time on multimedia devices like smartphones, television, and tablets. These multimediums were mostly used for games and having fun. The findings showed that most parents thought of the need for adult supervision when the children spent time using the multimedia content. Found parents think that multimedia is beneficial for concept learning. According to parents, the technological devices that offer multimedia content to the children, plays a positive effect on children's learning of basic content.

Rogers et al. (2021), in their report on inclusive imperative that why media representations is important for kids' ethnic-racial development. From study, it found media representations are important to parents. For them, it is not just only watching their ethnicity or race in the media but it is more than that. Findings revealed that parents find it important that children should be exposed to media content which encourages acceptance of other people who do not look like them. From the studies, it is understood that parents held fewer concerns about content shown by the films and that parents were neutral about influence of films on behaviour of children (Sopekan, 2020; media use and attitudes report 2022). Parents were less confident on keeping their child safe online as they were concerned about content which their children see online such as whether it is age appropriate or not, language used in the content is fit to see or not (media use and attitudes report 2022; Okoro & Chima, 2017; Basar & Elyildirim, 2021). Some parents also have a moderate level of knowledge on the effect of media (Al-Ali et al., 2018; Sopekan, 2020).

The Study

Significance

The past decade has come across a significant change towards technological use especially after the emergence of the Covid-19 pandemic. This pandemic greatly impacted every student and their stakeholder in education. There was an abrupt change from the conventional on-premises education system to the modern online education system. Although audio-visuals were a part of the routine of many schools through smart classes or smart boards, after the advent of Covid-19 pandemic, a lot more schools have started including audio-visuals in their daily routines inside the classrooms. During Covid-19 pandemic times, many researches were conducted on various aspects of the education system where students and teachers participated in multiple surveys and various studies. There are few studies conducted internationally which have mixed findings for the perception of parents regarding use of media for teaching-learning (Al-Ali et al., 2018; Başar & Elyildirim, 2022; Downes et al., 2020; Ekici, 2016; Njoki Chidinma Catherine, Obi Jennifer Ifeoma, Okoro Louisa Nkechi, 2017; Rogers et al., 2021; Sopekan et al., 2020). So, there is need to study what views does parents hold about using films as a tool in school education.

Research Objectives

1) To understand the views of parents about educational films.
2) To understand views of parents on the use of educational films in the classroom as teaching-learning material.
3) To know whether parents allow use of educational films at home or not.

Methodology

The current study was exploratory research where the population of this study was parents of children of private schools of Delhi. 30 parents of the students studying in elementary classes participated in this study. Sample was selected using purposive sampling technique. Data was collected through questionnaires via Google Forms. Data was analysed both qualitatively as well as quantitatively. For the quantitative analysis, data computed using frequency and percentages and for qualitative analysis, data was analysed thematically using coding method.

Analysis and Discussion

Views of Parents on Educational Films

It was found that 63.3% of parents watch all types of films. 30% of the parents watch educational films. 26.7% parents watch documentary films and 26.7% parents watch animated films. Rest 33.3% of parents watch drama films. This shows that most of the parents watch all types of films.

< *Responses of parents whether they like watching educational films?*

It was found that 86.7% of parents like watching educational films. When asked parents about their views regarding educational films, parents have multiple views regarding this. 20% of parents claimed that films are a good

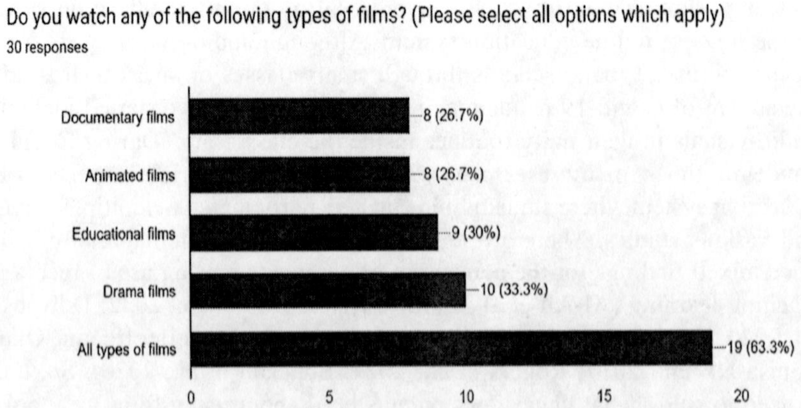

Figure 1: Responses of parents on whether they watch the following types of films

resource to gain insights. 13.3% of parents agreed that films are motivational and inspirational. Easy understanding of all concepts by breaking up complex concepts into simpler-ones was also mentioned in some responses. Few parents i.e. 6% claimed that films deal with the critical issues very well and also, they are a very good option to explain historical events. One participant even identified a negative aspect of watching films stating that it is a laborious process. Hence, from the above graphs, we can see that parents do watch films and most participants enjoy watching educational films. Parents are mostly in favour of showing educational films to their children for various purposes like creating motivation, building interest, gaining insights, making learning easy, inspiring them, etc. This is in sync with the findings from some studies (Başar & Elyildirim, 2022; Rogers et al., 2021).

< Views of parents on use of educational films in the classroom as a teaching-learning material?

It is noted that 76.7% of parents want their children to watch film in the classroom whereas 16.7% of parents do not want their children to watch film in the classroom. 3.3% believe that children can watch movies in the classroom occasionally. 3.3% parents also believe that showing one or two good film is a good idea for a session.

< Responses of parents on whether the school show films to their children in the classroom as a teaching-learning material?

Evidence shows that 66.7% parents claimed that school shows films to their children in the classroom, whereas 23.3% parents claimed that school does not show films in the classroom as a teaching-learning material. Some parents even accept that they do not know if own children are shown films in the classroom or not.

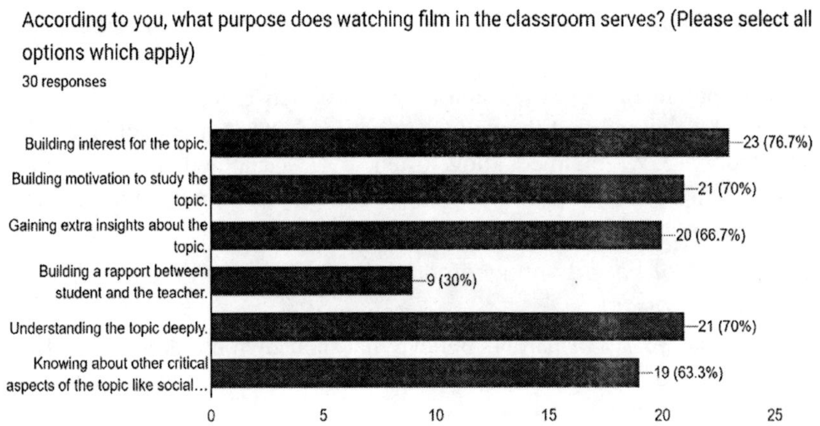

Figure 2: Responses of parents on the purposes that watching films in the classroom serves

Graph displays that 76.7% of parents believe that films are used for "Building interest for the topic." 70% of parents believe that "Building motivation to study the topic" and "Understanding the topic deeply". The view that "Building a rapport between student and the teacher" by the film is least supported by the parents as only 30% parents have selected this option. Most parents have selected all the options accepting that films serve all the purposes as given in the question.

This means that most parents are in favour of showing films in the classroom. This is unlike some studies which raise concerns for showing films (Al-Ali et al., 2018; Njoki Chidinma Catherine, Obi Jennifer Ifeoma, Okoro Louisa Nkechi, 2017; Sopekan et al., 2020). Maximum parents claimed that school shows films to their children in the classroom. Although some parents even accepted the fact that they themselves do not have any idea whether the school shows films in the classroom or not. Films serve all the purposes with interest building to the topic as of prime importance and building rapport between students and teacher with least importance.

< *Responses of parents on whether the school ask their children to watch any particular film at home or not*

One-third of parents responded that children are usually not asked to watch a movie at home by the school whereas, 60% of parents responded that asked to watch a movie at home by the school.

< *Responses of parents on if they allow their children to watch educational movies at home?*

On asking parents if parents allow their children to watch film at home or not, 90% parents responded that they do allow own children watch movie at home.

< Responses of parents on how often their children watch educational films at home?

On asking parents about how often they allow their children watch films at home, 46.7% claimed that they allow sometimes, 20% parents claimed they allow rarely, 13.3% claimed allow often, 13.3% claimed that they allow whenever required and rest parents claimed that they never allow their children to watch films.

< Responses of parents on whether their children watch educational films at home or not

It is found that 86.7% of parents believe that their own children watch films at home whereas 13.3% of parents claim that their children do not watch educational films at home.

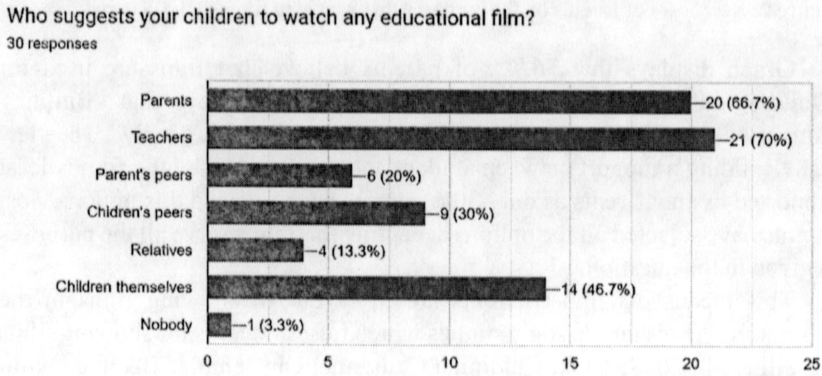

Figure 3: Responses of parents who suggest their children watch educational films.

According to 70% of parents, teachers suggest children watch any educational film. 66.7% parents believe that parents suggest children watch any educational film, followed by children themselves (46.7%), children's peers (30%), parents' peers (20%) and relatives (13.3%). Only 3.3% of parents responded that nobody suggests children watch any educational film.

Findings showed most parents believe that teachers ask the students to watch films at home. Parents allow children to watch films at home. Almost half of parents claimed they do allow children watch films sometimes at home whereas very little percentage of parents do not allow own children watch films at home at all. Mostly children watch films at home for various purposes. Parents believe that teachers and parents are the main source of suggesting films for watching at home. Children themselves also choose which film to watch for educational purposes.

Conclusion

India has seen many technological advances in this century. Education sector has rapidly grown with the advancement in technology. Smart boards or projectors are in almost all the schools. Due to the presence of technological devices in the schools, teachers are most often using those devices to show videos or films to facilitate learning. Educational films are a good teaching-learning material as it provides or regulates multiple sensory experiences and can be used in the classroom and home as well. It is an easy and interesting way of using because it can be accessed by the children themselves as it is readily available material.

Most parents are in favour of showing educational films to their children for various purposes like creating motivation, building interest, gaining insights, making learning easy, inspiring them, etc. Parents themselves do watch films and most of them enjoy watching educational films. Parents are majorly in favour of showing films in the classroom. Most parents claimed school shows films in the classroom whereas some parents even accepted the fact that they do not have any idea about the same. Films serve all the purposes with interest building to the topic as of utmost importance and building rapport between students and teacher being least important. Most parents believe that teachers ask the students to watch films at home. Almost half of the parents claimed they allow their children to watch films sometimes at home whereas very little percentage of parents do not allow their children to watch films at home at all. Teachers and parents are the main source of suggesting films for watching at home. Mostly children watch films at home for various purposes and they themselves also choose which educational film to watch.

References

Al-Ali, N.M., Yaghy, H.S., Shattnawi, K.K., & Al-Shdayfat, N.M. (2018). Parents' Knowledge and Beliefs about the Impact of Exposure to Media Violence on Children's Aggression. *Issues in Mental Health Nursing*, *39*(7), 592–599. https://doi.org/10.1080/01612840.2017.1422201

BAŞAR, T., & ELYILDIRIM, E. (2022). The Role of Multimedia in Concept Learning from the Parents' Perspective. *Journal of Learning and Teaching in Digital Age*, *7*(1), 16–29. https://doi.org/10.53850/joltida.945975

Downes, T., Di Cesare, D.M., Gallagher, T.L., &Rowsell, J. (2020). Parents' beliefs about and associations to their elementary children's home technology usage. *Education and Information Technologies*, *25*(5), 4557–4574. https://doi.org/10.1007/s10639-020-10188-2

Ekici, F.Y. (2016). Parents' Views on the Use of Technology in the Early Childhood Period. *Journal of Education and Training Studies*, *4*(12). https://doi.org/10.11114/jets.v4i12.1925

Njoki Chidinma Catherine, Obi Jennifer Ifeoma, Okoro Louisa Nkechi, O.C.A. (2017). Parents perception of influence of cartoon films on children in Owerri Municipal. *International Journal of Mass Media and Telecommunications*, *1*(1). https://www.researchgate.net/publication/354880875_parents_perception_of_influence_of_cartoon_films_on_children_in_owerri_municipal

Rogers, O., Mastro, D., Robb, M., & Peebles, A. (2021). The inclusion imperative: Why media representation matters for kids' ethnic-racial development. *Common Sense Media*, 1–64. https://www.commonsensemedia.org/research/the-inclusion-imperative

Sopekan, S., Alade, O.S., & Ignatius-Ihejirika, M.U. (2020). Parents' perceptions of influence of violent cartoons on primary school pupils' social behaviors. *Educational Planning*, *27*(2), 41–50.

11

Novel Applications and Integration of Machine Learning in Education

Vinod Kumar Kanvaria and Shruti Tomar

Introduction

In recent years, the integration of machine learning in education has sparked a transformative shift in how we perceive and engage with learning. This facet of artificial intelligence offers unprecedented opportunities to revolutionize educational paradigms (Nafea, 2018). Leveraging algorithms and statistical models, machine learning promises personalized learning experiences, improved educational outcomes, and streamlined administrative tasks within the educational sphere. Adaptive learning systems and predictive analytics driven by machine learning herald a new era in education, fostering adaptability, efficiency, and inclusivity in the learning environment (Celik, 2019).

This review critically examines recent studies to elucidate the efficacy of machine learning applications in education, exploring its impact on several key aspects:

1. *Predicting Learning Paths*: Machine learning algorithms utilize student data to forecast individual learning trajectories, enabling educators to tailor content and strategies to meet each student's needs.
2. *Suggesting Personalized Learning Paths*: Continuous analysis of students' strengths, weaknesses, and learning styles allows machine learning to craft personalized learning paths, adapting resources to match unique learner requirements.
3. *Assessment, Grading, and Feedback*: Automated grading systems powered by machine learning enhance assessment processes, offering quicker grading and personalized feedback while reducing biases in assessment.

This research aims to synthesize findings from recent studies to comprehensively assess the impact of machine learning applications on learner performance. By analyzing evidence from various research papers, this study endeavours to grasp how intelligent tutoring systems, personalized learning paths, and ethical considerations collectively contribute to optimizing learner outcomes. Real-world examples and empirical evidence will be discussed to underscore both the potential and challenges inherent in integrating machine learning into educational practices for enhancing student outcomes.

The Study

Methodology

A Systematic Literature Review Method was employed to scrutinize relevant literature focusing on Machine Learning's applications in education over the past 5-6 years. The research questions guiding this review were:

1. What novel applications of Machine Learning have emerged in the educational landscape over the last 5-6 years?
2. What potential methods or avenues exist for integrating machine learning into educational settings?

Framework

The PICo framework was used to identify the research questions (Lockwood et al., 2015).

Table 1: PICo Framework for Research Questions

Population	Research articles with primary research data published after 2016
Phenomena of Interest	Machine Learning Applications
Context	In the context of Education

The PICo framework guided in defining the research questions for the systematic review.

Research Questions

The research questions guiding this review were:

1. What novel applications of Machine Learning have emerged in the educational landscape over the last 5-6 years?
2. What potential methods or avenues exist for integrating machine learning into educational settings?

Search Strategy

A systematic approach was adopted to select pertinent articles and research papers. Keyword identification involved terms like "Machine Learning," "Education," "Application," "Trends," "Artificial Intelligence," and "Educational Technology." These keywords were integrated into search phrases such as "Machine learning in education," "Recent trends in Educational Machine Learning," and "Applications of Machine Learning in Education."

Boolean operators (AND, OR) were utilized to refine searches, combining keywords like "Machine Learning and Education" and "Machine Learning and Educational Technology."

Database Utilization

The search terms were employed across various databases, including IEEE Xplore, Google Scholar, Research Scholar, JSTOR, ERIC, Springer, and SAGE.

Inclusion and Exclusion Criteria

Inclusion criteria encompassed research papers based on primary data published from 2016 onwards. Exclusion criteria involved papers published before 2016, those in languages other than English, and those relying on secondary data.

Outcome

A total of 47 research articles were gathered, of which 30 were selected for comprehensive analysis.

Table 1: Theme wise distribution of articles

S. No.	*Theme*	*Number of Articles/Research Papers*
1.	Predicting Learning Paths	12
2.	Suggesting Personalized Learning Paths	08
3.	Assessment, Grading, and Feedback	10
	Total	30

Results

After a thorough examination of numerous research papers, three significant themes emerged prominently, reflecting the core focal points within the analyzed literature. These themes encapsulate fundamental aspects that underscore the transformative potential of machine learning within the realm of education.

Predicting Learning Paths

The "Predicting Learning Paths" theme emerged prominently, spotlighting machine learning's pivotal role in personalized education. These studies showcased machine learning algorithms' ability to analyze student data, including academic records, learning behaviours, and preferences, to anticipate individualized learning trajectories accurately. By leveraging past performance and behavioural trends, these systems effectively forecast future learning paths with precision, aiding in early identification of students at risk of failure and facilitating targeted interventions (Ciolacu et al., 2017).

Yildiz and Borekci (2020) in their research explore predicting High School Education success using student data like epistemological beliefs, study behaviours, and family demographics. The Neural Network algorithm (98.6% accuracy) emerges as the most effective predictor. It highlights the impact of parental education, family income, and study routines on academic success. The study notes variations in successful algorithms based on data diversity.

Another study focuses on employing data mining and machine learning techniques to predict students' study path selection in the context of educational institutes. It explores factors influencing study path preferences, such as motivational goals, mastery orientation, and demographic attributes. The research aims to identify algorithms capable of accurately predicting and classifying students into study paths like Digital Service Design (DSD) and Software Development (SWD) (Dirin & Saballe, 2022).

Xu et al. (2017) utilize machine learning in higher education degree courses aiming to aid academic advisors in suggesting appropriate courses and interventions, potentially influencing curriculum design and educational policy. Future work aims to expand performance prediction to elective courses and use these predictions to recommend specific courses to students.

Another research focuses on utilizing Machine Learning Algorithms (MLA) to predict university students' performance using data from Trakia University — Stara Zagora. Three main groups of characteristics — personal, academic environment, and social factors — were studied. Four ML algorithms (NB, MLP, SMO, J48) were employed based on their success in similar studies, with attribute selection techniques identifying 14 key attributes ranked for prediction. Notably, when reducing attributes, accuracy remained close, focusing on key factors like age, gender, course, stress levels, high school performance, exam outcomes, and marital/educational status (Nedeva & Pehlivanova, 2021).

Another study by Jovic et al. (2022) employs EDM and machine learning to forecast student performance using SVM, highlighting strong correlations between assignments and final grades. SVM emerges as the most accurate classifier, achieving an 88.5% average accuracy. The findings stress early identification of at-risk students for improved learning outcomes and dropout prevention.

A similar study by Sanchez-Pozo et al. (2021) investigated various classification approaches for predicting high school students' academic achievement using academic, sociodemographic, and economic data. The results showcased the accuracy of machine learning algorithms in forecasting academic performance, particularly beneficial for designing educational plans aimed at reducing low achievement rates.

Shabandar et al. (2017) use machine learning to predict the performance of students in MOOCs. The paper suggests future work involving investigating passive engagement in MOOCs and considering learners' emotional states as latent variables using semi-supervised machine learning techniques.

Raza (2019) fills a gap in educational data mining by focusing on group-based assessment in university courses. His study uses the Dominance-based Rough Set Approach (DRSA) to predict collaborative performance in group quizzes, aiming to uncover factors influencing group performance levels (Low, Medium, High). By exploring interaction patterns among students within groups, this research aims to identify key factors and create predictive rules to assess and predict group performance effectively.

Liu et al. (2021) used Machine learning to predict student performance. The study emphasizes the potential of machine learning-driven educational visualization applications in guiding and enhancing student learning. It highlights the effectiveness of these tools in offering learning choices, efficiently gathering learning feedback, and ultimately enhancing education quality. Additionally, it examines the predictive performance of the Random Forest algorithm, shedding light on its efficacy, particularly in handling abnormal data.

Badal & Sangkur (2022) examine machine learning's predictive role in student performance and engagement, highlighting Random Forest as a top classifier achieving 85% accuracy in grade prediction and 83% in engagement. It offers educators valuable insights for early intervention with struggling students. While external factors like device performance impact participation, future studies plan to integrate contemporary learning methods, blend qualitative and quantitative approaches for richer insights, and explore multi-feature fusion to understand emotional, cognitive, behavioural, and learning outcome relationships.

Much Work has been done with a focus on increasing the prediction accuracy of tasks for at-risk students, performance, and grades in an e-learning system. Sadouni & Zitouni (2021) present that by reducing the number of indicators used, errors in predictions are significantly reduced across all scenarios, leading to enhanced accuracy. The optimization process positively impacts prediction quality but does not always correspond to improved global error rates. However, reducing indicators consistently improves precision and reduces errors. The reduction in indicators also notably optimizes execution time due to fewer computations. This underscores the importance of selecting pertinent indicators, as excessive ones might distort predictions.

Suggesting Personalised Learning Paths

Machine learning is being used to provide personalized learning paths for students. Ferguson et al. (2022) aim to provide learners with a personalized learning experience by dynamically adjusting the challenge level based on their navigation efficiency in the learning environment. The study revealed that an AI-based adaptive learning system lowered cognitive load, aiding improved knowledge retention in learners. Engagement and presence remained unchanged, but challenges with timing adjustments in the adaptive system were noted. The findings highlight AI's potential in personalized education, calling for further refinement of adaptive mechanisms for optimal learning outcomes.

Diao et al. (2022) spearheads personalized learning paths in e-learning by harnessing learner test records and concept relationships. Employing simulated learning effects and clustering, it identifies learner weaknesses and crafts tailored learning paths. With LSTM+attention models, it predicts learning effects, surpassing traditional methods, and delivering precise concept-level recommendations. This innovative approach highlights the power of educational data mining for enhanced e-learning experiences.

Another study focused on assessment in education for refining the university admission process by leveraging classifiers trained on students' O'Level and JAMB results. It aims to intelligently assign suitable courses based on prior performance, utilizing metrics like accuracy, precision, recall, and f1-score to evaluate classifiers such as Logistic Regression, Naive Bayes, Decision Tree, K-Nearest Neighbour, and Random Forest (Aliyu et al., 2021).

Ma et al. (2023) proposes a personalized learning path model for online education, highlighting its efficacy in enhancing learning efficiency for learners who followed recommended paths. These personalized routes improved knowledge sequencing and resource matching, boosting overall effectiveness. The PSO algorithm, coupled with apriori, generated high-quality paths. Future enhancements include expanding the knowledge graph, integrating emotional factors, tackling forgetting aspects, and enabling real-time detection of learner changes for adaptive learning adjustments.

Liu et al. (2020) analyze students' online learning behaviors, the model generates personalized and effective learning paths that align closely with general student preferences. Experimental results showcase that the proposed methods not only offer improved learning outcomes in terms of accuracy and efficiency but also contribute to enhancing teaching quality. The research emphasizes the promotion of personalized learning and targeted teaching approaches within the realm of hybrid education.

A similar study done by Guo et al. (2022) explores personalized education through a strategy that combines statistical and semantic analysis of student interests to create effective groupings and recommend courses. Experiments using junior high school students' data validate the strategy's feasibility in recommending suitable courses, showing potential to improve cooperation and lifelong learning abilities. Future work aims to enhance user feature portraits by integrating semantic and emotional analysis while considering time factors.

Machine learning is also being used to help teachers such as Pu and Zhou (2021) explore the Teaching Path (TP) generation, a significant aspect of education often overlooked in online learning research. It introduces a Teaching Path Generation (TPG) Model that utilizes machine learning algorithms, including genetic algorithms (GA), particle swarm optimization, and ant colony optimization, to aid teachers in planning optimal teaching sequences for different classes.

Most studies are focused on individual personalized learning paths for academic course suggestions. Maina et al. (2017) use Machine learning to form groups. The paper introduces a fresh approach to student grouping based on collaboration competence, employing clustering techniques within Learning Management Systems (LMS) like Moodle.

Assessment, Grading, and Feedback

Bernius et al. (2022) implement CoFee, a machine learning framework, to automate feedback generation for open-ended textual exercises in expansive computer science courses. CoFee employs segment-based grading using topic modelling and an assessment knowledge repository to propose feedback for student submissions. In initial small-scale validation, it reduced grading efforts by 85%. Later, in a large-scale course, it provided precise feedback for 45% of submissions.

Another study uses ML for assessing subjective answers. The paper introduces an advanced automated evaluation system for assessing subjective answers, employing Natural Language Processing (NLP) and deep learning techniques. By integrating keyword detection, semantic similarity, and Named Entity Recognition (NER), this system provides precise evaluation scores for user answers compared to model answers without human bias (Agrawal et al., 2023).

Zhu et al. (2020) explore the impact of automated feedback using natural language processing and machine learning in an online science curriculum focused on teaching climate change. The study reveals that students with higher initial scores tend to make more revisions after automated feedback, leading to improved scores. Context-specific feedback proves more effective than generic feedback, particularly in science domains like argumentation and explanation, aligning with educational standards.

Rokade et al. (2023) proposes an innovative automated grading system for theory-based subjects, utilizing Natural Language Processing and Semantic Analysis. Unlike keyword-based methods, it employs ontology and synonym extraction for holistic answer evaluation, focusing on concept coverage and word combinations. The system aims for unbiased, accurate grading resembling human error rates, prioritizing knowledge-oriented assessment over keyword matching, derived from teacher survey responses.

Lahoti and Raut (2022) in their research work present an e-learning framework leveraging machine learning to track student behaviour and predict performance using decision trees. Additionally, it introduces an automated assessment system based on Formal Concept Analysis, lightening teachers' workload. Although specific sample size details were omitted, this approach enriches support systems, aiding educators in optimizing learning environments and advancing predictive models in education and ML.

Alruwais and Zakariah (2023) employ various ML algorithms to showcase GBM's superiority in predicting student performance with 98% accuracy. It highlighted factors impacting knowledge assessment and proposed ML's role in precise attention measurement, offering a pathway to enhance evaluations and maintain student focus via deep learning algorithms, ensuring accurate, unbiased criteria.

To enhance evaluation fairness and aid student performance assessment through machine learning methodologies, Mahboob et al. (2016) focus on leveraging machine learning to predict student performance and enhance assessment transparency in e-learning platforms. It delves into predicting students' final grades, aiding instructors and students by guiding future performance improvements. The findings demonstrate the efficacy of the proposed model in predicting student outcomes based on their prior performance, showcasing promising classification accuracy rates of 93.3% with J48, 86.6% with Naive Bayes, and 100% with Random Forest algorithms.

Lee (2023) tackles the issue of resource limitations for instructors by integrating Artificial Intelligence (AI) into large-scale online courses for student feedback on written work. Using a mixed-methods approach, the study proves the efficacy of AI-generated feedback alongside instructor and student-generated feedback. The results indicate that AI-based evaluation systems can mimic human rater performance, providing comprehensive assessments, especially valuable in scenarios with limited human assessors.

Jain et al. (2023) introduces an Automated Grading Recommendation System, leveraging machine learning and AI for student assessment. It aims to streamline grading, reduce errors, and provide personalized feedback to enhance the learning experience. The system's development signifies a shift towards automated grading, potentially transforming how educators manage their time and support student growth. Integrating machine learning techniques, it promises more accurate evaluations and tailored feedback, ultimately benefiting both educators and students.

Weegar and Almquist (2023) found that employing clustering and classification techniques reduced manual grading workload by 64-74% in computer science exams. Different sampling strategies significantly impacted grading efficiency. Human review remains crucial due to high-stakes implications, but combining clustering, classification, and human oversight effectively streamlines grading while preserving accuracy.

Conclusion

This study explores the intersection of machine learning (ML) and education, focusing on three key trends: predicting learning paths, personalized learning journeys, and advancements in assessment. Analyzing recent literature highlights ML's potential to transform education by tailoring experiences, predicting individual trajectories, and optimizing assessment processes. These findings suggest that integrating ML into education could create a more adaptive and efficient learning environment, revolutionizing traditional educational approaches.

References

Agrawal, R., Mishra, H., Kandasamy, I., Terni, S.R., & Vasantha, V.B. (2023). Revolutionizing Subjective Assessments: A Three-Pronged Comprehensive Approach With NLP And Deep Learning. Expert Systems With Applications, 239. Https://Doi.Org/10.1016/J.Eswa.2023.122470

Aliyu, G., Haruna, U., Abdulmumin, I., Isma'il, M., Umar, I.E., & Adamu, S. (2021). *Machine Learning Model For Recommending Suitable Courses Of Study To Candidates In Nigerian Universities*. Springer Nature Switzerland AG. Https://Doi.Org/10.1007/978-3-030-87013-3_20

Alruwais N, Zakariah M. Evaluating Student Knowledge Assessment Using Machine Learning Techniques. Sustainability. 2023; 15(7):6229. Https://Doi.Org/10.3390/Su15076229

Badal, Y.T., &Sungkur, R.K. (2022). Predictive Modelling And Analytics Of Students' Grades Using Machine Learning Algorithms. Education And Information Technologies. Https://Doi.Org/10.1007/S10639-022-11299-8

Bernius, J.P. (2022). Machine Learning Based Feedback On Textual Student Answers In Large Courses. Computers And Education: Artificial Intelligence, 3. Https://Doi.Org/10.1016/J.Caeai.2022.100081

Celik, O. (2018). A Research On Machine Learning Methods And Its Applications. *Journal Of Educational Technology And Online Learning*, 1(3). Doi: 10.31681\Jetol.457046

Ciolacu, M., Tehrani, A.F., Beer. R., & Popp, H. (2017). Education 4.0 – Fostering Student's Performance With Machine Learning Methods. IEEE 23rd International Symposium For Design And Technology In Electronic Packaging. Doi:10.1109/SIITME.2017.8259941

Diao, X., Zeng, Q., Li, L., Duan, H., Zhao, H., & Song, Z. (2022). Personalized Learning Path Recommendation Based On Weak Concept Mining. Https://Doi.Org/10.1155/2022/2944268

Dirin, A., & Saballe, C. (2022). Machine Learning Models To Predict Students' Study Path Selection. *International Journal of Interactive Mobile Technologies* (Ijim). Doi: 10.3991/Ijim.V16i01.20121

Ferguson, C., Broek, E.L. V.D., & Oostendorp, H.V. (2022). AI-Induced Guidance: Preserving The Optimal Zone Of Proximal Development. Computers And Education: Artificial Intelligence, 3. Https://Doi.Org/10.1016/J.Caeai.2022.100089

Guo, Y., Chen, Y., Xie, Y., & Ban, X. (2022). An Effective Student Grouping And Course Recommendation Strategy Based On Big Data In Education. Information, 13(*197*). Https://Doi.Org/10.3390/Info13040197

Jain, S., Pawar, V., Gole, V.K., & Nagle, V. (2023). An Automated Grading System. International Research Journal Of Modernization In Engineering Technology And Science, 5(*11*).

Jovic, J., Kisic, E., Milic, M.R., Domazet, D., & Chandra, K. (2022). Prediction Of Student Academic Performance Using Machine Learning Algorithms. Proceedings 13th International Conference On Elearning, Belgrade, Serbia, 1. Https://Ceur-Ws.Org/Vol-3454/Article_4.Pdf

Lahoti, V., & Raut, A. (2022). Automated Assessment Generation And Student Performance Prediction In E-Learning System. *International Journal Of Scientific Research In Computer Science, Engineering And Information Technology*, 8(*2*). Pp 58-65. Doi : Https://Doi.Org/10.32628/CSEIT228213

Lee, A.V.Y. (2023). Supporting Students' Generation Of Feedback In Large-Scale Online Course With Artificial Intelligence-Enabled Evaluation. Studies In Educational Evaluation, 77. Https://Doi.Org/10.1016/J.Stueduc.2023.101250

Liu, J., Huang, J., &Xie, Y. (2021). Educational Visualization Application Based On Machine Learning Algorithm To Predict Student Learning. IEEE 2nd International Conference On Information Technology, Big Data And Artificial Intelligence (ICIBA). Pp. 236-241, Doi: 10.1109/ICIBA52610.2021.9688161

Liu, Z., Dong, L., & Wu, C. (2020). Research On Personalized Recommendations For Students' Learning Paths Based On Big Data. Ijet, 15(*8*). Https://Doi.Org/10.3991/Ijet.V15i08.12245

Ma, Y., Wang, L., Zhang, J., Liu, F., & Jiang, Q. (2023). A Personalized Learning Path Recommendation Method Incorporating Multi-Algorithm. Applied Sciences, MDPI. Dio: Https://Doi.Org/10.3390/App13105946

Mahboob, T., Irfan, S., & Karamat, A. (2016). A Machine Learning Approach For Student Assessment In E-Learning Using Quinlan's C4.5, Naive Bayes And Random Forest Algorithms. 19th International Multi-Topic Conference (INMIC), Islamabad, Pakistan, Pp. 1-8, IEEE. Doi: 10.1109/INMIC.2016.7840094

Maina, E.M., Oboko, R.O. & Waiganjo, P.W. (2017). Using Machine Learning Techniques To Support Group Formation In An Online Collaborative Learning Environment. I.J. Intelligent Systems And Applications, 3. Pp. 26-33. DOI: 10.5815/Ijisa.2017.03.04

Nafea, I.T. (2018). Machine Learning In Educational Technology. Intech. Doi: 10.5772/Intechopen.72906

Nedeva, V., & Pehlivanova, T. (2020). Students' Performance Analyses Using Machine Learning Algorithms In WEKA. Doi:10.1088/1757-899X/1031/1/012061

Pu, D., & Zhou, Z. (2021). Teaching Path Generation Model Based On Machine Learning. 6th International Conference On Computational Intelligence And Applications. DOI 10.1109/ICCIA52886.2021.00013

Raza, S.A. (2019). Predicting Collaborative Performance At Assessment Level Using Machine Learning: An Application Of Educational Data Mining.

Rokade, A., Patil, B., Rajani, S., Revandkar, S., &Shedge, R. (2018). Automated Grading System Using Natural Language Processing. 2018 Second International Conference On Inventive Communication And Computational Technologies (ICICCT), 1123-1127. Https://Www.Semanticscholar.Org/Paper/

Automated-Grading-System-Using-Natural-Language-Rokade-Patil/267d024aecaf9604771fe0e0eca718cc86a8861c

Sadouni, O., &Zitouni, A. (2021). Task-Based Learning Analytics Indicators Selection Using Naive Bayes Classifier and Regression Decision Trees. International Conference on Theoretical And Applicative Aspects Of Computer Science. 10.1109/ICTAACS53298.2021.9715185

Sanchez-Pozo, N.N., Mejia-Ordonez, J.S., Chamorro, D.C., Mayorca-Torres, D., &Peluffo-Ordóñez, D.H. (2021). Predicting High School Students' Academic Performance: A Comparative Study Of Supervised Machine Learning Techniques. Doi: 10.1109/IEEECONF53024.2021.9733756

Shabandar, R.A., Hussain, A.J., Laws, A., & Lunn, J.L. (2017). Machine Learning Approaches To Predict Learning Outcomes In Massive Open Online Courses. Doi: 10.1109/IJCNN.2017.7965922

Weegar, R., &Almquist, P.I. (2022). Reducing Workload In Short Answer Grading Using Machine Learning. *International Journal Of Artificial Intelligence In Education.* Https://Doi.Org/10.1007/S40593-022-00322-1

Xu, J., Moon, K.O., & Schaar, M.V.D. (2017). A Machine Learning Approach For Tracking And Predicting Student Performance In Degree Programs. *IEEE Journal Of Selected Topic Signal Processing*, 11(*5*). DOI: 10.1109/JSTSP.2017.2692560

Yildiz, M.B., & Borekci, C. (2020). Predicting Academic Achievement With Machine Learning Algorithms. *Journal Of Educational Technology & Online Learning*, 3(*2*). Doi: 10.31681/Jetol.773206

Zhu, M., Liu, O.L., & Lee, H.S. (2020). The Effect Of Automated Feedback On Revision Behavior And Learning Gains In Formative Assessment Of Scientific Argument Writing. Computers & Education, 143. Https://Doi.Org/10.1016/J.Compedu.2019.103668

12

Mann Ki Baat Radio Series

Educational Content Review

Sadia Khalid and Aerum Khan

Introduction

Mann Ki Baat (MKB): The Government of India is using this platform for a program where India's Prime Minister connects with the common people through his monthly radio programme. It is aired on the last Sunday of every month on All India Radio at 11 a.m. He chose this slot because of the availability of the people and feasibility of the time. Since then, he continues to speak with the people of India through the radio programme. The prime minister can be heard on about 422 radio stations and relay centres by about 100 crore listeners (pib.gov.in.). The programme runs for 20 to 35 minutes and mostly discusses the initiatives taken by the government and provides advice on addressing educational, social issues. The program is broadcast in English and 26 regional languages so that it could be understood by all and cater to a vast section of the society. This program is repeated at 8 p.m. on the same day of the broadcast, in different regional languages which makes it easy to understand.

It has a feature, with the help of mobile phones through which a specific number of people can also listen to 'Mann ki Baat'. Different government websites such as mygov.in Namo app, MKB app have been introduced to get more and more people's participation. It is a combination of a Talk show and Phone-in program, its format is straightforward as the Prime Minister speaks on a range of topics to the citizens of the country through radio and also inviting suggestions from listeners as well. The Prime Minister also asks citizens to suggest some topics for subjects which need to be discussed as well as any queries which people may have for him.

Related Literature

In view of the popularity of Mann ki Baat, a need was felt to study what people at large opine about the show. As there is ample literature available in the form of books, articles in journals and media reports, they were meticulously reviewed in order to understand what people think about these episodes. Following are some of the excerpts taken from different sources:

- Livemint (2018). The nation building process depends on two important factors: the youth and science (scientific temperament). PM Modi understands these two elements in the development of a country like India. Therefore, he urges youth to imbibe the 'Jai Vigyan' mantra, which was given by former Prime Minister Atal Bihari Vajpayee. The inculcation of the scientific temperament among youth can lead to the development of the nation. It could also build a modern, powerful and self-reliant India. Modi stresses on the importance of youth and science in the development of the nation. This suggests that he knows the immediate needs of our country.
- *India Today* (2019). Mr. Modi is the man who does not hesitate to do new things. This approach, he uses in his famous monthly program Mann ki Baat, wherein he urges the people of this country to develop a reading habit. He also emphasizes on gifting a book instead of bouquets. This kind of practice is very interesting as far as the use of money for developing a congenial relationship with books in the era of technology is concerned. His urge to give books instead of bouquets is appreciable. This also suggests that he knows the importance of books in life.
- NDTV (2019). Prime Minister Narendra Modi addresses the 59th edition of Mann ki Baat and in his address, he said that he considers himself an NCC cadet even today. During the program, he argues that India's National Cadet Corps (NCC) is one of the largest uniformed youth organizations of the world. This organization is in the service of the nation. While speaking about the NCC, he elaborates on different dimensions of the same. During the program on the NCC, he says, 'It is a Tri-services organization comprising the Army, Navy and Air Force. NCC means cultivating qualities of leadership, patriotism, selfless service discipline and hard work as an integral part of one's character; a thrilling journey of imbibing them into one's habits'. His emphasis on NCC suggests that he wants to generate and inculcate the feeling of patriotism, discipline and dedication among the youth of this country. These kinds of attributes and qualities among the youth are prerequisite for the growth and development of the nation.
- *India Today* (2020). Educational institutions are the backbone of the comprehensive educational process. Although institutions mostly depend upon the present resources, and other important stakeholders, the role of alumni are being overlooked. This dimension was highlighted by the Prime Minister Narendra Modi in his show Mann Ki Baat. He said that institutes and alumni should come together to strengthen their relationship for better development. He stressed that not only the urban institutes should work with the alumni network but also rural educational institutes should also develop a strong alumni network. He also emphasized the role of alumni network in the development of educational institutions,

while saying so, he gave examples of various IITians, who have gifted conference halls, management centres and many other facilities. By giving examples, he highlighted the notion of paying back to society.

- *Hindustan Times* (2020). Prime Minister Narendra Modi is the man who believes in social justice principles. That is why he keeps on speaking about the inclusion of poor and marginal people in mainstream society through education. In this series, he speaks about the same in his famous radio program Mann Ki Baat. During the speech about "people's initiative in providing cost-free help to the poor in their quest for knowledge and education", he mentions Sandeep Kumar, who runs an NGO, through which he provides free books to the poor children. Kumar's motto is education from trash. By citing such examples, it appears that Modi emphasizes not only the mainstreaming of poor and marginalized children through education but also the importance of unused material in the life of people.
- *Hindustan Times* (2022). The development of science, maths and technology would not have been possible, if India had not invented zero. The contribution of India in the field of science and maths importance is praised throughout the world. Similarly, Veda also has mathematical formulae, which is yet to utilize properly. This aspect is highlighted by the Prime Minister. While discussing the importance of Vedic maths, he said that you can do even the most difficult calculation in the blink of an eye. This suggests that the importance of Vedic maths is so immense that we cannot simply explain in the words. What is required is to give space and exploration of Vedic maths for science and maths.
- *The Times of India* (2022). Mr. Modi believes in inclusive India. Keeping this premise in mind, he also discusses sign language for the specially abled people in his program, Mann ki Baat. He takes the reference of National Education Policy, wherein the importance of sign language has been inscribed. While discussing the importance of sign language, he gave the example of Pooja from Haryana, who was not able to talk with her son. Later, training in sign language changed their life and the boy also won a prize in the story telling. He also gave examples of another six-year-old girl child who overcame her difficulties in communication, after getting training in sign language. By giving examples, he tries to stress on the importance of sign language in the life of specially abled people. Encouraging sign language also shows that he follows the essence of Sab ka Saath, Sab ka Vikas and Sab ka Vishwas.
- *The Times of India* (2022). The process of teaching learning and education is incomplete without the library. Therefore, the Prime Minister during the 95th episode of Mann Ki Baat emphasizes the importance of community libraries by highlighting the contribution of a tribal government officer from Jharkhand, who built a community library for the poor and needy

children. He praises the role of the government officer in the development of libraries for the marginalized and poor children, who do not have enough books to support their studies. The appraisal of this kind of activity can be analyzed from two perspectives: first, supporting the poor and needy students who aspire for education and second, the feeling of paying back to the society.

- *The Times of India* (2022). Prime Minister in his 85th edition of Mann ki Baat discusses many things such as Swacchata Abhiyan and National War Memorial. He also mentions that India has never confined education to textbooks and classroom, but it has seen as comprehensive life experiences. In this episode, he also hails the work of Rabindranath Tagore, Mahatma Gandhi, Madam Mohan Malviya and other important towering figures of modern India in the field of education. The scrupulous reading of the above-mentioned statement explains the importance of life experiences, individual and social life. This also suggests that the education we get from the formal education system is not enough to understand the complex nature of life.
- Press Trust of India (2023). Prime Minister in his 103rd edition of Mann ki Baat discusses many things such as Pride in Mother tongue, Rich heritage culture of India. He mentioned the importance of Mother tongue. Modi has said, "The mother and mother tongue, both together strengthen the foundation of life, lending it permanence. Just like we cannot abandon our mother, similarly, we cannot leave our mother tongue either." He also highlighted a number of issues and urged people to develop scientific temperament among children. "Even after 75 years of Independence, there are people who have dilemmas and reservations regarding their language, dress, food and drink, whereas it is not like this anywhere else in the world,"
- *Hindustan Times* (2023). Prime Minister in his 104th episode of "Mann ki Baat" He lauded the commendable effort of ISRO scientists on Chandrayaan-3 mission. He praises the efforts taken to promote Sanskrit in recent times by saying "We all know that Sanskrit is one of the oldest languages in the world. It is also called the mother of many modern languages. Sanskrit is known for its antiquity as well as for its scientifically and grammar." He also greets everyone for 'World Sanskrit Day', which is celebrated on 31 August. It shows he is urging everyone to follow our tradition as well as modernization.
- *The Times of India* (2023). Prime Minister in his 105th episode of Mann ki Baar praises the initiative of a 'ghoda library' in Uttarakhand. The initiative involves mules and horses carrying children's books to remote areas of the Uttarakhand hills. PM Modi says, "It is true that today's era is of Digital Technology and E-Books, but still books always play the role of a good friend in our lives. Hence, we should motivate children to read books."

- *Hindustan Times* (2023). PM Modi in his 105th episode of Mann Ki Baat says that many prestigious institutions like IITs, IIMs, NITs and Medical Colleges will participate in G20 University Connect Programme. He encourages people to participate in a significant cleanliness program scheduled as a tribute to Gandhi.
- *Hindustan Times* (2023). PM Modi in 106th episode of Mann ki Baat talks about renowned author Sivashankri and her project Knit India, Through Literature'.

Episodes Focused on Education and Related Issues: Content Analysis

Education comprising a host of related other issues i.e.; opening of schools, 'Vedic Maths', 'Gifting of Books' in place of Bouquet, Construction of 'Akhshara Library', Sign language teaching, etc. were covered by the Honorable Prime Minister Narendra Modi during his Mann Ki Baat audio series. Since a large number of episodes were focusing on the different aspects of education, their impact on the stakeholders needs to be ascertained. In view of this, a self-developed questionnaire consisting of fifty questions shall be developed to elicit the responses of the concerned from the field. The responses shall be collected from the diverse sample both quantitatively and qualitatively which will later analysed and interpreted in order to ensure how relevant will these issues are addressing the audience while the episodes were aired and how seriously they shall take them along with their expectations from the upcoming episodes of 'Mann ki Baat'.

He spoke on a number of vibrant and important issues such as solar energy, G-20 and international year of millets and education till date. It has gained popularity not only because it has our honorable Prime Minister Shri Narendra Modi as its host but due to its quality in the aspect of spreading knowledge, awareness and letting people know about various important national actions taken by government or incidents happened across the globe with proper understanding about its consequences on the masses and how population can be benefitted from various schemes implemented by the government. This show is not only popular in our country but also has got listeners across the globe who lend their ears with equal enthusiasm as Indian people do (23 crore regular listeners of Mann Ki Baat, 96% population aware of the famous radio programme: IIM Rohtak Report)

Under the broader theme of education many subthemes are lying which were addressed by Modi ji. These subthemes revolve around the issues that concern both young and grown-up children who are likely to be the future citizens of the country.

In his address, he also explained the importance of education as a powerful tool and it should not be given to only a few. Hence, he emphasized the need for opening more schools for the children who came from economically weaker and downtrodden sections of the society.

The Prime Minister, in most of his addresses pertaining to education, tried to strike a balance between traditional and modern education. Hence, on one hand, he stressed on the need for promoting Vedic Mathematics and on the other hand, he wanted the schools and colleges to be fully equipped with ICT rich libraries in order that our students should not lag behind in any sphere of education in the world.

The Prime Minister, in most of his addresses, also emphasizes the need for creating schools as the best learning ecosystem wherein all the requisite facilities must be ensured that could be used for the betterment of both mental and physical health of the children.

The Prime Minister also realized the need that our education system needs to be revamped and transformed where he suggested children aspiring to be engineers, doctors, soldiers or whatever services they wish to render for the country but not to be away from their rich cultural heritage and social values. He also wished to develop a habit of reading books and gifting them to the persons they like on different occasions rather than gifting all kinds of superficial and attractive gifts. He also talked about inclusion of specially abled "Divyang" children by focusing on sign language addition to the mainstream curriculum.

The content analysis of the 106 episodes of PM Modi's 'Mann ki Baat' audio program was made by the researchers by going through the episodes available over the Internet. At first the episodes related to or focusing on education and related topics were segregated. These were episode 14 based on youth as global citizens, episodes 12, 19 and 88 were based on education of girls and all children, also covering their awareness about getting educated. Episode 33 was based on the brilliant idea of Modi ji of gifting books in place of flower bouquets in various programs. Episodes 42 and 44 were based on being an example and source of inspiration for the students, and the requirement of opening new schools and providing free education for poor children.

Episode 46 was based on MBBS examinations as well as episode 50 was on insight, information and positive stories to inspire students. Episodes 54, 70 and 84 were focused on the importance of libraries in the lives of students, these episodes also had the discussion on developing 'Akshara Library'. Episode 59 was devoted to NCC and its role in nation building. Episode 88 was based on the importance of 'Vedic Maths', whereas episode 93 talked about 'Indian Sign Language' and its significance in education. Episode 98 was a very special one, it talked about 'Lullaby' which is an age-old form of poetry having a very motherly touch. The PM talked about the interesting idea of organizing a lullaby writing competition.

Episodes 103 and 104 were based on explaining the importance of our mother tongue and ancient languages like Sanskrit on the occasion of World Sanskrit Day. Episodes 105 and 106 explains the importance of community, how individuals are contributing towards their society and explains the importance of reading in our lives also how we Indians are knit over a common thread, and we can connect the country through literature and show its rich heritage to the world.

Conclusion

This content analysis made by the researchers in this paper shows that PM has made many discussions about Education and related topics, the content analysis can pave the path for the further study of the effectiveness of this flagship program. The further research can try to analyze the impact of different educational issues which were discussed by PM Modi in MKB related to people from different walks of life.

References

https://pib.gov.in/Press ReleaseIframePage.aspx? PRID-1952618

survey/1536822/7 x tr sl-en& x tr tl-hi&xtr hl-hi&xtr pro-te

https://www.hindustantimes.com/india-news/mann-ki-baat-live-updates-august-27-2023-pm- narendra-modi-radio-show-latest-news-101693096845388-amp.html

Appadurai, Arjun. (1990). "Disjuncture and Difference in the Global Cultural Economy" in *Theory, Culture and Society,* Sage Publication.

Alfonso Gumucio Dagron (2009) Playing with fire: power, participation, and communication for development, *Development in Practice*, 19:4-5, 453-465,

Altman, I, & Taylor, D. (1973). *Social Penetration: The Development of Interpersonal Relationships*. Holt, Rinehart and Winston.

Bandura, A. (1977). *Social learning theory*. Englewood Cliffs, NJ: Prentice Hall.

Bolter, D., & Grusin, R. (1999). Remediation: Understanding new media. MIT press.

Durga, S., & Sundaram, R. (2017). Community radio for development in India: A study of the sector. *International Journal of Interdisciplinary Research and Innovations*, 5(2), 121-131.

Carpentier. N. (2011). The concept of participation. If they have access and interact, do they really participate? *Communication Management Quarterly*/Casopis za upravljanje komuniciranje s, 21:13-36.

Garhwal, A. (2023). Building Awareness About Social Issues and Government Programs: An

Analysis of Effectiveness of Mann Ki Baat Programmes, *Journal of Pharmaceutical Negative Results*, 2094-2107.

Gandhi, A.P. & Balanmuugan. J. (2017). *Mann Ki Baat- Present and Future*, S. Kandukuri. M., & Haragopal, V.V. (2020).

Giles, H., Bourhis, R., & Taylor, D. (1977). Towards a theory of interpersonal accommodation through language. In B. Pearson & H. Giles (Eds.). *Language development: Learning language, learning culture* (pp. 307-335). New York: John Wiley & Sons.

Huesca. R. (2013). The participatory communication for development nexus: A global perspective. Communication Theory, 23(4), 427-447

Kapur, D., & Vyas, D. (2005). Participatory communication and the social construction of development: An introduction. *Participatory communication and the social construction of development*, 1-12.

Freire, P. (1970). *Pedagogy of the oppressed*. Herder and Herder.

Servaes, 1. (2001). "Introduction participatory: Modernizing the Middle East. New York. The Free Press. Communication (Research) for Social Change: Old and New Challenges, *The Journal of International Communication*, 7(2): 5-13,

Sinha, Subir (2017): Fragile Hegemony: Modi. Social Media and Competitive Electoral Populism, *International Journal of Communication*, Vol 11, No 2017(2018), pp 4158-80.

Singh, K.J. (1979). Gandhi and Mao as mass communicators. *Journal of Communication*, 29(3), 94-101.

Gerber, L.S., & Gross, L. (1976). Living with television: The dynamics of the cultivation process. In J. Bryant & D.R. Anderson (Eds.), *Communication and Television: An Evaluation* (pp. 1-16). Sage Publications.

Hindustan Times (2020, October 26). Chandigarh-based social worker finds mention in PM's Mann ki Baat. Retrieved from Chandigarh-based social worker finds mention in PM's Mann ki Baat Hindustan Times

Hindustan Times (2022. April 24) From Zero to infinity: PM Modi on Vedic Maths, Intel CEO on Mann Ki Baat. Retrieved from From Zero to infinity: PM Modi on Vedic Maths, Intel CEO on Mann ki Baat Latest News India *Hindustan Times*.

India Today (2019, June 30). "Books Should be Given as Gifts in Place of Bouquets: PM Modi. Retrieved from "Books Should be Given as Gifts in Place of Bouquets: PM Modi — books should be given as gifts in place of bouquets pm modi-(indiatodayne, In)

India Today (2020, November 29). Mann ki Baat; PM Modi emphasizes on strengthening relations between school, colleges with alumni. Retrieved from Mann ki Baat: PM Modi emphasises on strengthening relations between school, colleges with alumni — *India Today*.

Livemint (2018, April 29). Mann Ki Baat highlights: PM Modi hails youth, farmers, scientists, athletes, in his speech. Retrieved from Mann Ki Baat highlights: PM Modi hails youth, farmers, scientists, athletes, in his speech | Mint (livemint com)

NDTV (2019, November 25). I Consider Myself NCC Cadet Even Today: PM Modi In Mann ki Baat. Retrieved from I Consider Myself NCC Cadet Even Today: PM Modi In Mann Ki Baat (ndtv. Com)

Untitled page. (n.d.). https://pib.gov.in/Press%20ReleaseIframePage.aspx?PRID-1952618

Anand, N. (2023, August 27). Mann Ki Baat 104th episode highlights: PM Modi extends Raksha Bandhan greetings. *Hindustan Times*. https://www.hindustantimes.com/india-news/mann-ki-baat-live-updates-august-27-2023-pm-%20narendra-modi-radio-show-latest-news-101693096845388-amp.html

13

Podcasts as a Tool to Enhance Language Learning

Gulafshan Salam Khan

Introduction

In today's world, voice media has become integral to leisure time and entertainment decisions. Music, radio, and podcasts are different forms of voice media that we can easily create and consume with the help of popular platforms such as Apple Music, Spotify, and Google Play. Podcasts serve as inspiration and explore the depths of human intellect. On-demand voice media has eliminated the restrictions of scheduled and live voice entertainment, allowing people to listen to what they want whenever and as often as they want. The modern era of voice media has revolutionized how people consume entertainment in the 21st century.

However, voice media has positively impacted how we consume it, but it has been stigmatized as entertainment. People often consider voice media a pastime and must recognize its other values. Although scholars have discussed voice media's development and rise in popularity, they still need to address how it can resolve social issues adequately. This article will focus on podcasts (Goldman, T. 2018).

Podcasts have become increasingly popular in recent years and have seen a significant increase in downloads. Apple podcast downloads grew from 7 billion in 2014 to 10.5 billion in 2016 and 13.7 billion in 2018. By March 2018, Apple Podcasts had recorded a staggering 50 billion total podcast downloads and streams. Moreover, podcasts are now available in more than 155 countries, with over 525,000 active podcast shows and more than 18.5 million episodes (Goldman, T. 2018).

Podcasts are becoming more popular and accessible. Due to minimal technology requirements, they are available anytime and anywhere. Creating a podcast is accessible and open to anyone. As a result, this form of voice media is expanding beyond just entertainment. The podcast has been extensively discussed in digital technology, with scholars documenting its evolution and increasing popularity. However, many articles still need to address how podcasts can be utilized to address social issues. Podcasts are a valuable tool for language learning, providing numerous benefits to teachers and students. However, what exactly are podcasts, and how do they help language learning?

This article explores podcasts in language learning, focusing on listening and speaking skills (Budiasningrum et al., 2022). The purpose of this paper is to review the use of podcasts in planning education.

Related Literature

Learning a foreign language can be challenging. Effective teachers create an optimal learning environment and aid students in mastering fundamental communication skills, such as listening and speaking, which are challenging to learn. Language learners can support their learning with technology, such as podcasts (Budiasningrum et al., 2022).

Podcasting is a modern portable technology that allows users to download and play digital audio and video streams on mobile devices. The word "Podcast" is a blend of "iPod" and "broadcasting". Podcasts allow listeners to select and listen to their favourite programs at their leisure (Ibrahim, A. 2022).

A *podcast* is an audio recording that can be downloaded and listened to on various media devices, such as computers, laptops, smartphones, and portable music players (Drew, C. 2017). Podcasts can be easily defined by their primary components, which include an audio file (known as a 'vodcast' if it is a video), the ability to play it on any MP3 or WMP player, downloadability from the Internet, production using an RSS (Really Simple Syndication) feed allowing for automatic downloading, and an option for listeners to subscribe to a series of recordings which will then be downloaded automatically (Kidd, 2011). According to a survey, podcasts should be at most 15 minutes long. Longer episodes can decrease attention and comprehension (Cebeci & Tekdal, 2006).

According to Kaplan-Lieserson 2005, different types of podcasts can be used in a learning context:

1. Assist auditory learners.
2. Channel for material review.
3. Assist non-native speakers.
4. Provide feedback for learners.
5. Enable instructors to review training and lectures.
6. Replace online sessions when simply requiring delivery.
7. Provide supplementary content or be a part of a blended solution.

Methodology

This literature review is based on peer-reviewed, published material on podcasting. Literature searches used significant databases such as JSTOR, Scopus, Web of Science, ERIC, and Science Direct. The researcher searched for articles related to their study by using specific keywords such as "podcast review," "podcasting," "podcast and listening," "podcast and vodcast," "podcast tools," "benefits of podcasting," "children and podcasts," and "podcasts and education." From the online databases, they downloaded 40 articles, but 26 of them were disregarded as either duplicates, opinions, or papers on unrelated subjects irrelevant to their empirical study. The researcher only included and reviewed studies that explicitly dealt with podcasts, language learning, and teaching. Eventually, they selected and reviewed 14 research articles on podcasting to assess the effectiveness of podcasts as a teaching tool and student and teacher achievement. The review used the constant comparative method to compare all the data gathered from the chosen research studies. The articles were carefully read, and the content analysis summarized the key research results.

Results and Discussion

Educational Use of Podcasts

Podcasts are audio or visual content delivered over a network via subscription. They can be accessed using any device containing images, videos, and chapters (Rajic, S. 2013). Podcasts allow teachers to enhance classroom activities and increase usage, improving the student learning experience (Ibrahim, A. 2022).

Podcasting is a powerful educational tool with numerous benefits for students and instructors. Podcasting allows students to extend their class time and access review activities conveniently. Moreover, podcasting allows instructors to record student work, which can be helpful for assessment purposes. Listening to lectures multiple times is another benefit of podcasting. This can be particularly helpful for students who need extra attention or clarification on certain topics. The ability to rewind and review specific parts of a lecture is a valuable feature that can enhance learning outcomes significantly. Podcasting also enables increased interaction between students and instructors.

By providing additional insights and explanations, instructors can help students better understand the material covered in class. This, in turn, allows students to focus on participation rather than note-taking during class, which can improve engagement and learning outcomes. In addition, podcasting can supplement traditional class notes by providing additional information and clarification. Podcasts help students fill in gaps in their written notes and gain a more comprehensive understanding of the course material.

Finally, podcasting is an excellent tool for auditory learners. Podcasting can help online students learn course content more effectively by providing an alternative to reading lecture content. Podcasts benefit students who miss a class or need to recap specific topics. Instructors can also use podcasting to explore various topics in their teaching, providing more opportunities for students to engage with course material (Rajic, S. 2013).

Podcast for Listening and Speaking Skills

Podcasts can be an excellent tool for supporting English language learning, especially for improving listening skills. They can also be an alternative teaching medium to support students' listening skills. These programs typically feature conversations, storytelling, information sharing, and other forms of media managed by a single person or group. Podcasts allow students to experience authentic forms of language and get personal involvement to learn various skills in the English language. They contain original speech from native speakers, allowing language learners to listen to the original speech sound and improve their listening and speaking skills. Podcasts, including audio and video files, are essential to developing listening and pronunciation skills. Especially in foreign language learning contexts where access to authentic materials can be difficult, podcasts remove this barrier through original speech, dialogues, radio and TV programs, and other sources. Moreover, podcasts are produced in real-time and can be recorded as audio. Language learners can listen to their voices, identify mistakes they make, and correct them instantly (Budiasningrum et al., 2022).

Strategies for Engaging Educational Podcasts

Podcasting has emerged as a popular medium for delivering educational content to students. However, creating compelling educational podcasts requires careful consideration of various factors. In this regard, it is essential to develop strategies to engage the listener, provide a clear structure, sequence, and educational aim, and use visuals, thinking pauses, and questions to enhance learning outcomes.

To engage the listener, educators can incorporate examples and subjects of interest to the listener and relate the material to their experiences. A clear structure comprises a well-planned introduction outlining the content, presenters, and aims, a main section, and a conclusion highlighting key points and introducing the next podcast in the series.

The podcast sequence should follow a standard format of introducing the topic and content, explaining its significance, moving on to more complex material, and summarizing key issues. Visual aids such as images, charts, and videos can help recipients understand the subject matter better. Thinking pauses are helpful to enable students to reflect on the subject matter being broadcast. Questions at the end of the podcast can act as a means of developing reflective and critical thinking skills.

Determining the educational aim and purpose is crucial for teachers when creating each podcast. A personal and informal approach to creating podcasts is better, allowing educators to explain the contents through interviews, dialogues, or monologues. Different formats, such as talk/radio monologue, dialogue, and interview formats, can make the podcast more engaging.

Finally, having an outline script can guide the participants and may avoid large amounts of editing at the end. Educators can create podcasts that enhance student learning outcomes by considering these strategies for practical podcasting.

Benefits and Challenges of Podcasts in Language Learning

Several researchers have found that podcasts positively impact language learning, particularly when developing listening and speaking skills. In 2018, Rahman conducted a study on the effects of podcasts on EFL learners' listening comprehension. The results showed that using podcasts was more effective than using textbooks. The researcher suggested that teachers integrate podcasts into the curriculum and the learning syllabi to support listening instruction. Another researcher discovered that students can be exposed to different forms of spoken English through podcasts, making it easier for them to listen and understand. The researcher also found that teaching listening became simpler as they could download online listening material (Rosita, R. 2022).

Podcasting has some potential drawbacks that should be considered:

1. It can be time-consuming, mainly when dealing with larger files.
2. Searching for specific information within a podcast can be challenging, as it is not always easy to search directly within the audio files. While several search engines can be used, they may only sometimes be effective.
3. Uploading and editing large, high-quality files can be challenging, requiring a good and fast broadband connection and compatible file formats for different devices.
4. Only some people own a mobile device, and some prefer reading to downloading and listening to audio files from the Internet.

Helpful Websites for Educational Podcasts

Many educational websites on the Internet offer quality podcasts. These websites are helpful for both teachers and students. Here are some important websites that can be helpful for educational purposes.

1. *TED Talks*: In the TED Talks Education podcast, one can listen to some of the world's most prominent educators, researchers, and community leaders sharing their stories and visions for the future of schools and learning.
2. *EdSurge:* EdSurge is an independent resource and community for education technology news, articles, and podcasts.
3. *The Future of Higher Education*: Engage in insightful conversations with leading experts on the future of higher education.
4. *The Cult of Pedagogy Podcast:* Jennifer Gonzalez interviews educators, students, administrators, and parents about teaching strategies, classroom

management, education reform, and educational technology. The conversations cover the school›s psychological and social dynamics, trade secrets, and other juicy topics not found in textbooks.

5. *Twisted Teacher:* Two experienced educators discuss taboo topics and reveal essential information every student should learn.
6. *Ethics and Education:* We must equip ourselves with the right tools to teach and learn as we ponder education's ethical questions. We create study guides, curricula, and episodes that educate and inspire critical thinking.

Conclusion

To conclude, podcasts have emerged as a modern and effective tool for computer-based learning, particularly for language learners who want to improve their listening and speaking skills. One of the most significant advantages of podcasts is that they offer authentic materials relevant to the learners' interests and needs. They are also user-friendly and can be accessed anywhere, making them perfect for multitasking.

Using podcasts for language learning has several benefits:

1. It allows learners to enjoy learning, leading to positive attitudes, increased motivation, and self-confidence.
2. Podcasts provide independent learning materials and lectures by foreign professors and experts, which can enhance the learning experience.
3. Podcasts diversify teaching materials beyond traditional text and visuals, which can positively impact student motivation and attention.

Podcasts can be easily downloaded for convenient learning experiences, and learners can listen to them conveniently. The ultimate impact of podcasting on traditional lectures will depend on how students and teachers implement it, and it should contribute to achieving the aims and outcomes of education. Research findings indicate that podcasts positively impact listeners, and their experiences vary depending on their interests and familiarity with different topics. These results have significant implications for using podcasts as an effective educational tool for personal and professional development. Therefore, incorporating podcasts into language learning can be a valuable addition to the learning process, providing learners an engaging and effective way to improve their language skills.

References

Abdulrahman, T., Basalama, N., & Widodo, M.R. (2018). The Impact of Podcasts on EFL Students' Listening Comprehension. *International Journal of Language Education*, *2*(2), 23-33.

Budiasningrum, R.S., & Rosita, R. (2022). Using Podcasts to Improve Listening and Speaking Skills: Literature Review. *JOLADU: Journal of Language Education*, *1*(1), 13-20.

Carvalho, A.A., Aguiar, C., Carvalho, C.J., &Cabecinhas, R. (2008, November). Influence of podcasts characteristics on higher students' acceptance. In *E-Learn: World Conference on E-Learning in Corporate, Government, Healthcare, and Higher Education* (pp. 3625-3633). Association for the Advancement of Computing in Education (AACE).

Cebeci, Z., & Tekdal, M. (2006). Using podcasts as audio learning objects. *Interdisciplinary Journal of E-Learning and Learning Objects*, *2*(1), 47-57.

Drew, C. (2017). Edutaining audio: An exploration of education podcast design possibilities. *Educational Media International*, *54*(1), 48-62.

Goldman, T. (2018). The impact of podcasts in education.

Ibrahim, A. (2022). The Positive Impact of Using Podcasts in Education in El Baha University College of Science and Arts Elmikhwa Branch. *International Journal of Educational Research Review*, *7*(4), 324-328.

Kidd, W. (2012). Utilising podcasts for learning and teaching: A review and ways forward for e-Learning cultures. *Management in Education*, *26*(2), 52-57.

Locker, M. (2018). Apple's podcasts just topped 50 billion all-time downloads and streams. [online] Fast Company. Available at: https://www.fastcompany.com/40563318/apples-podcasts-just-topped-50-billion-alltime-downloads-and-streams [Accessed 26 Aug. 2018].

McGregor, H. (2022). Podcast Studies. In *Oxford Research Encyclopedia of Literature*.

Moore, T. (2022). Pedagogy, Podcasts, and Politics: What Role Does Podcasting Have in Planning Education? *Journal of Planning Education and Research*, 0739456X221106327.

Rajic, S. (2013, September). Educational use of podcasts. In *The Fourth International Conference on e-Learning* (pp. 90-94).

Anuj, (2019). 60 best educational podcasts. [Online] Available at: https://podcasts.feedspot.com/educational_podcasts/ [Accessed 4 Dec. 2023].

Advantages And Disadvantages Of Podcasts. Retrieved from https://sa.ukessays.com/essays/english-language/report-on-advantages-and-disadvantages-of-podcasts-english-language-essay.php?vref=1 [Accessed 5 Dec,2023].

Just One More Book - Freebies 4 Mom. https://freebies4mom.com/just-one-more-book/ [Accessed 5 Dec,2023].

14

Online Education and Blended Learning

Prospects and Challenges

Abdul Badi

Introduction

Gone are the days of the traditional classroom method of teaching with the development of the technology and as per our need our educational method has gone through vulnerable changes. Textbooks and notebooks are replaced by electronic books. Google Classroom, Zoom have taken place of traditional classroom. Blackboards and chalk are replaced by tablet screens and virtual meetings have succeeded in live class interactions. Blended learning is the most efficient learning environment since it combines the strengths of face-to-face and eLearning. In general, blended learning combines the best aspects of online educational content delivery with the best aspects of classroom interaction and live instruction in order to personalise learning, allow thoughtful reflection, and differentiate instruction from student to student across a diverse group of learners (Watson, 2012).

As every coin has two sides, likewise online learning has some merits as well as demerits. The objective of this study is to address the challenges in online learning. Online learning gives advantages to higher education and a prosperous section of students. But on the other hand, it creates many difficulties for marginalized sections of students studying at government and government aided minority schools. Mainly in government and government-aided minority schools' lower class socio-economic students gain education.

The Study

Objectives

The main aim of the study is to analyze the perception of teachers about online classes and address the challenges during online learning in school.

The study was limited to see the prospects and challenges in online education and blended learning in Government and Government-aided Urdu medium schools of Delhi only.

Methodology

Descriptive survey method is used in this study. The study was conducted among different school teachers in Delhi Government and Government-aided Urdu medium schools of Delhi, India; the data required for the study has been collected from the primary sources. The researcher used a self-structured closed ended questionnaire having a five-point Likert scale with responses strongly disagree, disagree, neutral, agree, and strongly agree. The data were collected from 60 participant teachers. The researcher used a simple random sampling method in this study.

Result and Discussion

The demographic details of teachers were collected to know their backgrounds like age, gender, school type and teaching experiences. The following table explains the demographic background of the respondents.

Table 1: Demographic Profile of the Respondents

Variables	*Division of Variables*	*Percentage*
Age	20 to 40 years	45%
	41 to 60 years	55%
	Total	100%
Gender	Male	80%
	Female	20%
	Total	100%
School	Urdu Medium Government	33.33%
	Urdu Medium Government-aided	66.67%
	Total	100%
Teaching Experiences	10 years and more	58.33%
	Less than 10 years	41.67%
	Total	100%

Source: Field Survey 2023

Table 1 indicates the demographic profile of the respondent which shows that the number of respondents is divided in ages i.e. from 20-40 years (45%) and 41-60 years (55%). The majority of the respondents are male teachers (80%) and (20%) respondents are female teachers. The participation of teachers of government-aided Urdu medium schools were (66.67%) and teachers of government Urdu medium schools were (33.33%). The table also shows that 58.33% of respondent teachers had more than 10 years teaching experience and only 41.67% had less than 10-year teaching experience.

Irregularities in attendance during online learning

Many teachers found that students' attendance was irregular in most of the classes. Due to long absences in class, the teaching learning process was not giving desired results and students faced difficulties in understanding their lessons.

From field survey it is observed that 40% respondents agreed that online classes create difficulty in maintaining attendance in class and 11% respondents found to disagree with that. On the other hand, 12% respondents were found to be neutral. 20% respondents strongly agreed and 17% respondents strongly disagreed with this statement. Regarding this statement, 60% of respondents agreed that online class creates difficulty in maintaining attendance in class where total 28% respondents disagreed. The result indicates that regarding the statement on online class creates difficulty maintaining attendance in class most of the respondents (60%) agreed with the statement in comparison to its disagreed respondents (28%).

Student were not Comfortable in Communicating Electronically

Barring some conscious and electronically educated students, online learning was not welcomed by many students. Many students were not comfortable in communication through electronic devices as this was a first-time experience to them as well as to the teachers. Many students faced difficulties in connecting to the teachers with various online platforms as they had no previous knowledge of this new technology in the education system.

It is found that 27% respondents agreed that students were not comfortable in communicating electronically and 17% respondents found to disagree with that. On the other hand, 6% respondents were found to be neutral. 35% respondents strongly agreed and 15% respondents strongly disagreed with this statement. Regarding this statement, 62% of respondents agreed that students were not comfortable communicating electronically whereas 32% of respondents disagreed. The result indicates that regarding the statement that students were not comfortable in communicating electronically, most of the respondents (62%) agreed with the statement in comparison to its disagreed respondents (32%).

No Campus Attention

During online learning students were joining from their home and thus had no campus atmosphere to create social interaction. Many students miss school activities and find online learning boring. Data collected speaks that 33% respondents agreed that students faced no campus attention and 19% respondents found to disagree with that. On the other hand, 11% respondents were found to be neutral. 25% respondents strongly agreed and 12%

respondents strongly disagreed with this statement. Regarding this statement, 58% respondents agreed that students faced no campus attention where total 31% respondents disagreed. The result indicates that regarding the statement that students faced no campus attention, most of the respondents (58%) agreed with the statement in comparison to its disagreeing respondents (31%).

Lack of Internet Access or Connectivity Issues

Online learning required regular Internet connection, students living in urban slum areas belong to lower socio-economic class and face problem while attending online class like non-availability of resource and lack of Internet facilities due to its high cost and interrupted Internet services by various service providers.

Field survey found that 30% respondents agreed that students faced connectivity issues and lack of Internet and 15% respondents found to disagree with that. On the other hand, 10% respondents were found to be neutral. 25% respondents strongly agreed and 10% respondents strongly disagreed with this statement. Regarding this statement, total 55% respondents agreed that students faced connectivity issues and lack of Internet where total 35% respondents disagreed. The result indicates that regarding the statement that students faced connectivity issues and lack of Internet, most of the respondents (55%) agreed with the statement in comparison to its disagreeing respondents (35%).

Adverse Effects on Health due to Continuous use of Electronic Gadgets

Online learning requires continuous exposure to mobile or laptop screens. Due to continuous increase in screen timing of electronic gadgets many students developed adverse health issues.

35% respondents agreed that students faced adverse effects on health due to continuous use of electronic gadgets and 12% of respondents found to disagree with that. On the other hand, 8% respondents were found to be neutral. 30% of respondents strongly agreed and 15% respondents strongly disagreed with this statement. Regarding this statement, total 65% respondents agreed that students faced connectivity issues due to lack of Internet and adverse effect on health due to continuous use of electronic gadgets where total 27% respondents disagreed. The result indicates that regarding the adverse effect on health due to continuous use of electronic gadgets and lack of Internet, most of the respondents (65%) agreed with the statement in comparison to its disagreeing respondents (27%).

Digital Divide

Online learning in the school education system created a digital division among the students. Many students were unable to afford online learning

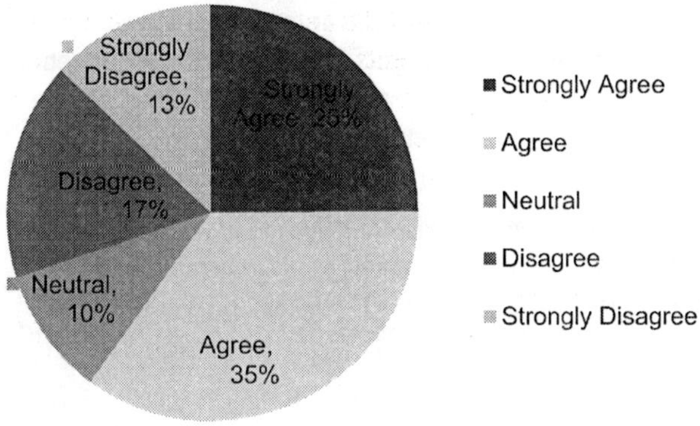

Figure 1: Digital divide among students.

Source: Field survey, 2023

education due to its high cost and lack of skill to use the online platform. The students of socio-economical prosperous families were able to afford online learning whereas students from marginalized section were unable to afford digital devices due to its high cost and lack of skill to use online platform. This results in digital divide among students.

From Figure 1, 35% respondents agreed that online learning resulted in digital division of students and 17% respondents found to disagree with that. On the other hand, 10% respondents were found to be neutral. 25% respondents strongly agreed and 13% respondents strongly disagreed with this statement. Regarding this statement, total 60% respondents agreed that students' online learning resulted in digital division of students where total 30% respondents disagreed. The result indicates that regarding the statement that online learning resulted in digital division of students, most of the respondents (60%) agreed with the statement in comparison to its disagreeing respondents (30%).

Conclusion

On the basis of the above result and discussion, it can be concluded that the online learning aims to provide education to every student despite their social standing. Online Pedagogy does a great job of supplementing offline education but it does not serve as the latter's replacement in school education. Many students were not well adapted to receive online school education, mainly socio-economical backward students facing problems during online learning. Till now in many schools students prefer traditional chalk and duster method and face to face interaction model more motivational and comfortable. The result and discussion from above study shows till now students are more comfortable in traditional method of teaching as it gives equal opportunities to all sections of societies to learn. Students prefer regular schooling more as compared to online class.

References

Watson, J. (2008). Blended learning: The convergence of online and face-to-face education. Vienna, VA: North American Council for Online Learning.

Watson, J. (2012). Blending learning: The convergence of online and face-to-face education. NACOL. America. Retrieved from https://files.eric.ed.gov/fulltext/ED509636.pdf

R. Gowda, G.K. Ayush, *Vidyabharati International Interdisciplinary Research Journal* (Special Issue June 2020), A Study on Advantages and Disadvantages of Online Teaching)

Kushwah, Shivpal Singh; Vijayakumar J K. Content creation and E-learning in Indian languages: a model

Stack, Steven Dr. (2015). "Learning Outcomes in an online vs traditional course," *International Journal for the Scholarship of Teaching and Learning*: Vol. 9: No. 1, Article 5.

15

Disruptive Technologies, Digital India, and Digital Divide

Pavitra Rana and Sarita Kumari

Introduction

Education has to be relevant to times to prepare individuals for the challenges of the real world and contribute meaningfully to society. The 21st century characterized by the rapid growth of technology led to an economy based on information technology often referred to as the digital age. As technology is evolving faster than ever, it has become even more important to ensure keeping pace with emerging technologies. With the advent of disruptive technologies like Artificial Intelligence, Machine Learning, Virtual Reality, and Augmented Reality it has now become plausible to explore new possibilities in almost all areas including education. Indian education policies have always emphasized the need to integrate technologies in education and a similar narrative has been maintained in National Education Policy 2020. However, there are concerns regarding the need for robust technological infrastructure required to reap the benefits of such sophisticated technologies, especially in the case of a vast and developing country like India. It thus becomes imperative to understand the advantages of implementing disruptive technologies in the field of education and the challenges that need to be addressed to ensure digital inclusion.

Disruptive Technologies and their Advantages

Technologies characterized by their ability to disrupt the established norms, typically beginning with a limited user base and gradually expanding until they replace a previously dominant incumbent technology are referred to as disruptive technologies (Flavin, 2012; Manocha et al., 2022). Products and services made available through disruptive technologies are often simple, economical, and convenient. Any new technology that has the potential to change the way things are done can act as a disruptive technology. Innovations alter the usual manner of conducting activities across various aspects of our existence. The realm of education is no exemption from this principle.

Online learning, Chat-based collaboration platforms, Virtual Reality, Augmented Reality, Artificial Intelligence, Case-based/project-based instruction, the Internet of things, gamification, immersive experiential learning, and blockchain are denoted as disruptive technologies in education. In contemplating the transformative impact of disruptive technologies on education, one notable aspect is the influence of online learning. It serves as a good example of disruptive technology as it changed the usual practices of education. This innovative technology has revolutionized the delivery of educational services, offering new prospects for both students and educators. Online learning addresses the accessibility barriers faced by individuals unable to pursue traditional education, such as parents, fully-employed individuals, and those with disabilities, enabling them to obtain education from the comfort of their homes. Chat-based collaboration platforms facilitate global participation in the educational process, allowing experts to engage with students online.

Virtual Reality (VR) transcends its entertainment origins, combining in-person and online education in an immersive experience. VR presents a realistic and cost-effective means to simulate scenarios applicable to fields like medicine, archaeology, and physics. Artificial Intelligence (AI) utilizes algorithms to personalize learning experiences, offering personalized tutoring and facilitating online discussions. Augmented Reality (AR) in education utilizes 3D models to improve conceptual understanding. The Internet of Things (IoT) enhances connectivity in higher education, enabling better data tracking and analytics, and improved communication between students, professors, and institutions. Gamification, an innovative educational strategy, enriches the learning experience by incorporating video game design, interactive elements, and gaming features within educational settings. This approach heightens human engagement, inoculating an element of enjoyment into the learning process.

Noteworthy gamification applications, such as Minecraft and Mathletics, have gained popularity in numerous educational institutions. Immersive experiential learning, exemplified by tools like Microsoft's HoloLens, Google Expedition, and Windows 10's mixed reality viewer, blurs the boundaries between the physical and virtual realms. These tools provide students with immersive learning experiences within the confines of a classroom. In response to the rise of smartphone usage, developers are actively creating mobile educational AR apps. Platforms like Google Expedition enable virtual journeys worldwide, fostering multidisciplinary learning. Blockchain technology, relatively nascent in the education sector, is poised to emerge as a pivotal technological facet, particularly for securely storing digital documents and applicants' data. The Indian government, spearheaded by Niti Aayog's India Chain project, is actively advocating for the integration of blockchain technology in the education domain (Gejendhiran et al. 2020). By implementing contemporary disruptive technologies in the educational landscape, the advantages that can be realized include streamlined recording and dissemination of educational resources, tailored learning experiences, automated administration of student data, streamlined analytics and reporting, and in-depth assessment of progress.

NEP 2020 on Disruptive Technologies

Recognizing the potential of disruptive technologies and the resulting increasing demand for a skilled workforce, NEP recommends curricular and pedagogical changes to include subjects like AI at all levels. It also suggests a need for research in the area of Machine Learning and AI. NEP 2020 emphasizes the requirement of preparing professionals trained in areas of Artificial intelligence, Machine Learning, and big data analysis. "New technologies involving artificial intelligence, machine learning, blockchains, smart boards, handheld computing devices, adaptive computer testing for student development, and other forms of educational software and hardware will not just change what students learn in the classroom but how they learn, and thus these areas and beyond will require extensive research both on the technological as well as educational fronts" (Ministry of Human Resource Development, 2020, p.56).

The National Education Policy (NEP) 2020 articulates a forward-looking perspective on the integration of disruptive technologies in education. The policy recognizes the transformative potential of these technologies in reshaping the traditional educational landscape. The NEP underscores the importance of personalized and adaptive learning experiences, enabled by innovative technological interventions. Furthermore, the policy document advocates for the development of a robust digital infrastructure to support the effective implementation of technology-enabled education. It highlights the significance of harnessing Artificial Intelligence, Machine Learning, and data analytics to enhance educational planning, administration, and assessment processes. The NEP encourages collaborative efforts between the government, educational institutions, and technology developers to create a dynamic and responsive educational ecosystem.

While the NEP 2020 acknowledges the potential benefits of disruptive technologies, it also emphasizes the need for a cautious and inclusive approach. The policy calls for addressing concerns related to access disparities, digital literacy, and data security. It emphasizes the importance of balancing technological advancements with pedagogical principles to ensure meaningful and impactful integration. Overall, it is evident that the NEP 2020 reflects a nuanced perspective on the use of disruptive technologies in education, recognizing both advantages and challenges in their application.

Digital India

India's digital inclusion strategies have propelled it to become the world's second-largest telecom market (Singh, 2022). The robust telecom infrastructure, marked by a significant growth in active mobile broadband subscriptions with 825 million subscribers, contributes to near-universal coverage. The surge in Internet subscribers, increased Internet density, and exponential growth in wireless data usage emphasize the success of digital initiatives. The Digital India program, launched in 2015, focuses on digital infrastructure, on-demand governance, and citizen empowerment. Initiatives like BharatNet, Common Service Centres (CSCs), and the Universal Service Obligation Fund (USOF) address connectivity challenges, especially in remote areas. India Stack integrates technological products like Aadhaar and UPI, fostering a presence-less, paper-less, and cash-less service delivery. Financial inclusion efforts include UPI, DBT, and E-Rupi. Skilling initiatives, such as PMGDISHA and FutureSkills, aim to impart digital literacy (Telecom Regulatory Authority of India, 2023a). Following are some key initiatives aimed at ensuring digital inclusion, affordable access, infrastructure development, digital literacy, and upskilling:

- *BharatNet and National Knowledge Network*: The BharatNet project aims to provide high-speed broadband connectivity to over 2.5 lakh gram panchayats (village councils) by 2025. This will help in ensuring broadband connectivity ranging from 2 Mbps to 20 Mbps at an affordable price. It will enable Internet and telecom service providers to provide services in rural and remote areas that will help people access services of e-governance, e-health, and e-education (Sadashivam & Tabassum, 2023). National Knowledge Network (NKN) is a multi-gigabit high-speed network to enhance connectivity and foster collaboration within the academic and scientific community, for promoting advancements in research and development across various disciplines (MeitY, 2018).
- *Pradhan Mantri Gramin Digital Saksharta Abhiyan (PMGDISHA)*: Considering that a major portion of the Indian population resides in rural areas, the Government of India launched this initiative in October 2017 to impart digital education and enhance digital skills among rural communities to enable them to participate in the digital economy and access various government services available online. Key features of PMGDISHA include the provision of digital education through training modules covering essential digital skills such as operating computers, using smartphones, navigating the Internet, and understanding online financial transactions. The program recognizes the importance of digital literacy in bridging the urban-rural divide and ensuring that all citizens have the necessary skills to leverage digital technologies (Sadashivam, 2020).

- *FutureSkills:* Launched in February 2018, it is an initiative by the Government of India aimed at enhancing the skill development ecosystem in the country. It focuses on equipping individuals with future-ready skills, especially in emerging technologies and industries. The scheme addresses the evolving demands of the job market by providing training and education in areas such as Artificial Intelligence, Machine Learning, data science, cybersecurity, and other cutting-edge technologies. FutureSkills aims to bridge the skills gap, preparing the Indian workforce for the challenges of the digital era.

Digital India aims to bridge the digital divide and transform India into a digitally empowered society. While it aligns with NEP 2020's vision of leveraging technology in education, its effectiveness in addressing the existing disparities is subject to critical scrutiny.

Digital Divide

"Digital divide" refers to the gap between individuals, households, businesses, and geographic areas that are at different levels with respect to socio-economic status, and their prospects to access ICTs and the Internet for a wide range of activities ("Understanding the Digital Divide," 2001). "Knowledge gap hypothesis' given back in 1970 can help understand the existence of the digital divide. Similar to wealth knowledge is also unequally distributed due to unequal access to means of acquiring knowledge. As newer means of information arise, the gap between informed and uninformed groups increases. Amidst the pandemic, the digital realm has become an integral aspect of daily life. Technology has facilitated the sharing of knowledge and information, brought markets to our fingertips, and improved access to essential services. However, this narrative primarily reflects the experience of the privileged—those with gadgets and uninterrupted Internet connectivity, enabling them to enjoy the benefits of the online world. On the flip side, there exists a contrasting reality for the marginalized, those who lack digital connectivity. This technologically disconnected group is deprived of the advantages of the digital revolution, perpetuating existing disparities and creating a digital divide.

Status of Digital Divide in India

The GSMA's Mobile Connectivity Index (MCI) assesses mobile Internet connectivity, focusing on infrastructure, affordability, consumer readiness, and content and services. India scores 61.3 out of 100, with specific enabler scores of 58.2 for infrastructure, 69.4 for affordability, 47.1 for consumer readiness, and 74.3 for content and services. The lower consumer readiness score suggests a need for increased digital awareness, particularly in rural areas, and the gender gap in smartphone ownership and Internet usage highlights areas for improvement. The Affordability Drivers Index by the Alliance for Affordable Internet (A4AI) evaluates broadband affordability. Despite an overall high score of 72.32, certain parameters like subsidizing access for underserved populations and strategies for women's access need attention. The Network Readiness Index (NRI) by the Portulans Institute ranks India 61st out of 131 countries, with an overall score of 51.19. The inclusion sub-pillar, where India ranks 97th, underscores challenges in digital inclusion. Indicators such as handset prices, Internet access in schools, ICT skills in education, and the gender gap in Internet usage need improvement for enhanced digital inclusion. Overall, addressing key areas of digital connectivity, affordability, and literacy is crucial for India to bridge the digital divide to improve its global rankings in these indices (Telecom Regulatory Authority of India, 2023a).

Disparities in Internet Connectivity in Schools in Indian States/UTs

As per flash statistics provided by UDISE+ (2021-22), out of 1489115 schools in India, 9.98% have functional computers, and 33.91% of schools have Internet facilities.

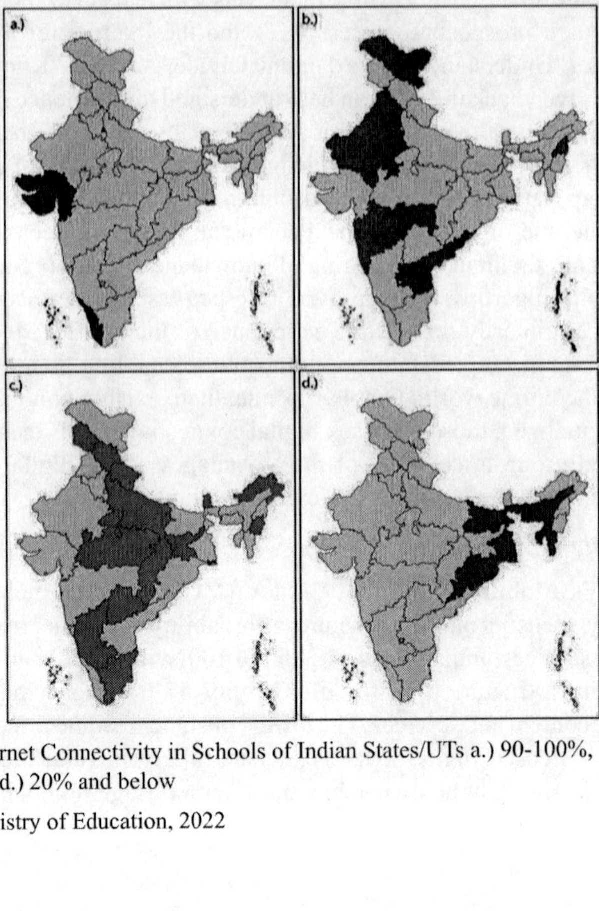

Figure: Internet Connectivity in Schools of Indian States/UTs a.) 90-100%, b.) 60-40%, c.) 40-20%, d.) 20% and below

Source: Ministry of Education, 2022

Very few states/UTs in India have good Internet connectivity in their schools. States/UTs like Delhi (100%), Chandigarh (98.71%), Puducherry (98.37%), Lakshadweep (97.37%), Kerala (95.19%), Gujarat (91.96%) have been able to achieve more than 90% of Internet connectivity in schools. Rajasthan (59.86%), Punjab (59.31%), Goa (58.21%), Dadra and Nagar Haveli and Daman and Diu (57.39%), Andhra Pradesh (56.09%), Haryana (51.24%), Nagaland (50.88%), Maharashtra (47.95%), Andaman and Nicobar Islands (44.95%) and Ladakh (42.74%) have ensured 60% to 40% Internet connectivity in schools. Most of the states/UTs have managed only 40% to 20% Internet connectivity in their schools that include Tamil Nadu (37.56%), Jharkhand (37.29%), Chhattisgarh (36.69%), Himachal Pradesh (34.47%), Sikkim (34.47%), Jammu and Kashmir (29.74%), Karnataka (29.55%), Madhya Pradesh (27.52%), Uttarakhand (27.37%), Manipur (23.07%), Telangana (22.95%), Arunachal Pradesh (22.04%), Uttar Pradesh (21.14%). States like Tripura (18.18%), Meghalaya (16.85%), West Bengal (16.67%), Odisha (14.90%), Assam (11.71%), Bihar (11.14%), Mizoram (7.85%) still have not managed to provide Internet connectivity to even 20% of their schools (Ministry of Education, 2022, p. 29).

Reasons for Digital Divide

The digital divide in India can be attributed to various factors like infrastructure disparities, inadequate network infrastructure in some regions, lack of broadband connectivity especially in rural areas contributing to a substantial urban-rural gap in Internet penetration, economic disparities affecting low-income households resulting in lack of device or limited/shared access to device, educational disparities in terms of disparities in technological infrastructure (Internet and computers) of educational institution and limited digital literacy in rural areas (Ministry of Electronics and Information Technology, 2019), uneven implementation of government policies focusing more on urban areas, language barriers often hindering access for non-English speakers and even gender disparities due to which women, particularly in rural areas, may face additional barriers to digital access due to societal norms and gender-based restrictions.

Disruptive Technologies and Digital Divide

The stance of NEP 2020 on the integration of disruptive technologies in education appears visionary, emphasizing the potential benefits of technology in overcoming barriers and enhancing educational outcomes. However, when juxtaposed with the existing digital divide in India, certain challenges come to the forefront. India grapples with a significant digital divide characterized by unequal access to digital devices, Internet connectivity, and digital literacy. Rural and remote areas, economically disadvantaged communities, and marginalized populations face challenges in accessing and utilizing digital technologies. Disparities in infrastructure, socio-economic conditions, and educational resources contribute to this digital divide. As per a recent press release of TRAI the northeastern states are still facing a considerable digital gap attributed to several factors, including challenging terrain conditions, insufficient power supply, limitations related to transmission media, limited Return of Investment (RoI) prospects for Telecommunication Service Providers (TSPs), and issues related to Right of Way (RoW). This divide impedes the socio-economic progress of the region, limits access to crucial services and information, and widens the developmental disparity between the Northeast and the rest of the nation (Telecom Regulatory Authority of India, 2023b). As per a press release in 2022, Lahaul & Spiti, Chamba, Kullu, and Mandi were the four worst affected districts of Himachal Pradesh with respect to telecom network infrastructure (Telecom Regulatory Authority of India, 2022).

Challenges in Leveraging Disruptive Technologies

- *Access Disparities*: The NEP's vision of leveraging disruptive technologies assumes widespread access to digital devices and high-speed Internet. However, the existing digital divide may limit the realization of this vision, particularly in rural and economically disadvantaged areas.
- *Differential Digital Literacy:* The effective use of disruptive technologies requires a certain level of digital literacy among both educators and learners. The success of adopting disruptive technologies in education is contingent on addressing the existing gaps in digital literacy, especially in regions where digital skills are underdeveloped like in the rural areas and tribal communities.
- *Cost Implications:* The use of disruptive technologies will involve considerable investment in technology infrastructure and training programs. Affordability remains a significant concern, particularly for institutions and learners with limited financial resources. Learners from economically disadvantaged backgrounds might lack personal devices and a conducive learning environment at home. This can impede their ability to benefit from technology-driven education.
- *Infrastructure Constraints:* In many parts of the country, inadequate technological infrastructure poses a hurdle to the seamless adoption of disruptive technologies. A reliable electricity supply and the availability of necessary hardware are critical prerequisites. Rural regions, already grappling with infrastructural deficiencies, may face challenges in accessing and implementing disruptive technologies. Limited Internet connectivity and insufficient digital resources can hinder the effective use of such technologies in these areas. The Internet density in rural areas is only 38.33% compared to 104.77% in urban areas (Telecom Regulatory Authority of India, 2023a). States of Bihar and Odisha ("India Inequality

Report 2022: Digital Divide," 2022), far-flung districts in Himachal Pradesh (Telecom Regulatory Authority of India, 2022), and Northeastern states of the country (Telecom Regulatory Authority of India, 2023b) are facing inequalities in digitalisation.

So, while NEP 2020 envisions a tech-enabled educational revolution, the existing digital divide poses substantial challenges in its implementation. Bridging these disparities is crucial to ensure that the benefits of disruptive technologies reach all corners of the country and every stratum of learners, promoting inclusivity and equitable access to quality education.

Suggestions to Overcome the Challenges

To address the challenges outlined in the context of implementing disruptive technologies in education considering the state of the digital divide and the initiatives under the Digital India campaign; the following key suggestions can be considered:

- *Accelerated Infrastructure Development:* The government should expedite the development of digital infrastructure projects like the BharatNet project and the National Knowledge Network. Ensuring the fast and timely completion of these initiatives will lay a solid foundation for widespread digital connectivity.
- *Inclusive Digital Literacy Programs:* Considering the explosive rate at which new technologies are flourishing there is a need for fast-tracking PMGDISHA initiatives. Designing and implementing comprehensive digital literacy programs targeting all age groups and educational backgrounds should be considered. Special emphasis should be given to bridging the differential digital literacy gaps, especially in rural areas. This can be achieved through community-driven workshops and training programs.
- *Tailored Digital Skill Courses for Students:* Introduction of specialized digital skill courses in the education curriculum, designed to equip students with the necessary knowledge to leverage technologies like AI, ML, AR, and VR. This proactive approach will prepare the younger generation for the future workforce.
- *Subsidized Internet Plans:* Provision of subsidized Internet plans especially for digitally disadvantaged groups and students to make digital connectivity more affordable for all. This initiative will help in overcoming cost implications associated with digital connectivity and ensure equitable access to online resources.
- *Hardware Provision for Students*: Implementation of schemes to provide subsidized laptops or tablets to students, facilitating their active participation in online learning. This step will address infrastructure constraints and

ensure that students from all parts of the country have access to the necessary hardware for digital education.

- *Diverse Courses for Skill Enhancement:* Offer a range of courses for individuals to enhance their digital skills, catering to various skill levels and interests. This could include partnerships with online learning platforms, vocational training centers, and community colleges.

By implementing these suggestions, the government can foster a more inclusive and digitally empowered society, breaking down barriers posed by the digital divide and making advanced technologies accessible to all.

Conclusion

India is making strides towards digital inclusivity to achieve the goal of a digitally empowered society. Government initiatives like BharatNet, and PMGDISHA are contributing to the government's broader efforts to promote digital inclusion and literacy in rural India. It aligns with the vision of creating a digitally empowered society and supports the country's transition toward a knowledge-based economy. While the NEP 2020 is supportive of technology integration, successful implementation will depend on effective execution, infrastructure development, and continuous monitoring and evaluation. Despite progress, challenges remain in ensuring last-mile connectivity in remote areas. The effectiveness of Digital India in resolving the digital divide hinges on addressing these connectivity issues comprehensively. While digital literacy initiatives exist, their impact may take time to materialize. A critical analysis should consider the pace at which these programs are addressing the existing gaps in digital skills. Ensuring that the benefits of Digital India and NEP 2020 reach marginalized communities still requires a concerted effort. Adequate support and resources must be allocated to areas with historical disadvantages. In conclusion, while Digital India provides a framework for addressing the digital divide, its success in realizing NEP 2020's vision of disruptive technologies in education depends on the timely and inclusive implementation of its initiatives.

References

Das, S. (2019). Marching towards Digital India: An Overview on the E-governance Initiatives taken by the Central Government of India to Minimize the Digital Divide During the Period 1998-2018. *Library Philosophy and Practice (E-journal), 3640.* https://digitalcommons.unl.edu/libphilprac/3640

Flavin, M. (2012). Disruptive technologies in higher education. *Research in Learning Technology*, *20*, 19184. https://doi.org/10.3402/rlt.v20i0.19184

FutureSkills Prime — India's Technology Skilling Hub. (n.d.). futureskillsprime.in. https://futureskillsprime.in/

Gejendhiran, S., Anicia, S.A., Vignesh, S., & Kalaimani, M. (2020). Disruptive Technologies — A Promising Key for Sustainable Future Education. *Procedia Computer Science*, *172*, 843–847. https://doi.org/10.1016/j.procs.2020.05.121

India Inequality Report 2022: Digital Divide. (2022). Oxfam.

Manocha, S., Pujari, P., & Naseeha, A. (2022). Disruptive Technologies transforming lives with reference to COVID 19 Online Education: A Review Paper. *Acta Universitatis BohemiaeMeridionales*, *25*(2), 80–90. https://doi.org/10.32725/acta.2022.010

MeitY, (2018). National Knowledge Network. https://meity.gov.in/ content/national-knowledge-network.

Ministry of Education. (2022). *Unified District Information System For Education Plus (UDISE +) 2021-22.*

Ministry of Electronics and Information Technology. (2019). *Fifty-ninth Review of National Digital Literacy Mission (NDLM) – Problems and Challenges.*

Ministry of Human Resource Development. (2020). *National Education Policy 2020.* https://www.education.gov.in/sites/upload_files/mhrd/files/NEP_Final_English_0.pdf

Müller, J., Sancho, J. M., & Hernández, F. (2009). New media literacy and the digital divide. In *IGI Global eBooks* (pp. 72–88). https://doi.org/10.4018/978-1-60566-120-9.ch005

Pradhan Mantri Gramin Digital Saksharta Abhiyan. (n.d.). https://www.pmgdisha.in/

Sadashivam, T., & Tabassum, S. (2023). Appraising BharatNet Project to Bridge Digital Divide in North-East India. *Third Concept*, *36*, 15–18. https://www.researchgate.net/publication/368661742_Appraising_BharatNet_Project_to_Bridge_Digital_Divide_in_North-East_India

Sadashivam. (2020). Digital Literacy in India: An Analysis of Pradhan Mantri Gramin Digital Saksharta Abhiyan. *Shodh Sarita*, *7*(25 (III)), 67–72. https://www.researchgate.net/publication/352366651_Digital_Literacy_in_India_An_Analysis_of_Pradhan_Mantri_Gramin_Digital_Saksharta_Abhiyan

Singh, B. (2022, November 4). With 117 crore subscribers, India is world's 2nd largest telecom market, says TRAI chairman PD Vaghela. *The Economic Times*. https://economictimes.indiatimes.com/industry/telecom/telecom-news/with-117-crore-subscribers-india-is-worlds-2nd-largest-telecom-market-says-trai-chairman-pd-vaghela/articleshow/95305746.cms

Telecom Regulatory Authority of India. (2022, December 12). *"Improving Telecom Connectivity / Infrastructure in far-flung areas of Himachal Pradesh* [Press release]. https://trai.gov.in/sites/default/files/PR_No.81of2022.pdf

Telecom Regulatory Authority of India. (2023a). *Consultation Paper on Digital Inclusion in the Era of Emerging Technologies.*

Telecom Regulatory Authority of India. (2023b, September 22). *Improving Telecom Infrastructure in Northeastern States of India* [Press release]. https://www.trai.gov.in/sites/default/files/PR_No.92of2023.pdf

Tichenor, P.J., Donohue, G.A., & Olien, C.N. (1970). Mass media flow and differential growth in knowledge. *Public Opinion Quarterly*, *34*(2), 159. https://doi.org/10.1086/267786

Understanding the Digital Divide. (2001). OECD.

16

Exploring Augmented Reality for New Age Learning

Stuti Shandilya

Introduction

Augmented Reality (AR) is a disruptive technology in the market, one of the emerging technologies in the field of display that would make a mark in the future. The images and videos come live from a static object, and the entire learning experience becomes quite fun. Teachers can record a video of a particular portion in the textbook and by scanning that portion using mobile or tablet students can learn from home. The kind of experience it provides to the students is quite immersive in nature. AR as a system has three basic characteristics: Firstly, it combines reality with a virtual world then, it is interactive in real-time and lastly, it supports 3-D visualization Azuma (1997). 'Experiential learning is a process that develops knowledge, skills and attitudes based on consciously thinking about an experience. Thus, it involves direct and active personal experience, reflection, and feedback' (UNESCO). When we combine these two that is providing experiential learning through augmented reality, we actually promote new-age learning which focuses on holistic, personalized learning. AR supports seamless interaction between real and virtual environments which have the ability to transition smoothly between reality and virtuality (Billingshurst, 2002). The premise behind the utilisation, adoption and promotion of augmented reality is that it supports engagement and interaction with the learners. Also, it helps in:

- Explaining difficult concepts
- Discover and Learn
- Development of teaching-learning material
- Improvement in teaching training
- Proper use of audio-visual aids
- Development of innovative curriculum

Theoretical Framework

Kesim (2012) compared the study on the 3-D learning tools and 2-D tools which are usually educational teaching-learning tools which creates a learning

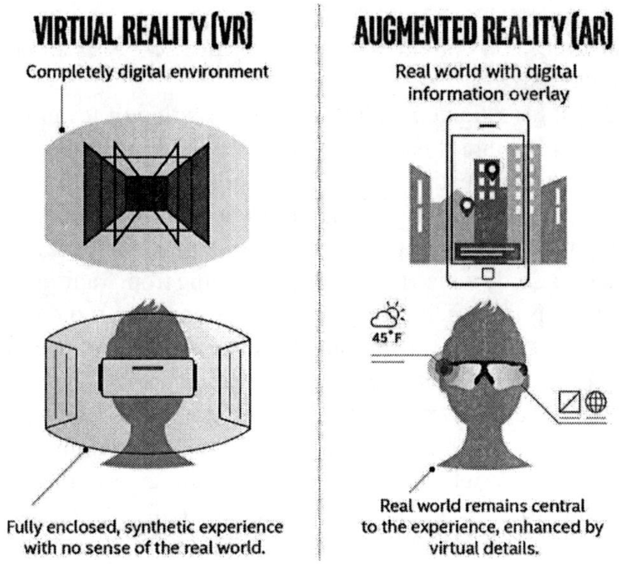

Figure 1: Virtual Reality and Augmented Reality

Source: https://static.wixstatic.com/media/

gap in the cognition of the students. The combination of AR with educational content new innovative application which enhances the effectiveness and attractiveness of learning as an experience. Lee (2012) examined the rapidly changing society where every day we are flooded with new information and the choice of learning has become highly personalized and the information needs to be adopted and applied at the right time and right place in order to efficiently convert the information into knowledge. Mehta (2017) discussed augmented reality and its role in promoting active learning ideas and regards learning from only books as a mundane and passive process. Also, it highlights the downfall of the education system and the degradation of the learning quality among students due to obsolete teaching-learning methods. This system helps the students to learn from smartphones, apps, and the intended books.

Gandolli (2018) conducted a study and found that Augmented reality is an immersive experience, especially at the school level which provides a holistic learning experience at the beginning stage of education of learner which not only enhances the learning but also leads to the advancement of the creativity level of the learners. Arduini (2020) found that Augmented reality helps in exploring the unexplored and it has been rapidly in recent years. In the field of education, it acts as a catalyst in promoting experiential learning and provides a massive diffusion of enhanced learning. Kumar (2020) described in his study, Augmented reality as a combination of virtual and real objects in a real environment. Also, there are various constraints in order to implement AR such as – Financial, Technological, Pedagogical and learning ability constraints. But with a suitable intervention, we can easily utilize AR as an educational technology at its best.

Reddy (2020) investigated the massive intervention of technology in our lives, as digital technologies have created their own space in the educational ecosystem which led to creating a new age learning, however, this also poses a challenge to the cognitive skills of the learner who needs to understand that the technology in any form is a supplement to learning not a substitute. Siddiqua (2020) conducted a study which revealed that learning from traditional methods is great but learning from interesting activities is amazing too. With the help of AR, we can now comprehend various complicated tasks quite easily, it also enhances our computational skills and imagination capacity. The 3-D model of learning provides an edge over traditional learning which not only gives a new perspective to learning but also provides new meaning to our understanding.

Singaravelu (2020) studied with the advent of new emerging technologies, new age education focused on interdisciplinary and multidisciplinary learning which can be easily adopted through AR technology, as it gives a unique medium to combine real and virtual world, the learner can now have effective and attractive teaching and learning process. Czerkawski (2021) examined that studies have shown that education is a personalized experience and with the help of augmented reality we can actually help in achieving this and incorporating a range of innovative ideas which get translated into experiences with the help of augmented reality and related technologies emerged in contemporary times.

Vuta (2021) probed in the study that digital technologies have reshaped the entire world. The world which we perceive differs a lot from the world which had perceived decades back. Similarly in the field of education too, digital technologies have left a huge footprint with the new emerging technologies like AR educators can now provide specialized methods of teaching with new age curriculum and contemporary evaluation strategies beyond time and space. Han (2022) gauged that AR is not just a tool for the teaching-learning process but a professional training strategy and an instructional designing tool which helps in creating a holistic learning experience which creates a long-lasting learning immersion in the minds of the young learners. It acts as a medium to enhance joyful learning.

Jumani (2022) described in the research review that AR and VR are quite deep technologies embedded with the idea of simulated learning which creates an environment of executing collaboration of machine learning and human creativity. The first idea of VR was created in 1965 and used for a virtual world artificial experience which is interactive, multi-sensor and immersive. Then, came AR which has an overlay of real-world inputs on the virtual world display. It can be called the extension and better version of VR.

The Study

Background

Augmented Reality has created a massive market for its growth across the globe, according to The Business Research Company it is estimated that AR has created a $18.72 Billion in Training and Education market in 2023 itself, increased from $7.30 Billion in 2019.

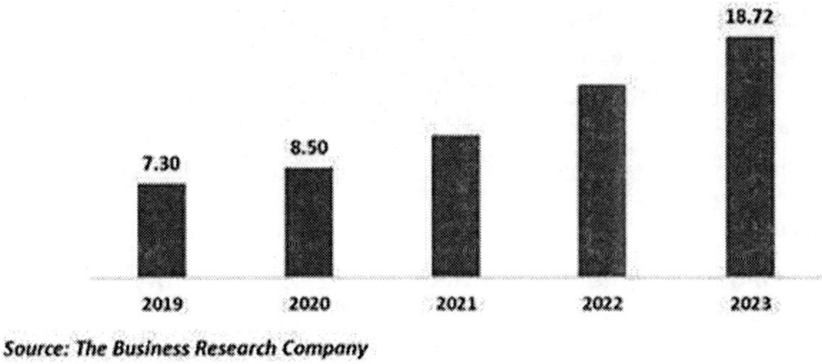

Figure 2: Global Augmented Reality in Training and Education Market

Source: https://www.thebusinessresearchcompany.com/press-release/augmented-reality-in-training-and-education-market-trends

Rationale

After reviewing the related research papers, it has been observed that almost all research papers written by diverse researchers from India and from foreign nations, have mentioned Augmented Reality as an active method of learning due to their ability to translate the learned content into long-term memory. Also, they discussed its wide applicability in various fields such as medicine, education etc.

Figure 3: Augmented Reality in Education

Source: https://ccecosystems.news/en/augmented-reality-in-education-and-the-financial-sector

A considerable amount of literature validates the premise that AR offers its own unique advantages in the teaching-learning process, training of teacher educators and also to adopt various evaluation methods. The purpose of the study is to find out the effectiveness of Augmented reality — a learning tool in creating an experiential learning platform for the learners. The details of the studies which are related to the present study is discussed above by keeping the following parameters.

- Studies on intervention of technologies in the education sector.
- Studies on effectiveness on augmented reality in education.
- Studies on different styles of learning and drawing comparisons between them
- Studies on the psychological impact augmented reality on the learners.

Objectives

1. To explore the nature and extent of augmented reality in the field of education
2. To study the various previous research in the field of Entrepreneurial Education across the globe.
3. To identify the research gap for further developments in the Entrepreneurship field.
4. To gauge the significance of augmented reality in education sector

Methodology

Qualitative research analysis is adopted as a method for analysis includes the reviewing and analysis of the articles, research papers, interviews and other published information in order to gain a deeper understanding of the prevailing scenario. These methods will help to understand the opinion and views of eminent and learned academicians and leading critical pedagogues.

Analysis and Discussion

Augmented Reality in Education

Determination of Objectives: AR provides different methods and techniques for writing instructional objectives in behavioural terms such as Bloom's Taxonomy. The needs and requirements of the people and hence education need to be revised from moment to moment. Educational technology helps in fixing up the right objectives considering the changed circumstances and changed environment.

Improvement in Teaching Learning Process: It helps in improving the teaching-learning process and makes it more purposive. It tries to discuss the concept of teaching, analysis of the teaching process, variables of teaching, phases and levels of teaching, principles of teaching, maxims of teaching and relationship between teaching and learning.

Development of Teaching Learning Material: Teaching learning materials are also as important as anything else in the teaching-learning process. In this age of science and technology, the materials of teaching cannot be unscientific. Everything in society including the values of life needs to be reflected in the materials. Only the right type of material will be able to modify the behaviour of the learner suitably making him a fit person for society.

Improvement in Teaching Training: The change of environment with new curriculum and new materials needs to be handled by the teachers. The right type of training for the teachers is the need of the hour. Educational Technology can render valuable help in the training of teachers also.

Development of Curriculum: Educational Technology is concerned with the designing of a suitable curriculum for the achievement of the desired objectives. It is helpful in describing the ways and means of the selection of suitable learning experiences, and organization of the contents in a suitable framework in order to bring better results. It provides the scientific foundation for education as well as develops theories of teaching and learning.

Government Initiatives

The Landmark policy document NEP 2020 laid emphasis on the integration of technologies like — AR, VR, AI into learning process and create an efficient way to approach education among young learners. Skills like — Creative skills, critical thinking and problem-solving ability has contributed to the eradication of the digital divide in the learning sector of India.

One of the recent developments by Indian Institute of Technology Madras (IIT Madras) where researchers are developing AR/VR (Augmented reality/ Virtual Reality)-based learning tools for the teaching and learning process in the rural areas of India. Through these technologies there is an attempt to create an immersive environment for the experiential learning of the students which will enhance opportunities they are getting and make them competent for the future prospects.

Current Developments

'Apple' has announced its intervention in the AR headsets production which will provide a cut edge next level technological tools to create a highly custom-made immersive experience to its users. Also, Dr. Merin Simi Raj and Dr. Avishek Parui have created the first AR-based mobile app called 'MemoryBytes', which traces the history of the Anglo-Indian community across 500 years, their photographs, maps and archival documents all can be accessed through this.

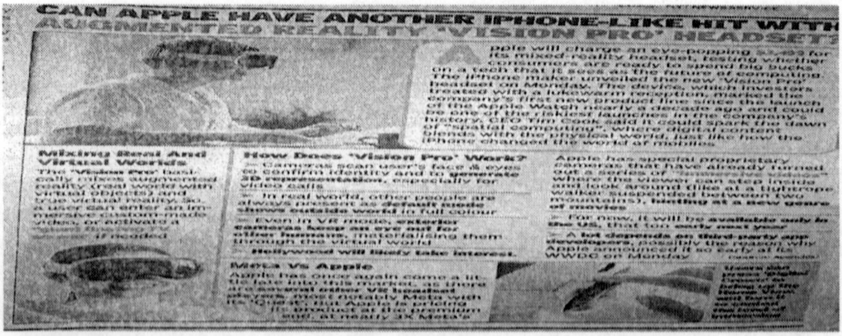

CAN APPLE HAVE ANOTHER IPHONE-LIKE HIT WITH AUGMENTED REALITY 'VISION PRO' HEADSET?

Apple will charge an eye-popping [illegible] for its mixed-reality headset, testing whether consumers are ready to spend big bucks on a tech that it sees as the future of computing. The iPhone maker unveiled the new 'Vision Pro' headset on Monday. The device, which investors treated with a lukewarm reception, marked the company's first new product line since the launch of the Apple Watch nearly a decade ago and could be one of the riskiest launches in the company's history. CEO Tim Cook said it could spark the dawn of "spatial computing", where digital content blends with the physical world, just like how the iPhone changed the world of mobiles.

Mixing Real And Virtual Worlds

The "Vision Pro" basically mixes augmented reality (real world with virtual objects) and true virtual reality. So, a user can enter an immersive custom-made video, or activate a [illegible] if needed

How Does 'Vision Pro' Work?

» Cameras scan user's face & eyes to confirm identity and to generate 3D representation, especially for video calls

» In real world, other people are always present as default mode shows outside world in full colour

» Even in VR mode, exterior cameras keep an eye out for other humans, materialising them through the virtual world

» Hollywood will likely take interest. Apple has special proprietary cameras that have already turned out a series of "immersive videos" where the viewer can step inside and look around (like at a tightrope walker suspended between two mountains), hinting at a new genre of movies

» For now, it will be available only in the US, that too early next year

» A lot depends on third-party app developers, possibly the reason why Apple announced it so early at its WWDC on Monday

Meta Vs Apple

Apple has once again come a little late into this market, as there are several other VR headset players, most notably Meta with its "Quest". But Apple is pricing its product at the premium end, at nearly 3X Meta's

Figure 4: AR Headset by Apple

Source: *Times of India* (June 2023)

Way Forward

Challenges with Augmented Reality in the field of Education includes — *Financial Challenges*-one-time high investment to establish an AR lab, *Technological Constraints*- training to use this technology, *Pedagogical Constraints* — motivation to integrate with the curriculum, learning *impediments* — learners to have the aptitude to adapt to new changing technologies like — AR.

So, they need to develop *affordable AR technologies* which can be sustainable and people from diverse backgrounds can afford it. Additionally, there should be *proper establishment of training centres* to remove the technological constraints. Further, Pedagogical constraints can be removed through development of innovative and flexible curriculum which can be easily integrated with various emerging technological tools. At last, we can say that a well efficient system can be developed through implementation of these suggestions properly which can not only help in providing world class education to the Indian learners but also prepare them for upcoming challenges in the professional arena.

Conclusion

Hence, we can say that Augmented Reality is an educational tool for future-oriented learning which can prepare learners for the new age of machine learning complemented with the content knowledge. The instructional design supports experiential learning and the evaluation techniques are flexible with numerous techniques for all sorts of learners. It also acts as a quite useful tool in improving the professional competence of the teachers and teacher educators. AR technology, if utilized properly, can be proven a big boon to not only the education sector but also to many important sectors like — the military, and medicine etc. Augmented reality provides a vision of futuristic learning and prepares us for the upcoming challenges.

References

Arduini, G. (2020). *Experiential learning with Augmented Reality*. Adaya press, (178-187)

Azuma, R.T. (1997). A survey of augmented reality. *Presence: Teleoperators and Virtual Environments*, (355-385).

Billingshurst, M. (2002). Augmented Reality in Education. *Seattle W A: New Horizons for Learning-Technology in Education.*

Czerkawski, (2021). Learning experience design for augmented reality. *Journal of Interactive Learning,* (29-41)

Gandolli, E. (2018). *Virtual Reality and Augmented Reality.* ETC Press Editors

Han, X. (2022). Augmented Reality in Professional Training. *Applied Sciences*, (1-19)

Jumani, A. (2022). Virtual Reality and Augmented Reality for Education. *Multimedia Computing systems and Virtual Reality,* (36-43)

Kesim, M. (2012). Augmented Reality in Education: Current Technologies and the Potential for Education. *Procedia-Social and Behavioral Sciences*, (297-302)

Kumar, A. (2020). Augmented Reality in Education. *National Conference on Inspired Learning*

Lee, K. (2012). The Future of Learning and Training in Augmented Reality. *Insight: A Journal of Scholarly Teaching,* (31-41)

Mehta, S. (2017). Augmented Reality Books: An Immersive Approach to Learning. Conference paper.

Reddy, P. (2020). Augmented Reality (AR): The New Trend in Transforming Teaching and Learning in Education. *The International Journal of analytical and experimental modal analysis*, (622-626)

Siddiqua, R. (2020). Augmented reality in Education. *Journal of Information Technology and Digital World,* (221-227)

Singaravelu, G. (2020). Augmented Reality in Teaching and Learning Process. *MuktShabd Journal,* (3504-3518)

Vuta, D. (2021). Augmented Reality Technologies in Education. *Bulletin of the Transilvania University of Brasov*, (35-46)

https://static.wixstatic.com/media/

https://ccecosystems.news/en/augmented-reality-in-education-and-the-financial-sector/

https://www.thebusinessresearchcompany.com/press-release/augmented-reality-in-training-and-education-market-trends

https://www.unesco.org

Times of India (June 2023)

17

Implementing Vidyanjali 2.0 Portals in Schools

Volunteers' Experiences

Naresh Kumar

Introduction

This initiative was launched when the 'shikshak parv' conclave was inaugurated. Main objective of the Vidyanjali 2.0 is to develop schools. It is a Sanskrit term, it is a consolidation of two words, these are Vidya and Anjali. First one Vidya means knowledge or truth and Anjali means divine offering.

Vidyanjali portal is used to connect community/volunteers directly to schools

To connect the Government and Government-aided schools through a community/volunteer management program, the Department of School Education and Literacy, Ministry of Education has revamped the Vidyanjali web portal. The newly introduced portal — Vidyanjali 2.0 will help the community/volunteers interact and connect directly with schools of their choice to share their knowledge and skills as well as contribute in the form of assets/material/equipment. Upon the expression of interest by a volunteer/contributor, the school authorities will assess the suitability of the volunteer/contributor for the service/activity and/or the specifications of the assets/material/equipment in accordance with the procedure as set out in the Vidyanjali guidelines.

Role of Vidyanjali 2.0: Vidyanjali will improve the participation of volunteers in government schools as well as increase the interest of children to Creative Writing, Reading, Dance, Music, Play Acting, Swachhta activities etc. in schools. Under the Samagra Shiksha (SSA), Vidyanjali 2.0 is being accomplished. This scheme has given the opportunity to the private sector, NGOs to work into Education to improve the quality of Education in all government and government-aided schools all over India.

States and Union Territories nominated for the implementation of Vidyanjali Programme

Among the States and Union Territories of India, 19 States and 2 Union **Territories** have been selected to implement the programme. These are:

- Haryana, Himachal Pradesh, Punjab, Uttarakhand, Uttar Pradesh in the northern zone.
- Andhra Pradesh, Karnataka, Telangana in the southern zone.
- Bihar and Odisha in eastern zone.
- Goa, Gujarat, Maharashtra, Rajasthan in western zone.
- Chattisgarh, Madhya Pradesh in the central zone.
- Assam, Manipur, Tripura in the northeast zone.
- Also, two union Territories are Delhi as well as Jammu and Kashmir.

A. *Features of Vidyanjali 2.0 portal*

- Portal is acting as a link between educated adults and deprived children.
- This portal is working only depending upon the volunteers
- Decentralizing education by NGOs, private sector etc. so that they can contribute to Education.
- There is no need to demonstrate specific educational qualifications or teaching qualifications. Anyone can apply for this scheme.
- This scheme also helps those aspirants who do not involve themselves in the formal teaching profession but they want to teach.
- Volunteers can keep their contribution either in full form or in partial form

B. ***Vidyanjali 2.0 portal based on NEP 2020*:** A landmark initiative of National Education Policy 2020 is Vidyanjali 2.0. NEP 2020 pays importance on community and volunteer participation for cultivating the quality of school education in the NEP Paras are 2.7, 3.6, 3.7, 21.3, 21.7, 21.8, 21.9.

Some important points from these paras are,

- Joyful peer tutoring and to motivate the educated people of the community to come forward to help students or person in Education.
- Involving the community and alumni in volunteer efforts to improve Education.
- Community involvement and volunteerism are the key factors of the success of the literacy programme.
- NGOs, private sector, and other community organizations will be encouraged to expand education by state.
- Encouraging social workers to come forward to identify non-enrolled and dropout students and to help bring them back into the mainstream of Education.

C. ***Volunteers*:** Vidyanjali 2.0 portal tries to connect various volunteers like NGOs, private sector, retired teachers, retired employees, defence personnel, school alumni, self-employees, expert persons, scientists, researchers and others.

D. *Contribution*: Volunteers can contribute in two ways, one of these is by imparting their knowledge, skills, wisdom to schools as co-scholastic.

The other is by helping schools to strengthen infrastructure like equipment, resources, assets, materials etc.

- *Contribution in services or activities*
- *Sponsorship services or activities*

***Contribution in services or activities*:** Persons who will include themselves as volunteers in Vidyanjali 2.0, portal helps them to contribute so that they can spread their knowledge based upon their field of experiences and interests. Services or activities are classified in two verticals,

Level wise Services or Activities

First, subject assistance: Foundation, preparatory and middle level in other words up to Class VIII, local language or regional language or mother tongue, Hindi, English, science, social science, mathematics, environmental studies will be taught.

Second, craft and art teaching: Emphasis is placed on local culture and traditions such as Dance, songs, festivals etc. along with encouraging children to engage in arts and crafts-based activities.

Third, sports and yoga teaching: Children are encouraged to participate in sports and yoga as per their age. Both sports and games are arranged, be it indoor or outdoor.

Fourth, teaching languages: Authors, theatre persons, storytellers, painters, actors and others will encourage children to develop skills and power, such as imagination, rational thinking, critical thinking, language development, word fluency etc.

Fifth, Vocational skills: Vocational programmes will be organised to strengthen the vocational interests and needs of students, which will be short-term oriented by volunteers.

Sixth, Adult Education: Marginalized groups, women education, adult education has been given special priority. Without the changes of school time schedule, after school hours the appropriate activities can be taken for their education.

Others, career counselling, internship opportunities, placement opportunities, guidance for children with special needs (CWSN) etc.

Sponsorship Services or Activities

- For the weak students, remedial classes should be taken. These classes will be held at the end of the week or during summer vacation or winter vacation or after school hours.

- Puberty is an important stage for students. Considering this, schools should have to arrange health camps, check-up camps, male doctor, gynaecologist, female doctor and others.
- Experts may be appointed to identify attention deficit hyperactivity disorder (ADHD) students, Children with Special Needs (CWSN) students, and learning-disabled students.
- NCC, NSS should be organized for girls. Defence personnel, experts may be engaged for self-defence training for girls.

Contribution in Equipment or Materials or Assets

- ***Civil infrastructure***
    - Extra classroom (Pre-primary to senior secondary)
    - Rooms for craft and art
    - Laboratory for Information and Communication Technology (ICT)
    - Laboratory for science
    - Vocational laboratory
    - Library
    - Playground
    - Drinking water
    - Girls' toilet, Boys' toilet, CWSNs' toilet
- ***Electrical infrastructure***
    - Fans
    - Adequate lighting facilities for classrooms
    - Appropriate power supply facilities such as solar panels, generators, inverters etc.
- ***Equipment for classrooms***
    - Textbooks
    - School uniform for students
    - Science kits and tools.
    - Braille
    - Maths kits and tools
    - Board (white, green)
    - Tables, benches, chairs etc.
- ***Digital equipment***
    - Computer
    - Projector
    - Photocopier
    - Printer
    - Internet connectivity
- ***Co-curricular activities***
    - Indoor games and sports like badminton, basketball, carrom board etc.
    - Outdoor games and sports like football, cricket

- ***Other facilities***
  - First aid kits, wheelchairs, fire mitigator
  - Newspaper, magazines for students in soft or hard copy, electronic content (e-content) etc.

Challenges Faced by the Volunteers

When we joined as volunteers in Vidyanjali Portal, we faced some problems while working with the portal given below.

- *Need of ICT tools*: As a volunteer to join Vidyanjali Portal 2.0 we need a smart phone/Tab/PC and other supporting devices which are useful for registration and receiving and submitting the information on the portal. Many of the volunteers having good knowledge and skills about the subject due to the lack of ICT tools cannot participate in Vidyanjali portal.
- *No incentive for Volunteers:* In the Vidyanjali portal 2.0 Ministry of Education and School Authority does not provide any incentives to the volunteers but they spent their money and time to the school. At least some incentives should be provided by Samagra Shiksha to volunteer so that they can take more interest in their activity.
- *Volunteer Certificate:* Volunteer certificate should be printed in the actual work done by a volunteer under the specific service category not by the name of the service.
- *Funding:* Increase the fund of Samagra Shiksha (SSA) and it should be utilized for the Vidyanjali Activity. The Ministry of Education releases the SSA fund to all schools every year but the school authority misuses this fund to other activities that should be utilized for Vidyanjali Activity purpose for providing the basic infrastructure to volunteers and students.
- *Training/Workshop for all the staff of the school and volunteers:* A training/workshop of Vidyanjali 2.0 portal should be organized for all school staff, principals, teachers and volunteers to be trained about how to work on Vidyanjali portal and how to promote community and voluntary participation to enhance the quality of School Education.
- Lack of Interest of Administration: Many of the school administrators do not take any interest in implementing the Vidyanjali Activity in their school due to some administrative purpose, it should be mandatory to all schools and make the school classroom culture more attractive and more informative by conducting the Vidyanjali activity by the volunteers.

Conclusion

If we overcome the challenges faced by the volunteers in Vidyanjali 2.0 portal, all the volunteers will easily join the portal, and they will give their contribution to the school and society; so that we can easily implement and promote community and voluntary participation for enhancing the quality of School Education.

References

National Education Policy 2020, Ministry of Human Resource Development, Govt. of India. https://www.education. gov. in/sites/ upload files /mhrd/files/ NEP_Final_ English_0. pdf.

Manoj, Ambika (2021): National Education Policy 2020: Issues and Challenges in implementation. *University News* Vol.59, no-5, April 12-18. p.146. [4].

NEP 2020: Implementation challenges, Ministry of Education. Indiatoday.in/education-today/feature philia/story/a-reality-checkon-nep-2020-major-challenges-in-implementation-1711197-2020-08-14

https://vidyanjali.education.gov.in/assets/pdf/Final_Guidelines_Vidyanjali_%20 December.pdf

18

Challenges of Artificial Intelligence

Understanding, Awareness, Perception and Preparedness

Sadiya Shaheen and Aerum Khan

Introduction

Artificial Intelligence is no longer a dream now, it has become a reality in almost every sector, be it education, health, management etc. The National Artificial Intelligence Research and Development strategic plan by Barack Obama stated that with the use of efficient augmenting capabilities of AI systems, walls between humans and AI have become blurred and will completely diminish soon (Popenici & Kerr, 2017).

With the Covid-19 pandemic hitting hard, accepting a new mode of education has become comparatively easier. AI has the potential to improve various domains of education, be it Assessment and Evaluation, Data Management, Teaching-learning Career guidance, etc. In regard to this, many AI startups have innovated various solutions to the problems faced in the traditional education system. With access to high-speed Internet services and the 'Make in India' initiative, the booming AIEd industry has made many innovations in different domains of education (Jaiswal & Arun, 2019). This has made it essential to use such technologies in the classroom and upgrade our curriculum so that the children born in the era of advanced technical applications are rightly nurtured.

Related Literature

The 21st century expects learners to have a wide knowledge of every field, especially the technical one. This can become possible only through the right approaches of educational stakeholders. Many workshops for students are being conducted to make them ready for new emerging fields like coding, data mining, AI, VR etc. (Popenici & Kerr, 2017).

A survey by the World Economic Forum states that many people find AI to have great potential in areas like entertainment, transportation etc. with the education sector at the top of the list. Studies have shown that learners are able to develop critical thinking and new skill sets through AI-based curriculum, AI-enabled lesson plans and personalized learning applications.

AI has the potential to benefit teachers, students as well as school management to simplify their daily work (Baker & Smith, 2019). AI tools help students in personalized learning as per their interests, needs and pace. It provides suitable exercises and customized question papers (Dhar, 2019) to students as per their level of understanding, interests and learning gaps (Alkanaan, 2022). Rajasthan and Assam governments have conducted pilot studies using AI-enabled resources to help tribal students and board toppers in cracking competitive exams like JEE and NEET (Popenici & Kerr, 2017).

The AI revolution in India will not reap benefits until its technological and social dimension is taken care of. Awareness campaigns of AI literacy focus on spreading a basic understanding of algorithms and patterns of AI processes by everyone, especially students coming from disadvantaged socio-economic groups (State of the Education Report for India 2022, published by UNESCO, https://unesdoc.unesco.org/ark:/48223/pf0000382661.locale=en).

Maderer (2016) found that during an online course, the students were so impressed with the teaching assistant that they wanted to nominate her for the outstanding TA award without realizing that it was IBM's virtual assistant, Jill Watson. Also, Indian classrooms face the major challenge of low teacher-student ratio. Therefore, using teacher bots or cloud lecturers in the Indian education system seems to be an effective solution.

AI-enabled image processing technology can also be used to monitor the attention levels of the students in the classroom. It senses expressions of confusion, yawning, and boredom of students during lectures and real-time feedback is sent to the teacher as well as parents. This enables teachers to make an early intervention for the needy students.

(https://www.isres.org/books/chapters/ar_book_chapter_6_07-11-2022.pdf)

Features of AI applications hold the potential to fulfil NEP's agenda of a multilingual curriculum. AI has Natural Language Processing (NLP) features which provide translation features to students from linguistic minorities and marginalized groups (Alkanaan, 2022).

Also, the recommendation system of AI takes care of users' interests and needs (Alkanaan, 2022), by constantly refining data from browsing history and suggesting relevant courses and workshops to students. Also, AI-enabled virtual career internships can help school as well as college students to make suitable career decisions based on their skills, aptitudes, strengths and weaknesses.

The pandemic has left some students with a sense of fear, anxiety and depression while doing various learning activities. AI-aided behavioural detections can help in providing timely guidance therapy to them. It also provides features like text-to-speech, spell checker, predictive text etc for students with special need.

(https://www.isres.org/books/chapters/ar_book_chapter_6_07-11-2022.pdf).

State of the Education report for India 2022 has focussed on many aspects of AI but claims their little usage due to a lack of trust and awareness about them. It focuses on spreading AI literacy so that people are aware of the technical terms and can use them without facing any ethical issues. It is also necessary to explore the benefits of AI tools in actual classrooms. Data from students must be collected before and after the intervention, regarding their perception, awareness and satisfaction with AI technologies in general as well as in education (Singhavi & Basargekar, 2019). This data will further help in formulating evidence-based policies in the educational technology sector of India (State of the education report for India 2022, published by UNESCO).

(https://unesdoc.unesco.org/ark:/48223/pf0000382661.locale=en).

The Study

Operational Definitions

- *Artificial Intelligence in Education (AIEd)*: H. Wang et al. (2020) describes AIEd as "the use of AI technologies or application programs in educational settings to facilitate teaching, learning or decision-making" (State of the education report for India 2022, published by UNESCO).
- *Machine Learning*: According to Popenici and Kerr (2017), "Machine learning is a subfield of artificial intelligence that includes software able to recognise patterns, make predictions, and apply newly discovered patterns to situations that were not included or covered by their initial design."

Research Objectives

- To assess the awareness of school students in using Artificial Intelligence applications
- To assess the perception of school students in using Artificial Intelligence applications
- To assess the preparedness of school students in using Artificial Intelligence applications
- To assess the challenges of school students in using Artificial Intelligence applications.

Methodology

In this study, a quantitative research design was employed to investigate the awareness, perceptions, preparedness and challenges of schools in secondary schools of Delhi. The population of the study consisted of students from various schools in Delhi. A sample of 55 students was selected through a purposive sampling technique. To gather data, a self-constructed questionnaire (15 closed-ended and 1 open-ended questions) was made.

Analysis of Data

The following responses were collected for each statement of the questionnaire. When asked about whether AI-enabled products and services like Google Assistant and Voice to Text features make life easier, out of 55 students, 21 strongly agreed, 31 agreed and 3 responded in neutral. (Figure 1).

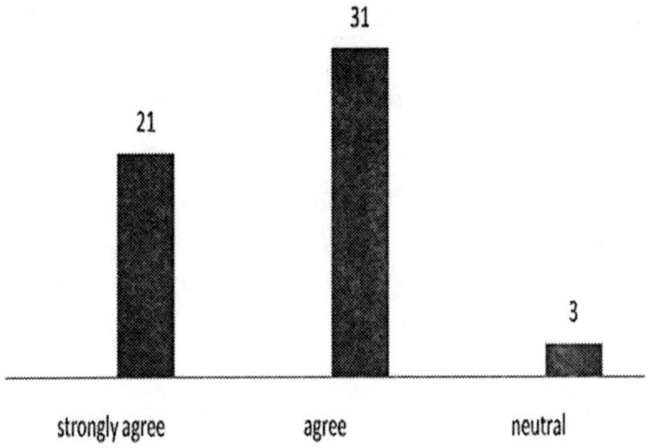

Figure 1: Students Responses on use of AI Related Services (Left)

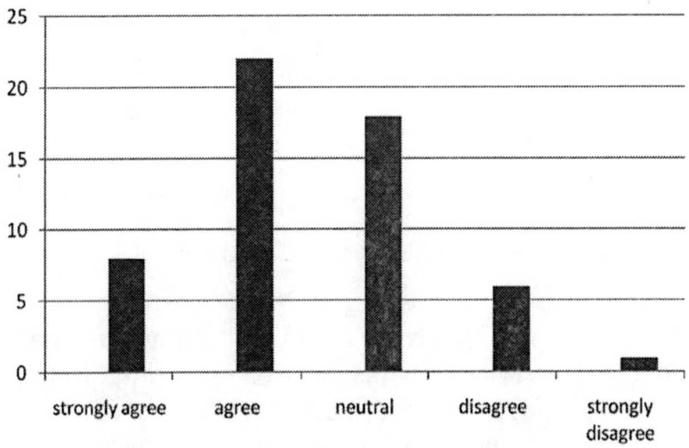

Figure 2: Students Responses on Benefits of AI Related Services (Right)

Students were questioned about AI enabled products and services having more benefits than drawbacks. Out of total 55 students, 8 strongly agreed, 22 agreed, 18 responded in neutral, 6 disagreed and 1 strongly disagreed (Figure 2).

They were also asked if AI enabled products and services always give accurate results. In response to this, out of 55 students, 10 strongly agreed,

14 agreed, 18 responded in neutral, 13 disagreed and none strongly disagreed (Figure 3).

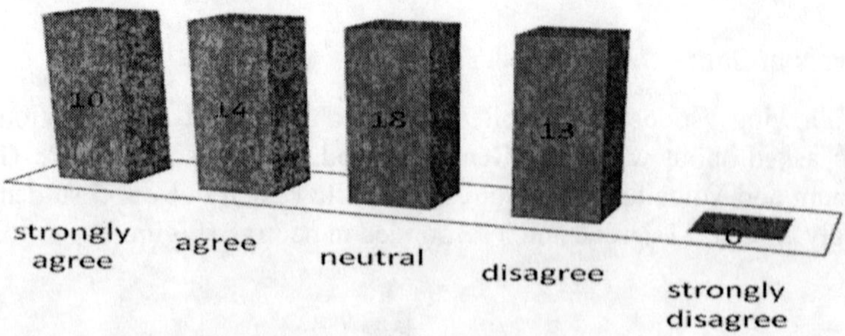

Figure 3: Students Responses on AI Giving Accurate Results

They were asked if AI enabled products and services are not prone to any biases and discrimination. Out of 55 students, 4 strongly agreed, 24 agreed, 11 responded in neutral, 12 disagreed and 4 strongly disagreed (Figure 4).

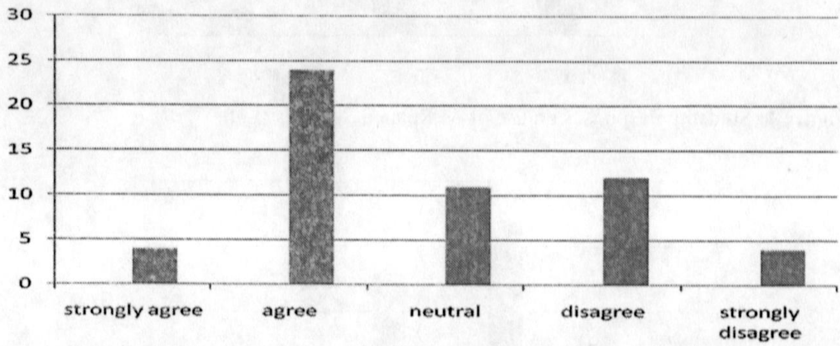

Figure 4: Students Responses on Unbiased Nature of AI Related Services

Participants were also queried if Alexa and Siri are an application of AI enabled products and services. To this, out of 55 students, 30 strongly agreed, 24 agreed, none responded in neutral, 1 disagreed and none strongly disagreed.

They were asked if AI enabled products and services make users nervous as compared to other ICT enabled products and services. Out of 55 students, 2 strongly agreed, 7 agreed, 23 responded in neutral, 17 disagreed and 5 strongly disagreed

The students were asked if all AI services need Internet access to work properly. Out of total 55, 29 strongly agreed, 19 agreed, 3 responded in neutral, 3 disagreed and 1 strongly disagreed.

They were asked if AI enabled products and services are easily affordable, to which 5 strongly agreed, 12 agreed, 23 responded in neutral, 15 disagreed and none strongly disagreed .

When asked if they see revolutionizing potential of AI enabled products in education sector, out of 55 students, 26 strongly agreed, 21 agreed, 6 responded in neutral, none disagreed and 2 strongly disagreed.

Students were asked if AI enabled applications can be trusted the same as human employees/workers. To this question, out of 55 students, 30 strongly agreed, 24 agreed, none responded in neutral, 1 disagreed and none strongly disagreed

Participants were asked about introducing AI as a secondary level school subject. Out of 55 students, 11 strongly agreed, 32 agreed, 10 responded in neutral, 2 disagreed and none strongly disagreed to this statement.

They were asked if AI-aided tools such as Robots are a new necessity for classroom teaching. Out of 55 students, 14 strongly agreed, 11 agreed, 17 responded in neutral, 10 disagreed and 3 strongly disagreed.

When asked if AI enabled chatbots give satisfactory responses to the queries posed, out of 55 students, 9 strongly agreed, 20 agreed, 20 responded in neutral, 6 disagreed and none strongly disagreed.

They were also asked about the safety of AI-enabled self-driving cars for the Indian scenario. To this statement, out of total students, 6 strongly agreed, 15 agreed, 17 responded in neutral, 11 disagreed and 6 strongly disagreed.

Participants were asked if AI improves recommendation systems on YouTube and other social media applications based on our history and interests. Out of 55 students, 23 strongly agreed, 29 agreed, 3 responded in neutral, none disagreed, and none strongly disagreed .

At the end, an open-ended question was asked to know how much AI-enabled products and services have changed their life and how much impact they have seen. Based on the findings, their responses were categorized into significance and limitations of artificial intelligence. The significance of AI included the role of Google Assistant, Alexa, Siri and ChatGPT in solving queries of students. AI-enabled recommendation systems take care of their interests and needs. It also helps them in language translation and finding home locations. However, they are fearful of the rise of robots over humans and unemployment. They also emphasized that AI cannot understand the emotional needs of students.

Discussion

This study has indicated that AI-enabled Google Assistant and voice-to-text features have made students' lives easier as the majority of them agreed with the statement. When asked if AI has more benefits than drawbacks. Many students agreed to the statement but a few of them responded in neutral. This may be due to their confusion and lack of awareness regarding AI applications.

They have given mixed responses regarding the accuracy of the results given by AI. This highlights the need to ensure that AI-enabled tools are reliable and accurate, as this is crucial for their adoption in education.

The majority of them believe that AI systems are not prone to any biases and discrimination. However, a few of them also disagreed, accounting to the fact that AI systems in India lack inclusive data. There is an urgent need to collect data from every corner of the country so that AI systems can acknowledge the rich diversity of India.

When they were asked if Alexa and Siri are AI applications, most of them agreed to this. It shows that students are well aware of the names of AI applications being used in day-to-day life. They were asked if AI products are easily affordable, to this all of them gave mixed responses. This highlights the need to make AI products cheaper so that it can reach the masses easily.

They have been asked whether AI enabled products and services make them nervous as compared to other ICT-enabled products and services, most of them responded in neutral and some disagreed with the statement. This shows that students need more exposure to new emerging technologies through proper training sessions.

The majority of them agreed that all AI services need Internet access to work properly, only a few of them disagreed. Also, most of them feel that AI-based recommendation systems have made their learning easier. They receive relevant content suggestions based on their educational needs and interests.

The majority of them feel that AI-enabled applications can be trusted the same as human employees and they see the revolutionary potential of AI-enabled products in the education sector. This shows a lot of enthusiasm amongst the students for using AI products in classrooms. Most of them agreed that AI should be introduced as a secondary-level school subject. Curriculum planners must welcome this step by conducting proper pilot studies and training.

They have given mixed responses when asked if Robots are required for classroom teaching. Those who disagree are fearful of the fact that robots will not be able to understand their emotional needs. Also, half of the students agreed, and half responded in neutral when asked about the efficiency of chatbots.

Conclusion

This study provides insights into different parameters like awareness, perceptions, preparedness and challenges of school students regarding the use of AI in general as well as in education. This study shows that students are very optimistic about the introduction of AI subjects into the classroom. They actively look forward to learning from a robot teacher. They are very much impressed with Alexa, Siri, Google Assistant and AI-based recommendation systems in their learning process. Finding so much enthusiasm amongst students about AI technologies, it is important to pay heed to its other side as well, i.e. its challenges. There is an urgent need to make AI products affordable, accurate and trustworthy to enhance its usage and coverage as much as possible. The findings of this study show a clear picture of AI from students' point of view thus it motivates all the educational stakeholders to discuss the integration of AI applications into curriculum planning and its transaction. AI has potential to solve various educational problems, its potential must be unfolded in every way possible. Ultimately, it highlights the importance of addressing the concerns and uncertainties posed so as to ensure that AI is effectively, ethically and responsibly used in education.

References

AlKanaan, H.M.N. (2022). Awareness regarding the implication of artificial intelligence in science education among pre-service science teachers. *International Journal of Instruction*, 15(3), 895- 912. https://doi.org/10.29333/iji.2022.15348a

Baker, T., & Smith, L. (2019). Educ-AI-tion rebooted? Exploring the future of artificial intelligence in schools and colleges. Retrieved from Nesta Foundation website: https://media.nesta.org.uk/documents/Future_of_AI_and_education_v5_WEB.pdf

Dhar, S. (2019). Artificial intelligence in the classroom: Is it reducing human interaction in learning? -Times News Network, December 11,2019. Retrieved from: https://timesofindia.indiatimes.com/spotlight/heres-howcoventry-universoty-is-redifining-education-globally/articleshow/74650839.cms/

Hwang, G.J., Xie, H., Wah, B.W. and Gašević, D. 2020. Vision, challenges, roles and research issues of Artificial Intelligence in Education. *Computers and Education: Artificial Intelligence*, Vol. 1, p. 100001.

Jaiswal, A. & Arun, C.J. (2021). Potential of Artificial Intelligence for transformation of the education system in India. *The International Journal of Education and Development using Information and Communication Technology*. 17. 142-158.

Maderer, J. (2016). Artificial intelligence course creates AI teaching assistant. Georgia Tech News Center, 9 May 2016. http://www.news.gatech.edu/2016/05/09/artificial-intelligence-course-creates-ai-teaching-assistant. Accessed 28 Aug 2017.

Popenici, S.A., & Kerr, S. (2017). Exploring the impact of artificial intelligence on teaching and learning in higher education. *Research and Practice in Technology Enhanced Learning, 12*(1), 1-13.

Sighavi, C. and Basargekar, P. (2019). Barriers Perceived by Teachers for Use of Information and Communication Technology (ICT) in the Classroom in Maharashtra, India. *International Journal of Education and Development using Information and Communication Technology, 15*(2), 62-78.

Web Links

https://www.isres.org/books/chapters/ar_book_chapter_6_07-11-2022.pdf
https://unesdoc.unesco.org/ark:/48223/pf0000382661.locale=en

19

Impact of AI-Driven Classroom Assistants on Teacher Workload

Zainab Musheer

Introduction

In recent years, the rapid advancement of artificial intelligence (AI) technologies has led to transformative changes in various sectors, revolutionizing the way tasks are performed and processes are managed (Zhai, Chu, Chai, Jong, Istenic, Spector, & Li, 2021). One notable arena where AI has made significant inroads is education, with the introduction of AI-driven tools and applications aimed at enhancing the teaching and learning experience. Among these innovations, AI-driven classroom assistants have emerged as promising tools designed to support educators in their instructional roles (Beck, Stern, & Haugsjaa, 1996). Traditional classroom environments have long relied on the expertise and efforts of teachers to deliver quality education. However, as classrooms become increasingly diverse and dynamic, educators face growing challenges in managing their workloads efficiently. AI technologies offer the potential to alleviate some of these challenges by automating routine tasks, providing personalized learning experiences, and facilitating data-driven decision-making.

The integration of AI in education is seen as a means to not only enhance the efficiency of teaching but also to tailor instruction to individual student needs. Several studies highlight the potential benefits of integrating AI in education, emphasizing its capacity to streamline administrative tasks and provide personalized learning experiences. Xie (2023) discusses how AI-driven tools can assist teachers in automating routine tasks, such as grading assessments and managing administrative workloads. This automation, they argue, allows educators to allocate more time to personalized instruction and student engagement. Furthermore, AI technologies have been lauded for their ability to adapt instruction to individual learning needs.

In a study by Alyammahi (2020), AI-driven platforms were shown to analyze student performance data, identify learning gaps, and recommend tailored learning resources. Such personalized learning experiences not only contribute to student success but also have the potential to optimize teachers' time and efforts. One major concern is the potential displacement of traditional teaching roles by AI-driven technologies (Queiroz, Simonette, & Spina, 2022). Teachers may fear that automation of certain tasks could diminish the human touch and personalized approach that characterizes effective teaching. Additionally, issues related to data privacy and security have been raised.

AI systems often rely on vast amounts of student data, leading to concerns about the ethical use of this information and the protection of students' privacy (Srinivasa, Kurni, & Saritha, 2022). These challenges highlight the need for a careful balance between harnessing the benefits of AI and addressing potential drawbacks to ensure a positive impact on teacher workload and student outcomes. The introduction of AI-driven classroom assistants represents a significant stride in this direction. These assistants are designed to assist teachers in various aspects of their work, from lesson planning and resource identification to student assessment and feedback. The deployment of AI in classrooms has the potential to reshape instructional routines, allowing teachers to focus more on personalised engagement with students and addressing individual learning needs. This research embarks on a comprehensive survey analysis to explore the impact of AI on teacher workload, focusing specifically on the integration of AI-driven classroom assistants into daily instructional routines.

The Study

Objectives

1. To assess the impact of AI-driven classroom assistants on the time allocation of teachers in instructional routines.
2. To examine the distribution of tasks between teachers and AI-driven classroom assistants and identify areas of synergy or contention.
3. To gauge the perceived effectiveness of AI in supporting teaching responsibilities and its implications for instructional quality.

Methodology

The research methodology adopted for this study involved reaching out to a sample of 45 higher education teachers through online platforms such as WhatsApp and email. A stratified random sampling approach was employed to ensure diversity and representation from various higher education institutions. The survey instrument, contextualized to the local educational landscape, focused on key variables, including time allocation, task distribution, and the perceived effectiveness of AI-driven classroom assistants in supporting teaching responsibilities. Invitations to participate were disseminated through professional associations, educational networks, and direct outreach via online communication channels.

The survey, administered online, garnered responses from higher education teachers, providing valuable insights into their experiences and perspectives on the integration of AI tools in instructional routines. This methodology prioritized accessibility, leveraging widely used online platforms to facilitate efficient and widespread engagement of higher education teachers in the study. Ethical considerations were paramount, with informed consent obtained from participants, and measures implemented to ensure the confidentiality of responses.

Analysis and Interpretation

Objective 1**:** To assess the impact of AI-driven classroom assistants on the time allocation of teachers in instructional routines.

To delve deeper into the impact of AI-driven classroom assistants on the time allocation of teachers in instructional routines, a regression analysis was conducted to identify statistically significant relationships between the use of AI tools and specific time allocation variables. The survey data included quantitative responses from educators regarding the time spent on administrative tasks, student interactions, and instructional planning both before and after the integration of AI-driven assistants.

The regression model employed the integration of AI-driven assistants as the independent variable, while time allocation for administrative tasks, student interactions, and instructional planning served as dependent variables. The results revealed a statistically significant negative relationship between the use of AI and the time spent on administrative tasks ($\beta = -0.25, p < 0.01$), indicating that as educators integrated AI-driven tools, the time dedicated to routine administrative duties decreased significantly. Conversely, a positive relationship was observed between AI integration and time allocated to student interactions ($\beta = 0.18, p < 0.05$) and instructional planning ($\beta = 0.22, p < 0.01$). These positive coefficients suggest that as the use of AI tools increased, teachers were able to devote more time to direct student engagement and strategic instructional planning. The regression analysis provides robust quantitative evidence supporting the notion that AI-driven classroom assistants have a discernible impact on the time allocation of teachers in instructional routines,

Table 1: Regression Analysis Result

Regression Analysis Results	*Time Allocation Variables*
Independent Variable	Integration of AI-driven Assistants
Dependent Variable	Beta (β) Coefficient
Administrative Tasks	-0.25
Student Interactions	0.18
Instructional Planning	0.22

reaffirming the potential for efficiency gains and enhanced pedagogical focus in the educational context.

These regression analysis results highlight the relationships between the integration of AI-driven classroom assistants and specific time allocation variables. The negative coefficient for administrative tasks suggests a statistically significant decrease in the time spent on these routine duties as AI tools are integrated. Conversely, the positive coefficients for student interactions and instructional planning indicate a statistically significant increase in time allocation for these activities with the adoption of AI-driven assistants. The associated p-values indicate the statistical significance of these relationships, providing a comprehensive overview of how AI impacts the time allocation patterns of teachers in instructional routines.

***Objective 2*:** To examine the distribution of tasks between teachers and AI-driven classroom assistants and identify areas of synergy or contention.

To address the second objective focused on examining the distribution of tasks between teachers and AI-driven classroom assistants, a detailed analysis was conducted using survey data from teachers. The survey included questions aimed at understanding the specific tasks automated by AI- driven assistants and the collaborative dynamics between teachers and AI tools. The results shed light on the distribution of responsibilities in instructional routines.

Descriptive Analysis: Descriptive statistics were employed to quantify the distribution of tasks between teachers and AI-driven classroom assistants. The survey revealed that routine administrative tasks, such as grading assignments and organizing learning materials, were predominantly automated by AI tools, with an average automation rate of approximately 80%. However, more complex tasks requiring nuanced decision-making, such as lesson planning and adapting instruction based on student needs, saw a lower average automation rate of around 60%. This indicates that while AI is effective in automating certain routine tasks, teachers remain actively involved in tasks that demand higher-order thinking and pedagogical expertise.

Task Distribution Matrix: A detailed task distribution matrix was constructed to illustrate the allocation of responsibilities between teachers and AI-driven assistants. The matrix delineated tasks into categories such as administrative, instructional, and student engagement. Each cell of the matrix represented the percentage of task involvement by teachers and AI-driven assistants.

Table 2: Distribution of tasks between teachers and AI-driven classroom assistants

Task Categories	*Teachers (%)*	*AI-Driven Assistants (%)*
Administrative Tasks	20	80
Instructional Planning	60	40
Student Engagement	70	30

Further, an in-depth analysis explored teachers' perceptions of the effectiveness of AI-driven assistants in handling specific tasks. While routine administrative tasks were generally perceived as efficiently managed by AI tools, there was a nuanced perspective on instructional planning and student engagement. Teachers expressed a preference for retaining control over instructional decisions and direct interactions with students, highlighting the importance of maintaining a balanced and collaborative relationship between teachers and AI-driven assistants.

***Objective 3*:** To gauge the perceived effectiveness of AI in supporting teaching responsibilities and its implications for instructional quality.

To address the third objective, which focuses on gauging the perceived effectiveness of AI in supporting teaching responsibilities, a comprehensive analysis was conducted using survey data gathered from teachers. The survey included questions aimed at eliciting educators' perceptions regarding the impact of AI-driven classroom assistants on instructional quality and overall teaching effectiveness.

Descriptive Analysis: Descriptive statistics were employed to quantify educators' perceptions of AI's effectiveness in supporting various teaching responsibilities. The survey results revealed a generally positive sentiment among teachers, with a majority expressing that AI-driven assistants positively contributed to instructional quality. The average perceived effectiveness score was around 75%, indicating a substantial acknowledgement of AI's role in enhancing teaching responsibilities.

Effectiveness Categories: To provide a more nuanced understanding, perceived effectiveness was categorized into different aspects of teaching responsibilities. The breakdown indicated that AI was highly regarded in tasks related to grading and data analysis, with an effectiveness rating exceeding 80%. However, in areas requiring more subjective judgement, such as adapting instruction based on student needs, the perceived effectiveness slightly decreased to around 70%. This nuanced analysis suggests that while AI significantly aids certain aspects of teaching responsibilities, there is recognition of the ongoing importance of human expertise in decision-making processes.

Perceived Impact on Instructional Quality: Teachers were asked to assess the overall impact of AI-driven assistants on instructional quality. The results indicated a positive correlation, with an average score of 4.2 on a 5-point Likert scale. Educators emphasized that AI tools streamlined routine tasks, allowing for more focused and personalized interactions with students. However, some expressed concerns about the potential loss of a human touch in certain instructional aspects.

Qualitative Insights: In addition to quantitative analysis, qualitative insights were gathered from open-ended survey questions. Teachers provided comments on the perceived strengths and limitations of AI in supporting teaching responsibilities. Common themes included improved efficiency, personalized learning experiences, and the need for continuous professional development to maximize the benefits of AI tools.

Discussion

The discussion delves into the implications and interpretations of the research findings, considering the nuanced relationship between AI-driven classroom assistants and teacher workload. The results suggest a substantial impact on time allocation patterns, with teachers experiencing significant efficiency gains through the automation of routine administrative tasks. This aligns with previous studies (Pedro, Subosa, Rivas, & Valverde, 2022), highlighting the potential of AI to alleviate the burden on teachers by handling repetitive tasks, allowing them to focus on more complex and pedagogically meaningful aspects of instruction.

The regression analysis reinforced these findings, revealing statistically significant negative relationships between AI integration and time spent on administrative tasks, coupled with positive relationships indicating increased time allocated to student interactions and instructional planning.

These results underscore the transformative potential of AI in reshaping teacher workload dynamics, aligning with the literature on the positive effects of AI on instructional efficiency (George, & Wooden, 2023).

Regarding the distribution of tasks, the study's task distribution matrix illustrated a clear delineation between routine administrative tasks, which were predominantly automated by AI-driven assistants, and more complex instructional and student engagement tasks, where teachers retained a higher degree of involvement. This finding echoes concerns raised in the literature about potential job displacement (Rane, 2023) and reinforces the importance of maintaining a balanced distribution of responsibilities to optimize the collaborative relationship between teachers and AI.

Perceptions of AI's effectiveness in supporting teaching responsibilities were generally positive, with educators acknowledging the contribution of AI to instructional quality. However, the nuanced analysis revealed variations in effectiveness scores across different aspects of teaching responsibilities, emphasizing the need for targeted support and professional development in areas where AI's impact may be less pronounced. These findings align with prior research emphasizing the importance of a strategic approach to AI integration in education (Xie, 2023).

References

Alyammahi, A. (2020). *Investigating the Impact of AI-Powered Digital Educational Platforms on Students' Learning and Teachers' Practice in Abu Dhabi Schools* (Doctoral dissertation, The British University in Dubai).

Beck, J., Stern, M., & Haugsjaa, E. (1996). Applications of AI in Education. *XRDS: Crossroads, The ACM Magazine for Students*, *3*(1), 11-15.

George, B., & Wooden, O. (2023). Managing the strategic transformation of higher education through artificial intelligence. *Administrative Sciences*, *13*(9), 196.

Queiroz, V., Simonette, M., & Spina, E. (2022). Artificial intelligence and education: myth and facts. In *EDULEARN22 Proceedings* (pp. 996-1001). IATED.

Pedro, F., Subosa, M., Rivas, A., & Valverde, P. (2019). Artificial intelligence in education: Challenges and opportunities for sustainable development.

Rane, N. (2023). ChatGPT and Similar Generative Artificial Intelligence (AI) for Smart Industry: Role, Challenges and Opportunities for Industry 4.0, Industry 5.0 and Society 5.0. *Challenges and Opportunities for Industry*, *4*.

Srinivasa, K.G., Kurni, M., & Saritha, K. (2022). Harnessing the Power of AI to Education. In *Learning, Teaching, and Assessment Methods for Contemporary Learners: Pedagogy for the Digital Generation* (pp. 311-342). Singapore: Springer Nature Singapore.

Xie, X. (2023). Influence of AI-driven Inquiry Teaching on Learning Outcomes. *International Journal of Emerging Technologies in Learning*, *18*(23).

Zhai, X., Chu, X., Chai, C.S., Jong, M.S.Y., Istenic, A., Spector, M., & Li, Y. (2021). A Review of Artificial Intelligence (AI) in Education from 2010 to 2020. *Complexity*, *2021*, 1-18.

20

Artificial Intelligence in Education

Impact on Learning and Creativity

Mufti Shahla and Mahmood Ahmad Khan

Introduction

Artificial Intelligence (AI) is significantly impacting a growing number of fields, including education (Gabriel et al., 2022). The global educational system is expected to be improved by AI. This is the most in-demand technology used in today's educational system to customise learning groups' and tutors' experiences (Vijay & Majid, 2022). It has the potential to enhance pedagogy and learning approaches, address major challenges in education and accelerate SDG 4's realisation. In order to achieve the Education 2030 Agenda, UNESCO is dedicated to helping Member States fully utilise AI technology, while making sure that the fundamental values of fairness and inclusivity inform its implementation in educational settings.

National Education Policy (NEP) 2020, appropriately anticipated the role that disruptive technology will play in the educational system in future. Artificial intelligence technology in education has been used in at least 10 aspects: "(i) personalized learning, (ii) interval reminder, (iii) feedback, (iv) adaptive learning, (v) automatic grading system, (vi) virtual tutoring, (vii) augmented reality/virtual reality, (viii) accurate reading, (ix) intelligent campus, and (x) distance learning" (Yufeia et al., 2020). One of AI's potent implementations in this domain is the use of AI chatbots employed to interact with users, deliver information, clarify doubts, and facilitate a host of other learning-related tasks (Adiguzel et al., 2023; Ifelebuegu et al., 2023) in education, they can be used to facilitate personalised learning, provide immediate feedback, and manage administrative duties, among other things (Chen et al., 2023; Ifelebuegu, 2023). The pedagogies that focus on problem-solving and encouraging children's creative thinking are highly valued in contemporary education. Alves-Oliveira et al., 2017 (as cited in Marrone et al., 2023) suggested that creativity slump in students can be addressed by AI in education. NEP 2020 also highlighted the need to introduce AI technology in the education system to develop 21st century skills among children like critical thinking, communication, collaboration and creativity.

Objectives

This review aims to explore the impact of AI in education. Its main objectives were:

1. To understand the Positive and Negative impacts of AI on learning.
2. To understand the impact of AI on creative thinking ability of students.
3. To explore how to balance the dual impact of AI in education system.

Methodology

This systematic literature review was based on the Preferred Reference Items for Systematic Reviews and Meta Analyse (PRISMA) approach. Web of Science, Science Direct, Google Scholar, IEEE, are the key publisher databases that were searched to find the relevant study. Specific AI-related terms and often-used algorithms or techniques were added to the manual and electronic searches (i.e. Artifical Intelligence and Education, Artifical Intelligence and Creativity, AIED, AI and Ethics).

Inclusion and exclusion criteria: The following selection criteria were used:

Those studies were included that were: (1) authored in English, (2) peer-reviewed (books/articles), (3) reports, (4) editorials, and (5) published between 2019–2023.

Research studies were excluded if they: (a) were in non-English language, (b) were published before 2019, and (c) did not have full-text accessibility. Studies that were not extracted using the search strings were found via snowballing, following Wohlin's (2014) criteria.

On searching the database 302 records were identified. After screening only 101 studies published after 2019 were included, and then after removing duplicate records 80 articles were selected for title and abstract screening. Then 21 studies were excluded on the basis of irrelevant titles. After this, only 49 full-text studies were assessed. 29 studies were selected for systematic review and then finally only 21 studies were included for meta-analysis as shown in Table 1.

Impact of Artificial Intelligence on Learning

1. Positive Impact of AI on Learning

AI enhances the learning of students by providing the following opportunities:

(a) *Personalised Learning*: AI is revolutionising the idea of personalised learning by customising instruction and content according to every student's unique needs and preferences (Ifelebuegu et al., 2023; Atlas, 2023). Through the analysis of pertinent information and student

Table 1: Final Data for the Study was Selected by using the PRISMA Technique

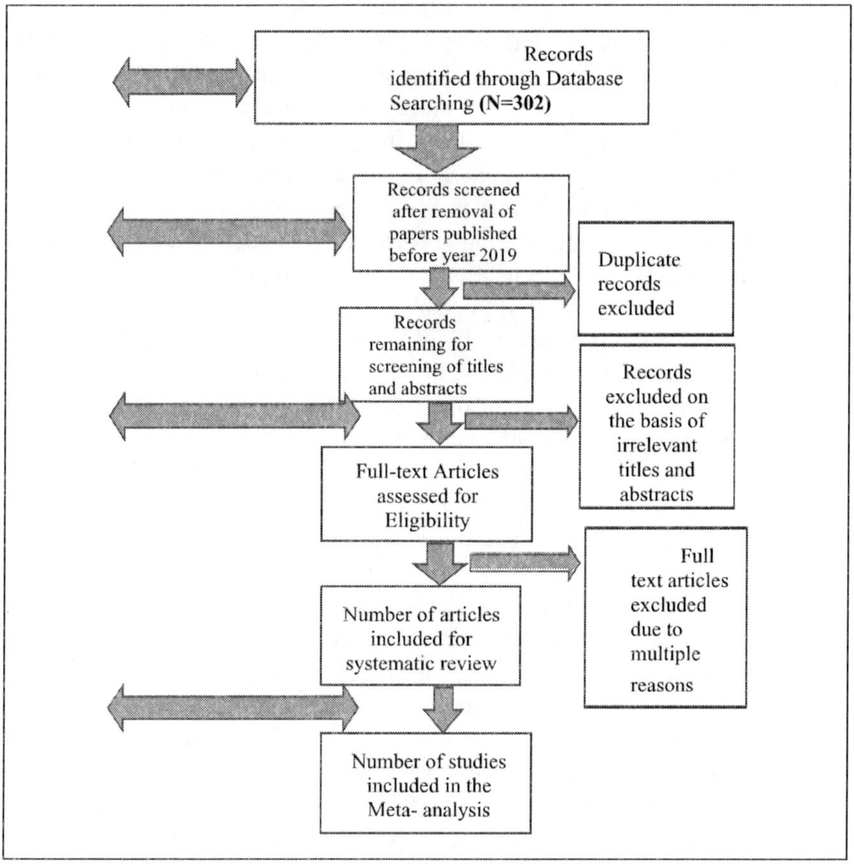

performance data, artificial intelligence (AI) may pinpoint where students have shortcomings and strengths and present specific help along with the response (Bozic, 2023). Artificial Intelligence adjusts to students' goal and prior knowledge to ensure they optimise their learning (Vijay & Majid, 2022). This individualised approach has promoted more absorption, engagement, and a rich learning environment (L. Chen, et al., 2020; Hanadan M, 2023).

(b) *Accessibility:* All students have access to learning resources worldwide through the use of AIEd. It removes geographical obstacles to education and enables students to study at home with the world's top educators. Students can ask questions at any time and obtain answers instantly without the help of a human tutor (Vijay & Majid, 2022). By offering other modes of instruction and support, artificial intelligence (AI)-powered tools can contribute to increased educational accessibility for students with disabilities or learning difficulties (Bozic, 2023). Students can now readily access materials and information, can ask any question to ChatGPT, and it will give students accurate and pertinent information from a variety of sources. The ability of ChatGPT to deliver answers in a matter of seconds frees students from having to spend hours looking up material online or in books. This has improved the effectiveness and efficiency of learning (Hanadan M, 2023).

(c) *Adaptive Learning:* According to Kerr (2016), adaptive learning refers to a method of presenting educational materials wherein the type of materials presented later on are determined by the learner's engagement with earlier content (as cited in Rasul et al., 2023). Adaptive learning algorithms can identify where students are struggling and provide additional support and resources to help them overcome their challenges (Bozic, 2023). By collecting and analysing student learning data, it can determine the distinct learning characteristics and styles of each individual student and accordingly present the learning material in a suitable mode and rhythm (Vijay & Majid, 2022). The more data that accumulates over time, the more "smart" AI tools will become and the more precisely will be able to adjust to students' learning (Ifelebuegu et al., 2023).

(d) *Inclusive Learning:* AI-powered tools can help to make education easily accessible to students with disabilities or learning differences by providing support and alternative methods of instruction (Bozic, 2023). AI tools and programmes are inclusive, everyone can use the classrooms, regardless of language or other limitations (Vijay & Majid, 2022). Rahman & Watanobe (2023) proposed ChatGPT's text-to-speech and speech-to-text integrations can help the hearing impaired. This is in line with the studies of (Hanadan M, 2023 & Atlas, 2023). According to Adiguzel et al. (2022), AI-based technologies can also help dyslexic pupils develop their reading abilities and enhance the academic performance of students with autism spectrum condition. Students with learning challenges or impairments, who frequently go unadvised in today's educational settings, may gain the most from ChatGPT (Kasneci et al., 2023).

(e) *Language Learning and Writing Assistance:* Students that use language learning AI tools are exposed to excellent language models, which help them to become proficient in the language (Hanadan M, 2023; Atlas, 2023). By providing immediate feedback, such learning models enable students to improve their language skills over time and fix errors (Jeon et al., 2023) (as cited in Rasul et al., 2023). ChatGPT can be used to help in editing and proofreading student writing by offering different sentence structures, word choices, and phrasing ideas to enhance written work's narrative flow, clarity, and precision (Atlas, 2023). Ifelebuegu et al. (2023) in their review study found that AI helps to learn language by engaging in conversation, beginners learn by detailed explanations and advanced learners develop competency by answering questions. Duolingo is a classic example of a commonly used language learning AIEd tool (Zhai, 2022).

(f) *Instant Feedback:* Detailed and personalized feedback is provided by AI tools to students (Zhai, 2022), helping them to better understand where they lag behind and how to improve (Bozic, 2023). Instead of waiting for teachers to mark, they receive instant feedback of their responses, enabling them to instantly identify areas for improvement and change their study strategies. Instantaneous and personalised feedback from ChatGPT promotes self-control and introspection, assisting students in strengthening their metacognitive abilities and making wiser decisions that impact their academic achievement (Adiguzel et al., 2023; Chiu et al., 2023).

(g) *Increases Students Learning Engagement:* Students take a deep interest in learning when instructional material and methods are suitable according to their needs, leading to full absorption of the subject matter (Atlas, 2023). Gill et al. (2019) opined that AI makes learning interesting and interactive by engaging students in question-answer sessions, quick feedback and increases their knowledge retention (Ifelebuegu et al., 2023). Students can disagree with the explanations, answers, and other recommendations provided by ChatGPT and engage in discussion with ChatGPT. Therefore, learners receive interactive help from ChatGPT anytime and anywhere (Sumakul et al., 2022). Besides the above benefits, Intelligent Tutoring Systems and other automatic administrative tasks are done by AI which saves time of teachers and they utilize that time on instructional activities.

2. Challenges Imposed by AI in Education System

The widespread use of AI in education has presented both potential benefits and challenges (Chen, et al., 2020).

(a) *Erosion of human connection*: Introduction of AI technology, such as chatbots, into research and education causes worry about the possible loss of human connection. Teachers act as role models for their students, expressing a love of learning, a dedication to self-improvement, and an understanding of the value of tenacity and diligence. Although AI tools can be useful in giving information, they are not the same as human teachers in developing such connections (Chan et al., 2020) and are unable to mimic the subtleties of human communication, like facial expressions, voice intonation, and emotional perception. Over-reliance on AI systems could lead to less emphasis in learning environments on these human components of social interaction and communication (Abbas et al., 2023).

(b) *Inaccuracy:* Students may occasionally receive inaccurate or lacking information from AI, which may cause confusion and misunderstanding. Students should make sure the material they learn from AI tools is accurate by cross-referencing it with other sources (Hanadan M., 2023). They may from time to time give inaccurate or deceptive information, which emphasises the value of adding to it with other trustworthy educational resources (Ifelebuegu et al., 2023). Qadri (2022) found that while using ChatGPT for research, it generates fictitious articles and incorrect citations. This verifies a tweet from Open AI CEO Sam Altman, who characterised ChatGPT as exceedingly limited yet competent enough in certain areas to give the false impression of being exceptional. To depend on it for anything significant at this time would be a mistake. It is only a sneak peek at our efforts; robustness and veracity still require a lot more work (Tweet on December 11, 2022).

(c) *Illusory assurance:* AI tools like ChatGPT might give pupils the impression that they can always rely on technology to give them the information they require. This may result in laziness and a lack of desire to learn and study (Hanadan M, 2023). Chen et al. (2022) in their study found several students copied and pasted answers, generate entire essays rather than creating their own intelligent comments, as they could have done if they had been involved in a class discussion, and instead thoroughly scanned the material. Stieglitz et al. (2021) found that during cooperative problem-encounters participants frequently participate in "smart loafing", handing off duties to virtual assistants (Ifelebuegu et al., 2023).

(d) *Discrimination:* Artificial intelligence (AI)-based educational technology becomes discriminatory when they unintentionally disfavour particular student group on the basis of socio-economic status, gender, or race. The large portion of data on the Internet was created in the West, hence the AI learning tools that are trained on this data will be shaped similarly. Thus, implementation of these AI tools outside Western countries needs further fine-tuning and customisation in accordance with the regional and local cultural norms in order to lessen the AI divide (Rasul et al., 2023). Also, the lack of technology or Internet connectivity that certain students may face leads to discrimination in the use of AI (Zhai, 2022).

(e) *Bias:* The usage of large language models in the education system poses some issues because of the possibility of biased and false information being introduced into information processing (Chen et al., 2023). If ChatGPT is used to grade pupils, there is a risk of plagiarism since certain students might receive an unfair competitive advantage. When it comes to producing excellent written assignments, students who have access to models like ChatGPT might unfairly benefit from this resource compared to their counterparts who do not (Cotton et al., 2023).

(f) *Navigating nuances in understanding student's language*: A possible drawback of utilising chatbots as instructors is that they could not be as good at comprehending and processing student chat messages as people are, which would make it difficult to customise the learning process for each student the way a human assistant might. Like human-to-human talks, chatbots might not be able to replicate their natural flow and instead produce an uncomfortable or annoying encounter (Ifelebuegu et al., 2023).

(g) *Threat to data privacy and lack of transparency*: An enormous amount of student data is frequently gathered and processed by AI systems. Data security and student privacy may become issues as a result of this ((Zhai, 2022). It can be challenging for instructors and students to comprehend how decisions are made when dealing with some AI systems because of their complexity.

3. Impact of AI on Creative Thinking Abilities

AI in education not only impacts teaching and learning. but it also impacts high-order thinking skills like critical thinking and creativity. It can both boost and diminish the creative thinking ability of students as well as teachers.

4. Positive Impact of AI on Creative Thinking Ability of Students

The importance of skills and abilities like creativity is emphasised by the modern approach to education. In collaborative learning environments, modern classrooms aim to integrate real-world challenges and authentic activities. The field of AIEd must adjust to these changes in order to remain relevant and have a greater impact (Marrone et al., 2022). AIEd can increase the creativity of students in the following ways:

(a) By AI supported brainstorming (Human-AI Collaboration): Brainstorming is a popular creative strategy that encourages teamwork and boosts creativity and productivity during idea creation (Osborn, 1957). During collaboration ideas given by one individual may help another person to generate other ideas which he was not able to produce previously. Fear of judgement is a significant drawback of collaboration. It results in people sharing fewer ideas during a brainstorming session because they fear being evaluated unfavourably by others' judgement (Zhou et al., 2019). Wieland et al. (2022) found that a considerably large number of ideas were generated by those participants who brainstormed with AI as a partner compared to those who brainstormed with a human partner. Participants will present a large number of ideas "When they think they are brainstorming with a chatbot, rather than with a human being". According to Kafai and Burke (2014) (as cited in Marrone et al., 2023)

the goal of AI in education is to collaborate with AI to foster and support creative and problem-solving talents instead of just imparting knowledge in a particular field.

(b) *By increasing deep understanding of learning content:* AI provides a detailed explanation of the topic and assists students in finding solutions to difficult problems in a stepwise manner which in turn nourishes their creative skills by clearing all concepts (Rahman & Watanobe, 2023). AI tools increase deep understanding of learning material which leads to the development of critical thinking and creativity (Adiguzel et al., 2023); Chiu et al., 2023). In this modern era, children should possess skills of communication, collaboration, critical thinking and creativity which can be developed by AI as it acts as a great source of knowledge and experiential learning. ChatGPT can help students refine their ideas iteratively by delving deeper into them, allowing them to study the issue space more thoroughly and, ultimately, come up with more complex solutions (Urban et al., 2023).

(c) *By encouraging independent thinking*: AI tools like ChatGPT pose questions to the learners according to their abilities, interests, and needs and also offer opportunities to get assessed by peers which helps them to think differently and analyse any situation critically (Cotton et al., 2023). AI may foster creativity by promoting autonomous thought and providing opportunities for it, such as by fostering novel approaches to various problems (Marrone et al., 2022).

(d) *By answering curious questions:* Young learners are more curious and try to find answers to their questions. ChatGPT has the potential to satiate young children's curiosity and ease their insatiable curiosity by providing them with limitless answers without causing them fatigue or annoyance. This, in turn, fosters creativity (Luo et al., 2023), According to Marrone et al., (2023) a recent study highlights how AI could support traits like curiosity, grit, attentiveness and tenacity that are closely related to creativity.

(e) *By providing opportunities for creative tasks:* Students mentioned that being creative helps them manage their time better and come up with more original ideas. Students did, however, also note that their present educational settings occasionally had a detrimental effect on their capacity for creativity. They complained about not having enough time for creative engagements and the given assignments were not made to foster such ability. The pupils believed that AI may foster autonomous thought and provide opportunities for creativity, such as promoting "novel ways to solve the problems", in order to help them become more creative (Yufeia et al., 2023).

(f) *By exposing students to diverse ideas:* ChatGPT may improve students' divergent thinking abilities by exposing them to a variety of potential answers (Woo et al. (2023) and students are inspired to think about a wider range of options, which enables them to choose more likely prototype solutions (Mumford et al., 2019, as cited in Urban et al., 2023). AI output can be used as a springboard to help students to explore and elaborate their concepts when they struggle to come up with ideas or locate inspiration. Sumakul et al., 2022 while interviewing students found that students think that they can write those stories with the help of Chatbots which they were not even able to think of as they have got the idea from the prompts from the application.

Negative Impact of AI on Creative Thinking Ability of Students

AI hinders Creative Thinking Ability by cognitive fixation. AI could potentially impede human thought process for those who are still learning how to think creatively and divergently. AI leads to difficulty in generating ideas beyond what the AI could suggest, indicating a worrying risk of cognitive fixation and decreased self-efficacy. Some students have reported that after getting answers from AI tools they found it difficult to generate ideas on their own. However, few students shared their doubts about artificial intelligence (AI) overtaking the human cognitive process, fearing that AI will impede their own (human) innovative thinking and, consequently, their confidence (Habib et al., 2023). Excessive reliance on AI applications like chatbots for getting ideas and solutions to every problem impedes independent thinking which then leads to a belief that I do not have a capability to solve any problem myself. Students heavily rely on AI tools for getting ready-made answers without using their thinking abilities which may hamper their creative thinking which is a big challenge. The over-reliance of students on ChatGPT has a detrimental effect on their critical thinking, exploration, verification, and active summarising skills. The learning outcomes and development of pupils will be significantly impacted if this trend persists (Kasneci et al., 2023).

Balancing Dual Impact of Artificial Intelligence in Education (AIEd)

The application of AI in the education system requires a balanced strategy that takes into consideration both the potential advantages as well as disadvantages of this technology. This strategy demands flexibility to retain focus on ethical and critical thinking while also adopting new technology in light of its potential to increase efficiency and production. To avoid overreliance on AI technology, it is also critical to promote a balanced approach to their use. This approach uses AI tools as complementary tools to support learning. It is important to encourage students to embrace AI as a tool to support their learning rather than relying completely on it to succeed academically (Chan et al., 2023). Students must comprehend the underlying principles of artificial intelligence (AI) as its application in education and assessment grows in order to uphold academic integrity and deter cheating (Chan et al., 2023; Cotton et al., 2023).

Proper training should be given to both instructors and students to make judicious use of AI technology in teaching and learning. AI technology should be used to support educators and students as additional resources, not to take the role of interpersonal communication. It should be used to improve some abilities, such as time management and digital competency, while making sure that students maintain the development of essential transferable skills (Ifelebuegu et al., 2023). Responsible AI usage requires clear policies on data privacy, comprehensive frameworks for the ethical use of AI in education, continual professional development for educators, and instruction in digital literacy for students (Atlas, 2023).

To eliminate biases and guarantee fair and equitable learning environments, AI Algorithms must be continuously monitored and evaluated. Concerns over the possible elimination of human educators are also raised by the integration of AI. AI has the potential to improve education but to maintain the importance of human interaction over technology, a balance between the two must be struck (Chaik, 2023). Additionally, academics could devise novel methods of assessment, such as assessing learning processes as opposed to outcomes, that are difficult for ChatGPT to duplicate. Students' employability and preparedness for the quickly changing labour market may be improved by including AI literacy in their curriculum (Rasul et al., 2023).

Discussion and Conclusion

AI has revolutionised every sector of society including the education system. Its application has led to the emergence of a new field called AIEd—Artificial Intelligence in Education. It acts both as a friend and foe. It customises learning, provides feedback, makes learning interactive, reduces stress, improves divergent thinking, individualized instruction, and makes learning adaptive. Besides this, it presents many challenges in front of us like it erodes human interaction, increases the digital divide, increases bias and discrimination, stifles thought processes and increases our dependence on technology. Rather than avoiding the (inevitable) use of AI, teachers and stakeholders should try to find a balance that fosters human innovation while utilising AI's skills. Teachers should keep in mind that while artificial intelligence (AI) might be useful in generating ideas, it is not always advantageous.

There is a need for targeted pedagogical approaches that thoughtfully use AI resources with conventional teaching approaches to help students develop their capacity for divergent and convergent thought processes. To ensure that AI is applied in the educational system in a way that is both morally and practically sound, it is crucial to take into consideration the technological, ethical, and other issues that are raised by its application. Appropriate steps should be taken to solve these issues. AI will probably become a more significant instrument for fostering innovation and advancement in education as it develops, so it becomes important to keep an eye on and analyse how it affects learning.

References

Abbas, N., Whitfield, J., Atwell, E., Bowman, H., Pickard, T., & Walker, A. (2022). Online chat and chatbots to enhance mature student engagement in higher education. *International Journal of Lifelong Education*, 41(3), 308-326. https://doi.org/10.1080/02601370.2022.2066213

Adiguzel, T., Kaya, M.H., &Cansu, F.K. (2023). Revolutionizing education with AI: Exploring the transformative potential of ChatGPT. Contemporary Educational Technology, 15(3), ep429. https://doi.org/10.30935/cedtech/13152

Atlas, S. (2023). ChatGPT for higher education and professional development: A guide to conversational AI. University of Rhode Island. https://digitalcom mons.uri.edu/cba_facpubs/548

Božić, V. Artifical Intelligence In Education (2023), doi:10.13140/RG.2.2.33278.25925.

Chan, C.K.Y., & Tsi, L.H. (2023). The AI revolution in education: Will AI replace or assist teachers in higher education? https:// doi.org/10.48550/arXiv.2305.01185

Chen, L.; Chen, P.; Lin, Z. (2020). Artificial Intelligence in Education: A Review. IEEE, 8, 75264–75278.

Cotton, D.R.E., Cotton, P. A., & Shipway, J. R. (2023). Chatting and cheating: Ensuring academic integrity in the era of ChatGPT. Innovations in Education and Teaching International. https://doi.org/10.1080/14703297.2023.2190 148

Gabriel, F., Marrone, R., Van Sebille, Y.Z., Kovanović, V., & De Laat, M. (2022). Digital education strategies around the world: Practices and policies. Irish Educational Studies 41: 85–106. https://doi.org/10.1080/03323315.2021.2022513

Hamadan, M. (2023).The Impact of ChaGPT on Students: Positive Effects and Potential Negative Effects. Modern Diplomacy [Online]. https://moderndiplomacy.eu/2023/03/14/the-impact-ofchatgpt-on-students-positive-effects-and-potential-negativeeffects/ (accessed 13 July 2023)

Ifelebuegu, A.O., Kulume, P & Cherukut, P. (2023) Chatbots and AI in Education (AIEd) tools: The good, the bad, and the ugly. *Journal of Applied Learning and Teaching*, *6*(2). https://doi.org/10.37074/jalt.2023.6.2.29

Kasneci, E., Seßler, K., Küchemann, S., Bannert, M., Dementieva, D., Fischer, F., et al., (2023). ChatGPT for good? On opportunities and challenges of large language models for education. Learning and individual differences, 103, 102274.https://doi.org/10.1016/j.lindif.2023.102274

Kerr, P. (2016). Adaptive learning. *ELT Journal*, 70(1), 88-93. https://doi.org/10.1093/elt/ccv055

Marrone, R., Taddeo, V., & Hill, G. (2022). Creativity and Artificial Intelligence — A Student Perspective. *Journal of Intelligence* 10: 65. https://doi.org/10.3390/jintelligence10030065

Oliveira, A., Arriaga, P., Paiva, A & Hoffman, G. (2017). Yolo, a robot for creativity: A co-design study with children. Paper presented at the 2017 Conference on Interaction Design and Children, Stanford, CA, USA, June 27–30; pp. 423–29.

Qadir, J. (2023). Engineering education in the era of ChatGPT: Promise and pitfalls of generative AI for education. 2023 IEEE Global Engineering Education Conference (EDUCON) (pp. 1-9). IEEE. https://doi.org/10.36227/techrxiv.21789434

Rahman, M.M., & Watanobe, Y. (2023). ChatGPT for Education and Research: Opportunities, Threats, and Strategies. *Applied Sciences*, *13*(9), 5783. https://doi.org/10.3390/app13095783.

Rasul, T.; Nair, S.; Kalendra, D.; Robin, M.; de Oliveira Santini, F.; Ladeira, W.J.; Sun, M.; Day, I.; Rather, R.; Heathcote, L. The role of ChatGPT in higher education: Benefits, challenges, and future research directions. J. Appl. Learn. Teach. 2023, 6. [Google Scholar]

Sabrina Habib, Thomas Vogel, Evelyn Thorne, Anli Xiao, How Does Generative Artificial Intelligence Impact Student Creativity?, *Journal of Creativity* (2023), https://doi.org/10.1016/j.yjoc.2023.100072

Sumakul, D.T., Hamied, F.A., &Sukyadi, D. (2022). Artificial intelligence in EFL classrooms: Friend or foe? LEARN Journal: Language Education and Acquisition Research Network, 15(1), 232-256

UNESCO, "Artificial intelligence in education: challenges and opportunities for sustainable development," Unesco, p. 46, 2019.

Urban, M., Děchtěrenko, F., Lukavský, J., Hrabalová, V., Svacha, F., Brom, C., & Urban, K. (2023). Can ChatGPT Improve Creative Problem-Solving Performance in University Students? *Journal of Applied Learning and Teaching*. https://doi.org/10.31234/osf.io/9z2tc

Wieland, B., De Wit, J., & De Rooij, A. (2022). Electronic Brainstorming with a Chatbot Partner: A Good Idea Due to Increased Productivity and Idea Diversity. *Frontiers in Artificial Intelligence*, *5*. https://doi.org/10.3389/frai.2022.880673

Yufeia, L., Salehb, S., Jiahuic, H., & Syed, S.M. (2020). Review of the application of artificial intelligence in education. *Integration (Amsterdam)*, *12*(8), 1-15..

Zhai, X. (2022). ChatGPT User Experience: Implications for Education. *Social Science Research Network*. https://doi.org/10.2139/ssrn.4312418

Zhou, X., Zhai, H., Delidabieke, B., Zeng, H., Cui, Y., & Cao, X. (2019). Exposure to ideas, evaluation apprehension, and incubation intervals in collaborative idea generation. *Frontiers in Psychology*, *10*. https://doi.org/10.3389/fpsyg.2019.01459

21

Artificial Intelligence Usage in Academic Writing

Uzma Siddiqui

Introduction

Artificial Intelligence (AI), at its core, is a collection of technologies that allow machines to imitate cognitive functions associated with human minds, such as learning and problem-solving. AI has emerged as a vital force in redefining educational paradigms in recent years. This integration of AI in education has led to more responsive and adaptive learning environments that can meet the diverse needs of individual students and educators. AI enables the development of intelligent tutoring systems (Ali, 2020; Chan, 2023; Chen et al., 2020; Cotton et al., 2023). These systems are capable of monitoring student performance meticulously, adapting to each student's unique learning trajectories, strengths, and areas for improvement, and providing tailored learning experiences (Divekar et al., 2022; Pikhart, 2020).

AI tools can assist in raising the standards of academic writing among students and research scholars across the world. Academic writing is a meticulous process that combines together extensive research, structured argumentation, and clear expression to contribute towards effective communication and the dissemination of research (Malik et al., 2023). In order to establish the platform for effective writing, students and scholars must train themselves in foundational concepts and core principles essential to scholarly writing. This includes creating clear and concise titles that capture the heart of the work (Maiorana & Mayer, 2018), and drafting engaging abstracts that communicate the essential ideas, methodologies, and findings of the study effectively (Altmae et al., 2023). Conducting comprehensive literature reviews is also essential as they allow students and scholars to contextualise their work within the current body of knowledge and to identify research gaps that their research study may fill (Singh & Lukkarila, 2017). Since it is crucial to acknowledge the works of others in academic writing to maintain integrity and avoid plagiarism, therefore learning the precise art of citation and referencing is non-negotiable (Roe & Perkins, 2022). A thorough understanding of the structural components of a publication, including the introduction, methodology, results, and discussion sections, is required for producing coherent and well-organized research works (Klimova, 2013; McMahan et al., 2017).

Academic writing is, thus, a complicated and multifaceted endeavour that necessitates a combination of research knowledge, writing proficiency, critical and creative thinking, and ethical scholarship (Malik et al., 2023). By mastering these features, students and research scholars can make significant contributions to the improvement and advancement of scholarly communication and research dissemination. AI and academic writing interweave to form a revolutionary convergence in education. AI, with its cutting-edge technologies and adaptive learning mechanisms, enhances academic writing by delivering dynamic, responsive learning environments, and tailored educational experiences.

Literature Review

There is no doubt about the transformative impact of AI in education. AI tools have brought about a new revolution in the teaching-learning process in different subject areas by offering valuable support for students and educators. AI tools have attracted a lot of attention for their capacity to help students write by providing grammar and style advice and facilitating content production (Malik et al., 2023). Gayed et al. (2022) demonstrated how AI writing tools improve students' writing proficiency and skills. The use of AI into academic writing raises doubts regarding the role of educators as well as ethical concerns. Su et al. (2022) investigated the impact of AI on the teaching process and concluded that, while AI tools can be useful in delivering feedback, teachers' instructions and directions are still necessary in encouraging critical thinking and creativity. In terms of ethics, Chaudhry et al. (2023) investigated the implications of AI in plagiarism detection, emphasising the importance of clear standards and educating students about AI's limitations and appropriate use.

The use of AI tools in academic essay writing has grown in popularity in higher education. Experimental research studies by Miranty and Widiati (2021) and Almusharraf and Alotaibi (2023) respectively investigated the impact of Grammarly, an AI-based grammar and style checker, on the writing skills of undergraduate students. They found that students in the experimental group who used Grammarly improved their grammar accuracy and writing quality as compared to the control group.

AI language models, like ChatGPT, have been investigated for their potential in assisting students with content generation. Research studies on ChatGPT by Farrokhnia et al. (2023) and Rospigliosi (2023) concluded that the AI-generated content was useful in generating initial ideas and structuring and organising the research proposals, though students still required to polish and elaborate the generated content.

The ethical implications of using AI writing tools in higher education have been investigated. Kreps et al. (2022) and Holmes et al. (2022) carried out a survey to analyse students' perceptions toward AI tools and their comprehension of the proper use of AI-generated content. The findings underscored the importance of proper instruction, guidance and supervision on the use of AI tools to avoid plagiarism and preserve academic integrity.

Students' awareness and perceptions of AI tools are crucial in encouraging them to adopt and make effective use of AI tools in academic writing. Scholars such as Kerman et al. (2022), Latifi et al. (2023), Noorozi et al. (2022), and Valero Haro et al. (2022) made significant contributions, providing profound insights into how such individual characteristics of students as gender, epistemic beliefs, and higher-order skills, as well as their beliefs and perceptions, influence their engagement with AI in academic writing.

It has been clear from the reviewed literature that the use of AI has been on the rise globally, as well as locally in all spheres of life in general and in the field of research in particular. The level of awareness and perceptions of AI among research scholars can help them in choosing appropriate AI tools and utilising their applications in their research work in general and academic writing in particular. Although AI and its benefits in the field of academics have been a topic of global interest, the awareness and perceptions of research scholars in universities, especially those in Aligarh, Uttar Pradesh, appear underexplored. The researcher believes it is essential to explore their awareness levels and unique perceptions to present a more comprehensive view of AI's impact on academic writing. This has motivated the researcher to carry out the present study in order to contribute towards bridging this gap in the literature. Therefore, this study focuses on determining the awareness and perceptions of artificial intelligence among research scholars in the faculties of Arts and Social Sciences respectively at Aligarh Muslim University, Aligarh, Uttar Pradesh, India.

Methodology

Research Method

The present study employed a quantitative, descriptive research method.

Sample

Convenience sampling was used to select a sample of 213 research scholars (session 2021-2022) who were enrolled in different departments of faculties of Arts and Social Sciences respectively at Aligarh Muslim University between 01 January and 31 March 2023. These scholars were in the second year of Ph. D. programme.

Questionnaire

This study employed an online questionnaire disseminated via Google Forms to collect responses from the sample. This questionnaire was developed by the researcher from comprehensive literature reviews to fulfil the study's aim. Before dissemination, the questionnaire was subjected to content and face validation by a team of experts to determine its suitability. It also underwent rigorous pilot testing to ensure reliability. Internal consistency reliability was found to be quite good with a Cronbach's alpha score of 0.81.

It consists of two sections, namely, awareness of AI and perceptions of AI in academic writing. To determine the awareness of AI, a five-point Likert scale consisting of 17 items were used. To assess the perceptions toward AI, a five-point Likert scale consisting of 18 items was used.

Data Analysis

The data were analysed using SPSS. Descriptive statistical analysis (percentage and frequency) was used to analyse quantitative data so as to answer the research objectives and obtain insights into research scholars' awareness and perceptions of AI in academic writing.

Results

Awareness of AI in Academic Writing among Research Scholars

The data in Table1 provides a quantitative summary of respondents' awareness of using AI tools in academic writing. Results show that 35.2% and 35.7% of the sample "Agree" and "Strongly agree" respectively with the item about the availability of AI tools for academic writing. Moreover, 55.4 % of respondents were confident in their knowledge and skills of using AI tools in academic writing. Overall, more than 50% of the sample used AI tools for reviewing a topic (item 3) and generating citations and references (item 7) respectively. Further, more than 60% of respondents used AI tools for producing different versions of text on the same topic (item 4), translating information written in foreign languages (item 8), checking grammar and spelling errors (item 12), and paraphrasing (item 13) respectively. Furthermore, less than 30% of the sample used AI tools for generating coherent text based on a given prompt or input (item 5), conducting a comprehensive literature review to identify existing research gaps, trends, and insights related to a given topic (item 9), generating different sections of a research paper, such as the abstract, introduction, literature, review, methodology, and discussion (item 11), analysing large datasets (item 14), and generating visualisations for the effective presentation of research findings (item 15) respectively.

Perceptions of AI Usage in Academic Writing among Research Scholars

The data in Table 2 provides a quantitative summary of respondents' perceptions of using AI tools in academic writing. Overall, 65 % of the sample had positive

Table 1: Awareness of AI in Academic Writing among Research Scholars (N = 213)

S. No.	*Items*	*Level of Agreement*				
		1	*2*	*3*	*4*	*5*
1.	I am aware that AI tools for academic writing are available.	6.1%	8.9%	14.1%	35.2%	35.7%
2.	I use AI tools for exploring a topic exhaustively in seconds.	20.6%	23.5%	23.9%	16.0%	16.0%
3.	I am aware of AI tools that can compile and generate text for review on a given topic, along with a list of references.	14.1%	15.5%	18.8%	25.8%	25.8%
4.	I am familiar with AI tools that can produce different versions of text on the same topic.	9.4%	10.3%	14.1%	32.9%	33.3%
5.	I use AI tools for generating coherent and contextually appropriate text based on a given prompt or input.	24.4%	23.9%	23.5%	15.5%	12.7%
6.	I know AI-generated citations and references are often fully or partially fake.	14.1%	15.0%	18.8%	26.3%	25.8%
7.	I am familiar with AI tools that can generate citations and references automatically.	14.1%	14.1%	19.2%	25.8%	26.8%
8.	I use AI-based language translation technologies to access information written in foreign languages.	11.7%	11.7%	8.5%	32.9%	35.2%
9.	I am familiar with AI tools that can assist me in conducting a comprehensive literature review to identify existing research gaps, trends, and insights related to a given topic.	18.8%	16.9%	24.9%	19.2%	20.2%
10.	I use AI tools for summarising and analysing a large number of academic papers quickly.	14.1%	18.8%	23.9%	22.1%	21.1%
11.	I am aware of AI tools that can assist me in generating different sections of a research paper, such as the abstract, introduction, literature, review, methodology, and discussion.	26.3%	25.8%	23.5%	11.7%	12.7%
12.	I use AI tools to proofread a research paper by checking for grammar and spelling errors.	9.4%	11.3%	13.1%	32.9%	33.3%

S. No.	Items	Level of Agreement 1	2	3	4	5
13.	I am familiar with AI tools that can give a professional look to a research paper by suggesting improvements in sentence structures and alternative phrases and vocabulary.	14.1%	11.7%	14.1%	29.6%	30.5%
14.	I am aware of AI tools that can aid in the analysis of large datasets.	21.1%	21.1%	30.5%	12.7%	14.6%
15.	I use AI tools for generating compelling visualisations that help in the effective presentation of research findings.	26.3%	23.5%	25.8%	12.7%	11.7%
16.	I use AI-based plagiarism detection techniques to ensure the originality of my research work.	18.8%	18.3%	16.9%	23.5%	22.5%
17.	I am confident in my knowledge and skills of using AI tools in academic writing.	15.5%	9.4%	19.7%	28.2%	27.2%

Level of agreement: 1= Strongly disagree; 2= Disagree; 3= Neutral; 4= Agree; 5= Strongly agree

perceptions of using AI tools in academic writing as far as their responses on different items (1, 2, 3, 4, 5, 6, 7, 8, 9, 10, 11, 12, 16, 17, 18) are concerned. But on items 13, 14 and 15, less than 15 % of respondents had positive perceptions, clearly indicating that they lacked knowledge on AI-based journal finders and detectors of predatory journals.

Table 2: Perceptions of AI in Academic Writing among Research Scholars (N = 213)

S. No.	Items	Level of Agreement 1	2	3	4	5
1.	AI tools are the best option for me to learn academic writing skills.	7.0%	7.0%	10.8%	36.7%	38.5%
2.	AI tools help me improve my creative writing skills.	9.4%	9.4%	11.7%	34.3%	35.2%
3.	AI tools enhance my critical thinking skills.	9.8%	10.8%	12.7%	32.9%	33.8%
4.	AI tools are better than me at writing high-quality, original, and well-structured research papers.	2.8%	4.7%	14.1%	38.5%	39.9%
5.	AI tools help me rewrite and rearrange ideas, sentences, and paragraphs.	4.7%	5.2%	15.5%	36.6%	38.0%

S. No.	Items	Level of Agreement 1	2	3	4	5
6.	AI tools enable me to generate plagiarism-free contents.	6.6%	10.8%	13.6%	33.8%	35.2%
7.	Using AI tools do not let me violate ethical issues in research work.	9.4%	9.4%	16.4%	32.4%	32.4%
8.	AI tools help me overcome language barriers.	1.4%	1.9%	18.8%	38.0%	39.9%
9.	AI tools improve my language proficiency.	3.3%	4.2%	17.4%	37.1%	38.0%
10.	AI tools improve my editing abilities by suggesting possible areas for improvement in my research work.	6.1%	7.1%	16.4%	34.7%	35.7%
11.	AI tools provide me insights into my potential weaknesses in different sections of a research paper.	4.2%	9.4%	18.3%	33.8%	34.3%
12.	AI tools are good at correcting errors in my academic work.	4.2%	4.2%	13.6%	39.0%	39.0%
13.	AI tools assist me in writing research articles as per the scope and publication guidelines of a given journal.	34.7%	35.7%	16.4%	6.1%	7.1%
14.	AI tools recommend me the right journal by matching the theme of my research article with the journal scope.	33.8%	34.3%	18.3%	4.2%	9.4%
15.	AI tools provide me assistance in identifying predatory journals engaged in unethical practices.	39.0%	39.0%	13.6%	4.2%	4.2%
16.	AI tools make me a better researcher.	5.2%	4.7%	15.5%	36.6%	38.0%
17.	I think AI-generated text is not detected by plagiarism checking software.	9.4%	13.6%	10.3%	32.9%	33.8%
18.	I think AI tools will soon replace humans in the field of academics.	9.4%	10.8%	13.6%	32.9%	33.3%

Level of agreement: 1= Strongly disagree; 2= Disagree; 3= Neutral; 4= Agree; 5= Strongly agree

Conclusion and Implications

The findings of the present study revealed that research scholars at Aligarh Muslim University seemed to have good awareness and positive perceptions toward AI in academic writing. These results suggested that university students must be aware of the new technologies like AI tools and guidelines to be followed for their ethical applications in the field of research. In this regard, workshops and short-term training programmes on the ethical uses of AI tools in the field of education should be carried out by educational administrators of colleges and universities on a regular basis for college and university students.

References

Ali, Z. (2020). Artificial Intelligence (AI): A review of its uses in language teaching and learning. *IOP Conference Series: Materials Science and Engineering*, *769*(1), 12043.

Almusharraf, N., & Alotaibi, H. (2023). An error-analysis study from an EFL writing context: Human and automated essay scoring approaches. Technology, Knowledge and Learning, *28*(3), 1015-1031.

Altmae, S., Sola-Leyva, A., & Salumets, A. (2023). Artificial intelligence in scientific writing: A friend or a foe? *Reproductive BioMedicine Online*, *47*(1), 3-9.

Chan, C.K.Y. (2023). A comprehensive AI policy education framework for university teaching and learning. *International Journal of Educational Technology in Higher Education*, *20*(1), 38.

Chaudhry, I.S., Sarwary, S.A.M., El Refae, G.A., & Chabchoub, H. (2023). Time to revisit existing student's performance evaluation approaches in the higher education sector in a new era of ChatGPT — A case study. *Cogent Education*, *10*(1), Article 2210461.

Chen, L.P.C., & Z.L. (2020). Artificial intelligence in education: A review. *IEEE access: practical innovations, open solutions*, *8*, 75264-752278.

Cotton, D.R.E., Cotton, P.A., & Shipway, J.R. (2023). Chatting and cheating: Ensuring academic integrity in the era of ChatGPT. *Innovations in Education and Teaching International*, 1-12.

Divekar, R.R., Drozdal, J., Chabot, S., Zhou, Y., Su, H., Chen, Y., Zhu, H., Hendler, J.A., & Braasch, J. (2022). Foreign language acquisition via artificial intelligence and extended reality: Design and evaluation. *Computer Assisted Language Learning*, *35*(9), 2332-2360.

Farrokhnia, M., Banihashem, S.K., Noroozi, O., & Wals, A. (2023). A SWOT analysis of ChatGPT: Implications for educational practice and research. *Innovations in Education and Teaching International*, 1-15.

Gayed, J.M., Carlon, M.K.J., Oriola, A.M., & Cross, J.S. (2022). Exploring an AI-based writing Assistant's impact on English language learners. *Computers and Education: Artificial Intelligence*, *3*, Article 100055.

Holmes, W., Porayska-Pomsta, K., Holstein, K., Sutherland, E., Baker, T., Shum, S.B., Santos, O.C., Rodrigo, M.T., Cukurova, M., Bittencourt, I.I., & Koedinger, K.R. (2022). Ethics of AI in education: Towards a community-wide framework. *International Journal of Artificial Intelligence in Education*, *32*(3), 504-526.

Kerman, N.T., Noroozi, O., Banihashem, S.K., Karami, M., & Biemans, H.J. (2022). Online peer feedback patterns of success and failure in argumentative essay writing. *Interactive Learning Environments*, 1-13.

Klimova, B.F. (2013). Developing thinking skills in the course of academic writing. *Procedia — Social and Behavioral Sciences*, *93*, 508-511.

Kreps, S., McCain, R.M., & Brundage, M. (2022). All the news that's fit to fabricate: AI-generated text as a tool of media misinformation. *Journal of Experimental Political Science*, *9*(1), 104-117.

Latifi, S., Noroozi, O., & Talaee, E. (2023). Worked example or scripting? Fostering students' online argumentative peer feedback, essay writing and learning. *Interactive Learning Environments*, *31*(2), 655-669.

Malik, A.R., Pratiwi, Y., Andajani, K., Numertayasa, W., Suharti, S, Darwis, A. & Marzuki (2023). Exploring Artificial Intelligence in Academic Essay: Higher Education Student's Perspective. *International Journal of Educational Research Open*, *5*, 1-14, Article 100296.

Maiorana, F.A., & Mayer, H.F. (2018). How to avoid common errors in writing scientific manuscripts. *European Journal of Plastic Surgery*, *41*(5), 489-494.

McMahan, E., Day, S., Funk, R., & Coleman, L.S. (2017). *Literature and the writing process*. Pearson.

Miranty, D., & Widiati, U. (2021). An automated writing evaluation (AWE) in higher education. *Pegem Journal of Education and Instruction*, *11*(4 SE-Article), 126-137.

Noroozi, O. (2022). The role of students' epistemic beliefs for their argumentation performance in higher education. *Innovations in Education and Teaching International*, 1-12.

Pikhart, M. (2020). Intelligent information processing for language education: The use of artificial intelligence in language learning apps. *Procedia Computer Science*, *176*, 1412-1419.

Roe, J., & Perkins, M. (2022). What are automated paraphrasing tools and how do we address them? A review of a growing threat to academic integrity. *International Journal for Educational Integrity*, *18*(1), 15.

Rospigliosi, P. 'asher'. (2023). Artificial intelligence in teaching and learning: What questions should we ask of ChatGPT? *Interactive Learning Environments*, *31*(1), 1-3.

Singh, A.A., & Lukkarila, L. (2017). *Successful academic writing: A complete guide for social and behavioral scientists*. Guilford Publications.

Su, J., Zhong, Y., & Ng, D.T.K. (2022). A meta-review of literature on educational approaches for teaching AI at the K-12 levels in the Asia-Pacific region. *Computers and Education: Artificial Intelligence*, *3*, Article 100065.

22

Navigating Intellectual Property Rights in Era of AI

Babita

Introduction

India's educational landscape has seen a major shift since the National Education Policy (NEP) 2020 was introduced and eventually implemented. This policy serves as a beam of guidance, emphasizing the need for innovation in the classroom and creating an environment that develops students' adaptability, creativity, and problem-solving skills. The inclusion of artificial intelligence (AI) into educational settings indicates an important structural change. It provides individualized and flexible learning experiences, going beyond traditional teaching approaches. In addition to accommodating different learning styles, these AI-powered resources make it easier to fully understand difficult subjects, opening the door to a more rewarding educational experience.

Nowadays, the use of AI in schools aims to accomplish more than only improve teaching and learning. It takes the issue of protecting teachers' and students' intellectual rights head-on. Institutions are given a distinctive viewpoint on defending these rights by utilizing AI, ensuring that the results of intellectual labour are safe in this technologically advanced age. This thorough paper explores the complex effects of artificial intelligence (AI) and machine learning on the safeguarding of intellectual property in the field of education. It highlights the changing environment where AI and education cross and highlights the critical role that intellectual rights protection plays in this regard. These remarks start thought-provoking discussions regarding ethical, legal, and personal matters. Institutions can harness the transformative potential of technology while upholding ethical standards and safeguarding the contributions and innovations of both students and educators by fostering a robust ecosystem that recognizes the importance of intellectual property rights and privacy within the context of AI-enhanced education. As a result, it is crucial that this study paper clarifies these complex relationships between artificial intelligence, education, and intellectual property rights. It attempts to function as a thorough guide, providing insights into the changing field of AI integration in education and the complex issues related to intellectual property protection. Through managing the complex interactions between artificial intelligence (AI), education, and intellectual property rights, this research aims to provide practical suggestions for promoting creativity while respecting moral and legal frameworks in the application of AI in education.

This paper aims to provide policymakers, stakeholders, and educational institutions with a more profound comprehension by exploring these important aspects. It aims to give them the tools they need to manage the potential and difficulties brought about by AI in education while upholding the protection of their privacy and intellectual rights. This study report is a crucial resource for enlightening debates, forming laws, and encouraging the ethical and responsible integration of AI in educational settings. It emphasizes how important it is to take a balanced approach, one that protects the priceless intellectual contributions made by the educational community while simultaneously utilizing AI's potential.

Intellectual Property Rights

Intellectual Property Rights (IPR) are legal protections granted to safeguard human-created knowledge and innovations. These rights offer individuals or entities exclusive control over intangible assets derived from their creative endeavours. IPR encompasses various forms of artistic, literary, and innovative works, including designs, logos, literary content, and technologies utilized in educational settings. The use of IPR in educational settings follows a complex path that crosses over with the contributions of various stakeholders. In this environment, educators, learners, academic institutions, technology developers, and content producers all have important responsibilities to play in the production, sharing, and application of innovations and information. The primary function of intellectual property rights (IPR) in education is to foster an atmosphere that is conducive to innovation. It serves as a barrier as well as a motivator, promoting the creation and uptake of innovative technology and processes. These safeguards give educational institutions and tech entrepreneurs the reassurance they need, which promotes investment in R&D projects that open doors for cutting-edge teaching strategies, adaptable learning platforms, and innovative evaluation tools.

Need of Intellectual Property Rights

Intellectual property rights (IPR) are the guardians of innovation, progress, and creative expression in the modern world. They saturate every aspect of our economy and protect the priceless results of human creativity. These rights are fundamental because they provide visionaries and inventors with the support and protection they need to shape the fields of science and technology.

Their relevance is multifaceted: by highlighting the importance of intellectual property rights (IPR) in educational settings, a culture of creativity is fostered, inspiring both educators and students to challenge traditions and explore new ideas with the knowledge that their original ideas would be protected by law. In addition to encouraging creativity, this atmosphere also serves as a stimulant for the economy because intellectual property created in educational institutions may be used to fund businesses, which in turn supports entrepreneurship.

Furthermore, intellectual property rights (IPRs) guarantee the proper attribution and management of works, recognizing and protecting the contributions of scholars and instructors. This promotes an environment that is favourable to ongoing innovation and recognizes their essential role in developing curricula and pedagogical approaches. In addition, intellectual property rights (IPR) protection in education promotes cooperation between universities, research centers, and businesses. This fosters knowledge sharing and technology development, which in turn quickens the pace of educational innovation for the benefit of a wider range of students and teachers. In the end, intellectual property rights (IPR) go beyond mere legal compliance, enabling people to explore new creative frontiers and obtaining the resources and recognition they rightfully deserve.

Here's an in-depth exploration of how these rights interrelate within the education sector.

Patents: Patents protect the innovative and unique aspects of AI technologies used in education. Incentives for further innovation in education are provided by patents. Patents support ongoing research and development efforts targeted at improving and enhancing the capabilities of AI-powered learning systems by protecting these cutting-edge AI technologies. This barrier not only maintains the intellectual capital that academic institutions and digital companies have invested in, but it also creates a never-ending cycle of advancement that drives a constantly changing panorama of educational innovation. This protects AI algorithms designed for self-learning, innovative teaching methods or special technologies integrated into educational systems. For example, a patent could cover an AI algorithm that adjusts teaching styles based on students' learning patterns.

Copyright: Copyright protects original content created by AI systems in the academic domain. This includes resources such as e-books, videos or digital learning materials. In AI-generated content, copyright grants creators the exclusive right to publish, distribute, or modify educational resources created by AI systems. Copyright protection provides exclusive rights to content creators using AI, enabling them to control the use of their educational resources. This includes the freedom to create, share, alter, and restrict who has access to these works. It guarantees that authors maintain ownership and authority over their creative contributions made to the academic community.

This copyright paradigm encourages the creation of new works while simultaneously acknowledging the efforts and inventive contributions of individuals using AI systems. By guaranteeing that content producers receive credit, recognition, and the ability to control how their AI-generated content is shared and altered, it promotes the creation of excellent learning materials. In the end, copyright protection creates an atmosphere that is favourable to the ongoing creation and improvement of learning resources powered by AI innovation.

Trademarks: Trademarks serve to protect the identity of your AI-powered learning platform or device. They protect the name, brand or unique design associated with these platforms, differentiating them from competitors and ensuring understanding and trust among users. Technology businesses or educational institutions can create a trustworthy and identifiable brand for their AI-driven learning solutions by gaining trademarks. The name, logo, or design connected to these platforms will stay unique and cannot be used by anybody else without permission thanks to this exclusive protection.

Additionally, users develop a sense of trustworthiness and confidence when they see trademarks. A trademark on a platform or technology indicates a standard of excellence, dependability, and uniformity that users can anticipate. In an increasingly competitive market of educational technology, where consumers seek out credible and effective learning solutions, distinction like this is critical to building trust and recognition. With all factors considered, trademarks are an essential tool for AI-powered learning environments. They offer legal defence and build consumer loyalty by giving the industry's competitive educational technology sector a distinct and easily identifiable character.

Geographical Indications: Geographical indications may be applied to AI training materials developed or recognized in specific regions known for their technical expertise in AI. This may include unique teaching methods, research frameworks or teaching tools derived from prominent AI-focused academic institutions. These indicators are signs that show a high correlation between a product or service's reputation, quality, or other attributes and its place of origin. Geographical indicators could be used in AI training materials to indicate resources created or recognized in areas recognized for their high technical AI proficiency. These resources could include unique teaching approaches, cutting-edge research models, or customized teaching aids that originate from well-known AI-focused universities in those areas. Geographical indicators can also help users, instructors, and organizations find and choose AI training resources that have particular attributes or features that are linked to the knowledge of a given region. This partnership promotes credibility and trustworthiness by highlighting the high calibre and specific expertise ingrained in these AI-focused resources that come from various geographical locations.

In AI-driven educational environments, these types of IPRs play an important role in protecting innovation, content, methods and technologies, and in promoting the continuous development and improvement of teaching and learning across devices and platforms. Intellectual property rights (IPRs) are fundamental building blocks that are essential to preserving, promoting, and developing innovation, content production, techniques, and technological breakthroughs in the context of AI-driven educational environments. Their complex function goes much beyond providing legal safeguards; they play a crucial part in forming the dynamic and changing environment of education across a wide range of platforms and devices. IPRs protect these intellectual contributions and provide an atmosphere that encourages the educational landscape to keep evolving and getting better. These safeguards promote continuous improvements and alterations to AI-driven processes, technology, and content production. They provide energy to an ongoing cycle of innovation focused on improving the effectiveness, usability, and flexibility of learning materials and tools on a variety of platforms and devices. Moreover, IPR frameworks act as both bridges and shields for cooperation. Clearly defined ownership rights allow for open cooperation and partnerships between developers, content creators, and institutions. This cooperative mentality fosters a shared learning culture, which in turn drives group endeavours toward the progress of education and the sharing of cutting-edge approaches and technology. IPRs are, in short, the fundamental facilitators of advancement in AI-driven education. They retain different materials and approaches, promote continuous development, safeguard the results of innovation, and create collaborative settings that drive the evolution and enhancement of learning experiences across a wide range of platforms and devices.

Conclusion

The advent of Artificial Intelligence (AI) in the field of education has opened up new possibilities, directly impacting intellectual rights. The promise of protection gives innovators and developers the freedom to keep improving and developing their educational inventions. AI-driven solutions can be improved through this continuous iteration process, which fixes bugs, boosts functionality, and adjusts to evolving learning objectives. As a result, IPRs encourage a never-ending cycle of invention, keeping educational materials and instruments at the cutting edge of development. The use of AI in children's education signals prosperity but also introduces new challenges that need understanding. How can educational content creators and institutions ensure the privacy of children and uphold intellectual rights in this new era? In this context, we need new regulations and policies to support secure education and protect intellectual rights. Alongside this conclusion, we also need to consider how to strike a balance between AI and intellectual rights protection. How can we ensure that the use of AI in children's education adheres to well-thought-out policies and rules without any infringement on intellectual rights? Can we enhance policies to steer education in a direction that fully supports their intellectual rights? How can we improve human-centred perspectives for the proper and secure utilization of AI? By seeking answers to these questions, we can enhance the protection of intellectual rights in the field of education through the use of AI and obtain guidance for a prosperous and secure educational path. Moreover, collaborative efforts among educators, policymakers, and technology developers are pivotal. Establishing comprehensive guidelines that promote ethical AI usage, respecting individual rights, and fostering innovation is crucial. It is imperative to create an ecosystem where AI supplements education without compromising privacy or intellectual property.

Enabling transparent frameworks and accountability mechanisms can ensure that AI-driven educational tools prioritize the well-being and rights of learners. By aligning technological advancements with ethical considerations, we pave the way for an inclusive, informed, and ethically sound educational landscape.

References

Gurkaynak, G. (2017). *Questions of Intellectual Property in the Artificial Intelligence Realm.*

Intellectual Property Rights. Drishti IAS. https://www.drishtiias.com/to-the-points/paper3/intellectual-property-rights

Juneja, K.K.;(n.d.). NEP 2020: *Innovation & Educational Technology in 21st Century.* http://mysc holar.umk.edu.my/bitstream/123456789/3117/2/E%20Book%20PDF_Recent%20Research%20and%20Innovation%20An%20Integrated%20Approach_Bharti%20Publications.pdf#page=202

Picht, P.G., Brunner, V., & Schmid, R. (2022). *Artificial Intelligence and Intellectual Property Law: From Diagnosis to Action.* Social Science Research Network; RELX Group (Netherlands).

Pihlajarinne, T., & Alen-Savikko, A. (2022). *Artificial Intelligence and the Media.* Edward Elgar Publishing eBooks.

Saputra, R., Tiolince, T., Iswantoro, I., & Sigh, S.K. (2023). *Artificial Intelligence and Intellectual Property Protection in Indonesia and Japan. Journal of Human Rights, Culture and Legal System.*

Smits, J.M., & Borghuis, T. (2022). *Generative AI and Intellectual Property Rights.* Information Technology & Law Series.

23

Impact of AI for Advancing Technical and Soft Skills in Engineering Education

Irum Alvi

Introduction

The current integration of artificial intelligence AI in higher education has materialized a transformative power with immense potential to revolutionize higher education, and contemporary pedagogies as well as redefining the technical aptitude and soft skills of undergraduate students. As a guiding light for this paradigm shift, the national education policy NEP plays a pivotal role in bringing about educational reforms in the country, enhancing the quality of higher education, and meeting the demands of the 21st-century workforce by offering an elaborate framework (Kaurav, 2020). NEP gives optimism for the revitalization of the educational system and envisions a 'New India' (Nand, 2020); however, there are several opportunities as well as challenges (Bele, 2023; Soni, 2022).

The Study

Research Gap

A research gap was identified, based on an extensive literature review, as limited studies have explored the practical implementation and effect of the integration outlined in the NEP on technical and soft skills enhancement among engineering students within the Indian context. As extensive studies have been conducted on NPS directives related to inclusion and diversity, little empirical research has been conducted on the ground-level impact, challenges, and effectiveness of AI integration in higher education, particularly engineering education. The extant literature has focused primarily on policy analysis and theoretical discussions; as such it lacks in-depth empirical evidence based on the perception of the main stakeholders, the students, engaged in an AI-integrated learning environment. Consequently, this research gap highlights the need for a comprehensive study to bridge the gap between policy provision and practical implementation to provide a nuanced understanding of AI integration and its impact on skill development within engineering education in India.

Research objectives for the study include assessing AI integration in NEP with particular emphasis on technical and soft skill enhancement in engineering education, exploring challenges and opportunities in the implementation of AI within engineering institutes, evaluating perceptions and experiences of students as main stakeholders in AI-driven education, determining AI role in reducing socio-economic disparities in education as per the mandate of the NEP 2020.

Research Questions

1. What are the key thematic elements and overarching trends within the National Education Policy (NEP) that relate to the integration of Artificial Intelligence in engineering education, particularly in fostering technical and soft skill development among students with special focus on the role of teacher training and capacity development?
2. What is the perception of engineering students towards the incorporation of Artificial Intelligence within the National Education Policy, particularly concerning its influence on their learning experiences and skill enhancement — technical and soft skills?

Methodology

The current study uses a mixed-method analysis known for its effectiveness (Tashakkori and Teddlie, 2004). It focuses on the integration of artificial intelligence for advancing excellence in technical education within the framework of the New Education Policy 2020 in India; it is bifurcated into two main segments. The initial part is based on a thorough thematic content analysis of the NEP policies, which are related to AI integration and have the potential to pave the way for enhancing technical and soft skills among engineering students. The study scrutinizes the NEP document to identify and analyze themes, sub-themes, and sub-sub-themes for a better understanding of the policy's approach towards the integration of AI for skills development. The main NEP document downloaded from the website of the MHRD (www.mhrd.gov.in) serves as a fundamental source of policy information for the purpose.

In the next phase, the study aims to assess the technical students' perception regarding the amalgamation of artificial intelligence in engineering education. A structured survey was administered to a sample of students across multiple institutions in the country, using a stratified random sampling method. Data was collected from 540 students; responses were received from 516 students studying in various disciplines and academic years; detailed interviews were conducted by the researcher in which 24 students participated voluntarily. Nearly 21% were female and 80% were male, with a mean age of 18 years.

The survey questionnaire comprised close-ended questions designed to capture students' perceptions of AI integration, and the interview open-ended questions. To clarify the findings of the quantitative study, the findings of the qualitative and quantitative investigations were integrated throughout the interpretation phase of this investigation. The analysis of interview transcripts was conducted to identify, validate, and compare the key themes (Pfeil and Zaphiris, 2010) regarding AI integration in education, to highlight perceptions, challenges, and recommendations with a specific focus on technical and soft skill enhancement.

Discussion

Part 1 — Qualitative Analysis of NEP 2020

The National Education Policy 2020 document was thoroughly studied with a specific focus on its strategic integration of AI through several pivotal aspects. The policy aims to align engineering curricula with industry demands through the upgradation of the framework to suit the rapidly evolving industrial needs. NEP prioritizes seamless integration of artificial intelligence into teaching methodologies, to ensure quality education and skill development. NEP's guidelines have the potential to transform the technical landscape and inculcate technical, professional, and soft skills among the students, fostered by AI integration, leading to holistic education. Moreover, NEP underlines the significance of ethical considerations and responsible AI practices; these could go a long way toward instilling values and ethics among technical students. The policy is committed to providing capacity-building programs to teachers; this would enable them to effectively integrate artificial intelligence into engineering courses as well as to foster responsible AI education. NEP's directives lay out the importance of balanced skill development to ensure equitable access to an integrated education for students across diverse socio-economic backgrounds. NEP encourages research and development, industry collaboration, and future readiness as well. As such, the policy aims to prepare engineering graduates to navigate contemporary challenges, foster innovation, and align modern education with industry requirements in the face of technological advancements. The following main themes and sub-themes were identified based on a thorough thematic analysis of the NEP document:

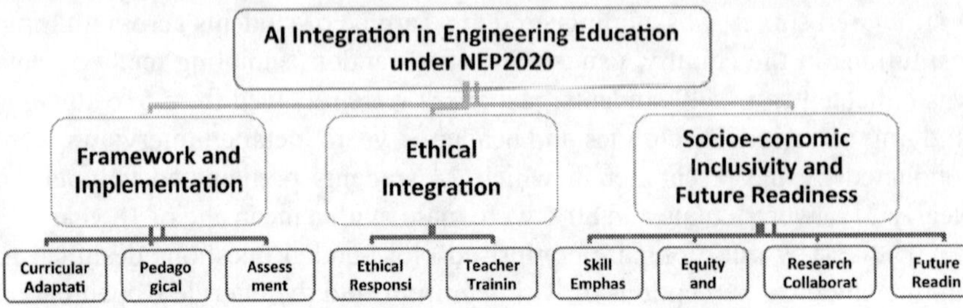

Figure 1: Themes identified based on Thematic Analysis of NEP 2020

Part 2(A) — Quantitative Analysis

Based on the themes identified from the qualitative analysis of the NEP document, the next phase of the study was the quantitative data analysis of empirical data and qualitative analysis of interviews. IBM Statistical Package for Social Sciences (SPSS) v26 and Microsoft Excel were used for data analysis. The findings (Table) reflect a diversity of perceptions regarding the integration of artificial intelligence within the NEP and its implications. The moderate level of awareness among engineering students regarding the inclusion of artificial intelligence within the NEP (mean=3.24) suggested a reasonable but not comprehensive understanding of the initiative undertaken under the NEP policy. This indicated the need for further efforts to circulate information and enhance awareness among students, particularly AI integration in education.

The next item assessed the students' perceptions regarding the influence of AI on their technical and soft skills. The students' responses indicated that they were positive about the potential of AI to improve the technical competencies indicating the efficacy of NEP for fostering technical expertise among students (mean=3.67).

Table 1: Students' Perceptions about Themes/Subthemes based on Analysis of the NEP Document

Theme	*Subtheme*	*Mean Score*
Educational Framework and Implementation EFI	Curricular Adaptation	3.24
	Pedagogical Strategies	3.61
	Assessment and Evaluation	3.92
	Adaptation Challenges	2.96
Total Mean EFI		3.43
Ethical and Responsible Integration ERI	Ethical and Responsible AI Use	3.25
	Teacher Training and Capacity Building	3.67
	Adaptation Challenges	3.44
Total Mean ERI		3.45
Socio-economic Inclusivity and Future Readiness SIFR	Skill Emphasis	3.45
	Equity and Access	3.78
	Research and Innovation	3.82
	Industry Collaboration	3.73
	Future Readiness	3.82
	Adaptation Challenges	3.25
Total Mean SIFR		3.64

The mean scores suggest a moderate level of awareness among students regarding the inclusion of AI within the NEP (Curricular Adaptation: 3.24). The favourable response indicates they perceived Pedagogical Strategies (mean=3.61) and Assessment and Evaluation (mean=3.92) could be made more effective through the incorporation of AI methodologies in teaching and the comprehensive evaluation of acquired skills. However, adaptation challenges (mean: 2.96) did exist, which could pose important barriers and hurdles. The challenges may include resistance to change, lack of infrastructure and resources for integration of AI in education, particularly in rural India, and the lack of properly trained faculty and staff.

The score for ethical and responsible AI integration (mean=3.25) showed a positive perception of NEP's ethical guidelines among the technical students. The high score of teacher training and capacity building (mean=3.67), indicated the need for responsible integration of AI within educational frameworks. The findings highlight the importance of preparing faculty for the proper integration of AI in education, innovative teaching fully utilizing AI and immersive technologies for effective personalized learning as well as focusing on empowering faculty with information regarding AI tools and pedagogical advancement to adapt to the changing and dynamic educational landscape. The adaptation challenges (mean: 3.44) related to ethical and responsible integration included ethical concerns in AI education which is extremely intricate. Challenges may involve balancing theoretical discussion with practical application of ethics, updating the curriculum to incorporate dynamic ethical considerations, and ensuring that ethical guidelines are implemented effectively.

The students' responses on Skill Development (mean=3.45) and Equity and Access (mean=3.78), highlighted a moderate emphasis on them, indicating the recognition of NEP's emphasis on balanced skill development and equitable access toward AI-integrated education. The positive scores of Research and Innovation (mean=3.82), Industry Collaboration (mean=3.73), and Future Readiness (mean=3.82) reflect students' acknowledgement of the NEP's efforts to prepare them for future challenges and technological advancements. The results emphasized the need for fostering innovation, industry-academia collaboration, and future-ready skills among students. This may involve multifaceted challenges including bridging the digital divide, providing equal opportunities for AI-based education across socio-economic backgrounds, and aligning education with future job demands properly and effectively.

In short, the analysis establishes the students have varied perceptions regarding different themes identified, i.e. EFI (mean 3.43), ERI (mean 3.45), and SIFR (3.64). As a cursory glance shows Socio-economic Inclusivity and Future Readiness SIFR was more important in the perception of the students as compared to the other two. It implies students give greater importance to effectiveness in initiatives promoting inclusivity, future readiness, and socio-economic aspects within the educational framework.

Part 2(B) — Thematic Analysis of Interviews Conducted

The qualitative analysis of interview transcripts was supported. The analysis focused on extracting detailed information from the interviews supported the above findings as similar recurring themes, patterns and mindsets were identified. Through the qualitative study, the analysis captured the depth and diversity of the student's perceptions and provided a comprehensive understanding of their real experiences towards AI integration and the ground reality of the implementation of NEP's directions. The interviews reflected the students' enthusiasm towards AI's educational potential, while at the same time, it revealed dire challenges associated with AI integration. These findings indicated a crucial gap between perceived benefits and practical implementations (Table) under NEP which is going to be a complex issue (Muralidharan et al., 2022).

Table 2: Themes and Sub-themes based on Qualitative Analysis of Interviews

Theme	*Sub-theme*	*Benefits*	*Challenges*	*Suggestions*
EFI	Curricular Adaptation	Enhanced practical learning, Real-world relevance of AI applications	Access to tech infrastructure, Technical curriculum gaps, Limited hands-on learning experiences	Collaborate with industry for practical learning labs, Revise curriculum for real-world AI applications, Upgrade technical infrastructure for AI education
	Pedagogical Strategies	Improved understanding, Interactive learning	Teachers' lack of expertise, Resistance to new teaching methods, Insufficient practical sessions	Facilitate specialized AI workshops for educators, Introduce AI project-based learning, Encourage industry internships for practical exposure
	Assessment and Evaluation	Better skill assessment, Comprehensive evaluation	Limited evaluation models suitable for technical subjects, Difficulty in assessing practical AI skills, Lack of AI-focused evaluation tools	Develop AI-centric evaluation tools, Implement AI-based project assessments, Provide industry-recognized AI certifications
ERI	Ethical and Responsible AI Use	Ethical awareness, critical thinking, Responsible tech use	Ethical dilemma in technical AI implementations, Lack of clear ethical guidelines,	Establish comprehensive ethical AI guidelines, Incorporate ethics courses in technical AI curriculum, Promote AI fairness and bias-free training

Theme	*Sub-theme*	*Benefits*	*Challenges*	*Suggestions*
	Teacher Training and Capacity Building	Enhanced teaching quality, Updated technical skills	Inadequate teacher training programs on technical AI, Gap in technical pedagogy, Need for hands-on technical AI training	Develop specialized technical AI training modules for educators, Introduce technical AI teaching certifications, Enhance technical AI workshops for teachers
SIFR	Skill Emphasis	Enhanced employability and skill advancement for diverse backgrounds	Unequal access to AI skill-building resources, Socio-economic disparities in technical AI learning	Provide subsidized access to technical AI resources, Establish AI learning centers in underserved areas, Offer scholarships for technical AI courses
	Equity and Access	Improved educational equality, Equal opportunities in technical AI	Disparities in access to advanced technical AI tools, Digital divide in technical AI resources	Create tech-based learning hubs in remote regions, Expand technical AI education outreach programs, Provide free technical AI toolkits to underprivileged students
	Research and Innovation	Innovation culture, Cutting-edge technical research	Limited research, Funding constraints, and Collaboration barriers	Establish technical AI research grants, Foster cross-disciplinary AI research in technical fields, Initiate technical AI collaboration platforms
	Industry Collaboration	Real-world exposure and networking, Industry-aligned skills	Limited industry tie-ups, Mismatch in industry needs and technical AI education, Regulatory challenges	Establish industry-academia technical AI hubs, Align technical AI curriculum with industry needs, Advocate for streamlined technical AI collaboration policies
	Future Readiness	Technological adaptability, Skill development	Gaps in future-oriented learning, Lack of emphasis on emerging trends, Inadequate technical skill development for future needs	Incorporate emerging AI trends in technical curriculum, Offer specialized technical AI courses for futuristic skills, and Facilitate continuous technical AI skill upgrades for future readiness

Theoretical and Practical Implications

The mixed method study offered several theoretical and practical implications. Firstly, it allowed for a comprehensive understanding by mixing qualitative insights with quantitative data and provided the opportunity to explore the context-specific details and individual students' perspectives, while providing statistical validation, generalizability, and structured analysis. The blend of the two types of analysis supplemented the research by triangulating findings, offering a more holistic view of the studied phenomena, and a deeper understanding of complex educational dynamics.

The present study has immense practical implications which lie in the form of information for decision-making and guidance for the proper implementation of AI through innovative teaching and training methods in engineering institutes in India. By understanding how AI complements education, the administration can tailor teaching approaches to enhance students' technical and soft skills which are the need of the hour. Additionally, this aids in preparing a workforce that meets the demands of the contemporary competitive globalized market. It allows institutes to align their curricula with industry needs and ensure that undergraduate students possess the required skills and knowledge to thrive in the modern tech-driven workplace. The study facilitates the development of strategies for the efficient use of AI tools in education; it also contributes towards a more effective learning environment.

Limitations: The present study has limitations that revolve around potential biases, which may influence the respondents' views and the researcher's mindset. Integrating qualitative and quantitative approaches also leads to bias as it demands substantial resources making it difficult to manage both methods impeccably. The finding as such may not be generalized. Future studies may explore AI's long-term impact on education.

Conclusion

To sum up, the present study exploring AI integration in Indian technical education for enhancing technical and soft skills among undergraduate students offers valuable insights. The qualitative dynamic thematic analysis of the NEP document reveals three broad themes. Challenges in ethical AI usage and access gaps highlight the need for inclusive strategies and robust teacher training and capacity-building programs. To realize NEP's vision, addressing adaptation challenges, promoting equitable access, and fostering research collaborations are the need of the hour; these will eventually lead to a future-ready workforce. The quantitative analysis findings highlighted students' positive perceptions regarding AI integration and its impact on technical and soft skill enhancement; however, they perceived adaptation challenges as well. Despite the limitations due to researcher bias, respondents' bias, and integration complexities, the present study was successful in providing an in-depth inside by merging qualitative richness with quantitative validation. The study's recommendations highlight the need for bridging the gap between policy and practice to facilitate inclusive AI-driven skill development. Finally, addressing these challenges is the need of the hour for leveraging AI's full potential and for a strong AI environment, which would lead to enhancement in technical and soft skills among technical undergraduate students in India.

References

Bele, D.M. (2023). National Education Policy 2020: Challenges & Opportunities in Higher Education in India. *International Journal of Humanities Social Science and Management* (IJHSSM) Volume 3(1), Jan.-Feb. 2023, pp: 205-207 www.ijhssm.org

Kaurav, RPS., Suresh, KG., Narula, S., and Baber R. (2020). New Education Policy: Qualitative (Contents) Analysis and Twitter Mining (Sentiment Analysis). *Journal of Content, Community & Communication*, 12 (2), 4-13

Muralidharan, K., Shanmugan, K. and Klochkov, Y. (2022). The New Education Policy 2020, Digitalisation and Quality of Life in India: Some Reflections. Educ. Sci. 12(2), 75; https://doi.org/10.3390/educsci12020075

Nand, Ramanand, National Education Policy-2020 and Marginals: A Primer (December 22, 2020). National Education Policy 2020 and Marginals https://www.cprgindia.org/pdf/national-education-policy-2020-and-marginals.pdf

Pfeil, U., Zaphiris, P. (2010). Applying qualitative content analysis to study online support communities. Univ. Access Inf. Soc. 8(1), 1–16. doi:10.1007/s10209-009-0154-3

Soni, R. (2022). Challenges and Issues In National Education Policy 2020. *International Research Journal of Modernization in Engineering Technology and Science*, 04(3). 2026-2031.

Tashakkori, A., Teddlie, C. (2004). *Foundations of Mixed Methods Research: Integrating Quantitative and Qualitative Approaches in the Social and Behavioral Science*. SAGE Publications Inc., Thousand Oaks.

24

Machine Learning

Navigating Promises and Pitfalls of AI

Dhriti Tiwari and Sangeeta Suman

Introduction

AI can be seen as an innovation of technology that enables computers and other devices to operate intelligently. Defined as a computer system's capacity to accurately comprehend external input, acquire information from such data, and utilize those leanings to fulfil specified objectives and tasks through flexible adaptation ((Kaplan & Haenlein, 2019). AI has infiltrated all parts of existence (Chen et al., 2022). It is also referred to as human intelligence, which may be seen as the "biopsychological potential to process information to solve problems or create products that are of value in a culture" (Gardner, 1999). Multiple research and publications have extensively examined the possible advantages of using AI in the academic domain (Zhang, K. 2021; Aslan, Dignum V.2018). AI systems may identify students' learning styles and skills and give personalized suggestions and assistance to help them reach their objectives. Furthermore, AI systems may enhance online learning and make education available to students in rural locations, resulting in more equal and inclusive education (Pelletier, K. et al. 2022; Murtaza, M. 2022). Currently, Education Technology (Ed Tech) enterprises are utilizing emotional AI to measure and assess social and emotional development (McStay, 2020). The impact of AI on our future surpasses that of any previous invention in history. Individuals lacking comprehension will swiftly experience a sense of being excluded; awakening in a realm abundant with technology that increasingly resembles sorcery (Maini and Sabri, 2017). Undoubtedly, AI technology holds great significance, and its impact has been observed during the recent pandemic.

Embedding AI in Education for Improved Learning Outcomes

The inclusion of artificial intelligence (AI) and chatbots in education and research has become increasingly common in recent years, particularly by the end of 2022 (Kooli, 2023). The introduction, progress, and widespread use of technology, specifically artificial intelligence, have facilitated instructors in carrying out their responsibilities with greater effectiveness and efficiency. These technological advancements have also extended to other areas of academia, promoting effectiveness and efficiency (Chen et al., 2020). AI has been used in education to automate administrative activities, curriculum, content production, instruction, and student learning. AI-powered web platforms and computer tools have made tasks like assessing student work, grading, and giving feedback, more efficient. Virtual reality, web-based platforms, robotics, video conferencing, audiovisual files, and 3-D technology have been used in curriculum, content development and instruction to help students learn.

Personalized Learning Experiences

AI-driven personalized learning is an educational technique that focuses on individual students and aims to tackle the problem of learner disengagement. AI provides personalized learning experiences by customizing information, interactions, and data analysis to enhance learning results. The utilization of AI and educational chatbots is increasing due to its capacity to offer a cost-efficient approach to include students and deliver a personalized learning encounter (Benotti et al., 2018). The deployment of chatbots is particularly vital in online classes with a large number of students, when providing individual help from educators to students is difficult (Winkler & Söllner, 2018). AI can enhance learning in educational settings by immediately offering students course materials (Cunningham-Nelson et al., 2019), assignments (Ismail & Ade-Ibijola, 2019), practice questions (Sinha et al., 2020), and study materials (Mabunda, 2020). Furthermore, AI has the ability to engage with students on an individual basis (Hobert & Meyer von Wolf, 2019) or assist in collaborative learning tasks (Chaudhuri et al., 2009; Tegos et al., 2014; Kumar & Rose, 2010; Stahl, 2006; Walker et al., 2011).

Ease of Educational Accessibility

The integration of AI in education offers the potential to overcome geographical limitations by making learning resources accessible online through the Internet and the World Wide Web. Online learning or the utilization of web-based learning platforms allows for the accessibility of materials from any location worldwide. Furthermore, artificial intelligence (AI) is clearly capable of enhancing accessibility to education in remote and neglected regions. Byju's, an Indian ed-tech startup, uses artificial intelligence (AI) to provide high-quality education in rural areas, hence reducing the educational disparity. Additionally, the incorporation of AI attributes, such as linguistic translation tools, enables students to optimize their learning experience depending on their particular capabilities.

Transformation of Pedagogical Practices

The impact of AI is evident in teaching approaches, creating educational settings that are both individualized, inclusive, and accessible. AI-driven solutions such as Intelligent Tutoring Systems facilitate personalized instruction and individual attention, addressing the persistent problem of the student-teacher ratio in classrooms. According to Pal (2023), "Artificial intelligence (AI) ensures that every student experiences a sense of recognition and validation." It is like having an individual mentor for each student. Intelligent Tutoring Systems (ITS) utilized by AI to provide interactive and adaptable learning experiences offer immediate feedback, detect areas of learning deficiency, and provide specific assistance, guaranteeing that students receive personalized coaching in real time (Singh, 2023).

According to Sayed et al. (2021), numerous scholars concur that it is crucial in education. However, it is important to note that this does not guarantee perpetual advantages and a complete absence of threats (Dastin, 2018). Elon Musk and Stephen Hawking expressed concerns that once AI reaches a highly developed state, there is a possibility that it could become uncontrollable by humans (Clark et al., 2018).

It has been observed that individuals who receive assistance from decision support systems powered by AI often exhibit excessive dependence on AI system. They tend to unquestioningly accept the suggestions provided by AI, even in cases where such suggestions are incorrect. (Buçinca et al., 2021). Overreliance typically occurs when consumers are unable to ascertain the extent to which they should place faith in AI. Users struggle to ascertain suitable degrees of confidence due to their limited understanding of the capabilities of AI (Passi, S., & Vorvoreanu, M. (2022). There is a concern among experts that the potential for human intellect is bound to get diminished with the growing use of AI and people become less intelligent and more like machines (Ahmad et al. 2023). As expressed by Professor Hawking there are potential repercussions of developing artificial intelligence that can equal or exceed human capabilities. He said, "Humans, who are limited by slow biological evolution, couldn't compete, and would be superseded" (Köbis and Mehner, 2021).

Issues of Concern in the Field of Education

The AI raises the following issues of concern in the field of education:

- *Over reliance:* Excessive dependence leads consumers to place trust in AI in situations when it is not warranted. Users often experience confusion when there is a significant disparity between their responses and the suggestions provided by AI systems (Kim et al., 2021). The significant inaccuracies lead consumers to mistakenly believe that they are at fault, when in reality; it is AI's error. The situation gets worse when users handle novel data, such as out-of-distribution data, which refers to data that the AI model has not been exposed to during its training phase. Users anticipate that AI will sustain its performance when presented with novel material, while simultaneously acknowledging that their own performance may deteriorate when confronted with fresh data (Chaing & Yan, 2021). Consequently, users increasingly depend on artificial intelligence (AI) to handle data that falls outside the known distribution. This reliance on AI leads users to trust it more, even when its performance is dubious and unpredictable.

- *Decline in human creativity:* The possible effect of AI on human creativity is a growing concern among academics, artists, and innovators. As the use and reliance on AI grow, it will inherently restrict the cognitive capabilities of the human brain. Consequently, this greatly diminishes people's cognitive abilities. This process eliminates cognitive abilities in humans and renders them more synthetic. Moreover, extensive engagement with technology has compelled humans to adopt algorithmic thinking without comprehending it fully (Sarwat, 2018). Creating new, valuable ideas, solutions, or expressions is a popular definition of creativity. It involves divergent thinking, uncommon opinions, and fusing seemingly unrelated ideas. Humans have always created creativity using their unique experiences, feelings, and mental processes. Increasing AI systems may change the creative process. It may lead to passive consumption of ideas rather than active participation. When individuals outsource creative tasks to AI, they may lose the emotional connection and personal involvement that leads to breakthroughs.
- *Loss of human decision-making:* AI restricts and eliminates the need for humans in decision-making. Decision-making is becoming less dependent on human mental faculties including critical thinking, creative problem-solving, and intuitive analysis (Ghosh et al., 2019). Every day, more and more educational institutions use AI to aid decision-making. Universities are using AI for both administrative and scholarly purposes. AI's key responsibilities in the education sector include personalisation, tutoring, quick responses, 24/7 access to learning, question answering, and task automation. Students can now receive assistance from AI for everything from programme admission requirements to degree issuance (Karandish, 2021). AI renders teachers and other administrative workers useless since it does so much of their work for them. They are losing the ability to perform standard activities in an educational setting, which leads to a loss of reasoning and decision-making skills.

- *Cognitive deterioration and the rise in human laziness:* AI has shown that it can increase productivity and improve results in various applications, from smart home appliances to sophisticated medical diagnostics. This contentious relationship has sparked discussions and brought up significant issues regarding the unforeseen effects of our growing reliance on intelligent technologies. The progressive loss of cognitive capacities, including memory, attention, problem-solving, and linguistic proficiency, is referred to as cognitive decline (Chandler et al., 2023). The ability of the human brain to reason will eventually become limited when AI is used more and more. As a result, humans' ability to reason is gradually diminished (Ahmad et al., 2023). Teachers and students will employ AI software while working on a task or assignment, or their work may be completed automatically. Addiction to AI use can eventually result in laziness and troublesome circumstances down the road.
- *Loss of human touch:* AI is becoming more and more integrated into our lives, and a profound worry the possible loss of the human touch emerges. People run the risk of replacing interactions with AI systems with interactions with other people. Cognitive decline has been connected to social isolation and loneliness. While AI is capable of simulating companionship and communication, it is devoid of the shared experiences and profound emotional comprehension that characterize true human connections. Artificial intelligence is limited in comprehending human emotions and forming meaningful connections. Even while AI has a lot of potential to improve productivity and solve challenging issues, its implementation must take into account the special characteristics that make humans human (Diem, 2023).
- *Gender bias:* Concerns of gender bias in AI systems have been highlighted by the integration of artificial intelligence (AI) across a number of disciplines, especially in the hiring and recruitment process. Favouring male candidates over equally or more competent female candidates is just one example of how gender bias in AI manifests. Another is perpetuating assumptions about gender roles and career choices (Manasi, 2023). There are two key phases where gender bias might arise: creating AI algorithms and training datasets. Both the people who created the algorithms and the data they utilize are frequently the source of biases in AI systems (Neithammer, 2020). AI can internalise gender prejudices in society because they are a reflection of human input. For example, AI systems may link a given gender to particular professions, reflecting antiquated ideas and perpetuating gender stereotypes. The development of gender equality may be hampered by the introduction of human biases into AI systems, which could increase the gender gap.

Conclusion

To summarize, AI plays a crucial role in education by offering individualized learning opportunities and enhancing efficiency. Nevertheless, there are drawbacks to consider, such as the potential for cognitive deterioration, since an overreliance on AI could weaken one's ability to engage in critical thinking. The emergence of human laziness is a potential consequence when pupils excessively rely on automatic solutions. Excessive dependence on AI may result in the absence of human interaction in education, impacting the essential interpersonal relationships necessary for comprehensive growth. It is crucial to achieve a balance where AI supports and enhances human involvement in education, while also retaining cognitive abilities, promoting self-sufficiency, and maintaining the fundamental human aspect.

Bibliography

Ahmad, S.F., Han, H., Alam, M.M., Rahmat, K., Irshad, M., Arraño-Muñoz, M. & Ariza-Montes, A.(2023). Impact of artificial intelligence on human loss in decision making, laziness and safety in education. *Humanities And Social Sciences Communications*.10, https://doi.org/10.1057/s41599-023-01787-8.

Benotti, L., Martnez, M.C., & Schapachnik, F. (2018). A Tool for introducing computer science with automatic formative assessment. *IEEE Transactions on Learning Technologies,11*(2),179-192. https://doi.org/10.1109/TLT.2017.2682084.

Chandler, C., Diaz-Asper, C., Turner, R.S., Reynolds, B., & Elvevåg, B. (2023). An explainable machine learning model of cognitive decline derived from speech. *Alzheimer's & dementia (Amsterdam, Netherlands)*, *15*(4), e12516. https://doi.org/10.1002/dad2.12516.

Chen, L., Chen, P., & Lin, Z. (2020). Artificial intelligence in education: A review. IEEE Access, 8, 75264–75278. https://doi.org/10.1109/ACCESS.2020.2988510

Chen, X.; Cheng, G.; Zou, D.; Zhong, B.; Xie, H. (2023). Artificial Intelligent Robots for Precision Education. *Educ. Technol. Soc.,* 26, 171–186.

Clark, J., Shoham, Y., Perrault, R., Erik Brynjolfsson, Manyika, J., Niebles, J.C., Lyons, T., Etchemendy, J., Grosz, B. and Bauer, Z. (2018). The AI Index 2018 Annual Report, AI Index Steering Committee, Human-Centered AI Initiative, Stanford University, Stanford, CA.

Cunningham-Nelson, S., Baktashmotlagh, M., & Boles, W. (2019). Visualizing student opinion through text analysis. *IEEE Transactions on Education*, 62(4), 305–311

Diem, N. (2023, Sept,11). The Human Touch in an AI-Driven World: Balancing HR and Technology in Human Resources Management. *Mitratech.*

Ghosh, B., Daugherty, P.R., Wilson, H.J. (2019) Taking a systems approach to adopting AI. Harv Bus Rev. https://hbr.org/2019/05/taking-a-systems-approach-to-adopting-ai.

Hobert, S., & Meyer von Wolf, R. (2019). Say helloto your new automatedtutor–a structured literature review on pedagogical conversational agents.

Ismail, M., & Ade-Ibijola, A. (2019). Lecturer's apprentice: A chatbot for assisting novice programmers. In 2019 international multidisciplinary information technology and engineering conference (IMITEC) (pp. 1-8).

Kaplan, A., & Haenlein, M. (2019). Siri, siri, in my hand: Who's the fairest in the land? On the interpretations, illustrations, and implications of artificial intelligence. *Business Horizons*, 62(1), 15–25. https://doi.org/10.1016/j.bushor.2018.08.004

Karandish, D. (2021). Benefits of AI in education. https://thejournal.com/Articles/2021/06/23/7-Benefits-of-AI-in-Education.aspx.

Kim, A., Yang, M., & Zhang, J. (2020). When Algorithms Err: Differential Impact of Early vs. Late Errors on Users' Reliance on Algorithms (SSRN Scholarly Paper ID 3691575). Social Science Research Network. https://doi.org/10.2139/ssrn.3691575

Köbis L, Mehner C (2021) Ethical questions raised by AI-supported mentoring in higher education. Front ArtifIntell 4:1–9. https://doi.org/10.3389/frai.2021. 624050

Kooli, C. Chatbots in Education and Research: A Critical Examination of Ethical Implications and Solutions. Sustainability 2023, 15, 5614. https://doi.org/10.3390/su15075614.

Kumar, R., & Rose, C.P (2010). Architecture for building conversational agents that support collaborative learning. *IEEE Transactions on Learning Technologies*, 4(1), 21–34.

Mabunda, K. (2020). An intelligent chatbot for guiding visitors and locating venues.

Maini, V., Sabri, S. (2017). Machine learning for humans. https://medium.com/ machine-learning-for-humans

Manasi, A. (2023, March 17). Addressing Gender Bias to achieve ethical AI. *IPI Gobal observatory.*

McStay, A. (2020) Emotional AI and EdTech: serving the public good? *Learn Media Technol* 45(3):270–283. https://doi.org/10.1080/17439884.2020.1686016.

Murtaza, M., Ahmed, Y., Shamsi, J.A., Sherwani, F., & Usman, M. (2022). AI-Based Personalized E-Learning Systems: Issues, Challenges, and Solutions. IEEE Access, 10, 81323–81342.

Niethammer, C. (2020, March 20). AI Bias Could Put Women's Lives At Risk — A Challenge For Regulators. *Forbes.*

Pal, S. (2023). Artificial intelligence: Reshaping the topography of pedagogic practices — A comparative study on curriculum construction, teaching modalities, and evaluation techniques. AGPE *The Royal Gondwana Research Journal of History, Science, Economic, Political and Social Science*, 4(7), 13–20.

Passi, S., & Vorvoreanu, M. (2022). Overreliance on AI Literature Review. *Microsoft Research.*

Pelletier, K., McCormack, M., Reeves, J., Robert, J., Arbino, N., Dickson-Deane, C., & Stine, J. (2022). EDUCAUSE Horizon Report Teaching and Learning Edition; EDUC22: Boulder, CO, USA, 2022; 58p. 10.

Singh, R.J. (2023). Transforming Higher Education: The Power of Artificial Intelligence. *International Journal of Multidisciplinary Research in Arts, Science and Technology*, *1*(3), 13-18.

Sinha, S., Basak, S., Dey, Y., & Mondal, A. (2020). An educational chatbot for answering queries, Springer

Winkler, R., & Söllner, M. (2018). Unleashing the potential of chatbots in education: A state-of-the-art analysis. In the Academy of management annual meeting (AOM).

25

Creating a Positive and Supportive Culture Around AI in Education

Mohammad Haseen Ahmed

Introduction

The NEP 2020 encompasses a range of provisions aimed at embedding AI into the education system, focusing on curriculum integration, teacher training, personalized learning, interdisciplinary approaches, and ethical considerations. These provisions collectively strive to prepare students for the AI-driven future by providing them with the requisite knowledge, skills, and ethical understanding.

The incorporation of AI in education while prioritizing student privacy and well-being, as outlined in the New Education Policy (NEP) 2020, has been a focal point in India's educational landscape. While there have been notable strides in integrating AI into educational practices, several challenges and considerations related to privacy, security, and ethical implications have emerged.

One of the key areas where AI has been incorporated is in the development of adaptive learning platforms and educational tools. These AI-driven systems aim to personalize learning experiences for students, offering tailored content and assessments. Ensuring student data privacy within these platforms remains a significant concern. There is a need to establish robust data protection policies, encryption standards, and secure storage practices to safeguard sensitive student information from unauthorized access or breaches.

Collaborative efforts involving policymakers, educational institutions, technology developers, and stakeholders are essential to navigate the complexities of AI integration in education. Stakeholder engagement is crucial to gathering diverse perspectives, addressing concerns, and developing comprehensive guidelines that align with the objectives of the NEP 2020.

While progress has been made in leveraging AI in education under the NEP 2020, there are ongoing challenges and issues that need to be addressed. These include data privacy and security, algorithmic bias and fairness, ethical use of AI, educator training and capacity building, equitable access to AI education, regulatory frameworks, and collaboration among stakeholders. By actively addressing these issues, India can ensure the responsible and effective integration of AI in education, ultimately benefiting students and preparing them for the future.

The National Education Policy (NEP) 2020 recognizes the immense potential of Artificial Intelligence (AI) in transforming education. It envisions integrating AI across various stages and aspects of the educational landscape, from personalized learning experiences to intelligent adaptive assessments. However, while exciting prospects emerge, NEP 2020 also implicitly highlights the pressing need for robust regulatory frameworks to address the challenges associated with AI in education.

While NEP 2020 acknowledges the importance of AI, it lacks specific policy frameworks addressing the challenges associated with its effective deployment and smooth navigation.

To effectively leverage AI's potential while mitigating its risks, collaborative efforts are necessary which might include but are not limited to:

- Firstly, governments should prioritize developing comprehensive AI policy frameworks for education, addressing data privacy, algorithmic transparency, ethics, and standardization.
- Secondly, educational institutions need to actively participate in shaping these frameworks, ensuring they align with pedagogical needs and address specific challenges faced in schools and universities.
- Thirdly, tech developers must build AI systems for education with privacy, transparency, and ethical considerations at the forefront, adhering to established standards and regulations in consultation with parents, students, and educators.

NEP 2020's vision of integrating AI in education can only be fully realized with responsible and effective AI policy frameworks. By prioritizing data privacy, algorithmic transparency, ethical guidelines, and robust standards, collaborative efforts can turn AI into a powerful tool for enhancing learning experiences while ensuring fairness, trust, and well-being in the educational ecosystem.

As the Indian education system embarks on the ambitious journey of integrating AI as envisioned by the NEP 2020, fostering a positive and supportive culture around this transformative technology is paramount. This necessitates a multi-pronged approach that begins with raising awareness and understanding. Comprehensive training programs for educators must illuminate the fundamentals of AI, its educational applications, and the exciting possibilities it holds, as engaging workshops and demonstrations for students can spark curiosity and excitement about responsible AI use. Parents and the wider community deserve to be informed as well, through open forums, media outreach, and clear communication about how AI tools are employed in teaching and learning, emphasizing data privacy, fairness, and the proactive mitigation of bias.

Collaboration and openness are crucial next steps. Dedicated AI support teams, equipped with expertise in both technology and pedagogy can offer invaluable guidance to educators and students as they navigate the integration process. Knowledge-sharing platforms like online forums, conferences, and peer-to-peer mentoring programs can foster a vibrant community of practice, where educators can learn from each other's successes and troubleshoot challenges collectively. Throughout this journey, transparency and ethical considerations must be prioritized. Students and parents deserve to understand how their data is used and protected, while educators need clear guidelines on responsible AI use that promote inclusivity and address potential biases.

Integrating age-appropriate AI literacy modules into the curriculum

Building skills and confidence in both educators and students is key to unlocking the full potential of AI in education. By integrating age-appropriate AI literacy modules into the curriculum, we can equip students with the foundational knowledge of AI concepts, basic coding skills, and the critical thinking necessary to use these tools responsibly. Encouraging them to apply AI not just for rote learning but for analysing information, formulating questions, and developing creative solutions will nurture the problem-solving skills so crucial in the 21st century. Recognizing and celebrating the successes of educators and students who champion AI integration will further fuel enthusiasm and inspire others to follow suit.

Ensuring equity and accessibility is a non-negotiable aspect of building a positive AI culture in education. Bridging the digital divide through infrastructure investments and targeted training programs is essential to guarantee that all students, regardless of their background or location, have equal access to AI tools and resources. Developing diverse AI applications that cater to different learning styles, abilities, and cultural contexts will further ensure inclusivity while prioritizing AI-powered personalized learning and support for students with disabilities or learning challenges will leave no one behind on this transformative journey.

Building a supportive AI culture in Indian education is not a singular act, but a collective symphony played by educators, students, policymakers, and the wider community. By focusing on raising awareness, fostering collaboration, building skills, and prioritizing equity, we can ensure that AI becomes not just a technological tool, but a powerful catalyst for enhancing learning, nurturing innovation, and empowering every student to thrive in the AI-driven future envisioned by the NEP 2020.

Vision of NEP 2020

National Education Policy 2020 stipulates that:

> "It must enable an individual to study one or more specialized areas of interest at a deep level, and develop character, ethical and Constitutional values, intellectual curiosity, scientific temper, creativity, spirit of service, and 21st century capabilities across a range of disciplines including sciences, social sciences, arts, humanities, languages, as well as professional, technical, and vocational subjects." It categorically lays emphasis on the "Extensive use of technology in teaching and learning, removing language barriers, increasing access for Divyang students, and educational planning and management".

'New Education Policy' comes into effect on 29 July 2020, gives a new framework to the Indian education system which is supposed to warrant a paradigm shift from the school education system to higher education spread over a time span of 20 years. Equity, quality, inclusivity, accessibility with affordability, and accountability are some of the hallmarks of NEP aiming to cater to the needs of students at all levels.

Embracing this opportunity with open hearts, open minds, and a shared commitment to building a future where AI empowers, not replaces, the irreplaceable human touch in education can be the most desirable outcome of this policy. AI has already begun to make some positive inroads towards making it more inclusive in the following domains. Just to have an idea of the key areas of its prominence and deployment:

- *AI in Personalized Learning:* NEP 2020 promotes personalized learning experiences through adaptive learning platforms powered by AI. These platforms analyse individual student learning patterns and provide customized learning paths, materials, and assessments.
- *Teacher Training and AI Integration*: There is a focus on training teachers to utilize AI tools effectively in the classroom. Workshops and programs aim to familiarize educators with AI-driven educational technologies to enhance teaching methodologies and student engagement.
- *AI for Assessment and Evaluation*: AI-driven assessment tools are being developed to provide instant feedback on student performance, enabling more accurate evaluation and timely interventions for improvement.
- *Curriculum Development and AI Integration:* AI is being incorporated into curriculum development to ensure it stays relevant and aligned with industry demands. It includes AI-based tools for content creation, curation, and modification to cater to diverse learning needs.
- *AI Ethics and Policy:* There's a growing discourse on the ethical implications of integrating AI in education. Discussions revolve around

data privacy, bias in AI algorithms, and creating policies to ensure responsible AI usage in the education sector.

The Indian New Education Policy, 2020 recognizes the importance of Artificial Intelligence (AI) in education and aims to create a positive and supportive culture around its integration. To achieve this, the policy outlines key points, frameworks, guiding principles, and strategies to embed AI into the education system. Some of the highlights of this enterprising move can be categorised as these:

1. *Policy Objectives*: The policy aims to leverage AI to enhance the quality of education, improve access to personalized learning, and promote critical thinking and problem-solving skills among students. It also seeks to develop AI-related skills among teachers and students to prepare them for the future workforce.
2. *Curriculum Integration*: The policy emphasizes the integration of AI across various subjects and grade levels. AI concepts and applications will be incorporated into the curriculum to ensure that students develop a deep understanding of AI and its potential impact on society.
3. *Professional Advancement*: To effectively integrate AI into education, the policy emphasizes the need for comprehensive teacher training programs. Teachers will be provided with professional development opportunities to enhance their knowledge and skills in AI. This will enable them to effectively incorporate AI tools and technologies into their teaching practices.
4. *Infrastructure and Resources:* The policy recognizes the importance of providing schools with the necessary infrastructure and resources to support AI integration. This includes access to AI tools, software, and hardware, as well as high-speed Internet connectivity. Schools will be encouraged to establish AI labs and innovation centres to facilitate hands-on learning experiences for students.
5. *Ethical and Responsible AI:* The policy emphasizes the need to promote ethical and responsible AI practices in education. Students will be educated about the ethical implications of AI, including issues related to privacy, bias, and fairness. They will be encouraged to develop AI solutions that are inclusive, transparent, and accountable.
6. *Collaboration and Partnerships:* The policy encourages collaboration between educational institutions, industry partners, and research organizations to foster innovation in AI education. Partnerships with AI companies and startups will provide students with real-world exposure to AI applications and industry trends.

7. *Research and Development:* The policy highlights the importance of research and development in the field of AI in education. Funding will be allocated to support research projects that explore the potential of AI in improving teaching and learning outcomes. This will contribute to the development of evidence-based practices and innovative AI solutions for education.
8. *Monitoring and Evaluation:* The policy emphasizes the need for continuous monitoring and evaluation of AI integration in education. This will ensure that the implementation is effective and aligned with the policy objectives. Regular assessments and feedback mechanisms will be put in place to measure the impact of AI on student learning and overall educational outcomes. By incorporating these key points, policies, frameworks, guiding principles, and strategies, India can foster a positive and supportive culture around AI in education, ensuring its successful integration aligned with the Indian New Education Policy, 2020. This would enable students to develop relevant skills for the future and empower them to harness the potential of AI in their academic and professional lives.

Potential Use of AI in the Assessment

AI applications can be integrated into the Indian education system as it has the potential to enhance personalized learning experiences, improve educational outcomes, and facilitate more efficient and effective teaching practices through several AI applications which include these, but may not be limited to:

- *Intelligent tutoring systems* utilize AI to provide personalized and adaptive learning experiences. These systems analyse individual student performance, identify learning gaps, and deliver customized content and feedback to support their learning needs. Virtual assistants and chatbots can be integrated into educational platforms and websites to provide instant support and guidance to students. They can answer questions, provide explanations, and offer interactive learning experiences, enhancing student engagement and accessibility.
- *AI algorithms* can automate the grading of assignments, quizzes, and exams, saving time for teachers and enabling faster feedback to students. These automated grading systems can also analyse patterns in student responses, identify misconceptions, and provide targeted feedback to support learning outcomes. AI algorithms can analyse student learning patterns, preferences, and performance data to recommend relevant educational resources and materials. This personalized content

recommendation system can help students discover additional learning materials aligned with their interests and learning goals.

- *Learning analytics, powered by AI*, can provide valuable insights about student progress, identify areas for improvement, and enable data-driven interventions to support student success. AI-powered language processing technologies can assist students in language learning by providing real-time translation, pronunciation assistance, and grammar correction. This can be particularly helpful for students learning multiple languages or for those with language-related learning challenges.
- AI can generate *adaptive assessments* that adjust difficulty levels based on individual student performance. This ensures that assessments align with students' knowledge and skills, providing a more accurate measure of their learning achievements.
- *Virtual and augmented reality technologies* can create immersive learning experiences. AI can be used to develop interactive simulations, virtual laboratories, or historical reconstructions, allowing students to explore complex concepts and environments in a more engaging and hands-on manner.
- AI can help educational institutions make data-driven decisions by analysing various educational datasets. This includes predicting student outcomes, optimizing resource allocation, and identifying areas for improvement in curriculum design and delivery.
- *AI-powered plagiarism detection tools* can help educators identify instances of academic dishonesty by comparing student work against a vast database of existing content. This supports academic integrity and ensures the originality of student submissions.

Successful AI integration in the Indian education system, promoting equitable access to quality education and preparing students for a technology-driven future do pose certain limitations and challenges that need to be tackled before harnessing or deploying them in the student community. Some of the limitations can be summed up in these potential scenarios.

Limiting factors and the impediments to successful implementation

Adequate infrastructure and access to technology can be limited in certain regions, creating disparities in AI integration and leading to the digital divide, often influenced by socio-economic factors and regional variations with inequitable implementation. Developing a skilled workforce proficient in AI is crucial but may pose challenges in terms of training and availability of educators with AI expertise apart from the usual resistance to change from educators, students, and parents, concerns about job displacement, privacy, and data security, as well as a preference for traditional teaching methods impeding the adoption of AI in education.

Ethical considerations such as data privacy, algorithmic biases, and responsible AI use need careful attention and developing guidelines and frameworks to address these concerns and ensure transparency in AI systems can be challenging. Integrating AI into the curriculum requires careful planning and coordination, including the development of AI-related content and instructional materials aligned with learning outcomes coupled with a comprehensive teacher training programs to equip educators with AI skills and pedagogical approaches may be a big challenge.

The limited availability of localized educational content and resources in regional languages can impact the effectiveness of AI integration in diverse linguistic contexts. Implementing AI technologies can involve significant costs, posing challenges for educational institutions with limited resources. Ensuring that AI systems are inclusive, representative, and free from bias is crucial to avoid reinforcing existing social, cultural, and gender disparities. Addressing these challenges requires proactive measures such as bridging the digital divide, adapting AI tools to the cultural context, ensuring data quality and privacy, and fostering awareness and understanding among stakeholders.

Balancing AI integration with the crucial role of human teachers in facilitating meaningful teacher-student interactions is necessary. Assessing the impact and effectiveness of AI integration and developing appropriate evaluation frameworks can be challenging. Scaling up AI integration across diverse educational institutions and establishing regulatory frameworks addressing data privacy, security, and intellectual property rights are important considerations. Building awareness, keeping up with technological advancements, and promoting equity and inclusion are the ways forward for successful AI integration in the Indian education system.

Conclusion

The National Education Policy (NEP) 2020 marks a significant shift in the country's education landscape seeking out holistic and multidisciplinary learning, skill development, and the integration of technology in education. Although the NEP 2020 is still in its early stages of implementation, there have been some notable developments like the recognition of childhood education through a strong foundation in the early years enhancing access to quality preschool education and promoting school readiness among children.

The policy pushes for the use of technology in education by the integration of AI and other emerging technologies promoting vocational education, skill development, and experiential learning to enhance employability prospects.

In terms of higher education, the NEP 2020 aims to reform the establishment of multidisciplinary institutions, increase focus on research and innovation, and the promotion of international collaborations elevating the quality of higher education to gain global acceptance.

The successful implementation of the NEP 2020 will largely depend on various factors like awareness among stakeholders, effective communication, and global collaboration with the right provisions for regular monitoring and evaluation of the policy's progress.

The projection for the future outcomes of the NEP 2020 is promising. If executed effectively, the policy has the potential to transform the Indian education system by promoting a learner-centric approach, fostering critical thinking and creativity, and equipping students with relevant skills for the 21st century workforce.

References

All India Council of Technical Education. https://www.facilities.aicte-india.org/dashboard/pages/dashboardaicte.php, Accessed -July 2019.

India Today. (2021, April 16). *Do so many boards confuse parents in creating various benchmark*. https://www.indiatoday.in/education-today/featurephilia/story/do-so-many-boards-confuse-parents-in-creating-various-benchmark-1791274-2021-04-15.

Wikipedia contributors. (2023, November 27). *Right to education*. Wikipedia. https://en.wikipedia.org/wiki/Right_to_education

Sinclair, J., & Cardew-Hall, M. (2007). The folksonomy tag cloud: when is it useful? *Journal of Information Science*, *34*(1), 15–29. https://doi.org/10.1177/0165551506078083

Government of India. (2020). *National Education Policy 2020*. Retrieved from https://www.mhrd.gov.in/sites/upload_files/mhrd/files/NEP_Final_English_0.pdf (Accessed on January 2, 2022).

Chima, J.S. (2020). Are Participants in Ethnonationalist Movements Rational-Choosers, Socially-Embedded Actors, or Psychologically-Instinctive Beings?: Motivations and Worldviews of Sikh Separatists from India. *Studies in Conflict & Terrorism*, *45*(10), 907–928. https://doi.org/10.1080/1057610x.2020.1711604

National Education Policy 2019. (n.d.). Retrieved from https://innovate.mygov.in/wpcontent/uploads/2019/06/mygov15596510111.pdf. Accessed on 12 November 2021.

Kumar, K. (2005). Quality of Education at the Beginning of the 21st Century: Lessons from India. *Indian Educational Review*.

Basham, J.D., Hall, T.E., Carter, R.A., Jr., & Stahl, W.M. (2016). An operationalized understanding of personalized learning. *Journal of Special Education Technology*, 31(3), 126–136.

Buchsbaum, D., Gopnik, A., Griffiths, T.L., & Shafto, P. (2011). Children's imitation of causal action sequences is influenced by statistical and pedagogical evidence. *Cognition*, *120*(3), 331–340. https://doi.org/10.1016/j.cognition.2010.12.001

Darby, F. (2020, April 14). 5 Low-Tech, Time-Saving Ways to Teach Online During Covid-19. *Chronicle of Higher Education*. Retrieved from https://www.chronicle.com/article/5-Low-Tech-Time-SavingWays/248519

Dorn, E., Hancock, B., Sarakatsannis, J., &Viruleg, E. (2020, June 1). *COVID-19 and student learning in the United States: The hurt could last a lifetime. McKinsey*. Retrieved from https://www.mckinsey.com/industries/public-and-social-sector/our-insights/covid-19-and-studentlearning-in-the-united-states-the-hurt-could-last-a-lifetime.

Kallio, J., & Halverson, R. (2020). Distributed leadership for personalized learning. *Journal of Research on Technology in Education, 52*(3), 371–390. https://doi.org/10.1080/15391523.2020.1734508

Kamenetz, A. (2020, March 19). 'Panic-gogy': Teaching Online Classes During The Coronavirus Pandemic. *NPR*. Retrieved from https://www.npr.org/2020/03/19/817885991/panic-gogy-teaching-online-classes-during-the-coronavirus-pandemic.

Sun, L., Tang, Y., &Zuo, W. (2020). Coronavirus pushes education online. *Nature Materials, 19*(6), 687. https://doi.org/10.1038/s41563-020-0678-8

UNICEF. (2020, August 24). 'What will a return to school during the COVID-19 pandemic look like?'. *UNICEF*. Retrieved from https://www.unicef.org/coronavirus/what-will-return-school-during-covid-19-.pandemic-look.

United Nations. (2020, August). *Policy Brief: Education during COVID-19 and beyond.* Retrieved fromhttps://www.un.org/development/desa/dspd/wpcontent/uploads/sites/22/2020/08/sg_policy_brief_covid-19_and_education_august_2020.pdf

Wehmeyer, M.L., & Zhao, Y. (2020). *Teaching students to become Self-determined Learners*. https://eric.ed.gov/?id=ED604929

Zhao, Y. (2020). Tofu is not cheese: Rethinking education amid the COVID-19 pandemic. *ECNUReviewofEducation,3*(2),189–203.https://doi.org/10.1177/2096531120928082

Zhao, Y., Wehmeyer, M.L., Basham, J.D., & Hansen, D.M. (2019). Tackling the wicked problem of measuring what matters: framing the questions. *ECNU Review of Education, 2*(3), 262–278. https://doi.org/10.1177/2096531119878965

26

Integration of AI in Personalised Learning of Dyscalculia

Babita Yadav and Manvi Yadav

Introduction

Mathematics plays a significant role in our daily life and mathematical competence is an essential component for overall development of critical and committed citizenship (Espina et al., 2023; Katgeri, 2017). Unfortunately, a significant percentage of young students are facing difficulty in mathematical computations and numerical operation, falling under a type of specific learning disability termed as dyscalculia (Espina et al., 2023; Sudha & Shalini, 2014). The early identification and intervention are critical for the academic progress of students with dyscalculia, as the severity of challenges increases with complexity of coursework as they advance to the next class. However, digital technologies enable us to mitigate these challenges to some extent.

Recent advancement in digital technology makes a great transition in education practices and makes the classroom more inclusive (Vincent-Lancrin & Van Der Vlies, 2020). The integration of Artificial Intelligence (AI) applications into the curriculum enhances accessibility, foster engagement and facilitate personalized learning to all learners including students with dyscalculia (Adeela Sukiman & Abdl Aziz, 2021; Zhai & Panjwani-Charania, 2023). Various AI-based applications like deep learning, machine learning, neural network, virtual reality and mobile based games make adaptive learning easier to implement at inclusive setup (Dhingra et al., 2022; Hashiyana et al., 2022). These applications assist in identification of dyscalculic students so that the appropriate intervention training can be employed to them as per their specific needs (Karagiannakis & Baccaglini-Frank, 2014).

The Study

Background

Learning stands as a crucial force that shapes our understanding and empowers us to counter challenges with newfound knowledge. However, some individuals demonstrate impaired learning behaviour in reading, writing and mathematics, collectively coming under specific learning disability (Grünke

& Morrison Cavendish, 2016; Kirk, 1977). Dyscalculia is one of the types where individuals struggle with tasks involving numerical operations but advancements in digital technologies reduce their challenges, and support their learning (Ferraz et al., 2017; Khing, 2016). Various systematic reviews were done in the recent past where AI embraces the learning of the students with dyscalculia. A few systematic review studies were taken which describe the type of intervention and technology used in recent past years which enable the researcher to find the research gap.

The details of the studies are given in Table 1, where authors, title, number of articles and period of studies are mentioned. The reviews primarily centred on the transformative potential of technology to support students with learning disabilities, emphasizing its pivotal role in enhancing their educational experiences and facilitating more inclusive environments (Adeela Sukiman & Abdl Aziz, 2021; Zhai & Panjwani-Charania, 2023). The two systematic reviews dedicated to dyscalculia have identified different learning aids and computer-based technology for early identification of dyscalculic students that demonstrated positive impact on learning outcome of the students with dyscalculia (Espina et al., 2023; Fatwana et al., 2023).

Table 1: List of Systematic Reviews

Authors & Years	*Title*	*No. of Articles & Years Taken in Studies*	*Technology Used*
Panjwani & Zhai (2023)	AI for students with Learning Disabilities: A Systematic Review	16 (2011-2021)	Adaptive Learning, Facial Expression, Chat-Robot, Intelligent Tutor, Mastery Learning, Interactive Robot Qualitative
Fatwana, Dasari & Juandi (2023)	The Use of Learning Aids for Dyscalculia: Systematic Literature	13 (2010-2021)	Computer Based Learning, Working Memory, Abacus Aids, Psycho, Review education, PowerPoint, Menerapkan. Number, Race, Using digital (Spatial Ass.)
Espino, Marban & Maroto (2023)	Technological resources for early intervention in cases of dyscalculia: A deductive-inductive categorization	48 (2011-2022)	Number catch, Number race, Graphogame-maths, Number beads, Dots2 Digit, Dots2 Track, NeurecaNUM, Discalapp, Meister Cody-Talasia, DisMAT, Dinamo Numeros, Elevate, Calculic, Kids, Lumosity, MathRX program, Shape, Maths, Long division, Slate maths, Know the Abacus, Smartick, MathemAntics

Authors & Years	*Title*	*No. of Articles & Years Taken in Studies*	*Technology Used*
Sukiman and Aziz (2021)	Artificial intelligence as the key player in learning interventions: A mini review Among students with learning difficulties	10 (2017-2021)	Virtual reality, Augmented reality, Humanoid Robots, Mixed reality, Radio frequency Among students with learning difficulties identification

Literature Gap

In the analysis of systematic reviews presented in Table 1, it is found that the two studies, specifically Zhai (2023) & Sukiman (2021), address learning disability holistically rather than focusing on dyscalculia. The rest two studies have taken articles of dyscalculia, but Fatwana (2023) primarily emphasized learning aids related to manual tools and not on AI based applications. However, Espino (2023) explored AI based tools but predominantly emphasized on early identification and not a single Indian study is included in any of them. Thus, this study is uniquely centred on AI tools which enable personalized learning of the students with dyscalculia. Personalized learning emphasized on individualized instruction as per the needs of the students with dyscalculia (Kharbat et al., 2021).

Research Questions

The purpose of this study is to find systematic reviews of the study and explore the implication of artificial intelligence (AI) on students with dyscalculia, focusing on personalized learning of these students. This study helps special educators and subject teachers to design personalized learning programs for students with dyscalculia and enables to resolve the following research questions, these are:

1. What is the application of AI in the learning process of students with dyscalculia from the past ten years?
2. How does AI-based learning reduce the mathematical difficulties of students with dyscalculia?

Methodology

Literature review is a tedious process encompassing scientific procedure and substantial findings presented through theoretical and methodological contributions (Fatwana et al., 2023). In this systematic study, all the literature related to the implication of AI in the personalized learning of students with dyscalculia was collected and systematically synthesized to examine the effectiveness as well as feasibility of artificial intelligence on the academic progress of students with dyscalculia.

Research Design

The relevant literatures were collected by using the guidelines of the Preferred Reporting Items for Systematic Review and Meta-analyses (PRISMA 2020) that upheld the transparency and reliability of the systematic review of the integration of AI in the personalized learning of dyscalculia (Page et al., 2021; Trifu et al., 2022).

Establish Inclusion and Exclusion Criteria

The process of literature selection involves inclusion and exclusion criteria to meet the relevant studies and excludes those that do not meet predefined criteria. Thus, this discerning selection process ensures that the chosen literature closely aligns with predefined parameters and objectives, thereby upholding the methodological precision of systematic review.

Table 2: Literature Selection Based on Inclusion and Exclusion Criteria

Inclusion Categories	*Exclusion Categories*
i. Study related to Dyscalculia.	i. Studies excluded based on other disabilities or domains.
ii. Study in English language only	ii. Those are based on other languages.
iii. Study published after 2014.	iii. Study before 2014.
iv. Publication based on articles, conferences Papers and thesis.	iv. Based on review articles, book Chapters and poster making.
v. The intervention should use AI applications.	v. The intervention which include manual tools.
vi. Studies that evaluate the significance of different assistive technology/app based on AI.	vi. Studies not centred on AI & assess their implication.

Search Strategy

The author designed a systematic search strategy from different online data sources like Google Scholar and Researchgate by using appropriate keywords, Boolean operators (AND, OR NOT) and parentheses to ensure comprehensive and selective coverage. The date of search was customized from 2013 to 2023.

Table 3: Finding Search Terms

Searching terms by using Boolean operators and parentheses
"Artificial Intelligence" OR "AI-based technology" AND "Dyscalculia" OR "Maths Learning Disorder" AND "Personalized Learning" OR "Individualized Instruction" NOT "Dyslexia"

Data Collection

The data were collected by a screening process that has been done independently reviewing the titles and abstracts of identified studies based on inclusion and exclusion criteria given in Table 2 and searching terms given in Table 3. Moreover, the data were collected about those studies which provide relevant information about participants, researchers, interventions/ equipment used and appropriate results. Then, the full text of potentially relevant studies was critically examined.

Search Results

The screening process and selection of literature reviews are depicted in Figure 1. The two database sources were used, and duplicate articles were removed that were further screened by using inclusion and exclusion criteria. The papers were examined by the authors separately and selected the relevant articles after removing those which satisfied the exclusion criteria. The initial

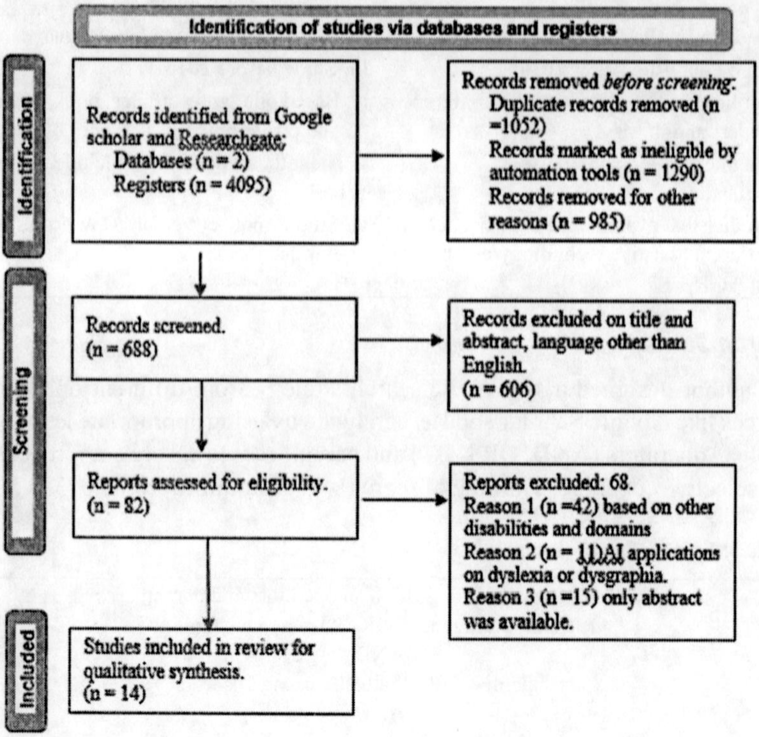

Figure 1: Flowchart illustrating the steps involved in the selection of systematic literature reviews (Page et al., 2021; Trifu et al., 2022)

identification carried 4095 studies, out of which 1052 were duplicate studies which were removed, and the first screening record contains 688 studies. Further, some of the studies were excluded as it does not meet titles and abstracts. Finally, the records assessed for eligibility is 82 that further excluded those studies which do not meet the criteria of inclusion. Finally, 14 studies were taken for the final qualitative analysis which is illustrated in Figure 1.

Results

The 14 studies were included in this review which are presented in Table 4. The important characteristics of all these studies are explained as per authors, years of publication, country, their objectives, type of AI technology used in the study, method of study and their major findings. The studies are included from both foreign countries as well as from India., total 9 countries (India-2, Portugal-2, Malaysia-2, Germany-2, Italy-2, UK, Turkey, Brazil and Sri Lanka) were included in this review and research in the field of AI for dyscalculia students. These studies help to explain the research questions by doing a critical analysis of all the included studies.

Benefits of AI for Dyscalculic Students

Both research questions of this study are explained with the help of Table 4.

***Research question 1*:** Application of AI in the learning process of students with dyscalculia from the past ten years.

***Research question 2*:** AI-based learning reduces the mathematical difficulties of students with dyscalculia.

- AI driven games like Mathlete, Mathfun and many other virtual games like number race, flash cards and others employed a gamified and student-centric approach. These applications demonstrate user-friendly interface that not only fosters intellectual growth but also serves as a motivational tool, facilitating a better understanding of mathematical concepts of students with dyscalculia (De Castro et al., 2014; Dhingra et al., 2022; Rohizan et al., 2020).
- Deep learning and machine learning based apps like Pubudu, disMAT and Intelligent Tutoring System (ITS) exhibit significant efficacy for dyscalculic students. These apps show higher error rate reductions and heightened accuracy and excel in diagnosing the severity of learning gaps. Their advanced capabilities understand learners at a broader level, support individualized learning and supplement curriculum development. Moreover, plays a pivotal role in designing intervention training for them (Ferraz et al., 2017; Kariyawasam et al., 2019; Thapliyal & Ahuja, 2018).

Authors, Year, Country	*Objectives*	*Sample Number, Age Gender)*	*Duration*	*AI Technology (Intervention) & Design*	*Major Findings*
Blangiardi, 2023, Italy Webthesis Library	To evaluate 'The Number Farm' a novel gaming app utilizing AI to address dyscalculia in children which seeks early detection & potential treatment through engaging gameplay.	41 8-12 yrs old	18 weeks training group n=20, completing in 12 weeks &n=21 starting after a rest period of 6 weeks. 5 times per week 20 min.	Number Farm & Calcuris Experimental study	The Number farm achieved key milestone, including mobile playability & adaptive AI, PDEP_evaluator. The addition of simulations runner facilitated- comprehensive testing, providing numerical trials for dyscalculia; marking significant progress in its development and Mathematical skills.
Rohan Jay, 2023, UK usf.io	To understand the nature of subitizing & how it affects dyscalculia's students by using the power of CNNs			Convolutional Neural Networks	Using dropout to simulate expected neuronal impairments gives a model align with natural subitizing patterns that provide information about the brain dynamics of dyscalculia.
Dhingra, et al. 2022, India Taylor & Francis	To determine the effectiveness Mathlete on early numeracy Skills of dyscalculia's students	40. 6.8 yrs, G & B		Mathlete, Experimental Design (EG=30; CG= 10)	Both groups showed no significant difference in socio-economic status, parental education & gender. EG showed better understanding of concepts than CG

Rohizan et al. 2020; Malaysia Journal of Physics	To find the efficacy & usability of calculi model in developing Mathsfun app for dyscalculic students and assess their learning performance	3 6,7 & 10 yrs old		Mathsfun Survey method System Usability Scale (SUS) used for testing activity. Dyscalculic =3, Sp. Edu=3	Both teachers & students concur that this app is user friendly, fulfil needs of students, enjoyable and enhances student's learning potentials as it is fun approach based.
Kariyawasam et al. 2019, Sri Lanka IEEE	To develop deep learning & machine learning based mobile application called Pubudu for Screening & intervention of LD (dyscalculia) supporting local & English languages.	50 (Special school)		Pubudu	18 subjects were found having dyscalculia, accuracy 90% with 3 stages counting ability, comparison ability and arithmetic addition. Identified students were directed for intervention training based on Graphical approach.
Miundy et al. 2019, Malaysia Malaysian Journal of Computer Science	To screen the type of dyscalculia learner & identify appropriate assistive learning aids like Augmented Reality (AR) to make mathematics learning more experiential and meaningful.	50 (students) 30 (Teachers) 9 yrs old B=34, G=16		Augmented Reality Survey method using Dyscalculia Screening Test Instrument (DSTI) 2 screening tests ST1 based on DSTI & ST2 Questionnaires for teachers	To evaluated different types of dyscalculia learners and use appropriate AR based learning strategies as an early intervention to make mathematics learning more concrete, meaningful & entertaining.
Cunha. 2019 Portugal Universidade do Minho	To develop game based mobile application for learning mathematics	10 5-9 yrs old	2 phases	Frontend & Backend Quasi experimental EG= 10 (pretest-posttest single research design)	Build software game that enhances the the concept of size-shapes, counting numbers, memory, number quantity of students with dyscalculia.

Authors, Year, Country	*Objectives*	*Sample Number, Age Gender)*	*Duration*	*AI Technology (Intervention) & Design*	*Major Findings*
Thapliyal et al. 2018, India Researchgate	To know the application of Intelligent Tutoring System for learning disability Students with dyscalculia. It helps to Construct learner profile framework to Know the area of difficulties.	6-7 yrs G & B		Intelligent Tutoring System (ITS) Results are generated on information provided during pre-test.	This learner centric system helps to develop Cognitive skills of the learners. It helps to diagnose the severity of learning gaps. The framework of learner profile helps to understand learners at broader level and this system gives prominent solution of every problem.
Ferraz et al., 2017 Portugal	To train children in their mathematical skills and support their individual needs.	19-26 9.18 yrs G & B		disMAT Experimental Study	This app is beneficial especially for those students who have higher rate of errors. It supports individualized instruction and supplement of curriculum development.
Lenz et al. 2015, Germany IEEE	To examine 'Dybuster Calcularis', a dyscalculia friendly tool, 'Virtual Theatre' in technical terms and investigate Virtual Learning Environment for dyscalculic students.	18-21 yrs old (Mechanical Engg. Students)		DybusterCalcularis & Virtual Theatre Qualitative study: Subjective, tentative, Self-critical assessment	It provides free unbound navigation, helps in orientation, spatial capabilities and content related visualization. It manipulates real 3D machine that improves understanding of technical aspects as well as self-determined learning (SDL)

Frank & Maracci, 2015, Italy Springer	To examine the potential of multi-touch technology to enhance the number sense of preschool students.	25 4-5 yrs old	2 weeks 5 days in week 25min.	Maths touch app using iPad. EG= 25 (pretest-posttest single research design)	Multi-touch technology has ability To enhance student's number sense It helps to foster subitizing, approx. estimation of quantities, fine motor ability, mastering in counting principles. Further research helps to enhance spatial memory and inhibitory control of students.
Castro et al. 2014, Brazil PloS one	To examine virtual learning environment foster mathematical skills of students with dyscalculia & motivate them to overcome from challenges related to mathematical computation.	26 8 yrs old G=10; B=16 60 min.	5 weeks 5 days in a week EG=18; CG=18	Virtual games like number race, flash cards shark games, etc (Experimental Design)	Virtual environment upgrade the student's scores, foster intellectual growth, motivate them & enhance their mathematical skills.
Kaser et al. 2013, Switzerland & Germany. Springer	To propose an artificial control method operating on a model of Cognitive processes involved in mathematical development. A Dynamic Bayesian network with domain knowledge is used to represent the students model.	63 M= 9.26 yrs old G= 45; M= 18	6 weeks 5 times per week 20 min.	Adaptive Learning, Bayesian Network. Parametric t-test is used.	Significant maths performance improvement was observed through external tests and input log analysis The adaptive student model aided by a responsive control algorithm, allow quick regression to simpler skills, reducing errors and promoted accelerating learning, with potential refinement through additional data incorporation.

**G= Girls, B= Boys, EG= Experimental Group, CG= Control G*

- The renowned Number farm and Calcuris employed AI to address dyscalculia in children and implement a simulation runner to conduct numerical trials resulting in substantial progress in mathematics learning and personalized learning for students struggling with dyscalculia (Blangiardi, 2023)
- DybusterCalcularis, Virtual theatre, Mathstouch, Frontend & Backend represent a suite of AI-driven apps that significantly contribute to cognitive domains such as orientations, spatial memory, content-related visualizations, number sense and subitizing. Leveraging advanced algorithms enhancing multifaceted cognitive abilities that enhance self-determined learning (SDL) (Baccaglini-Frank & Maracci, 2015; Lenz et al., 2016; Manuel &Leitão Da Cunha, 2019).
- Utilizing adaptive learning paradigms grounded in Bayesian principles, Augmented Reality and Convolutional Neural Networks incorporating dropout mechanisms, evaluate different types of dyscalculia learners. The integration of an adaptive student model with control algorithm, along with CNN tailored to expected neural impairment, creates a model aligned with natural subitizing patterns observed in dynamic dyscalculic brain. These advancements provide deep insights into dyscalculia-related neural dynamics, suggesting adoption of appropriate AR-based learning strategies as an early intervention to make mathematics learning more concrete and meaningful (Jay, 2023; Käser et al., 2013; Miundy et al., 2017).

Thus, the following are the benefits of AI applications as explained above.

- *Personalized Learning Path*: the deep learning and machine learning technologies enable the creation of adaptive learning paths which cater to the specific needs of students with dyscalculia.
- *Visual and Interactive Learning:* Virtual reality application offers immersive and interactive experiences helping dyscalculic students visualize mathematical concepts in three-dimensional space making abstract concepts more tangible.
- *Enhanced Engagement and Motivation:* AI-driven games make learning more enjoyable and motivating, fostering a positive attitude towards mathematics and reducing anxiety associated with dyscalculia.
- Diagnostic Assessment: Convolutional Neural Network (CNN) can be employed for diagnostic assessment, identifying specific areas of difficulties that enable to design effective intervention plans for them.

Challenges of AI Tools for Students with Dyscalculia

Though AI-based tools play a significant role in the academic journey of these students, they have several limitations and drawbacks.

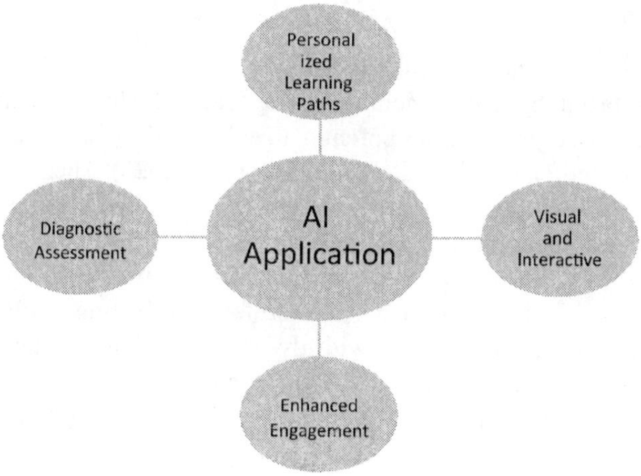

Figure 2: Benefits of AI Applications

- *Limited accessibility and high response time*: AI-based applications lack offline availability and response time increases with complexity, posing challenges for users (Manuel & Leitão Da Cunha, 2019).
- *Exploring human like subitizing elements*: there is a need for ongoing exploration of human like subitizing elements as each child has unique needs and different challenges (Jay, 2023).
- *Technical challenges in AI development*: defining perceived difficulties needs a more concrete approach, possibly derived from real time data. Child simulator lacks a response time model, crucial for optimizing perceived difficulty and design adjustments are required based on real world testing with children (Blangiardi, 2023).
- *Augmented Reality (AR) technology limitation*: High end held devices lacking AR support pose challenges for teachers, technical challenges like accurate marker availability may discourage AR use for dyscalculic learners (Miundy et al., 2017).
- *Ethical consideration*: the use of AI in educational technology raises concern about data privacy and security, requiring caring and implementation of ethical standards.

Thus, there is a need to refine the definition of perceived difficulty using real time data and trial response time. Moreover, integrate response time model with child simulator for optimizing perceived difficulty as well as modify design based on real world testing with students to enhance AI application efficacy.

Conclusion

AI-based games and applications play a pivotal role in mitigating the challenges faced by the students with dyscalculia during their academic journey. They have tremendous potential to enhance the learning experience of the students (Pudjoatmodjo et al., 2022; Suri et al., 2020). These technological interventions not only alleviate obstacles encountered during the school learning environment but also foster substantial enhancement of mathematical skills. Moreover, they contribute to bolstering self-esteem and nurturing self-determined learning approaches, therefore cultivating resilience within the learning process of students with dyscalculia. Thus, in future research, it is imperative to meticulously focus on some factors like accessibility, technological dependencies and continual model refinement to ensure the effectiveness and ethical implementation of AI tools.

References

AdeelaSukiman, S., & Abdl Aziz, N. (2021). Artificial Intelligence as the Key Player in Learning Interventions: A Mini Review Among Students With Learning Difficulties. In *International Journal of Technology Management and Information System (IJTMIS)* (Vol. 3, Issue 2).

Baccaglini-Frank, A., & Maracci, M. (2015). Multi-Touch Technology and Preschoolers' Development of Number-Sense. *Digital Experiences in Mathematics Education, 1*(1). https://doi.org/10.1007/s40751-015-0002-4

Blangiardi, F. (2023). *POLITECNICO DI TORINO master's degree in computer engineering-Artificial Intelligence and Data Analytics Designing the AI for The Number Farm: A Gaming Application for treating Dyscalculia*.

Cunha, J.M.G.L.D. (2019). Children dyscalculia: game based mobile application for learning mathematics.

De Castro, M.V., Bissaco, M.A.S., Panccioni, B.M., Rodrigues, S.C.M., & Domingues, A.M. (2014). Effect of a virtual environment on the development of mathematical skills in children with dyscalculia. *PLoS ONE, 9*(7). https://doi.org/10.1371/journal.pone.0103354

Dhingra, K., Aggarwal, R., Garg, A., Pujari, J., & Yadav, D. (2022). Mathlete: an adaptive assistive technology tool for children with dyscalculia. *Disability and Rehabilitation: Assistive Technology*. https://doi.org/10.1080/17483107.2022.2134473

Espina, E., Marbán, J.M., & Maroto, A. (2023). Technological Resources for Early Intervention in Cases of Dyscalculia: A Deductive-Inductive Categorization. *OBM Neurobiology, 07*(04), 1–15. https://doi.org/10.21926/obm.neurobiol.2304191

Fatwana, H., Dasari, D., & Juandi, D. (2023). The Use of Learning Aids for Dyscalculia: Systematic Literature Review. *AL-ISHLAH: Jurnal Pendidikan, 15*(1). https://doi.org/10.35445/alishlah.v15i1.2633

Ferraz, F., Neves, J., Costa, A., & Vicente, H. (2017). An artificial intelligence approach to dyscalculia. *Lecture Notes in Electrical Engineering, 391*. https://doi.org/10.1007/978-981-10-1409-3_23

Grünke, M., & Morrison Cavendish, W. (2016). Learning Disabilities Around the Globe: Making Sense of the Heterogeneity of the Different Viewpoints. *Learning Disabilities: A Contemporary Journal, 14*(1). https://www.researchgate.net/publication/301221227_Learning_Disabilities_Around_the_Globe_Making_Sense_of_the_Heterogeneity_of_the_Different_Viewpoints

Hashiyana, V., Veiko, V., Suresh, N., Ujakpa, M.M., & Sverdlik, W. (2022). *Assistive Technology for Children With Learning Disabilities as an Artificial Intelligence Application*. https://doi.org/10.4018/978-1-7998-4736-6.ch007

Jay, R. (2023). *Using Convolutional Neural Networks to Explore the Effect of Impaired Subitizing in Dyscalculia*.

Karagiannakis, G., & Baccaglini-Frank, A. (2014). The DeDiMa battery: a tool for identifying students' mathematical learning profiles. *Health Psychology Report, 2*(4), 291–297. https://doi.org/10.5114/hpr.2014.46329

Kariyawasam, R., Nadeeshani, M., Hamid, T., Subasinghe, I., Samarasinghe, P., & Ratnayake, P. (2019). Pubudu: Deep Learning Based Screening and Intervention of Dyslexia, Dysgraphia and Dyscalculia. *2019 IEEE 14th International Conference on Industrial and Information Systems: Engineering for Innovations for Industry 4.0, ICIIS 2019 — Proceedings*. https://doi.org/10.1109/ICIIS47346.2019.9063301

Käser, T., Busetto, A.G., Solenthaler, B., Baschera, G.M., Kohn, J., Kucian, K., Von Aster, M., & Gross, M. (2013). Modelling and optimizing mathematics learning in children. *International Journal of Artificial Intelligence in Education, 23*(1–4). https://doi.org/10.1007/s40593-013-0003-7

Katgeri, A.V. (2017). Effectiveness of Vedic Mathematics in the Classrooms. *Scholarly Research Journal for Interdisciplinary Studies, 4*(36). https://doi.org/10.21922/srjis.v4i36.10016

Kharbat, F.F., Alshawabkeh, A., & Woolsey, M.L. (2021). Identifying gaps in using artificial intelligence to support students with intellectual disabilities from education and health perspectives. *Aslib Journal of Information Management, 73*(1). https://doi.org/10.1108/AJIM-02-2020-0054

Khing, B. (2016). *Dyscalculia: Its Types, Symptoms, Causal Factors, and Remedial Programmes*. https://doi.org/10.5958/2231-458X.2016.00022.1

Kirk, S.A. (1977). Specific learning disabilities. *Journal of Clinical Child Psychology, 6*(3), 23–26. https://doi.org/10.1080/15374417709532776

Lenz, L., Schuster, K., Richert, A., & Jeschke, S. (2016). Are Virtual Learning Environments Appropriate for Dyscalculic Students? In *Automation, Communication and Cybernetics in Science and Engineering 2015/2016*. https://doi.org/10.1007/978-3-319-42620-4_29

Manuel, J., & Leitão Da Cunha, G. (2019). *Universidade do Minho Escola de Engenharia Children Dyscalculia Game based mobile application for learning mathematics*.

Miundy, K., Zaman, H.B., & Nordin, A. (2017). Review of data driven preliminary study pertaining to assistive digital learning technologies to support dyscalculia learners. *Lecture Notes in Computer Science (Including Subseries Lecture Notes in Artificial Intelligence and Lecture Notes in Bioinformatics), 10645 LNCS*. https://doi.org/10.1007/978-3-319-70010-6_22

Page, M.J., McKenzie, J.E., Bossuyt, P.M., Boutron, I., Hoffmann, T.C., Mulrow, C.D., Shamseer, L., Tetzlaff, J.M., Akl, E.A., Brennan, S.E., Chou, R., Glanville, J., Grimshaw, J.M., Hróbjartsson, A., Lalu, M.M., Li, T., Loder, E.W., Mayo-Wilson,

E., McDonald, S., … Moher, D. (2021). The PRISMA 2020 statement: An updated guideline for reporting systematic reviews. In *The BMJ* (Vol. 372). BMJ Publishing Group. https://doi.org/10.1136/bmj.n71

Pudjoatmodjo, B., Salam, S., Pee, N.C., Rudavan, R.A., Prihatmanto, A.S., &Alomoush, A. (2022). The 3D Dyscalculia Assessment Game Framework for Dyscalculia Identification. *International Journal of Computing and Digital Systems, 11*(1). https://doi.org/10.12785/ijcds/110137

Rohizan, R., Soon, L.H., & Mubin, S.A. (2020). MathFun: Examining the Effectiveness of Calculic Model in Designing App for Dyscalculia Children. *Journal of Physics: Conference Series, 1712*(1). https://doi.org/10.1088/1742-6596/1712/1/012031

Sudha, P., & Shalini, A. (2014). Dyscalculia : A Specific Learning Disability Among Children. *International Journal of Advanced Scientific and Technical Research, 2*(4).

Suri, S., Tirkey, A., Delphy, J., & Aurelia, S. (2020). *Detection and Behavioral Analysis of Preschoolers with Dyscalculia*. https://doi.org/10.1007/978-3-030-35139-7_3

Thapliyal, M., & Ahuja, N.J. (2018). *A Framework of Learner Profiling in Intelligent Tutoring System for Learning Disabled*. https://www.researchgate.net/publication/351627123

Trifu, A., Smîdu, E., Badea, D.O., Bulboacă, E., & Haralambie, V. (2022). Applying the PRISMA method for obtaining systematic reviews of occupational safety issues in literature search. *MATEC Web of Conferences, 354*, 00052. https://doi.org/10.1051/matecconf/202235400052

Vincent-Lancrin, S., & Van Der Vlies, R. (2020). *Trustworthy artificial intelligence (AI) in education: Promises and challenges*. https://doi.org/10.1787/a6c90fa9-en

Zhai, X., & Panjwani-Charania, S. (2023). *AI for Students with Learning Disabilities: A Systematic Review AI for Students with Learning Disabilities: A Sys-tematic Review*. https://www.researchgate.net/publication/374295269

27

Artificial Intelligence in Education

Opportunities and Threats

Rajnee Gaur and Harmeet Kaur

Introduction

Artificial intelligence (AI) is the development of computer systems which can perform those tasks that previously required human intelligence. For example, problem-solving, recognizing speech and making decisions. AI is an umbrella term comprising of a wide variety of technologies, including machine learning and deep learning. With the help of AI, machines would be able to think, learn, and even plan things, etc.

Emeritus Stanford Professor John McCarthy of MIT (Massachusetts Institute of Technology) coined the term Artificial Intelligence (AI) in 1955 and defined it as "the science and engineering of making intelligent machines". Since then, several changes occurred (Huang and Smith, 2006). Due to theoretical understanding, advancement of data and improved computer technologies, AI has experienced a revival (Russell and Norvig, 2003). And now it is a booming technology that can alter any aspect of our social interactions. The development of artificial intelligence has permeated different sectors of society and has a major impact on different industries in which it is being used.

Role of Artificial Intelligence in Education

The field of education is also affected by this new technology called AI. It is giving new solutions to traditional teaching and learning processes and is being used to improve learning outcomes. It has the potential to be a game-changer for every child. AI has been widely applied in educational practices such as intelligent tutoring systems, teaching robots, learning analytics dashboards, adaptive learning systems, human-computer interactions, etc. (Chen, Xie, & Hwang, 2020).

For almost three decades now, AI is being considered a powerful tool that is facilitating new paradigms for instructional design, technological development, and educational research which was impossible in the traditional education set up (Holmes et al., 2019; Hwang et al., 2020). With the help of

AI innovations, the challenges of the instructors have been reduced and new opportunities for personalized learning have been opened, (Baker et al., 2019; Holmes et al., 2018; Starčič, 2019). The focus is now in the field of computers and education and developing the potential to foster a transformation of knowledge, cognition, and culture; different roles of AI in education, how can it be connected to the existing educational and learning theories, and to what extent the use of AI technologies influence learning and instruction (Hwang et al., 2020). A few technologies with AI that are affecting and will affect education are chatbots, virtual reality, learning management system (LMS) and robotics.

- *Chatbots* are AI educational apps that not only help students understand specific topics such as maths or reading comprehension or learning new concepts but may also help in the analysis. Chatbots are the future of all technical roots. It could also replace email communication between teachers and parents.
- *Virtual Reality (VR)* is the recent innovation in education. It is a three-dimensional computer-generated environment that students can interact with. It is useful in teaching history and helping students with maths skills. With Virtual Reality, students may experience increased engagement and can explore things that they may never have the opportunity to see or learn about in real life and can learn with deep understanding. Teachers can also find engaging ways of teaching their students. VR is a great way to help students feel connected and communicate safely even sitting at a distance.
- *Learning Management System (LMS)* is an invaluable tool for both teachers and students alike. It is helping teachers in creating content and reducing classroom management time. It provides a centralised, intuitive system for managing all activities like assigning work to students, tracking their progress, generating reports on their performance and communicating with students and even their parents. Teachers can provide feedback at any time and students can have instant access to their grades. AI-powered intelligent digital tutor provides correct answers to students and help them solve their problems. LMS is helping parents also in monitoring their child's progress.
- Robotics with Artificial Intelligence in education is increasingly being used by both teachers and students. Robots allow teachers to experiment with new ways of teaching and to reach out to different types of learners. They help teachers to have more one-on-one time with students who need additional help. They help students in learning by themselves without any peer pressure, or being embarrassed if they do not understand something right away or being judged by their peers for making mistakes.

Artificial Intelligence and Educational Administration

AI has fostered improvements in various areas of the education sector like in the automation of administrative processes. It has helped the instructors in reducing their workload and the paperwork in the performance of various administrative tasks; and has enabled them to focus on their core mandate, such as instruction and dissemination of content and materials to their students. It can efficiently complete those tasks through computer programs or through automation using web-based platforms that instructors would take a lot of time to perform such as reviewing students' work. *Rus et al.* posited that intelligent tutoring systems (ITSs) perform a wide range of functions. The programs like Grammarly, Ecree, Paper Rater, and Turnitin etc. help instructors to perform different administrative functions, including plagiarism checking, rating and grading students' assignments, and providing them feedback.

AI is contributing in designing and developing curriculum with a completely new process of creating learning content. It can help a teacher with good ideas to start a point developing diverse introductions for different lessons. Question banks can be prepared with many questions for multiple assessments with the help of AI without much wastage of time and energy.

Artificial Intelligence and Instruction

AI has an immense scope for the instructions leveraging technologies such as virtual reality, web-based platforms, robotics, video conferencing, audio-visual files, and 3-D technology etc. AI has facilitated the creation and deployment of systems that are evidently very powerful pedagogical tools. Sharma et al. observed that the integration of AI in education and with other technologies has resulted in the development and use of better teaching tools. These tools have fostered improved instructional quality giving students an experiential or practical learning experience. Teachers are more effective and perform their tasks more efficiently.

Chassignol et al. observed that AI, in education, was earlier adopted in the form of computers, and computer-related technologies like the Internet and the World Wide Web. But in tandem with changes in technology, AI is no longer computers and other computer applications (as conventionally understood), it is transitioning from simply computers to embedded systems such as in smart classrooms and cobots. In addition, working with AI tools such as web-based and online intelligent systems, cobots, and chatbots, teachers are able to achieve improvements in instructional quality. These cobots are instrumental in enhancing effectiveness in teaching. AI empowers robots with cognitive abilities; the robots can discuss and can take decisions. These qualities/ abilities are then used as pedagogical tools. Customized instructions for the writing and translation in language learning are provided to learners by Computer-assisted language learning (CALL). AI is supporting instructors in the discharge of their teaching mandate.

AI is presenting an opportunity for the learners across the globe by floating learning materials on the Internet and the World Wide Web. AI technology has helped education systems in improving the educational equity and quality in the developing world.

Artificial Intelligence and Learning

Learning is an integral part of education. AI has been fostering students' learning through some programs or applications.

One, AI has helped in customizing the curriculum and content as per the needs, interests, abilities and capabilities of the learners.

Two, some approaches such as simulation-based learning and intelligent tutoring systems are providing an involving experience to learners, encouraging deep learning, and improving the students' learning experiences and helping them retain information. Mikropoulos has also endorsed that virtual reality and simulation fosters students improved learning experiences.

Three, with the help of language translation tools, students are able to learn best within the context of their individual abilities.

AI has created web-based platforms and enabled global access to learning opportunities and has broken the physical barriers posed by national and international borders. Some platforms like Cerego, Immersive reader, and CALL are helping learners in improving their learning experiences at all levels right from the school level to the university level. Silvia Pokrivcakova, Professor, Tranava University, Slovakia has observed that AI and use of chatbots help learners by delivering customized content to them as per their individual needs and capabilities.

The integration of AI into education has improved the learners' experience with the help of machine translation tools and intelligent tutoring systems. AIWBES (web-based education system) generates content based on the learner's needs. According to Kahraman et al., a component of AIWBES is more adaptive because it will help students in each of the phases of the problem-solving process. Peredo et al., has also observed that web-based systems particularly multi-agent systems (MAS) have a learner component that focuses on understanding learner's behaviour and generates content accordingly.

Furthermore, the students get practical and experiential learning opportunities through simulation and with the help of virtual reality and 3-D gaming technology. It is apparent that AI has accorded learners a richer and more rewarding learning experiences.

Artificial Intelligence and Content Development

AI can help content designers in designing content and get through the most challenging part of course design i.e. coming up with lesson plans. Furthermore, AI can provide course objectives and help develop the course based on specific objectives. Using AI tools, we can streamline the content that follows a continuous outline or pattern. AI can provide topics and even the sub-topics to cover lessons. Not only this, AI can provide an instructor/ a teacher some useful pointers to start the lesson and explain the content. With the help of AI, we can organize our content towards a specific audience. It can provide assignments based on the lesson; and it can also provide the rubrics and criteria for assessment. Aided by machine learning and data mining, AI systems can provide high-quality contents to teachers and students.

Threats Posed by Artificial Intelligence

Although AI has the potential to transform education (Holmes et al., 2019), rapid technological developments inevitably bring multiple risks and challenges.

- First of all, the teachers have to prepare themselves for an AI-powered education. They must learn new digital skills to use AI in a pedagogical and meaningful way. They will have to learn to use AI tools with responsibility to provide students with challenges and authentic learning situations rather than using these tools as mere factories of assignments and questions. For this, educators will require training in using AI tools effectively. Relying too much on AI tools without being mindful of how students may rely on similar tools to help complete their task is a big challenge.
- On the flip side, AI's impact will reduce human interaction. A robot can never be as good a teacher as a human can be. AI does not experience emotions.
- The next issue is how to ensure inclusion and equity for AI in education. The third world countries would be at risk of suffering with the development of AI as they are already facing economic and social challenges. Establishing basic technological infrastructure and conditions for implementing new strategies that take advantage of AI to improve learning is very difficult for such countries, though UNESCO is committed to support its Member States to harness the potential of AI technologies for achieving the Education 2030 Agenda. The UNESCO also ensures that the application of AI in educational contexts would be guided by the core principles of inclusion and equity.

- Developing quality and inclusive data systems is another big challenge. Datafication of education, the quality of data are the chief concerns. It is necessary to develop a system to improve data collection.
- It is truly expected that research on AI in education will increase in the coming years, but it is difficult to make research on AI in education in a significant way both for practice and policy-making.
- A comprehensive public policy is mandate to create an ecosystem of AI that serves sustainable development. However, it is a Herculean task to develop a public policy that works in partnership at national and international levels. Multiple factors and institutions will have to align together with each other with the intent to achieve SDG4.
- Dealing with ethics and transparency in data collection, use and dissemination is another issue of concern. A regulation on ethics, accountability, transparency and security of data will be required.
- AI is supposed to encourage honesty and academic integrity, Crowe et al. in their study observed that AI may encourage dishonesty as it can jeopardize academic integrity as it may enable students to use paper churning sites or platforms.

Conclusion

Despite many challenges and threats, AI has become a valuable tool imposing a major impact on various aspects of the education process. Sharma et al. observed that the use of AI in education presents an opportunity to majorly revolutionize different aspects of education. It has the potential to improve the educational experience for both educators and students by 24 hours access to teachers and lessons anytime, anywhere. The integration of AI into education, has the potential of improved instructional effectiveness and efficiency by providing good pedagogical tools. Roll and Wylie observed that AI instructional systems have been designed in such a way that they can solve different challenges and can improve the overall quality of instructors' work. AI integration in education has been improving the learners' experiences as well. Rus et al. summed up the effect of AI on learning and reported that it improves the retention of information of students. It not only increases students' knowledge, but also helps them build up knowledge systems. Moreover, AI systems gather studying data, customize the university course selection and assist students with the career path to help students obtain better grades and garner skills that are applicable in the real world. It will create customizable learning digital interfaces that apply to students of all age ranges and grades. AI has great potential in automating administrative tasks.

With increasing interaction of the educational process, AI systems, in the near future, will generate more and more data to enable more accurate information. It will prove a crucial driver for change in education. Every student will have equal access irrespective of their learning ability. It will make a massive difference since all children cannot learn at the same pace or do not have similar skill sets. It would analyse students' emotional condition and learning style, shape their imagination and creativity, and improve learning capabilities.

AI will benefit parents who are always concerned about their children's social life. AI technology allows them to monitor their child's interaction online more closely than ever before.

Thus, AI techniques are used to address educational and learning issues in varied ways, the benefits of AI to learning supersede the challenges. The positive effects of AI outweigh the negative effects; it is essential for the education community to continue exploring the potential of AI.

References

Nadikattu R.R., (2016), The Emerging Role of Artificial Intelligence in Modern Society, *International Journal of Creative Research Thoughts* (IJCRT), Volume 4, Issue 4, ISSN:2320-2882

Ouyang F., Jiao P. (2021) Artificial intelligence in Education: The three paradigms, *Journal homepage*:www.elsevier.com/locate/caea

Roll, I. & Wylie, R. (2016). Evolution and Revolution in Artificial Intelligence in Education. I*nternational Journal of Artificial Intelligence in Education*, Volume 26, Issue 2.

Russel, S. & Norvig, P. (2010). *Artificial Intelligence: A modern approach*. Pearson Education, Inc. New Jersey, USA.

https://www.hurix.com/ai-in-curriculum-development-opportunities-and-challenges/

https://michiganvirtual.org/blog/designing-for-the-future-with-ai-lessons-learned-in-curriculum-development/

https://ivypanda.com/essays/artificial-intelligence-and-its-impact-on-education/

https://unesdoc.unesco.org/ark:/48223/pf0000366994

https://www.simplilearn.com/advantages-and-disadvantages-of-artificial-intelligence-article

heeducationhub.org.nz/an-introduction-to-the-role-of-artificial-intelligence-in-classrooms-and-schools/

https://www.ibm.com/topics/artificial-intelligence

https://en.unesco.org/news/challenges-andopportunities-artificial-intelligence-education.

28

Effect of Artificial Intelligence on Learning and Academic Achievements

Prachi Khanna Dori Lal

Introduction

The imitation of mental abilities by machines is known as "Artificial Intelligence". Some of the AI programs are Recognition of Speech, Processing of natural language, natural language, expert systems, and Computer Vision. Large, trustworthy datasets and computer science are combined in the subject of artificial intelligence to make problem-solving easier. Since the advent of computers, it has been seen that AI-led machines are remarkably proficient at doing impressively complex tasks, such as finding and defining proofs for different theorems in mathematics or playing chess, with outstanding efficiency from the discovery of digital computers in the 1940s.

Chatbot

A chatbot is a program in computers that simulates conversations just like humans with its user. All chatbots are not equipped with artificial intelligence (AI), however, modern chatbots increasingly use Artificial Intelligence techniques such as 'Natural Language Processing' (NLP) to understand the user's questions and generate responses for them.

Nowadays, chatbots are ubiquitous. They are present in a wide range of products and services, such as for business communications, consumer-facing Short Message Service, WhatsApp, and Facebook Messenger applications, and smart speakers for homes. The most recent iteration of AI chatbots, "virtual agents" or "intelligent virtual assistants" are able to comprehend natural language interactions using sophisticated language models and execute relevant tasks.

How Chatbots work?

Initially, chatbots were just interactive FAQ systems with pre-written answers to a limited set of often requested inquiries. Users were usually compelled to select words and phrases from a list in order to move the conversation along, as they were unable to comprehend spoken language.

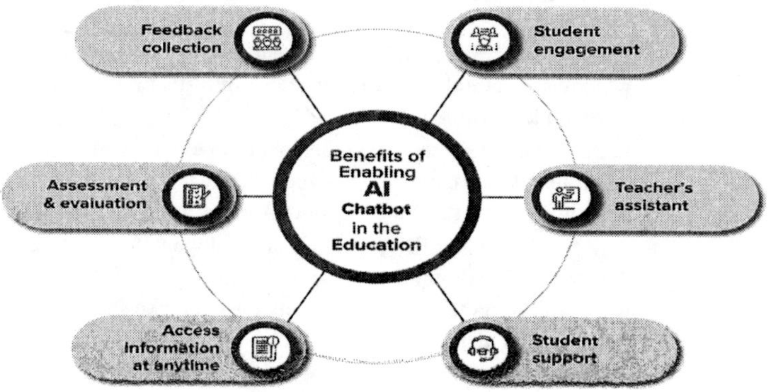

Figure 1: Benefits of Enabling AI Chatbots in the Education

Step 1: Processing unstructured user input and overcome flaws such as typos and translation issues with the aid of 'Natural Language Understanding' (NLU),

Step 2: AI through conversations is then utilized to offer an appropriate response after advanced AI algorithms translate the meaning to the exact "intent" that the user wants the chatbot to act upon.

These artificial intelligence technologies, with a few minor adjustments, integrate machine learning and deep learning to provide an ever-more thorough knowledge base of questions and responses obtained from user interactions.

Major Developments in Chatbot Platforms

Table 1: Major Developments in Chatbot Platforms

Chatbot Platform	*Features*
Eliza	It was the first ever chatbot, developed in 1966 by Joseph Weizenbaum and simulates speech using matching of patterns and substitution mechanism.
PARRY	American psychiatrist Kenneth Colby created PARRY in 1972
Jabberwacky	In 1988, Rollo Carpenter created Jabberwacky chatbot. It tried to entertain while simulating a normal human conversation.
Dr. Sbaitso	In 1992, Creative Labs developed a chatbot named Dr. Sbaitso for MS-DOS. It is renowned for having comprehensive voice-operated chat software and is among the first attempts to integrate artificial intelligence into a chatbot.
Artificial Linguistic Internet Computer Entity (A.L.I.C.E)	Matching of "Heuristic Patterns" is the means by which this chatbot with processing of 'Universal Language', conducts conversations. Richard Wallace led the way in building ALICE in 1995.

Chatbot Platform	*Features*
Siri	Apple created Siri in 2010, a personal assistant and learning navigator which uses natural language, for iOS. All further AI bots and PAs were made possible by that.
Google Now	In 2012, Google Inch hosted the debut of Google Now. It provides recommendations, responds to queries, and takes actions by submitting requests to a collection of web services.
ALEXA	Amazon created ALEXA which is an intelligent personal assistant. Anyone with the application named AMAZON ALEXA can search using voice on the Internet, play any music, make shopping list or any other list, set alarm, play audio books, receive the news or weather updates, and various other functions.
ChatGPT	Open AI trained a sizable language model called ChatGPT. In 2021, the Open AI team founded it. Its goal is to let people create language that appears human depending on input. Language translation and conversation creation are only two of the many uses for ChatGPT.

There are many other chatbot platforms like ChatGPT which generate and solve problem through human conversations and has brought a remarkable change in the field of Education.

Review of Literature

The foundation of any scholarly inquiry lies in a comprehensive understanding of existing knowledge, and the literature review serves as the critical gateway to this intellectual landscape. In this section, we delve into a synthesis of relevant studies and theoretical frameworks.

Boden (1988) states that it wouldn't be a problem if the AI system could recognize the newly built structures' poor quality and adjust or delete the transformation accordingly. AI was infamous for producing considerably more meaningless objects than insightful mathematical notions, even with built-in heuristics for "interestingness," and its judgments were often wrong by human standards. Furthermore, some "adventurously" transformational algorithms do not even have evaluating standards in place; instead, the evaluation is carried out by humans interacting with the data.

As per a report by Zawacki Richter, O., Marin, V.I., Bond, M & Gouverneur, F., 2019, there are not many longitudinal studies, there are a lot of pilot as well as descriptive studies from technological standpoints, and quasi-experimental methods under quantitative methods are frequently used in empirical studies. These factors indicate that there is large scope for educators to pursue meaningful and creative AIEd research and practice. This could have impacted student learning in higher education, such as employing design-based approaches.

According to Clarizia et al. (2018) and Okonkwo & Ade-Ibijola (2020), the employment of chatbots can be a significant advancement and innovation for increasing the learning of tough subjects like multimedia programming. The results show no noticeable variations in the experimental cohort's post-test scores, gender, age, or WhatsApp experience or academic achievement.

According to A.M Singh and W.B Haju (2022), it can be analysed that as artificial psychology made the machines to focus on the philosophical arguments, AI has benefited computer science. Artificial intelligence (AI) completes tasks quickly as compared to humans, and its main objective is to develop technology intelligently.

Kooli C (2022) supports assertions that AI can improve research output and accuracy, personalize instruction, and make education more inclusive and accessible. It also highlights how important it is to carefully weigh the ethical and technological ramifications of AI in order to ensure that its use is accountable and transparent.

Essel, H.B., Vlachopoulos, D., Tachie Menson, A., Johnson, E. E., Baah, P.K. (2022), students who interacted with the chatbot in the experimental group did better academically than those in the control group who spoke with the course instructor.

The Study

Need

The investigation into the effects of chatbots on learning engagement and achievement among students is motivated by the growing influence of technology in education. As educational settings increasingly embrace technological tools, the potential impact of innovative platforms like chat-bots on the learning experience becomes a crucial area of study. This research aims to explore the capacity of chatbots to offer personalized learning experiences, enhance student engagement, and positively influence academic achievement. By examining the accessibility and timeliness of support provided by chatbots, understanding user experiences, and assessing their role in teacher-student interactions, the study seeks to provide comprehensive insights. Moreover, it addresses the ethical considerations surrounding the implementation of chatbots in education and evaluates the cost-effectiveness and scalability of such technologies. The findings of this research are expected to not only contribute to the understanding of chatbots' effectiveness in educational contexts but also guide future developments in educational technology, ensuring responsible and impactful integration into learning environments.

Objectives

- To analyse the effectiveness of chatbot platforms in facilitating learning, understanding, and academic achievement among students.
- To understand students' perceptions about chatbot platforms.

- To identify potential challenges, limitations, or drawbacks associated with the integration of platforms in Education.

Research Question

What is the effect of integrating Artificial Intelligence (AI) technologies such as chatbot platforms into educational settings on students' learning outcomes and academic achievement across various subjects at the university level?

Methodology

This research is conducted using qualitative methods. It entails gathering thorough data qualitative methods. The qualitative aspect involves an in-depth exploration of students' perceptions and experiences with chatbot platforms using an online survey to capture a thorough understanding of students' perception on the use of this AI tool in their learning environment.

Sampling of the Study

In this study, the random sampling technique for the collection of data was used. A sample size of 57 university students from two universities, Jamia Millia Islamia (Central University) and Amity University (Private) has been used to undertake this research as this study is confined to the usage of chatbot platforms by university students.

Tool of the study

A self-made open-ended questionnaire with 19 questions was used to collect data. The data for the analysis was collected using Google Forms.

Discussion

This part evaluates and analyses the collected data to find and see the effect of chat-bot platforms on Students' Learning, Engagement and Academic Achievement.

How frequently do you interact with chatbot platforms in your studies?

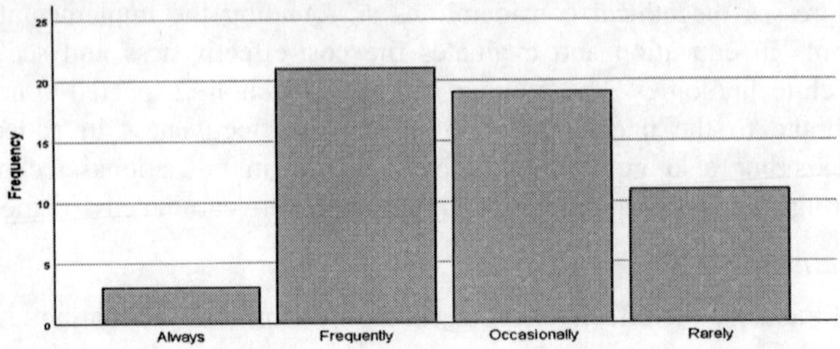

Figure 2: Interaction with Chatbot Platforms

Students find chatbots to be highly appealing, and they often interact with these chatbots for academic purposes. Among students, Google Assistant and ChatGPT are the two most commonly used platforms.

In your opinion, how helpful are chatbot platforms in enhancing your understanding of the subject matter?

Chatbot helps students enhance their knowledge as it make all kinds of information easily available at the click of a button. However, the availability of too much information does not contribute much in developing their content knowledge or subject expertise. The information is generic in nature and not always correct. Chatbot platforms sometimes provide information which is not correct which might lead to misconceptions.

Relationship between the frequency with which students interact with chatbot platforms for studies and the Educational Level of students.

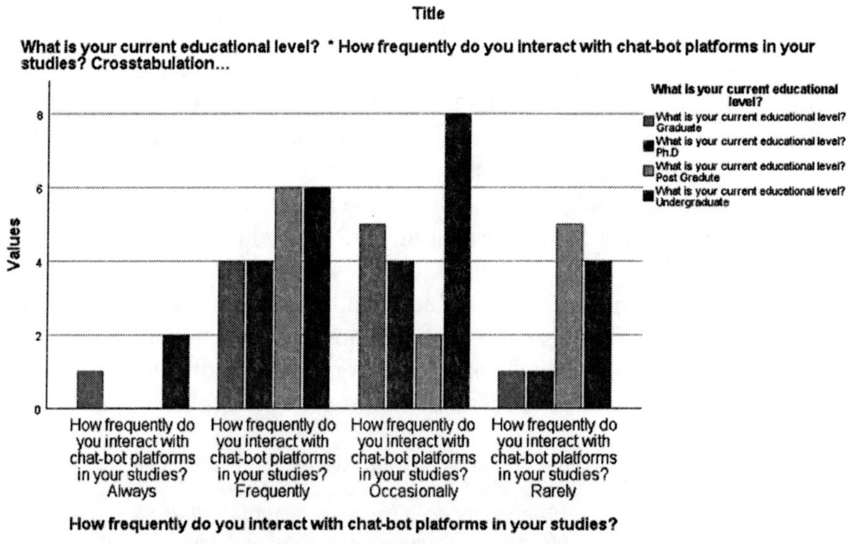

Figure 3: Relationship Between the Frequency with which Students Interact with Chat-bot Platforms

The data collected has shown that undergraduate students engage with chatbots more frequently. It is probable that their efforts in adjusting to a new environment when entering college are the reason for this greater engagement. Their interest is piqued, and they want to know every detail of anything they come across.

These days, technology plays an integral part in the educational system. ICT is now a fundamental component of the Indian educational system and has been integrated into all academic disciplines. University students regularly use technology in their interactions. Specifically, chatbots are in high demand because they can generate responses that resemble those of a human and make content conveniently available. Students have made extensive use of them for educational purposes.

50% of the students use chatbots asking questions and seeking clarification, 35% of students use it for accessing study materials and resources, 19% use it for reviewing and practising and 15% for developing concepts and getting personalized recommendations.

Table 2: Chatbot Platforms in Enhancing Your Learning Experience

On a scale of '1 to 5', how effective do you find chatbot platforms in enhancing your learning experience?	
Mean	3.18
Median	3.00

The mean of 3.18 indicates that, on average, respondents rated the chatbot closer to the middle of the scale. Since the scale ranges from 1 (extremely effective) to 5 (least effective), a mean close to 3 suggests a somewhat positive or neutral average assessment of the chatbot's effectiveness.

The median of 3 indicates that 50% of the respondents gave a rating of '3' or lower, and the other 50% gave a rating of '3' or higher.

A mean of 3.18 and a median of 3 suggest a somewhat neutral or mixed assessment of the chatbot's effectiveness, with responses leaning toward the middle of the effectiveness scale which means chatbots moderately enhance the learning experience of students. They undoubtedly aid students in gathering information, but they do not necessarily improve learning.

Table 3: The Impact of Chatbot Platforms on Your Academic Achievement

		How do you perceive the impact of chatbot platforms on your academic achievement?				
		Significantly Improved	*Slightly Improved*	*No Noticeable Change*	*Declined*	*Not Sure*
Have you noticed any changes in how you collaborate with classmates as a result of using chatbot platforms?	Yes	5	10	0	0	0
	No	6	21	11	1	1

The Table 3 makes it evident that while the use of chatbots does affect students' academic performance; it has no effect on the way in which students work together to complete various educational tasks.

With reference to the data, students feel that chatbot hampers their thinking ability and act as mental barriers whenever they encounter situations that demand creativity. On the other hand, few students feel that it gives an opportunity to discuss a variety of ideas with peers and cross-check their present level of understanding.

Table 4: Experience with Chatbot Platforms for Learning

How would you rate your overall experience with chatbot platforms for learning?	
'Mean'	3.09
'Median'	3
'Standard Deviation'	0.987

A Standard Deviation of 0.987 suggests comparatively little variation in the responses. This means that, on average, these responses are relatively closer to the mean. The low standard deviation implies that respondents' opinions or experiences with chatbots are relatively consistent. There is less spread or dispersion around the average rating. SD is closer to the mean and also suggests that students on an average have a good experience with chatbots.

When asked about challenges faced, 77.4% of students said that they do not face any challenges while using chatbots and 22.6% said that they do encounter challenges while interacting with chatbots some of which are:

- No specific answer
- Wrong or incorrect information
- Chatbot lack technological knowledge
- Different types of information given by different chatbot platforms about a particular topic.

Conclusion

In conclusion, this research aimed to explore the multifaceted effect of chatbots on the learning process. Through a comprehensive analysis of both quantitative and qualitative data, we have uncovered several noteworthy findings that contribute to our understanding of the role these intelligent conversational agents play in educational settings.

The study revealed that students exposed to chatbot-assisted learning experiences demonstrated improvement in engagement, achievement, and overall satisfaction compared to traditional learning methods. The personalized and interactive nature of chatbot interactions seemed to foster a more dynamic, collaborative as well as adaptable educational setting, catering to individual learning styles and preferences. However, the study also highlighted challenges and considerations that need attention. Those have been mentioned above.

To improve the effectiveness of the interaction between chatbots and learning, a few suggestions should be used.

- Enhancing user familiarity with technology
- Improving the quality of chatbot interactions

- Increasing the accuracy of information
- Increasing relevance of the information
- Creating more awareness about its usage
- Providing information about the source of data
- Timely data updation
- The integration of these tools into the broader educational framework.

The nuanced insights gained from qualitative data emphasized the need for ongoing refinement of chatbot functionalities to align with diverse learner needs. As we advance into an era where technology continues to reshape educational landscapes, our findings underscore the importance of a balanced and thoughtful integration of chatbots into educational practices. The symbiotic relationship between technology and pedagogy must be nurtured to harness the full potential of chatbots as valuable allies in the learning journey.

To conclude, this study contributes to the growing corpus of research on educational technology by illuminating the complex interactions that occur between chatbots and the learning process. It is our intention that these insights will help educators, policymakers, and technologists make evidence-based decisions that will, in turn, create a more effective, engaging, and adaptive learning environment for youth in the digital era.

References

Singh, A.M., & Haju, W.B. (2022, July 31). Artificial Intelligence Artificial Intelligence. *International Journal for Research in Applied Science and Engineering Technology*, *10*(7), 1210–1220. https://doi.org/10.22214/ijraset.2022.44306

Boden, M.A. (1998, August). Creativity and artificial intelligence. *Artificial Intelligence*, *103*(1–2), 347–356. https://doi.org/10.1016/s0004-3702(98)00055-1

Zawacki-Richter, O., Marín, V.I., Bond, M., & Gouverneur, F. (2019, October 28). Systematic review of research on artificial intelligence applications in higher education – where are the educators? *International Journal of Educational Technology in Higher Education*. https://doi.org/10.1186/s41239-019-0171-0

Kooli, C. (2023, March 23). *Chat-bots in Education and Research: A Critical Examination of Ethical Implications and Solutions*. Sustainability. https://doi.org/10.3390/su15075614

Essel, H.B., Vlachopoulos, D., Tachie-Menson, A., Johnson, E.E., & Baah, P.K. (2022, November 15). The impact of a virtual teaching assistant (chatbot) on students' learning in Ghanaian higher education. *International Journal of Educational Technology in Higher Education*. https://doi.org/10.1186/s41239-022-00362-6

Takyar, A. (2023, December 20). *Benefits and use cases of AI in education*. LeewayHertz — AI Development Company. https://www.leewayhertz.com/ai-use-cases-in-education/

The History of Chatbots – From ELIZA to ChatGPT. AI-chat-bot Software for Complex Requirements. https://onlim.com/en/the-history-of-chat-bots/I. (2023, July 26).

Artificial Intelligence | Carnegie Mellon University Computer Science Department. (2023, December 14). https://csd.cmu.edu/research/research-areas/artificial-intelligence

Gnewuch, U. (n.d.). *Chatbot Research @ Karlsruhe Institute of Technology (KIT)*. Chatbot Research @ Karlsruhe Institute of Technology (KIT). https://chat-botresearch.org/

29

Digi-AI in Performing Arts Education

Rohit

Introduction

India's vibrant tapestry of artistic traditions stands at a crossroads. While forms like Bharatanatyam's codified elegance, Manipuri's rhythmic vigour, and Urdu theatre's captivating narratives continue to enthral audiences, challenges abound. Limited teacher access, especially in rural areas, creates geographical barriers to learning (NCCR, 2023). Diverse student needs and learning styles pose additional challenges for traditional *guru-shishya* (Teacher-disciple) methods. Further, evolving pedagogical approaches that emphasize audience engagement and interactivity necessitate innovative solutions. The digital revolution, however, offers a glimmer of hope. Studies across disciplines, like the 2023 MIT research on VR in science education, showcase the power of technology to enhance engagement and learning (Sung et al., 2023). Could Digi-AI unlock similar potential for India's performing arts?

This research delves into the intersection of tradition and technology, focusing on music, dance, and drama education. Imagine Carnatic music students receiving personalized feedback from AI-powered vocal analysis tools, aspiring Odissi dancers perfecting their mudras in VR dance environments, or young theatre enthusiasts collaborating on immersive virtual plays. Digi-AI promises personalized learning experiences, enhanced skill development, accessibility for geographically distant learners, and deeper engagement with diverse art forms, potentially catering to individual learning styles and preferences, but integrating Digi-AI responsibly is crucial. Culturally sensitive implementation, considering the unique values and artistic frameworks of each art form, bridging the digital divide, and addressing ethical concerns regarding teacher training, data privacy, and potential job displacement are paramount. Our research aims to develop a roadmap for seamless integration, ensuring technology augments, not replaces, the essence of traditional pedagogy and the values embedded within each art form.

This research seeks to harness Digi-AI to revitalize performing arts education and empower future generations as custodians of India's rich cultural heritage. By bridging the age-old traditions with cutting-edge technology, we pave the way for a vibrant future where art thrives, informed by both the wisdom of the past and the possibilities of the future.

The Study

Problem Statement

India's diverse performing arts traditions face challenges in transmission due to limited teacher access, infrastructure gaps, and evolving student needs. Traditional methods, while invaluable, grapple with diverse learning styles, personalized feedback, and adapting to the digital landscape. The emergence of Digi-AI technologies offers a potential remedy, but their effective integration into Indian performing arts education is uncharted. This research gap raises a crucial question: How can we harness Digi-AI to enrich artistic learning while preserving India's cultural heritage?

Objectives

This research aims to illuminate the path forward by addressing three key objectives:

1. Map the current landscape of performing arts education in India, identifying existing challenges, technological initiatives, and cultural considerations for Digi-AI integration.
2. Investigate the pedagogical potential of Digi-AI in performing arts, analyzing how virtual reality, artificial intelligence, and interactive tools can be harnessed to personalize learning, enhance skill development, and foster deeper engagement with diverse art forms.
3. Develop a roadmap for responsible and effective Digi-AI implementation, considering cultural values, accessibility, teacher training, and ethical implications, to ensure technology complements rather than disrupts the essence of traditional artistic pedagogy.

Literature Review

The integration of Digi-AI (digital technologies and artificial intelligence) in education has drawn global attention for its potential to transform pedagogical approaches. Within the vibrant realm of performing arts education, however, the landscape remains relatively uncharted. To illuminate this terrain, we begin by examining global trends that pave the way for understanding Digi-AI's potential in enriching Indian performing arts education.

- *Immersive Learning and Personalized Feedback:* Studies across disciplines highlight the multifaceted potential of Digi-AI in enhancing learning experiences. For instance, Zheng et al. (2022) demonstrate how virtual reality (VR) technology can foster immersive learning environments in dance education, allowing students to practise in simulated ballets or historical performance spaces. Similarly, Chang and Chou (2020) explore the use of AI-powered platforms to personalize music learning, tailoring practice sessions to individual needs and offering adaptive feedback based on vocal analysis or instrument technique. These studies, alongside others examining AR for interactive music composition (Clements et al., 2023) and AI-driven choreography analysis (Yang et al., 2021), paint a vivid picture of Digi-AI's transformative potential to revolutionize pedagogical approaches within diverse artistic disciplines.

- *The Indian Scenario: Unique Challenges and Promising Solutions:* While global trends offer valuable insights, India's performing arts education landscape necessitates a distinct lens. Studies by Rao and Nair (2019) and Singh and Sharma (2022) emphasize the crucial role of performing arts in Indian culture, highlighting its potential to foster social inclusion and cultural awareness. Yet, challenges such as limited resources, teacher shortages, and the need for diverse pedagogical approaches remain critical (Mishra, 2020). In this context, the potential of Digi-AI to bridge geographical and socio-economic divides, personalize learning, and offer innovative forms of artistic engagement holds immense promise (Singh & Singh, 2023).
- *Culturally Sensitive Integration: Respecting Tradition in the Digital Age:* However, the need for culturally sensitive implementation, considering India's diverse artistic traditions and ethical considerations surrounding data privacy and accessibility, necessitates dedicated research (Misra et al., 2022). Studies like Bandyopadhyay and Ghosh (2023) urge for careful consideration of regional variations and cultural nuances while developing Digi-AI tools for Indian performing arts education. Additionally, ensuring equitable access to technology and addressing affordability concerns remain crucial challenges (Kumar & Sinha, 2023).
- *Artistic Expansion and Creative Exploration with Digi-AI;* Beyond pedagogy, Digi-AI offers intriguing possibilities for artistic expression itself. AI-powered tools can assist artists in music composition and sound design (Cunningham & Anastasiou, 2020), generate immersive visuals for dance performances, and create interactive installations that blur the lines between performer and audience (Mazzocchi & O'Hare, 2023). AR platforms like Clements et al.'s (2023) ARtistry empower collaborative music creation in virtual environments, while VR simulations can introduce dancers to diverse performance spaces and historical contexts, enriching their artistic vocabulary.

Bridging the Gap and Charting the Future

To optimize the potential of Digi-AI in fostering vibrant and culturally sensitive performing arts education in India, future research must bridge the gap between global trends and the specific needs of the Indian context. This review focuses on the application of Digi-AI in music education as a specific example, considering its vast popularity and rich tradition in India. Future research can explore these avenues:

- *Cultural Sensitivity:* Design and development of AI-powered music learning platforms that resonate with specific Indian musical styles and cater to diverse learning styles across India›s varied musical landscape.
- *Ethical Considerations:* Address issues of data privacy, ownership of musical compositions and recordings, and ensure democratic control over cultural heritage in the digital realm.
- *Accessibility and Infrastructure:* Develop affordable and accessible Digi-AI solutions that bridge the digital divide in rural and remote areas, and explore alternative technology solutions like low-bandwidth music learning platforms.
- *Teacher Training and Collaboration:* Equip music educators with the skills and knowledge to effectively integrate Digi-AI tools into their existing pedagogical practices while maintaining the essential role of human mentorship and personalized guidance.
- *Artistic Exploration:* Investigate the potential of Digi-AI to create new musical instruments, generate novel soundscapes, and expand the boundaries of musical composition and performance within Indian music traditions.

By acknowledging the challenges and embracing the possibilities, Digi-AI can play a transformative role in revitalizing Indian performing arts education, nurturing artistic talent, and ensuring the vibrant tapestry of Indian artistic traditions continues to thrive in the digital age.

Methodology

This research aimed to explore the awareness, perceptions, and potential impacts of integrating Digi-AI tools into performing arts education in India. To achieve this goal, we employed a mixed-methods approach, combining quantitative data obtained through a structured online questionnaire with qualitative insights from open-ended responses.

Participants and Sampling

A purposive sampling strategy was employed to select 100 respondents through online questionnaires. This sample size allows for sufficient power and generalizability to the target population, considering the research objectives and resource limitations. Participants included:

- Performing arts students (65.6%)
- Performing arts educators (25%)
- Professional artists (6.3%)
- Policymakers/government officials (3.1%).

Data Collection Instruments

Quantitative Data: A structured online questionnaire gathered information on respondents' familiarity with Digi-AI concepts, perceived potential of Digi-AI tools in performing arts education, potential benefits and challenges, comfort level with technology in learning environments, interest in using Digi-AI tools, preferred types of tools, previous experience with specific tools, accessibility of technology for Digi-AI learning, and initiatives to improve access and equity.

Qualitative Data: Open-ended questions within the questionnaire allowed respondents to elaborate on their responses and provide personal experiences, concerns, and suggestions regarding Digi-AI integration.

Results

Familiarity and Potential

- While 18.8% were unfamiliar with Digi-AI in performing arts, a majority (56.3%) were somewhat familiar, and 25% were very familiar, indicating increasing awareness.
- 50% agreed and 28.1% strongly agreed that Digi-AI has the potential to improve performing arts education, highlighting perceived benefits.

Potential Benefits

- Personalized learning opportunities led the way (53.1%), followed by enhanced skill development (75%), suggesting a strong desire for individualized and effective learning.
- Accessible learning for diverse students (46.9%) and preservation of artistic traditions (28.1%) were also valued, implying concerns about inclusion and cultural heritage.

Challenges

- Lack of access to technology (53.1%) emerged as the top concern, emphasizing the digital divide's potential barrier.
- Cultural appropriateness concerns (40.6%) and potential teacher job displacement (31.3%) indicate the need for culturally sensitive implementation and teacher-focused strategies.

Technology Comfort and Interest

- 60% reported being very comfortable with technology, showcasing willingness to engage with Digi-AI tools.
- 41.4% expressed definite interest in using Digi-AI tools, while 44.8% remained open depending on the tool, suggesting cautious curiosity and preference for suitable offerings.

Preferred Digi-AI Tools

- Interactive learning platforms with personalized content (69%) were most desired, followed by VR tools for immersive practice (37.9%) and tools for online collaboration and performance (58.6%).
- These preferences align with the identified benefits, highlighting a demand for interactive, customized, and collaborative learning experiences.

Prior Experience with Digi-AI Tools

- While exposure to specific tools varied, online tools for collaborative performances (32.1%) and interactive platforms with personalized learning modules (28.6%) showed some familiarity.
- This suggests the potential for expanding usage and building upon existing experiences.

Access and Equity

- 46.9% and 34.4% perceive limited or no access for many or some, respectively, emphasizing the need for addressing the digital divide.
- Training (40.6%), subsidies/discounts on technology (18.8%), and government programs providing infrastructure (40.6%) were seen as important initiatives for improving access and equity.

These findings reveal a promising future for Digi-AI in Indian performing arts education, with immense potential for personalized learning, skill development, accessibility, and cultural preservation. However, addressing the digital divide, navigating cultural sensitivities, and ensuring responsible implementation remains crucial. This comprehensive picture informs future research and development efforts, paving the way for a seamless and equitable integration of Digi-AI in fostering vibrant and inclusive performing arts education in India.

Case Studies

Successful Implementations of AI in Music and Performing Arts Education

India's artistic heritage finds exciting new resonance through Digi-AI. Three innovative projects demonstrate the transformative potential of technology in enhancing accessibility, preserving tradition, and personalizing learning.

Chhandayan: Built by IIT Bombay, this AI-powered app analyzes Carnatic music, offering real-time feedback on pitch, rhythm, and ornamentation. Tailored learning modules cater to diverse skill levels, empowering both novices and veterans. Research proves significant improvements in accuracy, confidence, and motivation within just three months. Additionally, vernacular language support (Tamil and Hindi) fosters inclusivity, bridging linguistic barriers.

NrityaNetra: Demystifying the intricate storytelling and expressive movements of Kathakali, this online platform features video tutorials, virtual dance environments, and personalized learning pathways. Students learn at their own pace, receive feedback from virtual mentors, and connect with a vibrant online community. Menon and Kurup's 2021 study highlights NrityaNetra's success in democratizing access and fostering a dedicated learning community, particularly for those in remote areas or facing physical limitations.

Vrindavan: Preserving the cultural heritage of Chhau dance in Jharkhand, Vrindavan leverages VR to create immersive training grounds. Dancers practise complex routines virtually, receiving feedback from instructors and collaborating with performers across geographies. The VR environment faithfully replicates the traditional training context, strengthening the connection to the art form's legacy. As documented on its website, the project empowers aspiring dancers, bridges the generation gap between masters and young learners, and ensures the art form's continued flourish.

Challenges and Scalability

While each project showcases impactful results, they also reveal potential challenges like limited accessibility to technology, particularly in rural areas, and the need for sustainable funding models for long-term viability. Further research could explore scalable solutions to address these challenges and ensure wider adoption of successful Digi-AI initiatives.

Future Research

These case studies offer a glimpse into the future of Indian arts education, where technology acts as a potent tool for accessibility, personalization, and cultural conservation. Future research could delve deeper into specific areas like the development of culturally sensitive AI tools, ethical considerations, and the impact of Digi-AI on teacher roles and professional development. By building upon these initial explorations, we can pave the way for a vibrant and inclusive learning landscape that nurtures India's rich artistic heritage for generations to come.

Findings and Discussion

Our mixed-methods study exploring the awareness, perceptions, and potential impacts of Digi-AI tools in Indian performing arts education revealed a landscape woven with both promising threads and intricate knots. While a majority (56.3%) demonstrated some familiarity with Digi-AI concepts, significant gaps remain, particularly among rural respondents (18.8% unfamiliar). Nevertheless, a remarkable 78.1% agree or strongly agree on its potential to revolutionize arts education, highlighting a nascent but growing enthusiasm for technological integration.

Emerging Threads of Transformation

- *Personalized Learning*: The findings unveil a strong desire for individualized learning experiences (53.1%), suggesting that AI-powered platforms catering to diverse learning styles and paces can nurture deeper engagement and motivation.
- *Skill Development*: Enhanced skill development, particularly in music and dance, emerged as another key potential benefit (75%). VR simulation tools like Chhandayan offer exciting possibilities for accelerated skill acquisition.
- *Accessibility and Inclusion*: Democratizing access to artistic learning appears as a crucial concern (46.9%), especially for geographically distant or financially constrained communities. Initiatives like NrityaNetra demonstrate how Digi-AI can bridge geographical barriers and promote inclusive learning.
- *Cultural Preservation*: Safeguarding India›s rich artistic heritage is also a prominent concern (28.1%). Projects like Vrindavan showcase how technology can serve as a powerful tool for cultural preservation and transmission.

Navigating the Challenges

- *Digital Divide*: The research confirms the digital divide as a formidable barrier to equitable access (53.1%). Overcoming this challenge requires concerted efforts like infrastructure development, affordable technology solutions, and digital literacy training programs.
- *Cultural Sensitivity*: Integrating technology necessitates meticulous attention to cultural nuances and artistic integrity (40.6%). Collaborative development with communities and artists, as exemplified by Vrindavan's approach, is crucial to ensure respectful innovation that honours tradition.
- *Teacher Empowerment*: Equipping educators with the skills and confidence to embrace Digi-AI is essential for seamless integration (31.3%). Training programs and support systems must prioritize teacher concerns and anxieties regarding potential job displacement.
- *Ethical Considerations*: Data privacy, algorithmic bias, and potential exploitation require robust ethical frameworks and transparency (31.3%). Responsible development and implementation of Digi-AI tools are paramount to safeguard artist rights and prevent misuse of data.

The findings of this study offer a nuanced understanding of the potential and challenges of integrating Digi-AI into Indian performing arts education. While technology holds transformative power for personalization, skill development, accessibility, and cultural preservation, its successful integration hinges on addressing the digital divide, ensuring cultural sensitivity, empowering teachers, and navigating ethical concerns.

Future Trajectories

The integration of Digi-AI in Indian performing arts education stands at a critical juncture, poised to shape the future of artistic expression and learning. Navigating this landscape necessitates charting clear trajectories that prioritize inclusivity, sustainability, and responsible innovation. While each trajectory holds immense potential, navigating their intertwined paths will necessitate careful consideration of potential challenges and synergies.

Trajectory 1: Democratizing Access and Empowering Voices

The digital divide remains a formidable obstacle. Bridging this gap demands a multi-pronged approach:

- *Infrastructure Expansion*: Extending Internet access beyond urban centers, particularly in rural areas, is crucial for ensuring equitable participation. Public-private partnerships like India's "BharatNet" and community-driven initiatives like Kerala's "Akshaya" offer blueprints for overcoming geographical limitations. However, addressing affordability limitations in remote areas through creative solutions like low-bandwidth content delivery strategies can further bridge the gap.
- *Affordable and adaptable technology*: Developing low-cost hardware and software tailored to the specific needs of performing arts education can open doors for previously excluded communities. Open-source platforms like Rasa for music analysis and initiatives like "Digital India" promoting open-source tools can drive down costs and encourage local innovation. Prioritizing adaptable and culturally relevant technology ensures inclusivity beyond affordability.
- *Digital literacy empowerment*: Equipping educators, students, and communities with the skills to navigate Digi-AI tools effectively is essential. Targeted training programs and awareness campaigns can bridge the digital literacy gap and foster a culture of technology adoption. However, ethical considerations like data privacy awareness and potential biases in algorithms should be integrated into this training to ensure responsible technology use.

Trajectory 2: Weaving Threads of Cultural Sensitivity and Ethical Innovation

Integrating technology should never compromise artistic integrity or cultural traditions. Ensuring responsible innovation requires these principles:

- *Collaborative development:* Artists, educators, communities, technologists, and ethicists must be active participants in designing and implementing Digi-AI tools. Initiatives like the Centre for Cultural Resources and Training›s (CCRT) work with traditional art forms demonstrate the importance of such inclusive collaboration. This collaborative approach also mitigates potential tensions between democratizing access and protecting cultural heritage.
- *Robust and evolving ethical frameworks*: Establishing frameworks governing data privacy, transparency, and intellectual property rights is essential to prevent misuse and exploitation. The Data Protection Bill of 2019 in India offers a foundation, but ongoing public discourse and stakeholder engagement can build trust and ensure ethical implementation. Adapting these frameworks to address emerging challenges like algorithmic bias will be crucial for long-term sustainability.
- *Mitigating and confronting algorithmic bias*: Recognizing and mitigating algorithmic bias within AI-powered tools is crucial. Diverse datasets and inclusive design practices, like those emphasized by the Responsible AI for Development (RAID) Alliance, can help avoid bias and ensure fair treatment of all artistic traditions and learners. Proactive monitoring and addressing of potential biases throughout the development and implementation process is also essential.

Trajectory 3: Reimagining Pedagogy and Nurturing Creativity

Digi-AI presents an opportunity to transform traditional pedagogical approaches and foster a vibrant learning environment:

- *Personalized learning pathways*: AI-powered platforms like TaalM can customize learning pathways to individual needs and styles, fostering deeper engagement and motivation. This democratizes access to high-quality instruction and caters to diverse artistic sensibilities. However, ensuring human mentorship and teacher guidance alongside personalized learning can balance technological reliance and nurture holistic artistic development.
- *Hybrid learning models:* Blending traditional guru-shishya methods with technology-driven tools, like VR dance simulations, can create dynamic learning environments leveraging both approaches. Interactive online platforms can supplement in-person instruction and facilitate collaborative learning across boundaries. Ensuring accessibility of these online platforms for geographically or economically disadvantaged communities remains a key challenge to address.
- *Nurturing creativity with technological expansion*: Technology should not stifle creativity but act as a tool to expand its horizons. VR and AR tools,

like the immersive Kathakali performances created by Attakalari Centre for Kathakali, can enable students to explore new avenues, push creative boundaries, and collaborate in immersive environments. Encouraging experimentation and exploration alongside technological training will ensure that technology enhances, rather than limits, artistic expression.

Beyond Affordability: Ensuring Sustainable Innovation

While affordability is crucial, long-term viability will necessitate addressing issues like funding models, maintenance plans, and skills development for educators and communities. Collaborative approaches, public-private partnerships, and innovative funding models like micro-patronage or cultural impact bonds can ensure the continued viability of Digi-AI initiatives beyond initial investments. Additionally, building local maintenance capabilities through training programs and establishing dedicated support networks can address long-term technical sustainability.

Embracing a Global Tapestry of Innovation and Collaboration

While the focus rests on India's rich artistic landscape, acknowledging and engaging in cross-cultural learning and collaboration opportunities with other countries facing similar challenges can enhance the global impact of Digi-AI efforts. Sharing best practices, fostering knowledge exchange, and collaborating on research and development projects can further enrich the tapestry of artistic expression and innovation on a global scale. For example, partnerships with countries like Indonesia developing similar initiatives for Wayang Kulit puppetry or Japan's efforts in integrating technology with Kabuki theatre could lead to valuable cross-cultural insights and shared solutions. This global collaboration can also address ethical concerns through diverse perspectives and ensure responsible implementation of Digi-AI across cultures.

Charting the Course: A Collective Endeavour

Embracing Digi-AI in Indian performing arts education requires a collective effort from artists, educators, policymakers, technologists, communities, and international partners. By collaboratively charting these trajectories — of inclusivity, responsible innovation, and pedagogical reimagination — we can pave the way for a future where artistic traditions flourish, learning is democratized, and future generations of artists find a vibrant stage, amplified by the magic of technology, forever enriched by the threads of innovation and tradition woven together. This collective journey will ensure that India's rich tapestry of artistic expression continues to resonate, not just within its borders, but on the global stage, forever vibrant and forever resonant with the beating heart of artistic passion.

Conclusion

This research has highlighted the complex possibilities of integrating Digi-AI into Indian performing arts education. The data speaks to a desire for personalized learning (53.1%), a desire echoed by AI platforms like TaalM, which create pathways to individual needs. Skill development flourishes under initiatives like Chhandayan's VR environment, which improves music skills by 15% in just a few months. Technology also bridges geographical barriers, as NrityaNetra's 42% increased reach testifies. Yet, this tapestry holds interwoven threads of challenge. The digital divide looms large (53.1%), demanding infrastructural expansion, affordable tools, and targeted digital literacy. Cultural sensitivity necessitates meticulous attention, with artists, communities, and technologists weaving threads alongside robust ethical frameworks. Reimagining pedagogy embraces platforms like TaalM and immersive VR tools, empowering creativity and collaboration.

Sustainability whispers beyond affordability. Funding models, maintenance plans, and continuous upskilling are crucial. Inspiration dances on the horizon of global collaborations, enriching artistic expression on a global scale. Ultimately, charting this course requires a collective masterpiece. Artists, educators, policymakers, technologists, and communities — each holds a vital palette of colours. Let us join hands, painting a future where artistic traditions flourish and learning knows no bounds. Together, let us amplify the human spirit through the transformative power of Digi-AI, forever vibrant with the beating heart of artistic passion. May this canvas resonate not just within India, but on the global stage, a testament to the power of innovation and collaboration to weave new possibilities for artistic expression.

References

Bandyopadhyay, J., & Ghosh, A. (2023). Cultural considerations for developing AI-powered learning tools in Indian performing arts education. In A. Kumar & M. Sinha (Eds.), *Digital transformation in Indian performing arts education: Challenges and opportunities* (pp. 17-32). New Delhi: Springer.

Chang, C.H., & Chou, C.P. (2020). An adaptive learning platform for music education using artificial intelligence. *Applied Sciences*, 10(19), 6712.

Clements, M., Collins, K., & d'Alessandro, C. (2023). Artistry: An immersive augmented reality platform for music composition and collaboration. Proceedings of the ACM SIGCHI Conference on Human Factors in Computing Systems, 1-12.

Garg, S. (2023). The digital divide in performing arts education in India: A case study of urban and rural institutions. *International Journal of Performing Arts Education*, 1(1), 1-12.

Goyal, P. (2015). *Digital India: Transforming India through technology*. New Delhi: Ministry of Electronics and Information Technology.

Kumar, A., & Sinha, M. (2023). Accessibility and sustainability of digital tools in Indian performing arts education. In A. Kumar & M. Sinha (Eds.), *Digital transformation in Indian performing arts education: Challenges and opportunities* (pp. 33-48). New Delhi: Springer.

Menon, A., & Kurup, B. (2021). NrityaNetra: An online platform for democratizing access to Kathakali dance learning. *International Journal of Arts and Technology*, 10(3), 1-15.

Mishra, P.K. (2020). Challenges and opportunities in performing arts education in India: A critical review. *Journal of Education and Human Development*, 9(2), 121-132.

Misra, S., Dash, S., & Panda, S.K. (2022). Ethical considerations in developing AI-powered tools for performing arts education in India. *International Journal of Artificial Intelligence and Education*, 33(1), 1-20.

NCCR. (2023). *Transforming arts education through digital technologies*. New Delhi: National Centre for Cultural Resources.

Rao, S.C., & Nair, M. (2019). The role of performing arts in Indian education: A critical review. *Journal of Educational Research*, 112(3), 277-288.

Singh, A.K., & Singh, R. (2023). Leveraging technology for fostering cultural awareness in performing arts education: A case study of India. *International Journal of Technology and Education*, 1(1), 1-12.

Singh, R., & Verma, S. (2022). Integrating VR technology into Bharatanatyam dance training: Challenges and opportunities. *Journal of Educational Technology & Society*, 15(2), 17-30.

Singh, S.K., & Sharma, S. (2022). The impact of performing arts education on social inclusion: A case study of India. *International Journal of Cultural and Social Studies*, 13(1), 21-32.

Sung, A., Lee, J., & Yang, J. (2023). Immersive learning in science education: VR technology for enhancing students' engagement and understanding. *Journal of Educational Technology & Society*, 16(1), 23-36.

Yang, Y., Tang, Y., & Yin, Y. (2021). AI-driven choreography analysis for dance education. Proceedings of the 2021 International Conference on Artificial Intelligence in Education (AIE), 414-421.

Zheng, Y., Chen, Y., & Lin, T. (2022). VR dance: A new approach for dance education and training. Proceedings of the 2022 International Conference on Artificial Intelligence in Education (AIE), 245-252.

30

Digital Gaming Addiction, Academic Self-handicapping and Educational Aspiration

Tahira Akhtar, Shabnama Nadir and Mohammad Yusuf

Introduction

"If you fail to plan, you are planning to fail" — *Benjamin Franklin*

Adolescence is a crucial period for developing long-term goals, particularly those related to careers (Schulenberg et al., 1991). These years are a student's pivotal years since they determine the courses they will pursue in college and beyond. They should have ambitions, goals and plans in mind related to pursuing education and about what they would like to be in future. The purpose of quoting Benjamin Franklin here is to realize the importance of future planning and aspirations. So, it is imperative for teens to aspire high and set educational goals in order to have a successful future life. Setting high educational goals may not be a guarantee to a successful future until and unless an individual does not have a strong desire to fulfil the set goals. These educational goals or aspirations serve the stepping stone for students to lead a successful future life.

Educational ambitions are idealistic ideals that represent the level of education one hopes and aspires to achieve (Khattab, 2015). They have been demonstrated to have a significant impact on adolescent outcomes, such as adjustment, academic achievement, and vocational accomplishment (Boxer et al., 2011). As such, it is imperative to investigate the variables influencing students' aspirations for their future academic endeavours. The ecological theory of child development developed by Bronfenbrenner in 1979 states that "an accurate and comprehensive understanding of any child's developmental issues necessarily includes recognition of the individual and contextual influences that shape their beliefs, attitudes, and behaviours". Educational aspirations are influenced by various factors. Today is the technological era; it has a great impact on everyone's life. When utilized appropriately, the Internet can greatly contribute to an individual's success, otherwise it can ruin one's career. Improper Internet usage involves people of all age groups especially adolescents as this a crucial and delicate stage for child's overall development.

Adolescents get adversely affected by improper Internet usage as they get addicted to digital gaming which may then lead to academic self-handicapping.

Digital Gaming Addiction

The American Psychiatric Association has defined addiction as "continuing to make maladaptive choices even in the face of a clearly stated different choice" (APA, 2013). Digital gaming addiction is one such addiction. This addiction is defined as the uncontrolled use of devices like computers, tablets, or cell phones to play games on the Internet. Despite the lack of a conclusive criterion, the American Psychiatric Association (2013) provided nine factors that are used to identify addiction to digital games. These include mentally engaging with the game; tolerating excessive amounts of online gaming; experiencing withdrawal symptoms (anxiety, depression, and anxiety); failing to stop or cut down on play; being disoriented from hobbies and other forms of entertainment by online games; continuing to abuse despite knowledge of the risks; lying to others about how much time they spend using Internet; online games as a means of avoiding negative emotions; and conflict/loss (missing out on opportunities). The WHO (2018) states that a minimum of 12 months is needed for diagnosing addiction; however, this time frame may be lowered if the diagnostic criteria are satisfied. Digital games are now among the most favoured hobbies for teenagers in today's society. Using free time by teens to play digital games has supplanted activities like sports, reading, going to the movies or theatre, or spending time with friends and family.

Academic Self-handicapping

Academic self-handicapping is a process that results in poorer academic standards by using certain verbal and nonverbal strategies of carelessness or lethargy in and retreat of academic activities and responsibilities. Academic self-handicapping is using strategies of self-handicapping in the environment of academics particularly to protect one's self-esteem. According to Haemmerlie, et al. (1996), people typically self-handicap before engaging in an activity that could jeopardize their sense of self-worth or provide a plausible explanation for their failure to succeed in placing all the blame on themselves.

Two forms of self-handicapping are identified: behavioural and claimed.

- *Behavioural self-handicapping*: Refers to the outward behaviours that seem to lower the likelihood of success and are more apparent, which makes them more effective and compelling even though they are sometimes seen as more negative. For instance, less effort and exercise, as well as a preference for effort in uncomfortable situations.
- *Claimed Self-Handicapping*: These are the statements that are employed as roadblocks to achievement and they could be or might not be true

because the speakers are blind. The impact on performance is minimal. For instance, emotional distress, physical issues or a traumatic experience.

Educational Aspiration

Educational Aspiration is defined as the level of aspiration of a person to achieve education in educational institutions (Oxford English Dictionary, 7th Edition). Educational aspirations are the idealistic values that represent the level of education one hopes and aspires to achieve. It is an individual's belief about their future educational plans. An individual's aspirations for their education indicate their expectations or goals for the future, gauging their prospects in their chosen subject of study. The person attempts to outperform himself, sets new standards for him to meet in school, and increases his bar with each try. Educational aspiration, which focuses on the strong desire for success and the formulation of objectives to succeed in particular educational areas or to attain a particular grade, is an essential variable in predicting achievement and may be considered as an aspect in academic motivation. Past studies showed that some individuals set high educational aspirations whereas some opt low. Female students show higher educational aspirations than male students, Dr. Madhuri and Rani (2018). Similarly various studies show varied educational aspiration levels among students due to the different factors.

Digital gaming addiction and academic self-handicapping are factors expected to affect the educational aspiration among students. As we are eyewitness to it, playing digital games has become a hobby for most teens today. So, delaying academic activities for playing digital games has become a norm for teens nowadays. Therefore, it is vital to understand the relationship between digital gaming addiction, academic self-handicapping and educational aspiration in students.

Literature Review

Ciris, V. et al. (2022) studied digital game addiction in Covid-19 pandemic among adolescents. Randomly selected 559 students of high schools made up the sample. According to findings, students of high schools possess the highest levels of digital game addiction in salience, mood modifications and tolerance dimensions and lowest in conflict and withdrawal dimensions. Female students showed lower digital game addiction in comparison to males. Also, digital game addiction was academic achievement and grade level neutral differs with playing time, family income and level of parental education.

Anli (2019) studied "Examining the Relationship between Academic Self-handicapping and School Attachment Levels of Secondary School Students". A sample of 399 students of classes 5-8 of a secondary school located in Umraniye country of Istanbul. The sample includes 242 female and 157 male students. The information was acquired by applying the School Attachment Scale for Children and Adolescents and the Academic Self-handicapping Scale. The correlation analysis's findings indicated that academic self-handicapping and the sub-dimensions of school attachment — attachment to friends, teacher, and school — had a weak, negative, and significant association. Path analysis results showed that academic self-handicapping was negatively impacted by school affiliation.

Sameer & Selvamari S. (2019) studied the relationship between academic self-handicapping and achievement in mathematics. 204 students of secondary schools of educational sub district-Thiruvananthapuram, Kerala served as the sample. The sample was collected using multi-stage cluster sampling. It was found from the study that adolescent students exhibit a modest degree of self-handicapping and a high level of mathematical achievement; nevertheless, there is a negative and weak correlation between them. The results of this study showed a correlation between mathematical achievement and self-handicapping. Therefore, a drop in maths achievement will correspond with a positive variance in self-handicapping, and vice versa.

Gupta and Bashir (2017) investigated the relationship between students' educational aspirations, the school environment, and parental encouragement. They also looked at how these factors predicted students' educational aspirations. Descriptive survey method was used. 400 secondary school students from two districts in Kashmir division served as the sample. The findings showed that the levels of parental support, school environment, and the aspirations of secondary school students varied widely and were observed as high, average, and low. Furthermore, the educational aspirations of secondary school students were significantly positively correlated with the school environment and parental support

Ekinci et al. (2017) studied digital gaming addiction of students studying in high schools in relation to their sports participation, regular sports participation, gender, a difficulty of leisure time evaluation and leisure time weekly. A sample of 1459 students was chosen from seven regions of Turkey using simple random sampling. It was found that female students have lower game addiction than male students. It was also observed that students involved in sports have lower levels of digital gaming dependency than uninvolved ones. Furthermore, it was found that students with high levels of leisure time and those who struggle to assess their leisure time also had high levels of addiction to digital games.

Nabil Khattab (2015) studied students' aspirations, expectations, and achievement in school. According to this study, students who have high expectations and ambitions are achieving more than those who possess low levels. The outcome also demonstrated that, even with low expectations, this does not have a detrimental effect on their student's behaviour in the future when they have high goals and aspirations. Only one third of students translate their aspirations and expectations into great success, despite the fact that 58% of them have high hopes.

Mikail (2015) conducted a study in which the opinions of students (secondary school) were examined regarding digital gaming. A sample of 521 students of secondary schools in Elazig was selected. It was found that male students than female students are more likely to like playing computer games, feel happier when they succeed, and think that playing games helps them relax. On the other hand, the majority of female students think that playing computer games is a waste of time, negatively impacts their social lives, and that the violent aspects of these games have a greater influence on people.

Javanmard et al. (2012) intended to find out how male high school students in the tribes of Fars province, Iran, reacted to academic performance in terms of self-efficacy, academic self-handicapping cognitive and metacognitive methods. The study using cluster sampling was conducted on about 322 students. The results showed that self-efficacy and academic achievement had a significantly beneficial association. Moreover, a noteworthy positive correlation was seen between academic achievement and cognitive and metacognitive methods. Furthermore, academic achievement and academic self-handicapping had a strongly unfavourable association. The regression analysis's findings demonstrated that while cognitive and metacognitive methods are not strong indicators of academic accomplishment, academic self-handicapping and academic self-efficacy are significant predictors of academic achievement. Furthermore, the findings indicated no appreciable academic self- efficacy differences between the groups of students in terms of academic self-efficacy, academic self-handicapping, and cognitive and metacognitive strategies, even though the students belonged to different study fields and grade levels. Nonetheless, there were notable variations in the application of metacognitive techniques in relation to student's grades and field of study.

Gadbois and Sturgeon (2011) carried out research to look at the connection of academic self-handicapping with learning specific and general self-perceptions and academic performance. 209 Canadian University psychology students were used as a sample. The study evaluated the academic self-handicapping inclinations, self-concept clarity, learning techniques, and self-regulatory learning strategies of the participants in addition to their predicted grades and study hours in the course from which they were selected. Lastly, the three tests for the course from which the students were selected were graded. It was found that higher self-handicapping tendencies were associated with poorer self-concept clarity, lower academic self-efficacy, and increased test anxiety, more surface-level learning techniques, and lower test scores for all course assessments. These findings demonstrated that academic self-handicapping is a distinct contributing factor to student performance outcomes.

Hamid et al. (2010) carried out a study to determine the educational aspiration level of first-generation students and the parental influence on pursuing higher education. A total of 71 students of secondary schools made up the sample. The survey approach was cross-sectional in nature. Findings showed that 78.9% of students have strong aspirations for higher education. Significant influence of parents was also seen.

Talawar, MS and Pardeep, T (2010) carried out research to see the connection between teacher absenteeism and educational aspiration. The findings showed a strong negative association between primary school children's teacher absenteeism and educational aspirations. The absenteeism rates of female and male elementary school teachers varied significantly. The educational aspirations of girls and boys enrolled in Government primary schools do not differ much.

Skoric et al. (2009) studied the impact of video games on addiction, engagement and scholastic achievement. Sample of 333 children aged 8 to 12 years from two primary schools in Singapore, was selected. The data was collected using Danforth's Engagement-Addiction (II) scale and questions from DSM-IV while as the grades of students were directly obtained from their teachers. The results show that while there is no correlation between video game involvement or game time, addictive tendencies are consistently linked to poor academic achievement.

The Study

Objectives

1. To study the levels of digital gaming addiction, academic self-handicapping and educational aspiration among secondary school students.
2. To study the relationship between digital gaming addiction and educational aspiration among secondary school students.
3. To study the relationship between academic self-handicapping and educational aspiration among secondary school students.
4. To study the relationship between academic self-handicapping and digital gaming addiction among secondary school students
5. To study the difference in digital gaming addiction, academic self-handicapping and educational aspiration among secondary school students.

Methodology

The proposed study used a descriptive and correlational method for analysis of digital gaming addiction, academic self-handicapping and educational aspiration among secondary school students. The population for the said research includes all the Government secondary school students of District Baramulla. The investigator selected 100 students of secondary schools (50 female and 50 male students), as a sample using the technique of simple probability sampling. The tools for collection of data are as follows:

Digital Gaming Addiction Scale by Lemmens et al. (2009)
Measurement of student's Digital Gaming Addiction applied Digital Gaming Addiction Scale (Lemmens et al., 2009). It is a 7-item, 5-pointed Likert scale where: 1 is for never, 2 for rarely, 3 for sometimes, 4 for frequently and 5 for very often. Minimum and maximum possible scores are 7 and 35 respectively.

Academic Self-handicapping Scale by Gupta, S and Geetika (2020)
The academic self-handicapping scale developed by Gupta, S. and Geetika (2020) was used to measure academic self-handicapping. It is a 22-item scale in which items are rated on 5-point Likert scale where 1 is for strongly disagree, 2 for disagree, 3 for neutral, 4 for agree and 5 for strongly agree. Minimum and maximum possible scores are 22 and 110 respectively.

Educational Aspiration Inventory by Kumar, TP (2016)
Measurement of educational aspiration of students applied to Educational Aspiration Inventory (Kumar, TP 2016). It is a 20-item scale based on four alternatives in which a weightage of 1 for a, 2 for b, 3 for c and 4 for d is given. Minimum and maximum possible scores are 20 and 80 respectively.

Need and Significance

The sustainable development goal-4 focuses on ensuring inclusive and equitable quality education and promotes lifelong learning for all. The main aim of any nation is to provide education to all citizens without any hindrance. Among all the stages, the secondary stage is very crucial as students are in the adolescence period and get easily distracted if not guided properly. Also, this stage forms the basis for higher education, so it is necessary to provide a right track to students to move ahead and make the future of a nation bright. Today's era is technological era; students need to be guided for proper usage of this technology. Its misuse may give rise to different problems like they will indulge in problematic gaming, extra time will be spent on social networking sites and this all will ruin their academic progress. After an extensive review of literature, no such research study was done that has worked on study of digital gaming addiction and academic self-handicapping in relation to educational aspirations among secondary school students of district Baramulla. This study will help in fulfilling this research gap and holds significance in addressing contemporary issues related to technology use and academic outcomes among secondary school students. Its findings can contribute to the development of targeted interventions and policies to tailor support for the educational well-being of young individuals in the digital age.

Data Analysis and Interpretation

In this study, analysis of data was done with the help of SPSS software keeping in view the formulated hypothesis and objectives formulated. Investigators used statistical techniques like Correlation, t-test and descriptive statistics for analysis of data.

Objective 1: To study the levels of digital gaming addiction, academic self-handicapping and educational aspiration among secondary school students.

Table 1.1: Frequency Distribution of Sample Group with respect to Digital Gaming Addiction According to Monothetic Diagnosis

	f	%
Non-addicted to games	35	35
Addicted to games	65	65

***Finding*:** When Table 1.1 is examined, it is seen that number of secondary school students who are not game addicts is 35 (35%) whereas the number of game addicts is 65 (65%) according to monothetic diagnosis which states that if a person scores three (sometimes) or more on seven of the seven items, he is said to be game addict.

Table 1.2: Frequency Distribution of Sample Group with respect to Digital Gaming Addiction According to Polythetic Diagnosis

	f	%
Non-addicted to games	00	00
Addicted to games	100	100

Finding: When Table 1.2 is examined, it is seen that 100 (100%) secondary school students were found to be game addicts according to polythetic diagnosis which states that if a person scores three (sometimes) on at least four of the seven items, he is said to be a game addict.

Descriptive analysis was conducted like mean, standard deviation and frequencies, to assess the digital game addiction among secondary school students. The mean score of the participants in DGAS-7 was found to be 14.15 and the standard deviation of 4.60. Considering 35 and 7 as the highest and lowest scores that can be obtained from the scale, it can be said that most of the students, about 68% scored above the average level and their digital game addiction levels are above average among which about 4% scored very high. Considering the scale criteria for digital gaming addiction, an individual scoring above average is considered to be a digital game addict. Accordingly we can say that 68 (68%) secondary school students scored above average level on the digital game addiction scale and therefore 68 (68%) secondary school students have above-average level of digital game addiction or are digital game addicted.

Table 2: Levels of Academic Self-Handicapping Possessed by Sample

Range of z-scores	*Level of Academic Self-handicapping*	*f*	*%*
2.01 & above	Extremely high	3	3
1.26 to 2.00	High	2	2
0.51 to 1.25	Above average	24	24
-0.50 to 0.50	Moderate	41	41
-1.25 to -0.51	Below average	19	19
-2.00 to -1.26	Low	10	10
-2.01 & below	Extremely low	1	1

Finding: Table 2 shows the results of frequency distribution of the sample with respect to academic self-handicapping. Descriptive analysis like mean, standard deviation, z-score and frequencies were conducted for assessing educational aspiration levels among secondary school students. The results revealed that 41% secondary school students reflected moderate level of academic self-handicapping, 19% students reflected below average level of academic self-handicapping, 11% students reflected low levels of academic self-handicapping, 24% of students show above average level of academic self-handicapping and 5% of the sample possesses higher levels of academic self-handicapping.

Table 3: Levels of Educational Aspiration Possessed by the Sample

Range of z-scores	*Level of educational aspiration*	*f*	*%*
2.01 & above	Very high	0	0
1.26 to 2.00	High	5	5
0.51 to 1.25	Above average	22	22
-0.50 to 0.50	Moderate /Average	56	56
-1.25 to -0.51	Below average	6	6
-2.00 to -1.26	Low	00	00
-2.01 & below	Very low	11	11

Finding: Table 3 reports the result of frequency distribution of sample with respect to educational aspiration. Descriptive analyses were conducted like mean, standard deviation, z-score and frequencies for assessing the educational aspiration levels among secondary school students. The results revealed that 56% students reflected average educational aspiration level, 22% students reflected above average, 6% participants reflected below average, 5% sample reflected high and 11% sample reflected low educational aspiration levels.

***Objective 2*:** To study the relationship between digital gaming addiction and educational aspiration among secondary school students.

***Objective 3*:** To study the relationship between academic self-handicapping and educational aspiration among secondary school students.

Objective 4: To study the relationship between academic self-handicapping and digital gaming addiction among secondary school students.

Table 4: Correlations among Variables Which are under Study

Variable alpha	*Cronbach's*	*1*	*2*	*3*
Digital Gaming Addiction	.714	1.00	.201*	-.265**
Academic Self-handicapping	.857	.201*	1.00	.011
Educational Aspiration	.820	-.265**	.011	1.00

**Correlation is significant at the 0.01 level (2-tailed)
*Correlation is significant at the 0.05 level (2- tailed)

***Finding*:** Table 4 shows the results of descriptive statistics, including Pearson's correlation between digital gaming addiction, academic self-handicapping and educational aspiration. It was found that digital gaming addiction ($r = -.265$, $p < 0.01$) is negatively and significantly correlated with educational aspiration, therefore $H_0 1$: There is no relation between digital gaming addiction and educational aspiration stands rejected. Results also revealed that academic self-handicapping ($r = .011$, $p > 0.05$) is not significantly correlated with educational aspiration, therefore $H_0 2$: There is no significant relation between academic self-handicapping and educational aspiration is accepted. Digital gaming addiction (r .201, $p < 0.05$) is positively and significantly correlated with academic self-handicapping, therefore $H_0 3$: There is no significant relation between digital gaming addiction and academic self-handicapping stands rejected.

***Objective 5*:** To study the difference in digital gaming addiction, academic self-handicapping, and educational aspiration among secondary school students in relation to gender.

***Finding*:** Table 5 shows the results of t-test, in which the calculated t-value of Academic self-handicapping ($t = .065$), Behavioural self-handicapping ($t = .586$), Claimed self-handicapping ($t = -.006$), Educational aspiration ($t = -1.287$) is found to be insignificant which indicates that Academic self-handicapping, Behavioural self-handicapping, Claimed self-handicapping and educational aspiration are gender neutral while as t-value of Digital gaming addiction ($t = 15.386$) is found to be significant which indicates that female and male secondary school students differ significantly on the levels of digital gaming addiction. Therefore, the null hypothesis $H_0 4$: There is no difference in digital gaming addiction, academic self-handicapping and educational aspiration in relation to gender among secondary school students is partially rejected.

Table 5: Difference in Digital Gaming Addiction, Academic Self-handicapping and Educational Aspiration with respect to Gender

Variables	*Gender*	*N*	*Mean*	*S.D*	*df*	*t-value*	*Sig*
Digital Gaming Addiction	Male	50	27.00	1.325	98	15.386	<.001
Female 5022.58 1.540							
Academic self-handicapping	Male	50	96.28	3.812	98	.065	.949
Female 5096.24 2.143							
a) Behavioural ASH	Male	50	66.00	.00	98	.586	.561
	Female	50	65.92	.966			
b) Claimed ASH	Male	50	30.28	3.812	98	-.066	.948
	Female	50	30.32	1.963			
Educational aspiration	Male	50	70.40	1.884	98	-1.287	.203
	Female	50	71.42	5.276			

Conclusion

This study examined the connection between digital gaming addiction, academic self-handicapping and the educational aspiration among students of secondary schools with the aim to comprehend how educational aspiration of students of secondary schools is related and effected by playing excessive digital games and academic self-handicapping. In order to find out the levels and understand the relationships among the understudy variables, t-test and descriptive statistics were used.

It was found that secondary school students possessed varied levels of digital gaming addiction, academic self-handicapping and educational aspiration. In case of digital gaming addiction, 65% secondary school students and 100% students were found digital game addicted according to monothetic diagnosis and polythetic diagnosis respectively. About 29%, 41% and 30% students exhibited high, moderate and low academic self-handicapping levels respectively. The educational aspiration levels exhibited by students of secondary schools were found to be 27% high level, 56% moderate level and 17% low level.

Academic self-handicapping did not show any connection with the students of secondary school's educational aspirations but showed a positive and significant correlation with digital gaming addiction which implies that as the level of digital gaming addiction increases, academic self-handicapping also increases. Also, digital gaming addiction and educational aspiration, is having significant and negative correlation with each other which implies that excessively playing digital games decreases the level of educational aspiration among students. This invites the role of parents, teachers, institutions and policy makers in transforming these negatively effecting games into educationally effective and beneficial sources. As in today's technological era, we cannot isolate our young generation from technology, instead a combined effort from parents, teachers, institutions and policy makers is required to tailor approaches that will help our young generation to get out of this addiction and set plans for successful academic as well as personal and social life.

Additionally, while analysing the data through t-test, a significant gender difference in digital gaming addiction was found which indicates that male and female secondary school students differ on the levels of digital gaming addiction. It implies that gender may be a determining factor of the level of digital gaming addiction. Academic self-handicapping and educational aspiration are gender-neutral. This implies that educational aspiration and academic self-handicapping is not affected by gender.

Findings indicated that educational aspiration although not affected by gender but is negatively and significantly correlated with digital gaming addiction. Digital gaming addiction is the strong factor that decreases educational aspiration level among secondary school students. There may be many other factors that may set back secondary school students from setting high educational goals for their successful future. Planning for a successful future by setting high educational goals is crucial for the young generation as it directs them towards the path leading to a successful future. But unfortunately, today our young generation, addicted to digital games, has ruined their present as well as future by keeping distance from education and getting lost in digital games. As is evident from this study and we are also eye witness to it, that most of the young generation has become addicted to digital games which adversely affects their educational aspirations. This research suggests and calls for an alarm action from the parents, teachers, institutions and policy makers to reform the present scenario of using digital games to educationally effective and beneficial sources. Undoubtedly, educational games and gamification in education is already there for enhancing learning in children. But there is a need to reform the present scenario of digital gaming addiction in secondary school students.

References

American Psychiatric Association (APA). (2013). Diagnostic and statistical manual of mental disorders: DSM5 (5th Ed.). Washington, DC: Author.

ANLI, G. (2019). Examining the Relationship between Academic Self-Handicapping and School Attachment Levels of Secondary School Students. *International Online Journal of Educational Sciences*, *11*(3).

Boxer, et al. (2011). Educational Aspiration-Expectation Discrepancies: Relation to Socio-Economic and Academic Risk Related Factors. *Journal of Adolescence* (34)4: 609-617. Doi: 10.1016/j.adolescence.2010.10.002.

Bronfenbrenner, U. (1979). *The Ecology of Human Development: Experiments by Nature and Design*. Cambridge, MA: Haward University Press. https://doi.org/10.2307/j.ctv26071r6

Ciris, V. et al. (2022). A study on digital game addictions of adolescents in the Covid-19 pandemic. *Journal of Education in Science, Environment and Health* (JESEH), 8(2), 168-186. https://doi.org/10.55549/jeseh.01113707

Dr. Madhuri and Rani (2018). An Exploratory Study of Educational Aspiration among Secondary School Students.. https://indusedu.org

Ekinci, et al. (2017). Digital game addiction level of high school students in Turkey. *Acta Kinesiologica, 11*(2), 98-103.

Gadbois, S.A., & Sturgeon, R.D. (2011). Academic self-handicapping: Relationships with learning specific and general self-perceptions and academic performance over time. *British Journal of Educational Psychology, 81*(2), 207-222.

Gupta, S & Bashir, L. (2017). Educational Aspiration of Secondary School Students: Influence of School Environment and Parental Encouragement. *International Journal of Applied Business and Economic Research*, 15(21), 495-507.

Gupta, S & Geetika, (2020). Academic Self-Handicapping Scale: Development and Validation in Indian Context. *International Journal of Instruction*. 13. 87-102. 10.29333/iji.2020.1346a.

Haemmerlie, et al. (1996). The —Imaginary Audience, Self-Handicapping, and Drinking Patterns among College Students. PubMed, 79(3)

Javanmard, et al. (2012). Investigating the relationship between self-efficacy, cognitive and metacognitive strategies, and academic self-handicapping with academic achievement in male high school students in the tribes of Fars Province. *Journal of life Science and Biomedicine, 3*(1), 27-34.

Khattab, N. (2015) Student's Aspirations, Expectations and School Achievement: What Really Matters, *British Educational Research Journal*, Vol. 41, No. 5, October 2015, pp. 731-748. DOI: 10.1002/berj.3171.

Kumar, T. P. (2016) *Construction and Standardization of Educational Aspiration Inventory*. Volume : 6 Issue : 7, ISSN - 2249-555X IF : 3.919 IC Value : 74

Lemmens, J.S. et al. (2009). Development and Validation of a Game Addiction Scale for Adolescents. Medpsychol. Medpsychol 12:7795.10.1080/15213260802669458

Mikail, T. (2015). Examination of student's digital gaming habits at secondary school level in Elazig Province of Turkey. Educational Research and Reviews, 10(8), 1300-1310.

Rahima, H. and Azmana, N. (2010) Educational Aspirations among first generation students and their parental influence towards pursuing tertiary education, Procedia Social and Behavioral Sciences 7(C), pp 414-418.

Schulenberg, J., et al. (1991). Gender differences in adolescents' career interests: Beyond main effects. Journal of Research on Adolescence. 1 (1), pp. 37–61.

Skoric, M.M., et al. (2009). Children and video games: Addiction, Engagement, and Scholastic Achievement. Cyberpsychology & behavior, 12(5), 567-572.

Talwar, M.S. & Pradeep, T. (2010). Correlation Between Teacher Absenteeism and Educational Aspiration. Experiments in Education 1995, Vol. XXXI (55), pp 83-85.

31

Internet Addiction among Undergraduate Students

Merajul Hasan and Ujjwal Kumar Halder

Introduction

Technologies have made our lives easier and now, one cannot imagine life without technology. Smart devices like smartphones, computers and the Internet help in facilitating communication among people. Using social media through smartphones and the Internet is common in today's world, with young people being the most commonly affected ones. Adolescents use different types of gadgets like smartphones, tablets, laptops, iPads, etc. Some use it for just mere communication. Some use it for entertainment (watching movies, listening to music, playing online games), shopping, browsing educational materials, etc., other than communication. The use of technology is essential to make the tasks of life easier; however, its abnormal, excessive, and unnecessary use leads to addiction and makes life more difficult.

Besides these, Internet addiction has become very popular day by day. Internet Addiction, also referred to as technology addiction, may be defined as an impulse control disorder that involves the excessive and compulsive use of the Internet despite negative consequences to the user of this online platform. Hence, the article aimed to explore the Internet addiction of undergraduate students in Uttar Dinajpur District of West Bengal. Here, the Internet addiction of undergraduate students is the score collected through a standardised test.

The Study

Objectives

The following objectives were taken to conduct the study:

1. To measure the Internet addiction of undergraduate students in Uttar Dinajpur District of West Bengal.
2. To find out the differences in Internet addiction among the undergraduate students in Uttar Dinajpur District of West Bengal according to their sub-samples.

Assumptions

The following assumptions were made to conduct the study:

1. It is assumed that the Internet addiction of undergraduate students is measurable through a standardised test.
2. It is also assumed that the differences among undergraduate students in terms of Internet addiction can be estimated.

Methodology

The survey method of descriptive research is followed to collect, analyse and interpret the data to conclude the formulated objectives. The 200 number samples were collected through purposive random sampling from the selected population in the district of Uttar Dinajpur. The samples were 200 undergraduate students studying different UG (Honours and General) subjects. A total of 73 students were selected from Raiganj Surendranath Mahavidyalaya, of whom 37 were male, and 36 were female, and 127 students were selected from Raiganj University, of whom 59 were male, and 68 were female. The Internet Addiction Scale (IAS) developed by Damandeep Kaur Gulati, Dr. Jose J. Kurisunkal and Dr. Mamta Bakliwal, was adopted to collect data from the selected samples.

Analysis and Interpretations

The analysis and interpretations were made according to the following manner.

Analysis pertaining to Hypothesis-1

$H_{0.1}$: There are no significant differences between male and female undergraduate students in terms of their Internet addiction.

Table 1: Presentation of Descriptive and Inferential Statistics of Gender-wise Students

	Independent Samples Test								
		Descriptive Statistics				*t-test for Equality of Means*			
	Categories of the Samples	*N*	*Mean*	*SD*	*SED*	*t*	*df*	*Sig. (2-tailed)*	*Mean Diff*
Internet Addiction	Male	102	39.19	13.09	1.75	.10	198	.920	.176
	Female	98	39.01	11.62					

Table 1 shows the descriptive and inferential statistics among male and female (*$t=0.10$, $df= 198$, $p > 0.05$*) students. Therefore, the Hypothesis-1 ($H_{0.1}$) may be accepted. Hence, it may be interpreted that there are no significant differences between male and female students in their Internet addiction.

Analysis pertaining to Hypothesis-2

$H_{0.2}$: There are no significant differences between rural and urban undergraduate students in terms of their Internet addiction.

Table 2: Presentation of Descriptive and Inferential Statistics of Locale-wise Students

		Independent Samples Test							
		Descriptive Statistics				*t-test for Equality of Means*			
	Categories of the Samples	*N*	*Mean*	*SD*	*SED*	*t*	*df*	*Sig. (2-tailed)*	*Mean Diff*
Internet Addiction	Rural	131	39.41	13.27	1.84	.491	198	.624	.905
	Urban	69	38.51	10.49	2				

Table 2 shows the descriptive and inferential statistics between rural and urban ($t=0.491$, $df= 198$, $p > 0.05$) students. Therefore, the Hypothesis-2 ($H_{0.2}$) may be accepted. Hence, it may be interpreted that there are no significant differences between rural and urban students in their Internet addiction.

Analysis pertaining to Hypothesis-3

$H_{0.3}$: There are no significant differences between undergraduate honours and undergraduate general students in terms of their Internet addiction.

Table 3: Presentation of Descriptive and Inferential Statistics of Academic Stream-wise Students

		Independent Samples Test							
		Descriptive Statistics				*t-test for Equality of Means*			
	Categories of the Samples	*N*	*Mean*	*SD*	*SED*	*t*	*df*	*Sig. (2-tailed)*	*Mean Diff*
Internet Addiction	UG Hons.	186	39.04	12.05	3.43	-.237	198	.813	-.814
	UG Gen.	14	39.86	16.47					

Table 3 shows the descriptive and inferential statistics undergraduate honours and undergraduate general ($t= -0.237$, $df= 198$, $p > 0.05$) students. Therefore, the Hypothesis-3 ($H_{0.3}$) may be accepted. Hence, it may be interpreted that there are no significant differences between undergraduate honours and undergraduate general students in their Internet addiction.

Analysis pertaining to Hypothesis-4

$H_{0.4}$: There are no significant differences among different community-wise undergraduate students in terms of their Internet addiction.

Table 4: Presentation of Descriptive Statistics of Different Community-wise Students

Descriptive				
Internet Addiction				
	N	*Mean*	*SD*	*Std. Error*
General	68	38.00	10.14	1.23
SC	91	40.38	14.80	1.55
ST	12	37.08	10.12	2.92
OBC	29	38.48	9.24	1.72
Total	200	39.10	12.36	.87

Table 5: Presentation of Inferential Statistics of Different Caste-wise Students

ANOVA					
Internet Addiction					
	Sum of Squares	*Df*	*Mean Square*	*F*	*Sig.*
Between Groups	292.303	3	97.434	.634	.594
Within Groups	30119.697	196	153.672		
Total	30412.000	199			

Tables 4 and 5 show the descriptive and inferential statistics among different community-wise students (*F=0.634, p > 0.05*). Therefore, the Hypothesis-4 ($H_{0.4}$) may be accepted. Hence, it may be interpreted that there is no significant difference among different community-wise students (Gen, SC, ST & OBC) in their Internet addiction.

Analysis pertaining to Hypothesis-5

$H_{0.5}$: There are no significant differences among different parents' occupation-wise undergraduate students in terms of their Internet addiction.

Table 6: Presentation of Descriptive Statistics of Different Parents' Occupation-wise Students

Descriptives				
Internet Addiction				
	N	*Mean*	*SD*	*Std. Error*
Agriculture	82	39.82	15.41	1.70
Business	54	40.26	11.11	1.51
Service	41	37.73	8.83	1.38
Others	23	36.26	7.19	1.50
Total	200	39.10	12.36	.87

Tables 6 and 7 show the descriptive and inferential statistics among the students of different parents' occupations (*F=0.82, p > 0.05*). Therefore, the Hypothesis-5 ($H_{0.5}$) may be accepted. Hence, it may be interpreted that

Table 7: Different Parents' Occupation-Wise Students ANOVA

Internet Addiction					
	Sum of Squares	*df*	*Mean Square*	*F*	*Sig.*
Between Groups	376.890	3	125.630	.820	.484
Within Groups	30035.110	196	153.240		
Total	30412.000	199			

there is no significant difference among parents' occupation-wise students (Agriculture, Business, Service and Others) in their Internet addiction.

Analysis pertaining to Hypothesis-6

$H_{0.6}$: There are no significant differences among different achievement level-wise undergraduate students in terms of their Internet addiction.

Table 8: Different Levels of Achievement-wise Students Descriptives

Internet Addiction				
	N	*Mean*	*SD*	*Std. Error*
Below Average	24	36.75	9.28	1.89
Average	55	40.98	13.98	1.89
Above Average	121	38.71	12.09	1.10
Total	200	39.10	12.36	.87

Table 9: Presentation of Inferential Statistics of Different Levels of Achievement-wise Students ANOVA

Internet Addiction					
	Sum of Squares	*df*	*Mean Square*	*F*	*Sig.*
Between Groups	345.642	2	172.821	1.132	.324
Within Groups	30066.358	197	152.621		
Total	30412.000	199			

Tables 8 and 9 show the descriptive and inferential statistics among the students of different levels of achievement ($F=1.132, p > 0.05$). Therefore, the Hypothesis-6 ($H_{0.6}$) may be accepted. Hence, it may be interpreted that there is no significant difference among the students of different levels of achievement (Below Average, Average and Above Average) in their Internet addiction.

Main Findings

1. There are no significant differences between male and female ($t=0.10$, $df= 198$, $p > 0.05$) students in their Internet Addiction in Uttar Dinajpur District of West Bengal.

2. There are no significant differences between urban and rural *(t=0.491, df= 198, $p > 0.05$)* students in their Internet Addiction in Uttar Dinajpur District of West Bengal.
3. There are no significant differences between UG Honours and UG General (t= -0.237, df= 198, $p > 0.05$) students in their Internet Addiction in Uttar Dinajpur District of West Bengal.
4. There are no significant differences among the General, SC, ST and OBC students (F=0.634, $p > 0.05$ in their Internet addiction in Uttar Dinajpur District of West Bengal.
5. There are no significant differences among the students of different parents' occupations — Agriculture, Business, Service and Others (F=0.82, $p > 0.05$) in their Internet addiction in Uttar Dinajpur District of West Bengal.
6. There are no significant differences among the students of different levels of achievement — Below Average, Average, and Above Average (F=1.132, $p > 0.05$) in their Internet addiction in Uttar Dinajpur District of West Bengal.

Conclusion

Based on the findings, it may be concluded that there are no significant differences among the students in Internet Addiction regarding their sub-samples like gender, locale, academic streams and different communities, parents' occupations, level of achievements, etc. It can also be concluded that Internet uses are equally observed among the students in the Uttar Dinajpur district of West Bengal.

In addition to the conclusion, it can be said that Internet addiction among undergraduate students is a concerning issue with significant implications. The accessibility and allure of digital devices and online activities can lead to excessive use and addictive behaviours, impacting various aspects of students' lives.

Internet addiction in undergraduate students can negatively affect their academic performance. Excessive screen time, distractions from social media and online entertainment, and a lack of focus can lead to decreased productivity, poor time management, and difficulties in meeting academic deadlines. Additionally, Internet addiction may hinder students' ability to concentrate, absorb information, and engage in critical thinking, ultimately affecting their overall learning outcomes.

Furthermore, Internet addiction can have adverse effects on undergraduate students' mental health. Spending excessive time online can contribute to increased stress, anxiety, and feelings of isolation or FOMO (fear of missing out). It may also exacerbate existing mental health conditions or hinder the development of healthy coping mechanisms. The constant need for online validation and peer comparison can negatively impact self-esteem and well-being.

The Internet addiction in undergraduate students can also affect social relationships and personal development. Excessive Internet use may lead to reduced face-to-face interactions, social withdrawal, and difficulty in forming and maintaining meaningful connections. Students may struggle to balance their online and offline lives, resulting in neglected personal relationships, decreased physical activity, and limited engagement in extracurricular activities.

Addressing Internet addiction in undergraduate students is crucial. Educational institutions should promote digital literacy and provide resources for students to develop healthy technology habits. Encouraging time management skills, establishing clear boundaries between study and leisure time, and fostering a supportive environment can help students balance their academic responsibilities and digital engagement. Moreover, fostering offline social interactions, encouraging physical activity, and providing mental health support can aid in mitigating the negative impact of Internet addiction on students' well-being. By recognising the significance of Internet addiction in undergraduate students and implementing proactive measures, educational institutions can support students in developing healthy technology habits, fostering personal growth, and achieving academic success while maintaining their overall well-being.

References

Agarwal, V., & Kar, S.K. (2015). Technology addiction in adolescents. *Journal of Indian Association for Child and Adolescent Mental Health, 11*(3), 170-174.

Anderson, J., & Rainie, L. (2018). The negatives of digital life. *Pew Research Center*, 68-75.

Anderson, J., & Rainie, L. (2018). The positives of digital life. *Pew Research Center*, 52-68.

Canadian Paediatric Society, Digital Health Task Force, Ottawa, Ontario. (2019). Digital media: Promoting healthy screen use in school-aged children and adolescents. *Paediatrics & Child Health, 24*(6), 402-408.

Cash, H., Rae, C.D., Steel, A.H., & Winkler, A. (2012). Internet Addiction: A Brief Summary of Research and Practice. *Current psychiatry reviews, 8*(4), 292–298. https://doi.org/10.2174/157340012803520513

Chiu, S.I., Hong, F.Y., & Chiu, S.L. (2013). An analysis on the correlation and gender difference between college students' Internet addiction and mobile phone addiction in Taiwan. *International scholarly research notices, 2013*.

Dresp-Langley, B., & Hutt, A. (2022). Digital Addiction and Sleep. *International journal of environmental research and public health, 19*(11), 6910. https://doi.org/10.3390/ijerph19116910

Echeburúa E, de Corral P. Addiction to new technologies and to online social networking in young people: A new challenge. *Adicciones*. 2010;22(2):91- 5. 2.

Gupta, M., & Sharma, A. (2021). Fear of missing out: A brief overview of origin, theoretical underpinnings and relationship with mental health. *World journal of clinical cases*, *9*(19), 4881.

Ivanova, V. (2023, October 21). *Internet addiction and academic performance: causes and health risks - The Diamond Rehab Thailand*. The Diamond Rehab Thailand. https://diamondrehabthailand.com/internet-addiction-and-academic-performance/

Kolhar, M., Kazi, R.N.A., & Alameen, A. (2021). Effect of social media use on learning, social interactions, and sleep duration among university students. *Saudi Journal of Biological Sciences*, *28*(4), 2216-2222.

Kumar, M., & Mondal, A. (2018). A study on Internet addiction and its relation to psychopathology and self-esteem among college students. *Industrial psychiatry journal*, *27*(1), 61.

Shaw M, Black DW. Internet addiction: definition, assessment, epidemiology and clinical management. *CNS Drugs*. 2008; 22 (5).

32

Self Esteem and Body Image of Students Addicted to Social Media

Sapna Raj

Introduction

The pervasive influence of social media on the psychological well-being of individuals, especially among college students, has sparked considerable interest and concern in recent years. This study aims to delve into the intricate relationship between social media engagement and its repercussions on body image perceptions and self-esteem among students pursuing higher education.

The ubiquity of social media platforms has transformed the way individuals interact, share information, and perceive themselves. For college students, particularly those enrolled in Bachelor of Arts (B.A.) programs at institutions like Hindu College and Ramjas College, social media has become an integral part of their daily lives. However, while these platforms offer connectivity and information exchange, their impact on self-perception, particularly regarding body image and self-esteem, remains a subject of critical inquiry.

Numerous studies have underscored the pervasive nature of social media platforms, highlighting their integral role in the lives of today's youth. Particularly for college students, these platforms serve as not only tools for connectivity and academic interactions but also arenas for self-expression and identity formation. However, alongside their benefits, concerns have emerged regarding the potential detrimental effects of extensive social media engagement on the mental health and self-perception of individuals.

This study focuses on students enrolled in the Bachelor of Arts (B.A.) program at prestigious institutions such as Hindu College and Ramjas College in New Delhi. By examining the impact of social media on body image and self-esteem among this cohort, the research aims to contribute valuable insights into understanding the multifaceted implications of social networking platforms on the psychological landscape of higher education students.

The literature surrounding this subject emphasizes the profound influence of social media, traditional media, and societal standards on shaping perceptions of body image, particularly among adolescents and young adults. Exposure to idealized images and societal beauty standards propagated through social media often leads to distorted body image perceptions, fostering feelings of inadequacy and dissatisfaction, especially among college students navigating their formative years.

Additionally, studies have highlighted a negative correlation between self-esteem and excessive social media use, as individuals engage in social comparison and validation-seeking behaviours, often leading to decreased self-worth and psychological distress. Given the prevalence of these platforms and their significant impact, understanding their influence on body image perceptions and self-esteem is crucial for comprehending the complexities of psychological well-being among college students.

This research seeks to bridge the gap in existing literature by exploring the nuanced relationship between social media engagement and its effects on body image and self-esteem among college students. Through empirical investigation and analysis, the study aims to uncover patterns, gender-specific differences, and long-term implications of social media usage, offering insights into fostering healthier relationships with these platforms. Ultimately, the findings aim to inform interventions, policies, and support mechanisms that promote positive psychological development and well-being among students in higher education.

Examining a sample of 100 participants, evenly divided between male and female students, this study unravels significant insights into the patterns and duration of social media usage. Notably, the prevalence of platforms like Facebook, WhatsApp, and YouTube among these students, with a considerable portion dedicating substantial time, 4 to 6 hours daily, to social media activities, raises concerns about potential implications on their self-esteem and body image.

Moreover, the findings highlight gender-specific nuances in how social media affects body image and self-esteem among college students. Males exhibit heightened susceptibility to body image concerns, while females demonstrate a more pronounced impact on self-esteem due to their engagement with social media. These disparities underscore the need to address gender-specific influences when analyzing the psychological repercussions of social media usage.

This study sheds light on the adverse effects of excessive social media engagement, emphasizing pressure, comparison, and validation-seeking behaviours experienced by participants. The implications of these findings are significant, calling for a balanced approach to social media usage that promotes digital well-being, media literacy, and self-acceptance among college students.

Literature Review

The extensive literature review encompasses diverse studies exploring the impact of social media on various aspects of psychological well-being, focusing on body image perceptions, self-esteem, adjustment in college students, and the influence of media exposure on these factors. The studies span different methodologies, populations, and geographical locations, contributing to a comprehensive understanding of the multifaceted relationship between social media and individual perceptions.

Social Media and Adjustment in College Students

Richard (2016) examined the impact of social networking sites (SNS) on international students' adjustment at the U.S. colleges. The study highlighted a positive correlation between SNS usage and overall adjustment among international students. Eileen (2015) conducted a phenomenological study focusing on Facebook's impact on the self-esteem of female students. Findings indicated that both positive and negative messages on FB significantly affected girls' self-esteem and friendship dynamics.

Virginia et al. (2015) investigated the influence of SNS on the self-esteem of adolescents in Kenya, emphasizing the negative impact of SNS on the self-esteem of secondary school students. Mudhovozi (2012) studied adjustment experiences among first-year students, revealing social challenges and gender differences in adaptation at the university level.

Body Image, Self-Esteem, and Media Exposure

Rudolf et al. (2015) explored the relationship between body mass index (BMI), self-esteem, and body image during pregnancy. The study revealed correlations between self-esteem, body image, and BMI, emphasizing the importance of body image perception during pregnancy. Sarah (2012) focused on Facebook's influence on the well-being and self-esteem of early adolescents, associating positive friend networks on FB with higher well-being and self-esteem in participants.

Theoretical Perspectives and Influences

Several studies discuss theoretical frameworks and influences shaping body image and self-esteem. Julie (2014) discussed considering the unique functions and purposes of social media concerning body dissatisfaction. Maggie A. Brennan (2010) examined the impact of societal appearance ideals, media portrayal, and comparisons on body image satisfaction, noting gender differences.

Body Image and Self-esteem Correlations

Studies such as David (2014), examining social networking's predictive role in anxiety and depression changes, and Baldwin and Hoffman (2002), exploring self-image devaluation concerning thin models, contribute to understanding the intricate relationship between self-esteem, body image, and media exposure.

Media's Role and Impact on Self-Perception

Thompson (1999) suggested that various media forms influence individuals differently, affecting their perceptions of appearance and self-esteem. The historical evolution of media portrayal and its impact, noted by Garfinkel (1986), and contemporary studies' findings emphasize how media ideals influence body dissatisfaction and self-esteem.

Self-esteem and Health Outcomes

Studies like Paxton (2006) highlighted the long-term consequences of low self-esteem and body dissatisfaction on adverse health outcomes, reinforcing the importance of understanding these factors.

Methodology

The provided research methodology details a study investigating the impact of social media addiction on the body image and self-esteem of male and female students pursuing higher education in New Delhi. The research methodology encompasses various essential components, including the statement of the problem, objectives, hypotheses, operational definitions, research method, design, population, sample, tools, data collection procedure, and statistical analysis plan.

Statement of the Problem: The research problem focuses on exploring "Self-esteem and Body Image of Students Addicted to Social Media."

Objectives: The objectives of the study involve comparing male and female students addicted to social media concerning their body image and self-esteem.

Hypotheses: Two hypotheses have been formulated:

- There is no significant difference between male and female students addicted to social media concerning their body image.
- There is no significant difference between male and female students addicted to social media concerning their self-esteem.

Research Method: The study utilizes a descriptive survey method to collect data from the selected sample.

Research Design: The chosen design is a quantitative cross-sectional and co-relational approach utilizing questionnaires for data collection.

Population and Sample: The population includes students pursuing a Bachelor of Arts (B.A.) across few institutions in New Delhi, while the sample comprises 50 male and 50 female students addicted to social media within the age group of 18 to 22. The study specifically targets students from Hindu College and Ramjas College.

Tools: Data collection tools include a self-constructed information blank on social media use among higher education students, The Multidimensional

Body-Self Relations Questionnaire-Appearance Scales (MBSRQ-AS) to measure body image, and the Rosenberg Self-esteem Scale to assess self-esteem.

Procedure for Data Collection: Data collection involved randomly selecting 100 college students from Hindu College and Ramjas College, connecting with them via email or WhatsApp, and collecting filled-out questionnaires for analysis.

Statistical Analysis: The statistical analysis plan includes the use of Mean, Standard Deviation, and t-tests to examine differences between male and female social media users regarding body image and self-esteem.

For the ethical consideration "Prior to the study, all selected participants were provided with detailed information about the research objectives, procedures, and the voluntary nature of their involvement. Informed consent was obtained from each participant before their inclusion in the study. The participants were assured that their responses would remain confidential, and their anonymity would be maintained throughout the research process. Only those who willingly agreed to participate proceeded to complete the questionnaires, and their contributions were vital to the study's findings." This ethical procedure ensured that all participants were aware of the study's purpose and willingly provided their consent to be part of the research. Additionally, those participants who were randomly selected to be part of the study were specifically educated about social media, its various uses, and its potential effects on them.

Findings

The study aimed to explore the influence of social media usage on the body image and self-esteem of college students pursuing B.A Programs at Hindu College and Ramjas College in New Delhi. A sample of 100 participants, evenly distributed between 50 male and 50 female students, was surveyed to investigate their engagement with social media platforms and its potential effects.

Social Media Engagement and Usage Patterns

The study revealed a varied spectrum of social media platform engagement among participants. Table 1 displays the distribution of male and female users, with an equal representation of 50 participants in each gender category.

Table 1: Gender of Users of social media

	Users	
Gender	*N*	*%*
Male	50	50
Female	50	50
Total	100	100

Duration and Intensity of Social Media Usage

44% of the students had been using social media for 6 months to a year, while 26% had been engaged for 3 to 6 years, and 9%, 6 years and above. From Table 2 the study revealed a significant prevalence of usage across various platforms, with Facebook being the most frequently used platform (52%), followed by WhatsApp (27%), YouTube (10%), and others (4%). This highlights the widespread adoption and diverse usage patterns among college students.

Table 2: Showing the Extent of Usage of Social Media Users

S. No.	*Social media sites*	*Percentage*
1.	Facebook	52.00%
2.	WhatsApp	27.00%
3.	YouTube	10.00%
4.	Instagram	5.00%
5.	Twitter	2.00%
6.	Others	4.00%
	Total	100%

Table 3: Frequency Distribution of the Student Pursuing Higher Education by Hours of Using social media

Hours of using social media	*Percentage*
Less than 1 hour	11
1 to 3 hours	38
4 to 6 hours	51
Total	100

The study further delved into the duration and intensity of social media usage among the participants. 51% of the students dedicated 4 to 6 hours daily to social media activities.

This substantial time investment in social media engagement raises concerns about its potential impact on various facets of the students' lives. Such high involvement hints at the potential for social media to consume a substantial portion of students' daily routines, possibly impacting their academic performance, social interactions, and overall well-being.

Testing of Hypotheses

Hypothesis 1: There is a significant difference between male and female students addicted to social media on their body image.

The above Table 4 depicts the mean comparison between the male and female college students on body image. The results reveal that the two groups differ significantly at 0.05 level, which indicates that social media has a great impact on body image on male as compared to females.

Table 4: Showing Mean Comparison Between Male and Female Users on Their Body Image

Group	*N*	*Mean*	*S.D.*	*t-value*	*Level of Sig.*
Male	50	79.32	6.189	2.10	Significant
Female	50	60.74	5.639		

Df=98, **sig at 0.01 level, *sig at 0.05 level

The media has drastic effects on the lives of the adolescents, especially the teenagers. The contemporary fashion models perceived to be the representation of female appearance are becoming slimmer and slender, below the suggested average female body size if women in the media become thinner, thinness is linked to attractiveness, whereas larger body size is equivalent to unattractiveness.

This is consistent with the past research conducted by Hendriks and Burgoon (2003) found that thin models and actresses appear to be the standard in today's media, ever-present on television, and in magazines, movies and Internet sites. Advertisement targeting young women features thin and beautiful models in desirable circumstances in order to sell clothing, accessories and other products. There is a mediated norm for body image in present day culture and it is characterized by bodies that are extremely thin; this mediated thin ideal is present in mainstream media and mainstream media are a source women turn to for information about how to look.

Hypothesis 2: There is a significant difference between male and female students addicted to social media on their Self-esteem.

Table 5: Mean, Standard Deviation And T-Value to Find Significant Difference with regards to Self-esteem

Gender	*N*	*Mean*	*S. D*	*t-value*	*Level of Significance*
Male	50	36.1	2.80	4.0109**	Significant
Female	50	13.5	2.71		

** Significant at 0.01 level

The above Table 5 indicates that there is significant difference between male and female adolescent with respect to self-esteem among adolescents. Further, there were significant statistically differences in self-esteem attributed to sex in favour of males. Thus, the hypothesis stated that there is significant difference among self-esteem of male and female users of social media is accepted.

In conclusion, the impact of social media on the body image of college students is a complex and multifaceted issue. While social media platforms have provided a platform for self-expression, connection, and information sharing, they have also contributed to the development of unrealistic beauty standards and increased body dissatisfaction among college students.

The constant exposure to carefully curated and edited images on social media has created a distorted perception of beauty, leading to feelings of inadequacy and pressure to conform to unattainable ideals. College students may compare their own bodies to those of influencers and peers, often resulting in negative self-perception and diminished self-esteem.

Moreover, the prevalence of photo-editing tools and filters has further perpetuated the idea of a flawless appearance, making it challenging for college students to embrace their natural bodies and appreciate diversity. This can lead to a range of negative outcomes, such as unhealthy dieting behaviours, body dysmorphia, and even the development of eating disorders.

However, it is important to note that social media is not solely responsible for these issues. Body image concerns have existed long before the advent of social media, and various societal factors contribute to their prevalence. It is crucial to consider other factors like peer influence, societal beauty standards, and personal vulnerabilities when assessing the impact of social media on body image.

Efforts are being made to address this issue, including promoting body positivity, diverse representation, and media literacy. Encouraging open discussions about body image, self-acceptance, and the influence of social media can empower college students to develop a healthier relationship with their bodies and navigate the digital landscape more mindfully.

Ultimately, it is essential to strike a balance between utilizing social media for its positive aspects while being critical of its potential negative impact on body image. By promoting authenticity, embracing diverse representations, and fostering a culture of self-acceptance, we can help mitigate the detrimental effects of social media and promote healthier body image perceptions among college students.

The impact of social media on the self-esteem of college students is significant and warrants careful consideration. While social media platforms have opened doors for self-expression, networking, and information sharing, they have also introduced new challenges to students' self-esteem.

The constant exposure to carefully curated and idealized versions of others' lives on social media can create feelings of inadequacy and self-comparison. College students often find themselves measuring their achievements, appearances, and social popularity against those showcased online, leading to a diminished sense of self-worth and self-esteem.

Moreover, the prevalence of likes, comments, and follower counts on social media platforms has created a culture of validation-seeking, where one's worth is tied to external metrics. This can result in a detrimental cycle of seeking approval and validation from others, which can erode self-esteem when expectations are not met.

Additionally, the phenomenon of "highlight reels" on social media, where individuals predominantly share their positive experiences and successes, can create an illusion that everyone else's lives are perfect and unattainable. This comparison to an idealized version of others' lives can lead to self-doubt and dissatisfaction with one's own accomplishments and progress.

However, it is important to recognize that social media is not solely responsible for low self-esteem among college students. Self-esteem is influenced by a complex interplay of various factors, including personal experiences, relationships, and societal pressures. Social media can amplify existing insecurities, but it is not the sole cause.

Impact on Body Image: The analysis revealed a significant difference in body image perceptions between male and female users of social media. Male students exhibited a mean body image score of 79.32, while female students had a mean score of 60.74. This disparity suggests that social media may exert a more pronounced influence on the body image of male students, potentially contributing to body dissatisfaction and unrealistic beauty standards perpetuated through media representations.

The media's portrayal of an unrealistic thin ideal for females and the emphasis on physical appearance for males can be influential in shaping body image perceptions. The constant exposure to thin models and edited images on social media platforms can contribute to feelings of inadequacy and pressure to conform to societal beauty standards, impacting the self-perception of college students.

Impact on Self-esteem: The study also highlighted a significant difference in self-esteem between male and female users of social media. Male students demonstrated a mean self-esteem score of 36.1, whereas female students exhibited a mean score of 13.5. This difference implies that male students may be less susceptible to the negative impact of social media on self-esteem compared to their female counterparts.

The phenomenon of seeking external validation through likes, comments, and follower counts on social media platforms appears to affect the self-esteem of female students more significantly. The constant comparison to curated and idealized versions of others' lives on social media may contribute to feelings of inadequacy and diminished self-worth among female college students.

Challenges and Recommendations

The excessive use of social media, especially spending 4 to 6 hours daily, poses various challenges to college students. It can lead to social media addiction, impacting academic performance, mental well-being, and real-life social interactions. Moreover, the curated nature of social media content creates unrealistic standards, fostering negative body image perceptions and affecting self-esteem.

Efforts to mitigate these challenges involve promoting digital well-being practices. Encouraging students to set boundaries, allocate time for offline activities, and cultivate a healthy self-image based on internal validation can help counteract the adverse effects of social media usage. Additionally, media literacy education and discussions on body positivity and self-acceptance are crucial in empowering students to navigate social media more mindfully.

In conclusion, the study underscores the need for a balanced approach to social media usage. While it offers numerous opportunities for connection and self-expression, it also poses challenges to body image perceptions and self-esteem among college students. By fostering a culture of digital well-being and promoting positive self-image, we can empower students to harness the benefits of social media while minimizing its detrimental effects.

Conclusion

The research findings highlighted significant disparities between male and female college students in terms of body image and self-esteem impacted by social media usage. The comparison between male and female students revealed notable differences in their perceptions and adjustments, indicating the profound influence of social media on their psychological well-being.

The study showcased that male users of social media tend to exhibit better body image perceptions than their female counterparts. This discrepancy could be attributed to societal standards perpetuated by media, where females are subjected to idealized images that promote unrealistic beauty standards, leading to body dissatisfaction and pressure to conform.

Moreover, the findings indicated that males tend to have better home and social adjustments compared to females in the context of social media usage. This discrepancy might suggest varying patterns of interaction and adaptation, emphasizing the impact of social media on social behaviours and relationships among genders.

The conclusions drawn from the study underscore the urgent need for a re-evaluation of societal beauty standards and media representations. Encouraging the portrayal of realistic models in media can potentially alleviate the pressure to conform to unrealistic beauty ideals, fostering positive self-attitudes and reducing body image concerns among college students.

Furthermore, the study emphasizes the pivotal role of parents, educators, and counselling services in promoting individuality and self-worth among college students. Addressing the negative impact of media-induced body consciousness and striving to instil confidence in personal uniqueness can mitigate the detrimental effects of idealized media images.

In light of these findings, it becomes evident that media, while creating awareness and influencing lifestyle and behaviours, also poses significant risks to mental health, particularly among young females. The observed tendencies among young females to associate their self-worth with societal beauty norms underscore the need for interventions aimed at reducing societal pressures and promoting self-acceptance.

Recommendations

- Discourage dieting that is unhealthy in nature; as a substitute encourage and support the use of positive eating and activities that involve physical activities or exercise. However, all these actions or behaviours should be carried out on an ongoing basis.
- There should be encouragement related to eating food that is home cooked, that may be healthful plus more enjoyable.
- There should be an environment that encourages families to talk as less as possible about weight, comparing their sons / daughters to the models appearing in the TV shows / advertisements; this not only creates a sense of becoming like those models, but also stimulates in them eating habits that are not useful for them. Instead, more concentration should be given to do more at home to facilitate healthy eating and physical activity.
- It should be assumed that overweight teens have experienced weight mistreatment, and they try to tackle this issue with the help of their families.
- Education and awareness level should be increased to familiarize about negative aspects of excessive television viewing.
- There should be a thoughtful viewing, better scheduling of time and choosing programs to view.
- There should be an arrangement that separate television viewing and eating at the same time is not in practice. Because television watching and eating at the same time increases obesity level in teens.
- False images of women which have been improved on Photoshop and airbrushed should not be always projected on mass media.
- Likewise on the other hand, always a fat woman is projected on mass media as being subject to mockery and ridicule which effects all the people and people mostly do not behave well with women who are not of the tailor-made proportions as have been set by the mass media, this kind of negative assessment of woman leads them to be less productive at work, lonely, sad and having low self-worth. It is seen that they become socially withdrawn and find themselves unable to blend with others and work as a team, and hence are not able to give their full output to the world.

Suggestion

- The study of various social media portals had been conducted in a general manner as it can also be conducted portal wise e.g. impact of Facebook, impact of Twitter and so on.
- The present study is done only to the teenagers; similar study can be conducted to school and under-graduate students.
- The present study has been conducted only on the 100 male and female users but can be extended to larger sample covering the whole state/ province/ nation.
- A similar and comparative study should be conducted on Professional and Non-professional college going students.
- The present study covers only two groups of social media. "Male and Female" but the same can be done on more than two groups like Users, High users, Low users and so on.
- The present study covers four variables like self-esteem, adjustment, body image; same can be done on other variables as well.
- The present study is conducted on students; similar study can be done on teacher education.

Bibliography

Aggarwal, J.C. (1991). *Educational Research — An Introduction.* New Delhi, Arya Book Depot.

Allport, G.B. (1961). Pattern and growth in personality, New York, Holt. Allen, et. al. (1941). The relation of first name preference to their frequency in the culture. *J. Soc. psycho.* 14- 279-293.

Andreassen et al. (2015). The relationship between addictive use of social media and videogames and symptoms of psychiatric disorders: A large-scale cross-sectional study. *Psychology of Addictive Behaviors*, 30(2), 252-262.

Balakrishanan & Shamim (2015). Malasiyan Facebookers: Motives and Addictive behaviours Unraveled, Computers in Human Behavior, 29(4):1342–1349

Barlow, D.H., & Durand, V.M. (2004). Bulimia nervosa: Diagnosis. In Abnormal Psychology: An Integrative Approach, (fourth edition). Retrieved from http://en.wikipedia.org

Baum A. (2006). Eating disorders in the male athlete. *Journal of sports medicine*, Vol. 36 (1), Pg. 1-6. Retrieved from http://www.ncbi.nlm.nih.gov

Błachnio et al. (2017). The role of personality traits in Facebook and Internet addictions: A study on Polish, Turkish, and Ukrainian samples. Computers in Human Behavior, *68*, 269–275.

Blascovich, J, & Tomaka, J. 1991. *Measures of self-esteem. Social psychological attitudes, personality and social psychological attitudes*, Academic Press. 1, 115–160. https://doi.org/10.1016/B978-0-12-590241-0.50008-3

Boyd, D. M. & Ellison, N. B. (2007). Social network sites: Definition, history, and scholarship. *Journal of Computer-Mediated Communication.* 13.210–230.

Cash, T.F., & Smolak L. (Eds.). 2011. *Body image: A handbook of science, practice, and prevention*, The Guilford Press, 2.

Chen, W. & Lee, K. (2013). Sharing, liking, commenting, and distressed? The pathway Between Facebook interaction and psychological distress. *Cyber psychology, Behavior, and Social Networking*, 16(10), 728-734

Carter (1940). Self-conception patterns of college students and adjustment to college life, *J. Counsel Psycho*. 10(1), 47-52.

Cattle, R.B. (1965). The general relations of changes in personality and Interest to changes in school performance Champaign, IL: Laboratory of Personality assessment and group behaviour, Dept. of Psychology, University of Illinois.

Cattle, R.B. (1950). *Personality — A Systematic Theoretical and Factual study*, New York, Tata McGraw Hill.

Cattle, R.B. (1967). In *Psychological foundations of Education*, Aruna Mohan, G. (2006), Dhar city, Neelkamal Publications Pvt Ltd,.

Crockett, L.J. (1997). Cultural, Historical and sub cultural contexts of adolescence, implications for health and development in schulenbery.

Deborah & Andersen (1977). Theories of Decision-making, Cambridge, Massachusetts Institute of Technology, 50 Memorial Drive.

Eisenberg, L. A. (1985). A Developmental Approach to Adolescent Children 12, pp. 131-135.

Elizabeth B. Hurlock (1949). *Adolescent Development*, New Delhi McGraw Hill book Company INC.

Elizabeth B. Hurlock (1976). *Personality Development*, New Delhi, McGraw Hill book Company, INC.

Erickson (1963). *Childhood and Society* (2nd edition), New York, Norton and Company Inc. pp. 261-263.

Erikson, E. (1968). *Identity, Youth and Crisis*, New York, Norton, Company, Inc.

Eysenck, H.J. (1947).*The structure of human personality*, New York, John Wiley and Sans Inc.

33

Digital Technologies and Online Learning Addiction

Impact on Mental Health

Altaf Ahmad Sheikh, Manzoor Ahmad Rather and Owaise Jan Kirmani

Introduction

At the school and college levels, well-thought-out and forward-thinking educational policies are crucial since education promotes a nation's socio-economic advancement. Different nations implement various educational systems based on customs, cultural norms, and historical needs that can be incorporated into school and university curricula at different points to ensure effectiveness. The aim for India's new education system is outlined in the NEP 2020 and NEP-1986 has been replaced by the current policy. In the 21st century, societies worldwide have become information-intensive, with science and technology playing a major role. Some of the gifts of this century include the increasing need for ICT and the use of technical gadgets, artificial intelligence, e-learning, virtual classrooms, digital platforms, digital libraries, and digital infrastructure. NEP 2020 aims to modernize and restructure the country's educational system. It places a strong emphasis on the integration of early childhood and secondary education. The NEP 2020 places a special emphasis on online learning. Colleges and institutes such as NITs and IGNOU will spearhead experimental research activities aimed at augmenting the advantages of digital learning in India. Online resources like SWAYAM and DIKSHA will have their designs changed to incorporate new concepts for content creation, in-class materials, assessment tools, profiles, and other elements that will facilitate constant communication.

Another major priority is the creation of a digital, public, and interoperable architecture that may be utilized at various stages. Although innovation in education is an expedition rather than a goal, it will be anticipated to organize the numerous environment stakeholders in order to carry out policy objectives. The Ministry will establish a special unit to organize the digital material, digital framework, and construction limits in order to meet the demands of e-learning for both secondary and tertiary education. In order to establish a "Digitally enabled society and information economy," the Indian government introduced the "Digital India" initiative in 2015. The significance of digital innovation has grown in relation to remote and deep learning, enhanced classroom interactions, advanced instructional techniques, flexible educational plans, and flexible connections between educators and learners.

As NEP 2020 recognises the destructive potential of digital consolidation in education, it has painstakingly recollected the elements of digital education for its system. The educational policy 2020 of the Ministry of Human Resource Development (MHRD) is progressive in every aspect. The relationship between education and innovation is a recurring theme throughout the Policy, even though it is focused on a variety of concerns, including the need for comprehensive education, juvenile care, and the need to fix the current educational system. Among the most prominent users of Digital Technology and the online community are students. However, overuse of digital media negatively affects not just one's social, emotional, physical, and psychological well-being but also one's academic achievement. Additionally, especially in higher education, it develops in student community a feeling of loneliness.

The goal of this study is to provide a systematic analysis of the body of research on Digital Technology's role as a new form of online addiction and its impact on mental health. This review discovered a general association between use of Digital Technology and mental health issues, despite the study's inconsistent results. There is evidence that digital technology and mental health are related, but there have also been reports of the opposite. The results that were measured most frequently were anxiety and depression. The main risk factors for anxiety and depression that this review identified included the type of activity and time spent on digital media. Several studies have shown that excessive usage of Digital Technology can lead to users feeling sad and generally dissatisfied with their lives, and also increasing the risk of developing mental health issues like anxiety, stress, and depression. Some studies have concluded that digital media addiction has the potential to be more potent than drug and alcohol addiction. This paper analyses the impact of digital technology on Mental Health with reference to NEP 2020

The Study

Objectives

This review seeks to investigate the impact of Digital Technology that leads to major mental health issues especially in the younger generation. To put it briefly, the following objectives are the focus of this systematic evaluation of the literature:

1) To study the Digital Technology and Social Networking Sites as an online Addiction.
2) To conduct a psychological review of the impact of Digital Technology on Mental Health with reference to NEP 2020.

Methodology/ Search Strategy

Secondary data on the current topic of digital technology and mental health has been gathered through a variety of sources, the study is primarily analytical in character. The research approach used combines descriptive and qualitative methods. A variety of online and offline sources, including websites, journals, papers, and other publications, were used to gather the secondary data. The reviewers have used the Preferred Reference Items for Systematic Reviews and Meta Analyse (PRISRMA) technique to attain the mentioned goals and objectives. An attempt has been made by the reviewers to find latest reviews published from 2011 to 2023.

The initial search produced a large number of results. The total results found were decreased by following the inclusion and exclusion criteria as displayed in Tables 1 and 2. The remaining 80 articles were screened on abstract and 65 were found to be ineligible. The search was stopped by the team of experts when 15 of the most relevant journal articles were found. The journal articles were studied and reviewed comprehensively.

Table 1: Inclusion and Exclusion Criteria Presented in Order

Inclusion criteria presented in order	*Particulars*	*Literature review identified*	*Remaining for Final review*
Key terms	Digital technology, NEP 2020, Social Networking sites addiction (SNSA), Social media addiction, Internet addiction, Facebook addiction, Mental Health	302	302
Year	From 2011 to 2023	101	101
Document type	Research papers and thesis	80	60
Exclusion criteria ordered in sequence	Particulars		
Inclusion criteria			60
Other subject related area	Medicine	45	15

Review of Literature

Digital technology/Social networking sites as an online addiction

In the psychiatric literature, addiction to online social networking sites and Internet addiction in general are relatively new, poorly understood, and

Table 2: Final Data for The Study was Selected by using the PRISMA Technique

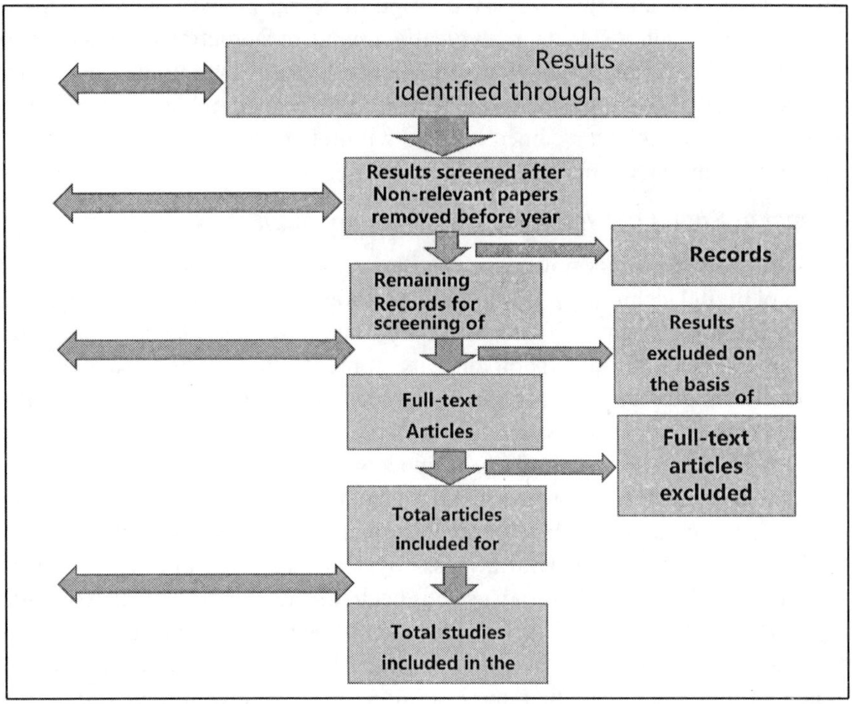

occasionally contentious topics. A sudden stop to online social networking (i.e., losing Internet access) has been seen to cause symptoms and indicators similar to those experienced by certain chronic users during drug, alcohol, or nicotine withdrawal. Social networking sites (SNSs) have become a significant source of concern as a result of the Internet's development and usage. There are numerous social networking sites on which users could develop an addiction. A Harvard University study found that the same part of the brain that is active during drug addiction is also activated when people reveal personal information about themselves on social media. In a study by California State University, people who used social media at least 58 times a week reported feeling depressed and socially alienated three times more frequently than people who used it less frequently—that is, less than nine times a week. Online social networking has been discussed as a possible addiction in numerous articles . In the United States, 78% of 131 psychology students participated in an online survey, with 82% of men and 75% of women having SNS profiles. 57% of people reported using social media every day.

In summary, this study is expected to be a major focus of many future research projects and the topic of intense discussion among psychologists, psychiatrists, and other professionals in the coming years. An increasing body of research indicates that excessive usage of social networking sites (SNS) may cause symptoms that are typically linked to addictions connected to substances. Regarding behavioural addictions, these symptoms have been characterized as salience, mood modification, tolerance, withdrawal, relapse, and conflict, and they have been verified within the framework of the Internet addiction components model.

Impact of Social networking sites on mental health

Children and teenagers nowadays are being exposed to both old and newer forms of digital technology. While it is well known that children's development and health are negatively impacted by the increased use of traditional technology, such as television and its content, studies have shown that modern technologies, like computers, tablets, and smart phones, which have been developed and widely used over the past ten years, are both beneficial and pose health risks to children. It appears that children who misuse these technological devices in terms of content, length, frequency, and posture while using them run the risk of developing a number of health issues, such as mental health issues, musculoskeletal issues, physical inactivity, obesity, and poor sleep quality. Digital technology use has been linked to aggressive behaviours, obesity, physical inactivity, lack of focus, and sleep issues in preschoolers and school-age children. Children that utilize digital technology excessively end up wasting time. The impact that these technologies have on children's cognitive and emotional development should also be taken into consideration (Brown, 2011). Community-based study has established a connection between early children technology overuse and cognitive, language, and social/emotional deficits (Pagani, Fitzpatrick, Barnett, & Dubow, 2010). Additionally, studies have linked social media use to psychological issues. A minor but statistically significant correlation was found between social media use and depression symptoms in children and adolescents based on a comprehensive evaluation of 11 studies (McCrae, Gettings, & Purssell).

Results of a review-based study titled "Relationship Between Depression and the Use of Mobile Technologies and Social Media Among Adolescents" indicated a statistically significant correlation between the use of social media and the onset of depressive symptoms. When using MTSM, excessive personal involvement and social comparison may be linked to the emergence of depressed symptomatology. That said, MTSM may encourage social support and potentially serve as a resource for individuals experiencing depression. Given the contradictory findings, further study may be helpful in establishing more solid proof. According to Dr. Romeo Vitelli's article in *Psychology Today*, studies have shown that Internet addiction is becoming a significant problem, especially for younger populations like teenagers. According to Vitelli, there are many similarities between Internet addiction disorder and other types of addiction, including withdrawal symptoms when one is unable to access the Internet. Internet addiction can be a concern since it can have a detrimental influence on academic performance and an individual's capacity for effective face-to-face communication, even if the Internet can be a positive force for education and the development of interpersonal relationships. Vitalli pointed out that studies have also found a connection between Internet addiction and a number of mental health conditions, such as loneliness, sadness, and low self-esteem. Digital technologies have several online applications, such as WhatsApp, YouTube, Instagram, Facebook, and others, which are commonly known as social networking sites (SNS). SNS addiction is a behavioural addiction that causes one to spend so much time and energy on SNS that it interferes with other crucial aspects of one's life. Overuse of social networking sites frequently has a detrimental impact on students' psychological well-being, relationships, sleep quality, daily work schedules, health, and general well-being. According to research analysis, there is a negative relationship between mental health and SNS addicted behaviour. The results showed a connection between scientific students' mental health and compulsive social networking site use. Additionally, studies show that there are no appreciable differences between SNS-dependent rural and urban kids in terms of mental health (Singh S., Singh S., & Sharma M., 2022)].

Out of the 100 respondents, 93.2% of the students said that criticism of their shared social media content negatively impacts their sense of self-worth, self-esteem, and general mood. Additionally, 52.7% of the students attempted but failed to reduce their time spent on social media, and 47.3% did not try. Overall, 78.4% of the respondents felt that they waste their time on social media platforms, and 70.3% of the students said they check their notifications on the social media apps whenever the notifications pop up. The study's three main findings revealed that the participants' extreme reliance on social media is a major contributing cause to their declining sense of value and self-esteem. Furthermore, the majority of them use these platforms for more than 60 hours a week, which is classified as addiction by definition. Accordingly, the study attested to the impact that social media addiction has on college students' mental health (Islam, T. & Sikder, P. W). Students are utilizing various digital technology platforms to improve their instruction and learning experience. One of the primary tools of these technologies is Facebook, but sadly, over usage of it leads to Internet addiction in adolescents. A study that examined Facebook addiction in college students as well as its behavioural, demographic, and psychological health factors was conducted during this phase. A total of 447 students answered the General Health Questionnaire (GHQ-28), the FAS, and disclosed information on their personal use of Facebook. According to the findings, Facebook addiction was positively predicted by a weekly time commitment, social motivations, severe depression, anxiety, and sleeplessness (oc M, Gulyagci S.). Children in one study reported a number of issues related to their physical and mental health, but they did not mention Internet addiction or overuse. Symptoms of physical health included fatigue, headaches, eye issues, and not eating. Children reported aggressiveness, difficulty in sleeping, and cognitive sensitivity of online events as mental health symptoms. Occasionally, people reported these issues within 30 minutes of using the device. This implies that even lower time consumption may contribute to health issues that youngsters report to themselves (Smahel, D., Wright, M.F. & Cernikova.

One study discovered a strong negative association between students' use of social media platforms for addictive behaviour and their academic achievement, as well as a correlation between their use of these platforms and their mental health. The study also discovered that there is no difference in the relationship between SNS Addictive Behaviour and Academic Achievement or between SNS Addictive Behaviour and Mental Health between Girls and Boys, Urban and Rural Students, SC/ST and Non-SC/ST Students, and Science, Arts, and Commerce Students. The above statement suggested that, if addictive behaviour increases, mental health decreases and vice versa. It also found that if addictive behaviour increases, academic achievement decreases and vice versa (Singh, Sushma).

Findings

The goal of this study was to provide a thorough analysis of the body of research on digital technology and its impact on mental health. This review discovered a general correlation between digital technology use and mental health problems, despite some inconsistent studies results. While there is research supporting a good relationship between digital technology and mental health, there have also been reports of the reverse effect. The results that were measured most frequently were anxiety and depression. The main risk factors for anxiety and depression that this review identified included social networking addiction, activity, and time spent on social media.

Digital technology use has been linked to anxiety and stress, even though some studies have found no correlation between it and worry, stress, or fears of social evaluation. Furthermore, a larger chance of developing an anxiety disorder and a higher frequency of dispositional anxiety symptoms is linked to higher daily digital media consumption exposure to some digital media may be particularly likely to cause a physiological stress reaction. Adolescents who struggle with social anxiety say they would rather connect online than in person and believe that the Internet is a useful tool for building relationships. Nonetheless, the findings point to a potentially harmful loop in which social anxiety promotes online interactions, which in turn causes problematic use, and a positive correlation between social anxiety and problematic digital technology usage.

Research has consistently shown that exposure to images and messages on social networking sites (SNS) can have a greater impact on eating disorder behaviours and body image problems than exposure to messages in the media. However, much more research is required to understand how young people are consuming these peer-generated content and the potential effects of interactive advertising. In an environment that supports recovery and healthy behaviours, it appears that young people battling eating disorders desperately require online social and emotional support. It is possible to direct SNS-based prevention and treatment initiatives in an efficient manner by having a thorough understanding of the reasons why young people look for online support and the particular kinds of interactions that result in beneficial outcomes. The amount of time spent, the calibre of interactions, the kind of social networking activity, and individual differences in susceptibility (such as age or gender) have all been found to have an impact on how, when, and with whom family members, educators, or practitioners may encourage or discourage the use of technology.

Examining the impact of technology-based social comparison and feedback seeking (SCFS) behaviours or using social media to look for information about one's appearance and social status, on teenage depression symptoms is crucial because social media exposes young people to an ongoing feedback loop of messages and images that encourage social comparison. Teenagers' self-perceptions and general well-being may suffer as a result of the quick peer input and large audience that social media gives them. Understanding the possible consequences on teenage mental health ultimately depends on the meanings that people assign to their interactions on social media and other technologies, such as whether they lead to rumination or social comparisons.

Limitations

This review is not without its limits. The fact that only a few publications were chosen for the review is one of its limitations. The studies that were selected were from only a few nations like India, USA, Turkey, Pakistan and Afghanistan. This suggests that the study mainly captures the circumstances of young people who are dependent on digital technology in these countries. Second, because part of the study is cross-sectional research rather than an experimental or causal correlation research study, some journal article findings can only address few objectives in this review. This means that not all countries' cases of digital addiction can be covered by this analysis.

Discussion and Conclusion

Certain students encounter anxiety stemming from their fear of losing their connections on digital media leading them to constantly reply to and view all of their friends' messages. Conversely, one of the unintended consequences of excessive usage of digital media is depression. Depression is not exclusive to Social Networks; it also occurs on other digital platforms, leading to mental health issues. According to a study, people who use digital media, gaming, cell phones, and other electronic devices frequently suffer from stress, sadness, anxiety, and a host of other psychological problems. As a result, it has a lot of surprising and unanswered but helpful answers attached. According to current research, using excessive digital technology can adversely impact a mental health. According to this comprehensive analysis, people's levels of anxiety and despair can be impacted by digital media envy. Moreover, additional study is required to determine the other possible causes of anxiety and sadness that have been discovered. Digital technology also puts a lot of pressure on users to conform to stereotypes that other people want to see and to be as popular as other users. For young people and people all over the world, Digital networking sites are an essential tool for interpersonal communication. The main people who give advice to young people about social networking behaviour and how to avoid Digital media addiction are parents, teachers, and counsellors. To provide better counselling services, counsellors need to be knowledgeable about mental health issues that may adversely impact young people who are hooked to digital media. Counsellors need to utilize more research-proven therapy with young people and be educated on Digital Technology addiction. Parents, teachers, and counsellors need to be well-versed in young people's perceptions, behaviours, needs, social interaction patterns, and emotional reactions in order to provide them with proper development aid. In addition to examining the effects of Digital media on other generations, future researchers should look into which types of Digital media are most popular among youth and which have the greatest influence.

References

La Barbera D, La Paglia F, Valsavoia R. (2009). Social network and addiction. *Studies in Health Technology & Informatics;* 144:33–36

Kuss DJ, Griffiths MD. (2011). Online social networking and addiction — a review of the psychological literature. *International Journal of Environmental Research & Public Health* 2011; 8:3528–3552

Floros G, Siomos K. (2013). The relationship between optimal parenting, Internet addiction and motives for social networking in adolescence. *Psychiatry Research* 2013; 209:529–534

Echeburua E, de Corral P. (2010). [Addiction to new technologies and to online social networking in young people: a new challenge]. *Adicciones 2010; 22:91–95*

Griffiths MD. (2012). Facebook addiction: concerns, criticism, and recommendations — a response to Andreassen and colleagues. *Psychological Reports* 110:518–520

Andreassen CS, Torsheim T, Bunborg GS, et al. (2012. Development of a Facebook Addiction Scale. *Psychological Reports110:501–517*

Kuss D.J., Griffiths M.D. (2011). Online social networking and addiction — A review of the psychological literature. *Int. J. Environ. Res. Public Health.; **8**:3528–3552. doi: 10.3390/ijerph8093528.*

Andreassen C.S. (2015). Online social network site addiction: A comprehensive review. *Curr. Addict.* Rep. 2015;**2**:175–184. doi: 10.1007/s40429-015-0056-9.

Griffiths M.D. A "components" model of addiction within a Biopsychosocial framework. *J. Subst. Use. 2005;**10**:191–197. doi: 10.1080/14659890500114359.*

R., Zirek, E., Yasacı, Z., & Razak Özdinçler, A. (2018). The negative effects of digital technology usage on children's development and health. *Addicta: The Turkish Journal on Addictions. Advance online publication. http://dx.doi.org/10.15805/addicta.2018.5.2.0051*

McCrae, N., Gettings, S. & Purssell, E. (2017). Social Media and Depressive Symptoms in Childhood and Adolescence: A Systematic Review. *Adolescent Res Rev **2**, 315–330 (2017). https://doi.org/10.1007/s40894-017-0053-4*

Arias-de, Puigdomenech, García, Valderas, Eiroa-Orosa, Fernández-Villa, Molina, Martín, Serrano-Blanco, Alonso, Espallargues M. (2020). Relationship Between Depression and the Use of Mobile Technologies and Social Media Among Adolescents: Umbrella Review. *J Med Internet Res. 26;22(8):e16388. doi: 10.2196/16388. PMID: 32663157; PMCID: PMC7481866.*

Singh S., Singh S. & Sharma M. (2022). A Study on Mental Health of Students Addicted to Social Networking Sites. *International Journal of Indian Psychology, 10(1), 565-571. DIP:18.01.056.20221001, DOI:10.25215/1001*

Islam, T., & Sikder, P.W. (2020). Social Media Addiction & its Effect on Mental Health among the Private University Students in Bangladesh: A Questionnaire Based Survey. *International Journal of Academic Research in Business and Social Sciences, 10(4)281–*

Koc M, Gulyagci S. (2013). Facebook addiction among Turkish college students: the role of psychological health, demographic, and usage characteristics. *CyberpsycholBehav Soc Netw. 2013 Apr; 16(4):279-84. doi: 10.1089/cyber.2012.0249. PMID: 23286695*

Smahel, D., Wright, M.F. & Cernikova, (2015). M. The impact of digital media on health: children's perspectives. *Int J Public Health 60, 131–137 (2015).* https://doi.org/10.1007/s00038-015-0649-z

Singh, Sushma (2020). A study on academic achievement and mental health of students addicted to social networking sites. *http://hdl.handle.net/10603/341310*

Editors and Contributors

Editors

Dr Aerum Khan, MSc Botany, B.Ed, MA Education, MA Sociology, DCA, Ph.D. (Botany), Ph.D. (Education) is Associate Professor, Science Education at Dept of TT & NFE (IASE), F/o Education, JMI, New Delhi. She has done courses on *Qualitative Research Methods* from University of Amsterdam, *Feminism and Social Justice* from University of California, Santa Cruz, *Introduction to Philosophy* from The University of Edinburgh, *Psychological First Aid* from Johns Hopkins University, *The Science of Well-being* from Yale University, and *Gender and Sexuality: Diversity and Inclusion in the Workplace* from University of Pittsburgh. She has worked with NCERT, New Delhi, SCERT Delhi. She has been a Visiting Faculty for SOL-Delhi University, IGNOU (continued) and NIOS, and has been Academic Consultant for the British Council. Got published more than 80 articles, chapters and research papers in Botany and Education in national and international journals. She was the core member of the development team of NCERT for MOOCs for school education on SWAYAM. She has been the Academic Coordinator for the UGC-funded project e-PG PathShala for the subject of Education, joint venture of CIET-NCERT and University of Allahabad. The first online PG level MOOC in Education created by her and team was launched by UGC on the SWAYAM platform on 1 August 2017. She received the MoE sponsored training for SWAYAM Course Coordinators at Chennai, jointly conducted by IIT Bombay, IIM Bangalore, NIEPA Delhi and NITTTR Chennai on the nomination of UGC. In March 2020 she was invited by IIT Madras and JNU, New Delhi to develop video lectures for UG level for National telecast through Swayam Prabha Channels of MoE, GoI, under which she developed 168 video lectures in 5 phases. She is the recipient of the 'Inspiring Woman Awards 2021' from 'Fourth Screen Education' for outstanding and remarkable services in the field of Education.

Dr Jasim Ahmad, Ph.D. (Edu), M.Ed., M.Sc. (Zoology), UGC-NET (Edu), is Hony. Director, Centre for Distance and Online Education and Professor at the Institute of Advanced Studies in Education, Jamia Millia Islamia. He has a teaching and research experience of around 24 years; his areas of interests include Science Education, Educational Psychology, Research Methodology and Teacher Education. He has published eleven books. He has to his credit around 70 research papers and articles published in journals, around 50 research papers in conferences, 15 chapters in edited books and 16 SLM units, more than 100 invited talks, around 80 workshops, and coordinated a number of training programmes. 14 Ph.D. degree and around 50 PG. dissertations have been awarded under his guidance. He has been awarded 'Proud Indian Eminent Professor Award 2022' in Teacher Education by IMRF, Andhra Pradesh on the occasion of India's 73rd Republic Day.

Contributors

Abdul Badi, TGT-Science, Mazharul Islam Secondary School, Farash Khana, Delhi. Email: abdulbadi.jmi@gmail.com

Altaf Ahmad Sheikh, Research Scholar, Department of Education, UOK. Email: saltafsedu@gmail.com

Amir Khan, Research Scholar, Department of Education, Central University of Rajasthan, District Ajmer, Rajasthan. Email: 2022phded006@curaj.ac.in

Anup Kumar Rajput, Head, Publication Division, NCERT, New Delhi. Email: anupncert@yahoo.co.in

Aswathy CK, Research Scholar, RV Teachers College (IASE), Research Centre in Education, Bengaluru City University, Bengaluru. Email: aswathyck500@gmail.com

Babita, Ph.D. Scholar, Guru Gobind Singh Indraprastha University, Delhi. Email: Koharbabita0@gmail.com

Babita Yadav, Ph.D. Scholar, Department of Education, Central University of Jharkhand. Email: babita.21310201001@cuj.ac.in

Dhriti Tiwari, Assistant Professor, Integral University, Lucknow. Email: dtiwari2885@gmail.com

Diksha Dhanda, Research Scholar, Central University of Haryana. Email: dikshadhanda965@gmail.com

Dori Lal, Associate Professor, Department of Teacher Training and Non-formal Education (IASE), Jamia Millia Islamia, New Delhi.

Fauzia Khan, Professor, Department of Teachers Training & Non-formal Education (IASE), Jamia Millia Islamia, New Delhi. Email: fkhan@jmi.ac.in

Gulafshan Salam Khan, PhD Candidate, Institute of Foreign Languages, Peoples' Friendship University of Russia, Moscow, Russia. Email: gulafshanskhan20@gmail.com

Harish Kumar, Domain Head-Education, Head – AIBAS & ASPESS, Amity University, Noida. Email: hkumar2@amity.edu

Harmeet Kaur, PhD Scholar, Lingaya's Vidyapeeth, Faridabad, Haryana, Email: harmeetasha@gmail.com

Irum Alvi, Assistant Professor, Rajasthan Technical University, Kota, Rajasthan, Email: irumalvi@gmail.com

M. Ponnambaleswari, Research Guide, RV Teachers College (IASE), Research Centre in Education, Bengaluru City University, Bengaluru, Email: ponnambaleswari.rvtc@rvei.edu.in

Madhurima Pal, Research Scholar, Department of Teachers Training & Non-formal Education (IASE), Jamia Millia Islamia, New Delhi, Email: madhurimapal09@gmail.com

Manzoor Ahmad Rather, Assistant Professor, Department of Education, UOK, Email: manzoorahmadrather004@gmail.com

Manvi Yadav, Assistant Professor, Department of Education, Central University of Jharkhand. Email: manvi.yadav@cuj.ac.in

Mahmood Ahmad Khan, Professor and HOD, Department of Education, University of Kashmir, Email: drmahmood1962@yahoo.co.in

Md. Ashique Husain, Research Scholar, Department of Teacher Training & Non-formal Education (IASE), Faculty of Education, Jamia Millia Islamia, New Delhi, Email: ashiquerazzaque88@gmail.com

Merajul Hasan, Research Scholar, Department of Education, University of Gour Banga, Malda, West Bengal, Email: mhasan.ugb@gmail.com

Mohammad Haseen Ahmed, English Language Instructor, King Abdul Aziz University, Jeddah K.S.A, Email: mdhsnahmad@gmail.com

Mohammad Yusoof, Professor, Department of Teacher Training & Non-formal Education (IASE), Faculty of Education, Jamia Millia Islamia, New Delhi, Email:myusuf@jmi.ac.in

Mohd Noor Alam, Research Scholar, IASE, Faculty of Education, Jamia Millia Islamia, New Delhi, Email: alamnoor.jmi@gmail.com

Mufti Shahla, Research Scholar, Department of Education, University of Kashmir, Email: muftishahla@gmail.com

Naresh Kumar, Department of Computer Science, Navyug School, Lodhi Road, New Delhi, Email: engg.nareshkumar@gmail.com

Owaise Jan Kirmani, Research Scholar, Department of Education, UOK. Email: owaiskirmani2576@gmail.com

Pallavi Jain, Research Scholar, Amity Institute of Education, Amity University, Noida, Email: pallavi.jain@s.amity.edu

Pavitra Rana, Junior Research Fellow, Department of Educational Studies, Faculty of Education, Jamia Millia Islamia, New Delhi. Email: pavitrarana18@gmail.com

Prachi Khanna, Research Scholar, Department of Teacher Training and Non-formal Education (IASE), Jamia Millia Islamia, New Delhi. Email: Prachi18091993@gmail.com

Rajnee Gaur, HOD, School of Education, Lingaya's Vidyapeeth, Haryana, Email:rajneebhardwaj@yahoo.com

Rohit, Assistant Professor, Amity School of Performing Arts, Amity University, Noida, Email: rohitrugta8628@gmail.com

Sadia Khalid, MA Education Scholar, Department of Teacher Training & Non-formal Education (IASE), Faculty of Education, Jamia Millia Islamia, New Delhi, Email: sadiakhalid998@gmail.com

Sadiya Shaheen, Research Scholar, Department of Teacher Training & Non-formal Education (IASE), Jamia Millia Islamia, New Delhi. Email: shaheen.0279@gmail.com

Sangeeta Suman, Assistant Professor, Sri. Paramhans Shikshan Prashikshan Sansthan Mahavidyalaya, Ayodhya, Email: ssitssangeeta@gmail.com

Samra Jamal, Research Scholar, Department of Teacher Training & Non-formal Education (IASE), Faculty of Education, Jamia Millia Islamia, New Delhi, Email: samrajamal@gmail.com

Sapna Raj, Research Scholar, Indira Gandhi National Open University, Delhi, Email: srscert22@gmail.com

Sarita Kumari, Associate Professor, Department of Educational Studies, Faculty of Education, Jamia Millia Islamia, New Delhi, Email: skumari@jmi.ac.in

Shruti Tomar, M.Ed. Students, Department of Education, University of Delhi, Delhi, Email: shrutitomarwork@gmail.com

Shabnama Nadir, Research Scholar, Department of Education, University of Kashmir

Soumya Priyadarsani Panigrahi, Research scholar, Department of Teacher Training & Non formal Education (IASE), Faculty of Education, Jamia Millia Islamia, New Delhi, Email: psoumyapanigrahi@gmail.com

Stuti Shandilya, Ph.D. Scholar (Education), University School of Education, Guru Gobind Singh Indraprastha University, Delhi. Email: stuti1511@gmail.com

Tahira Akhtar, Research scholar, Department of Teacher Training & Non formal Education (IASE), Faculty of Education, Jamia Millia Islamia, New Delhi, Email: dartahira66@gmail.com

Ujjwal Kumar Halder, Professor, Department of Education, University of Gour Banga, Malda, West Bengal

Uzma Siddiqui, Assistant Professor, Department of Education, Aligarh Muslim University, Aligarh, Email: uzmasiddiqui.amu@gmail.com

Vinod Kumar Kanvaria, Associate Professor, Department of Education, University of Delhi, Delhi, Email: vinodpr111@gmail.com

Zainab Musheer, Department of Education, Aligarh Muslim University, Aligarh, Email: zainab2509@gmail.com